# ADVANCE PRAISE FOR *RAW*

"Ricky Varghese's *Raw: Prep, Pedagogy and the Politics of Barebacking* is an important and timely contribution to a decade long debate over bareback sex, its meanings and it representations. The collection draws together a range of voices and critical frameworks ranging from the biopolitical to the pornographic, the embodied to the psychoanalytical. The book is essential reading for anyone interested in the politics of sex, sexuality and sexual representation in the 21st century." —JOHN MERCER, author of *Gay Pornography: Representations of Sexuality and Masculinity*

"This collection makes a major contribution to research. It opens up the discourse on barebacking to a variety of perspectives and theoretical arguments, and makes clear that the topic remains relevant, unsettled, and shifting in response to a series of changing circumstances. It is also a call for thinkers of sex and gender, pornography and queer theory to contend with the effects that the discourse and practices of barebacking can have on these fields." —JOHN PAUL RICCO, author of *The Decision Between Us: Art and Ethics in the Time of Scenes*

"Finally, queer theory returns to a topic it has had surprisingly little to say about: sex! Varghese's collection goes where others fear to tread, treating barebacking variously as a subcultural practice, an allegory, and a limit case for thinking, in the wake of the new sexual revolution unleashed by the advent of PrEP. Underpinning these essays is a thrilling wager: that desire demands discourse but resists rationalization." —DAMON R. YOUNG, author of *Making Sex Public and Other Cinematic Fantasies*

# THE EXQUISITE CORPSE
## BOOK SERIES

Publishing works from both emerging and established scholars,
The Exquisite Corpse book series challenges readers with
questions that are often left unasked about the human body. Like
the Surrealist's parlour game, for which the series is named, these
books present the body in all of its unruly and corporeal glory.

### PREVIOUS BOOKS IN THE EXQUISITE CORPSE SERIES

*Reading from Behind: A Cultural Analysis of the Anus,*
by Jonathan A. Allan

*Virgin Envy: The Cultural (In)Significance of the Hymen,*
edited by Jonathan A. Allan,
Cristina Santos, and Adriana Spahr

FOR MORE INFORMATION, PLEASE CONTACT:
Karen May Clark, Acquisitions Editor
University of Regina Press
3737 Wascana Parkway
Regina SK S4S OA2
Canada
PHONE: 306-585-4664
EMAIL: karen.clark@uregina.ca

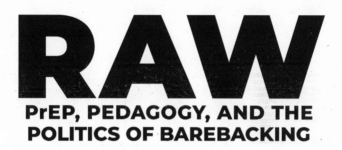

# RAW

## PrEP, PEDAGOGY, AND THE
## POLITICS OF BAREBACKING

edited by RICKY VARGHESE
afterword by TIM DEAN

**University of Regina Press**

Printed and bound in Canada at Friesens. The text of this book is printed on 100% post-consumer recycled paper with earth-friendly vegetable-based inks.

Cover art: "whole peeled banana," vicif / istockphoto
Cover and text design: Duncan Noel Campbell, University of Regina Press
Copy editor: Ryan Perks
Proofreader: Dallas Harrison
Indexer: Patricia Furdek
Epigraph: sam sax, "Risk," in *Bury It* (Middleton, CT: Wesleyan University Press, 2018). Reprinted with permission.

*Library and Archives Canada Cataloguing in Publication*

Title: Raw : PrEP, pedagogy, and the politics of barebacking / edited by Ricky Varghese ; afterword by Tim Dean.

Names: Varghese, Ricky, editor.

Series: Exquisite corpse book series.

Description: Series statement: The exquisite corpse | Includes bibliographical references and index.

Identifiers: Canadiana (print) 20190140879 | Canadiana (ebook) 20190140917 | ISBN 9780889776838 (softcover) | ISBN 9780889776869 (hardcover) | ISBN 9780889776845 (PDF) | ISBN 9780889776852 (HTML)

Subjects: LCSH: Unsafe sex. | LCSH: Pre-exposure prophylaxis. | LCSH: Gay men—Psychology. | LCSH: Risk-taking (Psychology) | LCSH: Male homosexuality—Psychological aspects.

Classification: LCC HQ76.115 .R39 2019 | DDC 306.77086/642—dc23

10  9  8  7  6  5  4  3  2  1

University of Regina Press, University of Regina
Regina, Saskatchewan, Canada, s4s 0a2
tel: (306) 585-4758 fax: (306) 585-4699
web: www.uofrpress.ca

**U OF R PRESS**

We acknowledge the support of the Canada Council for the Arts for our publishing program. We acknowledge the financial support of the Government of Canada. / Nous reconnaissons l'appui financier du gouvernement du Canada. This publication was made possible with support from Creative Saskatchewan's Book Publishing Production Grant Program.

*This book is for Umair and Gautam.*

## RISK

how harrowing the paradox of latex. on one hand the paragon of intimacy,
on the other a glove like a father loved more in his absence. my paramour,
my minotaur, my matador flashing his red sword. dear condemnation, i have
read all the commentaries of *raw*, how the forbidden fruit grows less sweet
the more you gorge on it. i've seen the formal debates where two gaping wounds
stand behind podiums + reach into each other's mouths. discourse, its own
form of pleasure. pleasure at its most broken down, a series of shapes.
ethnographies bleed from the ivory tower, the tower made of animal teeth.
the distance between theory + practice is a slick laceration. it's right there
in the name, *unprotected*, to be laid out before the animal in him, to be defenseless
+ deforested. perhaps this is worked out better in myth:

> he pilots my body across a waterbed
> full of drowned squid. in the distance, women
> sing us toward shore.

or perhaps, it's best to end in images:

> a handful of gravel, the open ground,
> a groveling mouth, a grave half full of water
> with my body not in it yet.

—sam sax

# CONTENTS

## PSYCHOANALYTIC AND PEDAGOGICAL LIMITS

# ACKNOWLEDGEMENTS

I t is intriguing to trace the formation of a work of this nature—to assess its genealogy, so to speak. When my colleague Christopher Smith and I co-organized From Raw to Real: Sexual Economies in the Age of Barebacking at the University of Toronto back in May 2014, little did I know that I would go on to helm this subsequent book project. I am immensely grateful to Christopher, my co-conspirator from those days at the Ontario Institute for Studies in Education (OISE), for joining me in organizing and participating in that heady afternoon symposium. I am grateful as well to the brilliant participants of that conversation—Rinaldo Walcott, Christien Garcia, Evangelos Tziallas, and John Paul Ricco—some of whom made their way into this volume. Damon Young, along with his partner Michael Forrey, flew all the way in from Berkeley to moderate and facilitate that event, which was more than I could have asked for. Damon has been an immense source of support and a significant interlocutor since we met at the Cornell School of Criticism and Theory back in 2008, and his participation in the 2014 symposium only helped push the conversation further.

Little did I know, as well, that that symposium would be the first of other similarly charged dialogues regarding barebacking—most notably, after I was granted the opportunity to organize panels concerning the subject at the annual meetings of the Sexuality Studies Association in both 2014 and 2015 and of the American Studies Association in 2015. I am thankful to those who participated in those panels (most of whom have also found their way into the pages of this book) and to those associations for opening up the space for these conversations to occur.

Since we met in 2007 as doctoral students at the University of Toronto, Jonathan Allan has been an ever-present fount of support, insight, nuance, and dialogue. It was his unwavering support and his introduction to the brilliantly rigorous editorial staff at the University of Regina Press that turned the fertile grounds sowed by the aforementioned symposium and panels into a book. He believed in this project's necessity long before I myself had realized its merit. He went above and beyond the call of duty when he went on to solicit Demetrios P. Tryphonopoulos, the dean of arts at Brandon University, where Jonathan teaches, to secure a subvention grant that could be put toward the production of this book. Rinaldo Walcott also aided this project by helping to secure funds that could be put toward making this project come to life. I want to acknowledge my gratitude to Jonathan, Rinaldo, and Dean Tryphonopoulos. Being a scholar working on a book like this from the outside, without any affiliation to a university, their support has been of immeasurable value to me.

Rinaldo's role in my intellectual formation has, to say the least, been invaluable. We met when I took an elective course with him at OISE while I was pursuing my master's in social work at the neighbouring Factor-Inwentash Faculty of Social Work of the University of Toronto. Immediately, Rinaldo—along with Roger Simon, who would go on to become my doctoral supervisor at OISE—took me under his wing, saw something in me that I didn't, and gave me a rigorous space to pursue my eclectically interdisciplinary set of academic interests. When Roger became ill and passed away in 2012—an incredibly devastating loss of a friend and mentor—Rinaldo stepped in and took over the reins of my dissertation process and helped me finish at a time when I was quite certain I was going to walk away from academia. I can hardly begin to say how appreciative I am of Rinaldo's steadfast presence in my life.

Since I met him, now almost a decade ago, John Paul Ricco has been a wonderful interlocutor and friend. Even after my doctoral studies were completed and I moved on to start my practice as a psychotherapist, he kept me abreast of various talks, lectures, workshops, and other scholarly events that were happening in Toronto and elsewhere. He has always known how pivotal staying connected to intellectual and scholarly communities has been for me, and he was instrumental in introducing me to Tim Dean.

When I first met him, I had been following Tim's work for the better part of a decade. Working with his input, feedback, and constant support in connection to this project has been an experience unlike any other I have had. Tim is a consummate professional in every sense. In addition to being one of the earliest conscripts to the book that you now hold in your hands, he was also one of its closest readers and most responsive and incisive critics. Put simply, working with Tim has been simultaneously pleasurable and pedagogical. I've learned so much about how to be a thorough, steadfast, and committed scholar from him, and there has been so much pleasure in this learning. I am grateful for his participation in this work and his ongoing support of my endeavours, and I could not have asked for a more fitting person to comment on—and write the afterword to—this text.

I also want to thank the brilliant and discursively diverse range of scholars that I was able to assemble herein. Each one of them has worked toward building a community of sorts through the site of this text, and this book is stronger for it.

The editorial team at the University of Regina Press has been nothing short of excellent. Since Jonathan Allan introduced us, Karen Clark has been a pleasure to work with. Her thoroughness has been greatly appreciated, as has been her gentleness and patience with me, qualities so immensely valued in an editor. Her ability to envision the bigger picture and the larger context in which this work might find itself, to imagine, think, and conceive of the afterlife of this book beyond its publication, has been astounding, to say the least. Kelly Laycock shepherded this project along so brilliantly through the production phase, and I am deeply appreciative of the care she took in doing so. Ryan Perks, who copy-edited this work, did so with a beautifully deft attention to detail. I could not have asked for a more finely honed and skilled set of eyes. Amani Khelifa, URP's editorial assistant, deserves thanks for the final touches and fine-tuning she did with regards to the editing process. I am also greatly appreciative of the careful manner with which Dallas Harrison proofread the entire manuscript and Patricia Furdek organized the final index for the book, both with such superb watchfulness to the most nuanced of details.

I also want to thank sam sax for graciously permitting me to use his poem "Risk" as a fitting epigraph to this book; I could not have hoped for a more compelling and evocative opening to *Raw*. When I was asked by the editorial team about what I had hoped for as far as the cover of this book was concerned, I had suggested that it would be nice to have something simple and elegant, but perhaps also witty and even somewhat irreverent. Duncan Campbell captured all of these effects in one fell swoop so marvellously, as can be seen in the finished product. I also want to take this opportunity to thank the two anonymous readers to whom an earlier draft of this manuscript was assigned. Their close reading of it and the constructive criticism they offered were the sort of gifts that any editor or author would appreciate.

In the course of working on this project, of course, life continued at its own enigmatic pace beyond the pages of this work. In the midst of preparing this text, I was busy setting up my clinical practice and commencing my training to become a psychoanalyst at the Toronto Institute of Psychoanalysis. The colleagues I met in my cohort of trainees, and the greater community of psychotherapists and psychoanalysts amidst whom I find myself presently, have enriched my thought process with regard to this work. The rigour and commitment they show to considered exegetical work have influenced me deeply in my own reading, rereading, and preparation of the manuscript for this project.

A work of this nature is also prone to bring up all sorts of affective registers and to bring to the fore the headiness of complex psychical processes, responses, and emotions. Over the years, since before this project was even a mere germ of an idea, I have had the pleasure of experiencing analyses with three different psychoanalysts at varying points of my intellectual development, all the way up to the present instance, where I find myself in the process of becoming an analyst myself. I feel the insights I have gained from the years I have spent on the couch, thinking and playing with my ideas and my curiosity, cannot be underestimated. As such, I want to acknowledge that seemingly interminable work of analysis and my analysts who appeared at different stages of my life, starting with Dr. Oren Gozlan, Dr. Jacinta O'Hanlon, and, most recently, Dr. Ronald Ruskin. Each of them has opened up something profoundly cached in me that allowed me to understand my commitment to this project and to bringing it to life.

Many friends have been part of this long journey as well, and I want to acknowledge their presence and efforts in supporting me through all the time it took to prepare this collection. I want to thank Libby Zeleke, Joshua Synenko, Gemma Charlebois, Svitlana Matviyenko, Christien Garcia, Francisco-Fernando Granados, Kurt Kraler, James Murray, Mic Carter, David Seitz, Yaseen Ali, Maita Sayo, Nick Hauck, Christine Korte, Concetta Principe, Fan Wu, Kevin Leung, Vince Rozario, Vincent Chevalier, Brien Wong, Nishan Karuna, Natasha Chaykowski, and Yury Simkhaev. Friends like these know when and how to be present as a source of much-needed support and solace and don't take it personally when you have to become reclusive in order to complete the task at hand. I am also grateful to the space that my family offered me in the process of getting this work done. My parents, Raju and Sara, and my brother Ronnie and sister-in-law Vijaya have known how to be present, and I appreciate them all the more for it. I am especially thankful for the arrival of my nephew Gautam, born in 2015, in the very early stages of putting this together. He has, as his name rightfully suggests, lit up my life in ways he has yet to learn about. This book is partly dedicated to him, and I hope that someday he might come across it in some or other archive and be surprised and possibly moved to find his name in here.

Without Umair, I don't think any of what I have done in the last few years would have been imaginable or possible. This collection of essays is as much a product of his keen, astute, and prudent copy-editing and close proofreading as it has been of my efforts at bringing it all together. He so carefully and cogently combed through each of the chapters assembled here, and this work is stronger and richer for it. This book is, as well, a testament to the numerous politically and philosophically charged conversations we have shared over the years and to the promise of hopefully many more to come in the future. His constant support in everything I do and have worked for is showcased here, and I am so grateful for his presence in my life.

# THE MOURNING AFTER: BAREBACKING AND BELATEDNESS

Ricky Varghese

Pleasure seems to be everywhere and nowhere. Late capitalism, with its overinvestments in cultures of seemingly uninhibited mediation—say, in the form of advertising—would have us believe that pleasure is everywhere, instantaneously accessible and gratifying, that it can be bought and sold, borrowed and appropriated, colonized and decolonized. And yet, sustained conversations concerning pleasure—what gives us pleasure, how we might seek it out or retrieve it, what it says about our deepest desires or our most intimate fantasies—still seem to be a matter of taboo. A kind of silence shrouds any rigorous examination of pleasure. And if not silence, then conversations regarding pleasure are oftentimes substituted by, sublimated into, or submerged under the tedium of ideological underpinnings or utilitarian imaginings. Under these headings, it would seem that we want our pleasure to do something, be put to work, be worth something to us (and, perhaps, to others as well), and possibly be meaning-making. And if not meaning-making of its own volition, then we appear to want to impose meanings upon it, contingent meanings that are either informed by the ideological bandwidths that exist in our current historical conjuncture or that serve to produce a use-value out of this very pleasure that we attempt to access.

I generally hesitate to use the collective "we" in my writing. There are a few reasons for this hesitation—one might even call it a "resistance." Partly, I am well aware of the complexities implicit in the notion of an imagined or fantasized collective, that which nonetheless might still feel materially real and viable: complexities mired by the layered and multifarious histories of injustice and oppression that various and variable bodies have had to contend with in different and differing historical, socio-political, economic, and geographical contexts. Still another reason for my apparent resistance comes from a simpler, more straightforward investment: an investment in psychoanalysis, the study and examination of sub-jective—dare I say individual—desire. I have had a long-drawn-out fascination with finding the voice of the individual subject in the scene of the collective and how these voices play off and inform one another. This is not, in any way, an attempt at privileging the neoliberal, individualized, and seemingly all-consuming subject of the free market but rather a move toward understanding how an individual subject's desires, fantasies, and pleasures evolve, become historically understood and/or collectively mediated and mandated, and come to gain a sense of recognition, both by themselves and by others that exist in the world they inhabit.

In the late nineties, as a plucky undergraduate in the Department of Psychology at Queen's University in Kingston, I came across Gay-atri Chakravorty Spivak's now canonical essay, "Can the Subaltern Speak?" I was attempting to figure the ways by which a study of the psyche, of the psychological, of the emotive and affective landscape of the subject—both conscious and unconscious—might be informed by aesthetics and aesthetic practices, be it in the form of the literary, the cinematic, or the artistic. As a student of psychology heavily invested in the humanities, I found the question Spivak posed rather arresting, to say the least. Apart from the essay's indispens-able critique of "the interested desire to conserve the subject of the

West, or the West as subject,"[1] the title itself felt as though it was blowing the cover off of this very "interested [Western] desire" by asking: Can, in all honesty, the subaltern speak? More to the point, can the subaltern speak its desire (f)or pleasure? Can this speech be heard and, if so, by whom? It felt as though the subject of desire was being rerouted or located elsewhere. Surely, "the subaltern," or its speech, could metonymically stand in for both the collective and subjectively individual voice of the most destitute and marginalized within the social sphere. However, in thinking more closely about the question, I observed something else rather specific and significantly more particular. In Spivak's attempt to reposition and recalibrate the debate about subjectivity and its incumbent "interested desires," I heard a move toward wanting to privilege the desires of those on the margins. The question felt at once both urgently political and deeply psychoanalytic. And, to this day, it serves as a motivating force in my work as a therapist, as a psychoanalyst-in-training (at the time of writing), and in my overall approach to research in the field of psychoanalytic theory.

What, then, does any of this have to do with sex and, more immediately, with bareback sex? To be sure, I am not suggesting that the barebacker and the subaltern are co-extensive figures. Nor am I suggesting that the barebacker can be read so easily as a subaltern figure on the margins of historical time or on the fringes of any given socio-political landscape. A reader of this collection will quickly discern the contradictory position that barebackers occupy; that, in some cases, they are presumed to be a radical figure precisely on those very fringes of the social sphere (perhaps even of history itself), while, in other instances, they come to occupy a rather mainstream, even normalized/normative, position. Rather, I invoked Spivak's question about the subaltern as a way to enter into a conversation about speech, voice, desire, and, perhaps most important of all, the question of pleasure, precisely because of the attention she drew to the notion of "interested desires" always already in operation in the

---

1    Gayatri Chakravorty Spivak, "Can the Subaltern Speak?," in *Marxism and the Interpretation of Culture*, eds. Cary Nelson and Lawrence Grossberg (Chicago: University of Illinois Press, 1988), 271.

social world. Amidst the clamour of this conservationist project, she attempted to locate—or rather attempted to assess the conditions for the very possibility of locating—the speech, the voice, and even the desire of the figure of the subaltern. If the array of essays assembled here—written from vastly divergent and at times discursively opposing or even contradictory vantage points—has taught me anything, it might be that a similar query could be posed in attempting to locate the barebacker, and more specifically the barebacker's pleasure, against the backdrop of queer theory.

Like any discipline in search of institutional and social forms of legitimacy, queer theory's investments in conserving a particular subject, perhaps a political and politicized subject most "at home" in the context of the urban centres of the Global North/West, has dealt an interesting blow to the question of pleasure. Matters concerning pleasure—what gives one pleasure, how one seeks it out, why one might search for a specific form of pleasure as opposed to another—have been substituted by questions pertaining to use-value, utility, and utilitarianism in the scene of queer theory. It would seem that "we" want our theory to be recognized as rational, as having rationales, at least slightly informed or touched by subtle forms of positivism or even scientism; we want it to be socially just, politically salient, and pragmatically or practically expedient. On the other hand, a queer theory that reckons with pleasure—its irrationality, the drive, need, wish, or want behind it, its inexplicability, its unquantifiable nature, its seeming incommensurability—feels antithetical to the noble goals that queer theory has set for itself.

Sure, pleasure is never innocent, nor can it be meaningless. Even in its most irrational or seemingly nonsensical or violent manifestations, there is, at its core, a sense and sensuality to it that makes sense—pun intended—to the subject. This is not to say that we can't be moral or ethical arbiters of pleasure—we already engage in the work of such judgment, taste, and arbitration—but to say that pleasure always has a meaning to it, a psychical historicity on whose foundation it is built. However, much like the space of the unconscious where it seems to reside, at times dormant and at other times in search of a pathway for release, pleasure appears to know no time or contradiction. Any sense of time, temporality, history, or contradiction that we might use to describe pleasure comes after, as an afterthought. These categories—time and contradiction, sociality, historicity, and politics—end up taking precedence in the space of queer theory. Pleasure is rarely, if ever, studied for its own sake. The jury is still out as to whether pleasure even can or should be studied for its own sake. It is as though pleasure becomes its own afterthought. Belated, deferred, set aside for further examination on another day or at another time, always already mourned, while shards of it melancholically remain untouched, unanalyzed. I hesitate to rely on the notion of the messianic, but Kafka appears to be useful here. His dictum concerning the question of hope, that there is "plenty of hope, an infinite amount of hope—but not for us,"[2] might very well be applicable to the question of pleasure. In the ideologically imbued scene of queer theory, one might be wont, if only for a brief moment, to rework Kafka and suggest that there is, indeed, plenty of pleasure, even an endless reserve, a bottomless pit as it were—just none for us.

This dragged-out, perhaps somewhat (self-)indulgent pontification on the question of pleasure in the scene of queer theory is not for naught. In a way, by doing so, my intention, as the editor of this collection, has been to pre-emptively highlight this project's central shortcoming—a launch pad, so to speak, for further research, which perhaps consciously or unconsciously—on the part of both myself and the brilliant contributors assembled here—rehearses a shortcoming of queer theory itself. A reader will immediately see that the writers of the various chapters can't agree on what barebacking is or what it is not. As suggested earlier, coming from rather different disciplinary, theoretical, and analytical vantage points, these authors reach no clear agreement on what the practice means or could entail. This, in itself, is perfectly fine and welcome as a way to expand the debate on the practice. It allows for a sort of widening of the field of study. However, the common thread that seems to tie together all the chapters assembled here is the absence or hidden nature of any sustained reference to the pleasure behind

---

2    As quoted in Dagmar Barnouw, *Weimar Intellectuals and the Threat of Modernity* (Bloomington: Indiana University Press, 1988), 187.

the practice. Instead, each of the authors in this project provides a rigorous examination of the ideological, socio-political, ethical, and moral ramifications and repercussions connected to barebacking. It would appear that barebacking, both as a potentially pleasurable, self-made sexual choice and as an ontological practice, must always already mean something.

I want to clarify that, when I invited the scholars who ended up contributing to this project, I never solicited any of them to speak explicitly to or about the question of pleasure. My concern with pleasure was, rather, something I culled from these contributions as a kind of question (hanging in the air) that readers of this book should carry with them as they read what follows. In these introductory remarks, I wanted to foreground my argument that queer theory, studies of sexuality, critical sexology, and even porn studies seem unsure of how to talk about pleasure (or desire, for that matter) on easy terms. In a way, this collection showcases that very difficulty, because it can be seen that, while many of us are great at theorizing sex and barebacking, there is a hesitation in discursive circles to address the slippery topic of pleasure. My hope is that a reader of this book will be able to continue the work done here as a kind of a jumping off point for further research.

It is also important that we not give in to the seemingly easy temptation of wanting to define the emergence of a field per se—that is, a field that could potentially be referred to as bareback studies. Certainly, one might get a sense of such a field having developed from a quick assessment of the essays that make up this book; however, such an assessment might be a sleight of hand, a simplified distraction from the seriousness of the endeavours undertaken by its contributors. The study of barebacking as conceived of here is an attempt at grasping at its profoundly semiotic potential. Exploring barebacking as a project of semiotics entails acknowledging its divergent and even conflicting signs, symbols, meanings, and affective registers. Some of the authors in this collection, for instance, valorize the act or gesture as politically progressive, revolutionary, and radical, while, at other times, it is given over to a certain amount of critique, speculation, doubt, or skepticism regarding its socio-political potential or its efficacy in facilitating the building of communities based on new ways of imagining kinship, filiation, and consanguinity. The act or gesture can't be pinned down to have a universalized meaning, and it resists being essentialized despite every possible attempt to do so. Even my own present use of the term "act" or "gesture"—a linguistic and verbal back-and-forth on my part—showcases the challenges inherent to trying to describe barebacking in easy terms. Is it an act? Or is it an attempt at a gesture? Or is it a practice? What kind of symbolic values do we adhere to it? How do we develop or arrive at these values? Does barebacking account for the complexities of sexual difference and the fluid ways by which gender identity and expression become sites for further deliberation and expansion? Has barebacking, or the values that inform it, evolved historically or changed as a result of generational shifts and of shifts in and across time? Has the very meaning of barebacking shifted as a result of biomedical advancements made in the form of pre- and post-exposure prophylaxes? As a certain reputed scholar of queer theory asked in a brief exchange I had with him in 2015, as I was just conceiving this project, "[Might] the question not be outdated? With so many young gay men with health coverage taking PrEP, and no apparent explosion in new HIV infections, the problematic status of barebacking may be diminishing, no?"[3] These are but some of the queries and concerns addressed by the various contributors to this volume.

The initial working title of this collection was Sex at the Limit: Essays on Barebacking. When I came up with this early title, I had in mind simply the colloquially accepted clinical and epidemiological understanding of what bareback sex comprised: sex without condoms, primarily presumed to be penetrative in this case (variously referred to as "raw," "unprotected," "unsafe," "real," sex "without limits," "unlimited"), practised mainly between men who have sex with other men. As such, one "limit" I had in mind was quite literally the barrier or the sheath—a technology of sex, as it were—that the condom itself came to represent as an easily accessible manner by which to curtail exposure to sexually transmitted forms of contagion. Psychoanalytically speaking, I am generally

---

3    I have decided to withhold the name of this respected scholar.

weary of subscribing to the notion of limit experiences: not because there are no such things as limits, but, more to the point, because the notion of a limit feels incredibly subjective. The ascription of such a subjective nature to the idea of limits, therefore, can neither be ignored nor dismissed and works to lay the subject bare (again, pun intended), open, or vulnerable to the risks that may come with pushing up against or undoing the limits that they, the subjects, have set for themselves. Simply put, it would seem that any discussion about limits might require the incorporation of a discussion concerning the risks implied, either implicitly or explicitly, in what it might mean to cross those limits. Any discussion addressing a limit appears to be informed by a need to account for what comes after the limit, beyond it, or even before it—in the form of conversations subjects have with themselves or with others about how they come to make certain and specific choices with regard to the practices they engage in. Sex at the precipice of such limits, or at least at the limit of fantasy, thus serves—it may be hoped—as a way to think productively and creatively about sex at the edge of risk itself or the fantasy of the presumed and/or real fear of risk.

Still, there seems to be another limit at work here, which I only came to realize in the process of compiling these essays and which pertains to the very ways by which we talk about sex and sexual practices. This limit appears to be concerned with the question of pleasure. While the writers that have been convened for this project approach the subject of barebacking from a series of differently innovative and rigorously argued positions, the blurriness of pleasure as an analytical category is evident. It is as though, in the effort to theorize, historicize, and make meaning and sense out of barebacking, every effort has been deployed to talk around it, to talk around the psychically complicated pleasures that inform the practice of barebacking. Talking about sex here comes to mean talking around it, swirling around or orbiting it, avoiding or resisting talking about it, or talking about everything but. Here barebacking is rendered as a legible and legitimate object of (queer theoretical, historical, archival, socio-political, pornographic, pedagogical, or epidemiological) study—either it is politically salient, radically cutting-edge, non-normative, on the fringes, other, and/or subaltern, or it is construed as already regressive, already normative and normalized, already something to be nostalgic about and, thus, perhaps even mourned, especially as technologies of sex continue to evolve to protect individuals and communities from the perceived or real threat of disease or illness.

Thus, the Freudian category of "belatedness" or "afterwardness" comes to be rather useful here in understanding how sex, and how we talk about it in this volume, has hit a sort of wall or limit. Belatedness, in psychoanalytic parlance, refers to how "the effects of [a] scene [become] deferred, but [have] the same effect as though it were a recent experience."[4] Barebacking itself, or the possibility of any discourse regarding how pleasure circulates and operates within its enactment, appears to always already be overdetermined by that which seems to weigh it down, the anxious scene of meaning-making that the impulse to theorize exposes any category to. Pleasure, or any discourse emerging from it, feels excised from the conversation as though it is either in excess of the conversation or a vestigial part of it. It is as though the pleasurable aspect of the act is in a state of constant deferral when it comes to talking about it. And yet, one has to wonder, why do people engage in it? What pleasure does it offer a practitioner? What meanings do such a practitioner imbue the practice with?

I thought it might be prudent, then, in light of the conscious and unconscious divestments from the matter of pleasure in relation to barebacking made here by the various contributors, that I included a short narrative specifically regarding it. This is a narrative culled from the therapeutic work I was doing with an erstwhile patient of mine. As one will be quick to note, it is not merely a narrative about pleasure but also a narrative about voice, about the desires that lead one in search of certain pleasures and the limits or the prohibitions—both personal and external—that one might have to engage with with respect to that search and concerning the ways by which certain risks are structured and understood in relation to the pursuit of pleasure itself.

4    See Sigmund Freud, *Case Histories II*, trans. James Strachey (London: Penguin Books, 1991), 276–77.

O is a cisgendered gay man in his late twenties.[5] He came out of the proverbial closet in his early twenties. Over the course of our therapeutic encounter, he would discuss at length a certain pattern he found himself repeating time and again within the context of his sex life. O occasionally, as he described it, enjoyed having sex under the influence of certain substances, namely alcohol and MDMA. More specifically, he claimed to enjoy penetrative sex in these instances and identified—more or less—as a submissive bottom with respect to the kind of sex that he sought out. He described how the use of these substances lowered his inhibitions, made him "feel looser with [himself], freer, a lot more comfortable with [his] body." In a way, the consumption of these substances appeared not only to heighten any physiological and affective pleasure he derived from sex but also to contribute to the very experience of having his inhibitions considerably lowered. The pattern that he found himself repeating, which left him feeling unsettled in how he appeared to describe it, was that he would forgo the use of condoms in these sexual encounters while his inhibitions were lowered. Unless they volunteered to do so, he would not ask or force the tops he had sex with to use protection. Something about this seeming passivity, the loss of control, and how these relate to the notion of risk in the scene appeared to be arousing to him.

Oftentimes when he was narrating such a scene to me, he would do so in a lowered voice infused with what felt like a tinge of guilt. It was as though any pleasure he derived from the experience was balanced or even cancelled out by an equal and seemingly opposing amount of guilt. He would go on to express concern for his physical well-being, stirring up fear in himself that he might have contracted this or that infection, and to feeling rather ashamed about the choices he had made. It was as though he was already mourning the pleasure he had derived from the sex he had had in the very act of narrating the incident to me the "morning after." The pleasure was, in this telling, transformed into a belated sense of either self-doubt, guilt, or shame. Coming to know a bit about

---

5     The patient's identity has been withheld and certain details pertaining to his identity altered so as to maintain confidentiality.

the challenging relationship O had with his highly critical father, I wondered if he was expecting me to take on a similar role, that of a highly critical paternal or authority figure, in our therapeutic relationship. I wondered whether the pleasure O felt might lay in being critiqued, being made to feel bad, because it had become normalized for him to be reprimanded for so-called bad behaviour or poor choices. When he did not receive the sort of critique that I felt he was expecting from me, his penitence would intensify, or it would turn into a sort of anger directed at me for seeming to withhold the desired-for critique. It was as though in the trans-ferential scene of therapy, a mnemonic dance he engaged me in with regard to his own desire and pleasure, he always had to or expected to be "wrong." In a way, one might argue that his desire was a desire to be "wrong," having presumably done the "wrong" thing, to be seen as "wrong," but also to be seen as worthy of the care that someone was entrusted with—his father or me—to tell him that he was "wrong." To an extent, he appeared to experience concern and critique as one and the same.

I recount this story not so much to further interpret, analyze, or examine the course that this treatment took; rather, I describe it to showcase the profoundly intriguing and fascinating ways by which pleasure as it relates to barebacking takes shape, gets talked about, and gets circulated when we tarry with it as a topic worthy of our intellectual energies. In listening to O's story, what was revealed to me was a profoundly compelling yet highly subjective way by which O understood, internalized, and accessed pleasure. It was as though any possibility for a theory, a deeply subjective theory at that, or rather the precise conditions for theorizing itself, emerged from the patient. What I was trying to lay out was that in this scene the practice was neither valorized as a radical act nor vilified as a regressive gesture in how I chose to hear O present it to me. Sure, he felt a sense of guilt attached to it, but he also appeared to find a certain amount of pleasure in it, a pleasure he arrived at through certain complex psychical and affective choices. I was also attempting to hold up certain contradictions, contradictions that he himself revealed to me, to show how barebacking can be layered in how it is experienced, in how it is personally understood, and in how sense can or cannot be made out of it. A discussion about pleasure in any such scene would have to take account of each of these layers and treat each of them with the utmost care.

In his trenchant afterword to this collection, Tim Dean reasserts what he was attempting to do in his field-defining text *Unlimited Intimacy*: to approach barebacking with "judgment suspended." Nearly a decade has passed since his book came out, and numerous essays, journal articles, and studies examining barebacking have since been published, both in response to and in conversation with the thoughtful interventions he laid out there. This collection, while not in any way exhaustive, was organized in the hope that it would serve simultaneously as a sort of survey of the field—what has occurred within it, how it has evolved over time, and how it has taken the conversation surrounding barebacking in increasingly different directions—and as an opportunity to build upon the initial provocations that Dean and the others who came after him have made.

The interventions made here serve not to close the chapter on the topic of barebacking but rather to expand the ongoing debates surrounding it. This feels especially pertinent in light of the new technologies of sex that are being created to make sexual practices safer. More to the point, these interventions work to highlight the differing and differential forms of psychical, affective, and socio-political meanings we bring to sex, how it is desired, how it is practised, and how it provides for complicated forms of pleasure. For instance, despite my aforementioned colleague's concern about the very merit of having these conversations anymore—"[Might] the question not be outdated?"—what might these discussions mean for men who, precisely because they are on PrEP, still contract HIV? What might these conversations hold for men who, while they might be protected against HIV, may also find themselves exposed to other forms of STIs? What value might these debates have for still other populations as well, like the trans-identified, lesbians, or heterosexuals? What might they offer, as well, in the name of recalibrating categories like health, stigma, risk, illness, danger, or debility? Furthermore, to echo Dean, might it be important to ask whether we are even barebacking anymore[6] as a result of new technologies of sex? Is barebacking still barebacking with the invisible barrier of chemical prophylaxes? And what does it mean to have one's life, one's sex life, always already medicalized?

Thinking alongside the aforementioned notion of limits and considering what it might mean to think sex precisely alongside such limits, both in being governed by them and in exceeding them, this collection, then, has been organized on the basis of a few limits around which, it is presumed, barebacking might operate. My hope is that the sections, in how they have been divided, read as intuitive choices made in my role as editor and that they work to highlight certain thematic strands of thought that might connect the various chapters in any given section. The overall intention was to think of barebacking in terms that are both interdisciplinary and multidisciplinary in tone, nature, and thematic cohesiveness. Taking Dean's challenge seriously, my desire was to suspend judgment, at least minimally, when approaching the subject of barebacking. One manner, albeit quick and dirty, by which I have attempted to do so throughout this project (which unto itself might be a form of value judgment and therefore be subject to critique) has been to encourage writers, whenever possible and necessary, to "simply" describe barebacking as "(penetrative) sex without condoms." As will be proven time and again here, this is no easy feat. And yet it was nonetheless emphasized as a challenge against describing barebacking in terms that appear significantly more value-laden, such as "unprotected" or "unsafe," to name a few such descriptors. Importance has also been given to the question of how the practice has evolved, with regard to its multiple meanings, across space, time, history, and various socio-political scenes, such that it becomes nearly impossible to find a unified meaning and understanding of it. Barebacking is consequentially shown, then, to be a profoundly malleable, tactile, and tensile category, simultaneously overdetermined and self-contradicting. In the final analysis, perhaps, my hope is that we not think necessarily or always (though sometimes

---

6    This is a reference to the opening line of Tim Dean's afterword to this collection of essays: "Are we still barebacking?"

this might be unavoidable and/or unconscious) about barebacking belatedly, mournfully, or nostalgically as an already-in-the-past subcultural or cultural node in the *longue durée* of human sexuality.

The first part, "Bio-Political Limits," sets the stage by outlining some of the biological, political, and sociological concerns around which barebacking as a practice might orbit. Jonathan Allan leads the collection by addressing the very materiality of that "extra" bit of skin that surrounds the penis, the foreskin. In politically and nationally situating the anxieties that the foreskin might or might not produce, Allan regards, with a keen eye for detail, the manner by which bodily parts, or the fragmentary body and the fragmented bodily part, become placed in service of tying together fantasies about masculinity, nationhood, national security, health, and contagion. Octavio González, writing about PrEP and the resulting sexual revolution that men who have sex with men find themselves in, attempts to offer us the genealogical coordinates for identifying the contemporary figure of the so-called Truvada whore. He locates this figure alongside a long list of other highly charged and historic AIDS panic icons, such as the mythic figure of a presumed Patient Zero, who has served to play a role in the fantasized origin story of HIV/AIDS, and the late-nineties figure of the barebacker, an outlaw on the supposed fringes of queer sociality. What does the emergence of these AIDS panic icons mean for how sexual relations are formed? How might we reckon with the precise formation of this new figure alongside the development of new technologies of sex that claim to make sex a safer endeavour? How might a figure such as this be promulgated in order to issue a warning or a prohibition against the circulation of certain sexual choices and practices such as barebacking? These are but some of the queries that González seamlessly attempts to tackle. In the final chapter in this section, Frank Karioris quite literally flips the script by reimagining the practice of barebacking as existing beyond the realm of its usually presumed practitioners—men who have sex with men—by considering its existence within the scene of heterosexuality. In what turns out to be an evocative study, he delineates how categories such as gender, masculinity, virility, and virality play off one another when the choice is made to relinquish the condom.

The second part, titled "Bodily Limits," starts off with what is perhaps the closest attempt in this volume to addressing my own aforementioned interest—the question of pleasure or rather of the uses of pleasure when thinking about barebacking. Here Rinaldo Walcott attempts to effectually and necessarily redeem the figure of the "Black cumjoy," yet another figure that could easily be (or, in some instances, has already been) subsumed under the heading of being or becoming an AIDS panic icon. In his capacious analysis, Walcott asks if a virus could be racist or construed as such. He explores what it means to simultaneously desire the pleasures of cum—swapping and sharing it, giving and receiving it—while also situating the history of HIV/AIDS alongside the history and the present of anti-Black racism. Walcott asks after the question of what happens to pleasure in a scene that is already imbued with the profoundly racist notion that systematically constructs the Black man as a harbinger of death and dying. Elliot Evans, writing on the work of Monique Wittig and Patrick Califia, closes off this section with their chapter about fantasies of lesbian bleeding. Moving simultaneously away from and alongside the theorizing that is often informed by the breeding fantasies of queer or gay male sex to other sites where skin may touch skin, where wounds may be exposed to wounds, where fluids—blood, saliva, and sweat—may be shared and passed between sexual subjects, Evans's reflection homes in on the eroticized potential of corporeal commiseration at the very site of flesh. By considering trans and lesbian forms of embodiment and identification, Evans opens up the body as a whole to become a zone for erotogenic vulnerability and openness to both intense risk and profound need and desire, where this risk and desire appear to feed off one another.

"Pornographic Limits" tackles the question of the visual and mediated representation of penetrative sex without condoms. The writers in this section approach the study of pornographic representation from discursively different perspectives. Evangelos Tziallas, in his analysis of the Raging Stallion film *Focus/Refocus*, addresses the difficult line that the consumption and production of bareback porn straddles between professional productions and amateur ones. With the influx of websites that showcase amateur work, suddenly everyone can occupy all three positions—porn producer, porn star, and porn consumer. Accordingly, for Tziallas, amateurism brings new meanings to how porn might be imagined, while also impeding the distribution and consumption of more professional productions. The coordinates for what excites us about porn might necessarily shift as who produces it and how it is distributed or accessed change over time. Next we have an epistolary exchange of sorts between a bareback pornographer and a media theorist. Keen observers of the genre of bareback pornography will immediately recognize the name of Paul Morris, founder of Treasure Island Media (TIM). Neither Morris nor his production house is a stranger to controversy and public scrutiny due to the highly charged nature of TIM's films depicting bareback sex. In a prior conversation with Susanna Paasonen, published in the *Gay and Lesbian Quarterly*, he described "TIM [as] two things . . . a developing and living archive of real male sexual experience . . . [and] a genetic laboratory exploring the vital sexual symbiosis of human and viral DNA."[7] Morris and Paasonen build on this earlier conversation to address the ways TIM exists within, and sees itself negotiating the larger contexts of, capitalism, market forces, and queer and sexual community formations. One will immediately pick up on the (potentially) radical, or even revolutionary, value that Morris offers to the thinking of bareback sex, both in its practice and in the scene of its pornographic representation. This part concludes with a chapter by Gareth Longstaff, who conducts a rigorous psychoanalytic analysis of the representation of *jouissance* in bareback and chemsex pornography. Chemsex—the use of substances to enhance sexual experience—has a long and, at times, problematized association with the practice of barebacking. I described this association, to a certain extent, in my earlier discussion of a case history from my clinical practice. Longstaff tackles the question of what happens to the body, and how it experiences *jouissance*, precisely at the intersection of sexual practice and substance use. Even in the most progressive of discursive spaces that claim to study barebacking, there is often an attempt to "clean up" and

---

7    Paul Morris and Susanna Paasonen, "Risk and Utopia: A Dialogue on Pornography," *GLQ: A Journal of Lesbian and Gay Studies* 20, no. 3 (2014): 215–39.

redeem the practice by distancing it from chemsex, which is often understood as taking alleged depravity one step too far. Longstaff's attempt at thinking barebacking and chemsex in tandem with each other is insightful in getting to the bottom of what may be desired (or occluded) in bringing the two together.

The final section of this book, "Psychoanalytic and Pedagogical Limits," endeavours to take the conversation further still, to' other terrains—to the realm of the unconscious and the scene of the classroom. My intention in formulating such a section was to encourage the writers therein to think critically and carefully about how sex and sexuality are sites of learning, ambivalence, reflexivity, and possible insight. The assumption here is that barebacking can presumably teach us something, something about our desire, or rather about how we desire, or, still, that we are always already learning from it about the experience of bodily fragility, resilience, and vulnerability. Diego Semerene's Lacanian assessment of barebacking alongside the structuration of masculinity and male violence attempts to think of the practice in line with conversations relating to drag, cross-dressing, and performativity. The symbolic weight of barebacking and of the constitution of viral transmission and transferability is given primacy in Semerene's discussion. There are other sites that have similar forms of symbolic weight attached to or imposed upon them. One might argue that the classroom is one such space wherein the conscious lives of subjects are trained and tamed against systematized ways by which risk circulates or is thought of. In his chapter, Adam Greteman explores what it might mean to update the sex education curriculum to incorporate a rigorous discussion of barebacking. What kind of systemic, structural, societal, and socio-political issues may be opened up or unravelled by looking more closely at how barebacking as a practice moves from being subcultural to being cultural and/or mainstream or normalized? What kind of parameters might be set up to understand how barebacking informs community formation and ethical forms of filiation? Christien Garcia, in the chapter that rounds off this book, locates what could only be assumed to be the unconscious and ethical kernel of barebacking by slowing down the very act or rather slowing down our analysis of it. By examining an incredibly short scene, one that lasts no more than a few seconds, from a Paul Morris film, Garcia wants us to think alongside the auteur about the question of "mereness." In this short scene, a lot transpires, and Garcia recounts how an incisive attention to detail in examining the moment can allow us to slow down sex in a temporal sense and give it a value that exceeds any theorizing that we might subject it to. The slowing down of sex, or more specifically the slowing down of an examination of it, goes beyond any attempt that can be made to contain or capitulate it under the pressures of meta-narratives.

As can be seen, barebacking as a queer theoretical concept, or as a representational category, or as a complex sexual practice, does overtime here. It comes to mean so many different things to the authors brought together here under the heading of thinking sex at, before, and beyond the notion of any limits we may be able to place upon it. My hope is that readers of this collection will at once relate to something they find in these pages while immediately asking, as I did regarding the question of pleasure, "Well, what about this . . . ? Or that . . . ?" As is the case with any other subject that merits attention, so too might be the case with barebacking, that thinking belatedly is still a thinking worth tarrying with. Or, in other words, it might never be too late to think more, a lot more, or think limitlessly about it.

**REFERENCES**

Barnouw, Dagmar. *Weimar Intellectuals and the Threat of Modernity*. Bloomington: Indiana University Press, 1988.

Freud, Sigmund. *Case Histories II*. Translated by James Strachey. London: Penguin Books, 1991.

Morris, Paul, and Susanna Paasonen. "Risk and Utopia: A Dialogue on Pornography." *GLQ: A Journal of Lesbian and Gay Studies* 20, no. 3 (June 2014): 215–39.

Spivak, Gayatri Chakravorty. "Can the Subaltern Speak?" In *Marxism and the Interpretation of Culture*, edited by Cary Nelson and Lawrence Grossberg, 271–313. Chicago: University of Illinois Press, 1988.

# BIO-
# POLITICAL
# LIMITS

CHAPTER 1

# IS THE FORESKIN A GRAVE?

Jonathan A. Allan

Every so often, we receive a particularly valuable comment from the peer review of an article; and sometimes—though, sadly, this is even less frequent—that comment takes us down a path that we had not imagined and, indeed, that ultimately causes us a kind of "was it worth it" anxiety. This chapter, in many ways, was provoked by an all-too-brief comment asking that I merely add a footnote to the article contending with how "anti-circumcision" activists often share much in common with "men's rights activists" or how these discourses slip into one another. (Little did I know that this would be a common question when research-ing my book *Uncut*.) Easy enough, I thought. However, in searching for the "perfect" or the "ideal" quotation, I quickly came across a number of phrases about the foreskin that caught my attention. I jotted these down, set them aside, and kept adding to this list of phrases. And yet I continued to think about these statements. This chapter, then, is an attempt to make sense of the plethora of prose surrounding the foreskin, and subsequently to think through the role played by the foreskin in the discourses on barebacking, especially given how often the foreskin is imagined as diseased or risky while circumcision is imagined as a prophylactic measure.

On March 28, 2007, the United Nations "endorsed male circumcision as a way to prevent HIV infections in heterosexual men"; at the same time, the World Health Organization and UNAIDS "said increasing male circumcision could prevent 5.7 million sub-Saharan African men from contracting HIV over the next two decades, and save 3 million lives."[1] Male circumcision—"the partial or total removal of the foreskin, or prepuce, of the penis"[2]—has been determined by these global organizations to be medically relevant and beneficent, and has been framed in a variety of places as a kind of "natural condom," though surely not infallible.[3] Nevertheless, "these [circumcision] proposals have attracted high levels of international support, including philanthropic endorsement and funding, notably from the Bill and Melinda Gates and Clinton Foundations."[4] Brian J. Morris, a professor of molecular medical sciences at the University of Sydney and the author of *In Favour of Circumcision*, arguably one of the most vociferous voices in favour of circumcision, goes so far as to argue that

> although condoms reduce risk by 80–90% when always used, they are not infallible, nor used universally, and do not protect during foreplay when the inner prepuce may come into contact with infected fluids. Circumcision in contrast is once only, so does not need to be applied each time sex is contemplated, is permanent, and *when coupled with condom use should virtually guarantee complete protection from infection by HIV.*[5]

---

1    Laura MacInnis, "U.N. Recommends Male Circumcision to Prevent HIV," *Reuters*, March 28, 2007, https://www.reuters.com/article/us-aids-un-idUSL2862367220070328.

2    Lawrence S. Dritsas, "Below the Belt: Doctors, Debate, and the Ongoing American Discussion of Routine Neonatal Male Circumcision," *Bulletin of Science, Technology & Society* 21, no. 4 (August 2001): 298.

3    Kate Bonner, "Male Circumcision as an HIV Control Strategy: Not a 'Natural Condom,'" *Reproductive Health Matters* 9, no. 18 (2001): 143. In her article, Bonner critiques the idea of the "natural condom."

4    Marie Fox and Michael Thomson, "The New Politics of Male Circumcision: HIV/AIDS, Health Law and Social Justice," *Legal Studies* 32, no. 2 (2012): 262.

5    Brian J. Morris, "Why Circumcision Is a Biomedical Imperative for the 21st Century," *Bioessays* 29, no. 11 (2007): 1150 (emphasis added).

For Morris, a condom and circumcision would seemingly provide Fort Knox–like security for the penis. Circumcision becomes, to Morris's mind, a "biomedical imperative."[6] The phrase "biomedical imperative" caught my attention as representative of the kind of language used to describe the removal of the foreskin.

Instead of focusing on circumcision itself, this chapter will focus its attention on what is being removed: the foreskin. In particular, I set out to think about how the foreskin is represented or not. Consider, for instance, the following examples. In an article in *Men's Health*, readers learn that the "advantage of the foreskin is not clear," which immediately sets in motion a kind of cost-benefit analysis. Readers will subsequently learn that "some scientists speculate that [foreskin] protected the prehistoric penis as it swung, naked, through thick forests and over tall grasses; and unless you take your penis on that sort of excursion, they argue, you don't need foreskin."[7] In this specific scene, taken from the popular press, the foreskin is framed as primitive, a historical remnant from a time gone by, a time from which we have evolved.

In another telling example, Marie Fox and Michael Thomson note that the foreskin has been called a "piece of prehistoric human culture that now only exists as a *reservoir of infection*,"[8] a claim echoed by Gerald N. Weiss, who called the foreskin a "cesspool."[9] In these cases, the foreskin is intimately tied to infection and disease. Melvin Anchell has suggested that "the foreskin is an anatomical remnant from a previous stage of evolution when it served a purpose. Today it is *useless and may cause physical harm*."[10] One cannot help but note the proximity between primitivism and infection or illness to which these descriptions of the foreskin allude.

---

6    Ibid., 1147.

7    Charles Hirshberg, "Should All Males Be Circumcised?," *Men's Health*, January 28, 2009, https://www.menshealth.com/health/a19531693/debate-over-circumcision/.

8    Marie Fox and Michael Thomson, "Foreskin Is a Feminist Issue," *Australian Feminist Studies* 24, no. 60 (2009): 204 (emphasis added).

9    Kimberly K. Updegrove, "An Evidence-Based Approach to Male Circumcision: What Do We Know?," *Journal of Midwifery and Women's Health* 46, no. 6 (2001): 416.

10   Daniel M. Harrison, "Rethinking Circumcision and Sexuality in the United States," *Sexualities* 5, no. 3 (2002): 303 (emphasis added).

Still another voice adds that the "foreskin turns out to be a sponge for the virus [HIV]."[11] In Cassell's *Queer Companion*, under the entry for "cut," we read this:

> Men seem prepared to go to war in defence of their fore-skin, or lack of. Cut men smugly announce that their way is healthy, since reports suggest that having a foreskin can leave one more open to certain forms of cancer and that cuts to foreskin can lead to greater vulnerability to HIV transmission.[12]

Similarly, Robert C. Bollinger specifically notes that foreskins are "magnets for HIV."[13] If one thing is certain, it would seem that the foreskin is, at least in these writings, tied to illness, infection, viral politics, and disease and is, of course, oriented toward the chronic and toward death. Foreskins seem naturally inclined to absorb the virus in all of these descriptions. Circumcision is thus construed as "a lifesaving STD stopper (for men and women)."[14]

Other critics, such as the aforementioned Morris, have noted that, in the United States, "those not circumcised are *mainly immigrants* from cultures in which circumcision is unfamiliar," a comment that follows his earlier remark in the same article that "when humans roamed naked on the African savannah, the prepuce [foreskin] protected the glans penis. But once humans started to cover genitals with clothing, that benefit was lost."[15] Here, then, the foreskin is presented as a kind of presumed threat to national security coming from abroad: the fantasy of "dirty" immigrants with foreskins. Moreover, and again, we see a clear, if imagined, delineation between "civilized" penises (those that have been

---

11   Bill Andriette, "Cocks Aquiver," *The Guide* 27, no. 3 (2007): 69.

12   William Stewart and Emily Hamer, "Cut," in *Cassell's Queer Companion: A Dictionary of Lesbian and Gay Life and Culture* (London: Continuum International Publishing Group, 1995), 62.

13   Bollinger in Nathan Seppa, "Better-Off Circumcised? Foreskin May Permit HIV Entry, Infection," *Science News*, March 31, 2004, 213.

14   Hirshberg, "Should All Males Be Circumcised?"

15   Morris, "Why Circumcision Is a Biomedical Imperative," 1147.

circumcised) and "primitive/immigrant" penises (those that have foreskins).

What is certain, as James Boon reminds his reader, is that "foreskins are facts—cultural facts—whether removed or retained. Absent versus present prepuces have divided many religions, politics, and ritual persuasions," and "(un)circumcision involves signs separating an 'us' from a 'them' entangled in various discourses of identity and distancing."[16] The foreskin is a fact insofar as it is there or it is not, but in its presence or absence it takes on meaning, which becomes, in Boon's estimation, a "cultural fact." These "cultural facts" are full of meaning and signification that cannot be denied: even the most cursory review of the word *foreskin* in scholarly and popular prose reveals a great deal about cultural ideas and ideals regarding its presence or absence.

Ultimately, as Peter Cuckow and Pierre Mouriquand argue, it would seem that "no other part of the body has aroused so much passion and misconception as the foreskin."[17] However, Cuckow and Mouriquand also summarize for their readers a series of "cultural facts":

> Attitudes towards the foreskin depend largely on civilisa-tion and culture. Muslims and Jews want to get rid of it for religious reasons; Americans want (wanted?) to get rid of it for hygienic reasons and for the hypothetical reduced risk of penile cancer in the circumcised population; Latins love to play with it, like to keep it, and are taught to mobilise it often; the British would like to ignore it, not to touch it, and eventually get rid of it when it causes too much trouble.[18]

How Cuckow and Mouriquand came to these conclusions is unclear, as no precise citations have been provided. Their argument, how-ever, does seem to summarize a range of presumed perspectives on

---

16    James Boon, *Verging on Extra-Vagance: Anthropology, History, Religion, Literature, Arts . . . Showbiz* (Princeton, NJ: Princeton University Press, 1999), 43.

17    Peter Cuckow and Pierre Mouriquand, "Saving the Normal Foreskin," *BMJ: British Medical Journal* 306, no. 6875 (1993): 459.

18    Ibid.

the foreskin, though again, it is not clear precisely what those are. When, for instance, Cuckow and Mouriquand speak of Latins, are they speaking in a fashion similar to Morris, who notes that it is "mainly immigrants" who remain uncircumcised? Or, conversely, is the argument here about the difference between being disciplined and controlled (American/British) versus pleasure-seeking and un-controlled (Latins)? Nonetheless, what is certain is that the foreskin "arouses" a great deal of "passion and misconception."[19]

Given all of this negative discourse, perhaps it is unsurprising that we have witnessed the rise of "intactivism" (anti-circumcision activism), which explicitly responds to those who have gone so far as to speak about the "stigma associated with the foreskin"[20] and presumably the corollary stigma of having a foreskin. For instance, we now frequently see the presence of "Foreskin Pride" at many Pride marches across North America.

Given all of this information, it should hardly be surprising that we have seen such an interest in foreskin as a site of difference, consternation, and curiosity. Indeed, it is perfectly natural in this context that men are seemingly "prepared to go to war in defence of their foreskin, or lack of,"[21] whether it is perceived as a source of shame, pride, or, perhaps for some, maybe even resignation. What is surprising, however, is that queer theory has yet to take up the foreskin as a site of critical interest. How, then, are we, as queer theorists, to think about the foreskin?

To be fair, of course, the foreskin has surely not been a terribly pressing or urgent issue for queer theory. Or perhaps its virtual absence in American culture—which, at one point (specifically in the eighties), boasted a circumcision rate between 80 and 90 percent—has led to its omission from discussions within queer theory.[22] How, though, can queer theory miss how intimately the

19  Ibid.
20  Sarah E. Waldeck, "Social Norm Theory and Male Circumcision: Why Parents Circumcise," *The American Journal of Bioethics* 3, no. 2 (2003): 57.
21  Stewart and Hamer, "Cut," 62.
22  See, for instance, Bonner, "Male Circumcision," 144; Harrison, "Rethinking Circumcision," 300; as well as Mary E. Buie, "Circumcision: The Good, the Bad, and American Values," *American Journal of Health Education* 36, no. 2 (2005): 102;

foreskin has been tied to discussions concerning HIV/AIDS? How can we neglect the ways that circumcision might be advocated as a safety mechanism for heterosexual men? This further begs the question what happens to bisexual, queer, and homosexual men in these discourses? In attempting to answer these questions, I work alongside and with queer theory to think about the foreskin.

When thinking about the foreskin, it seems nearly impossible not to return to Leo Bersani's provocative essay "Is the Rectum a Grave?"—especially at a moment when some suggest that circumcision provides the penis with a kind of "natural condom." Of course, we might turn to a range of queer theorists, particularly those thinking about questions of security, bio-politics, illness, nations and nationalisms, chronopolitics, temporality, and so on—all of which find their way into discussions of foreskins and circumcision. How might we think about the politics of colonialism, imperialism, racism, and primitivism in discussions concerning the foreskin? What might a sustained queer-of-colour critique offer the study of the foreskin, especially when the foreskin is figured as being primitive, perhaps uncivilized, and pertaining to "mainly immigrants"?[23] And, of course, how do we contend with the relationship between affect and the foreskin—for instance, that of stigma, shame, or pride? To be clear, I am speaking here exclusively about the language and representation of the foreskin: I am not, under any circumstances, speaking from the position of the biomedical sciences (I leave that work to those in the field). Moreover, this exploration should not be understood as "taking sides" in the larger debate over foreskins and circumcision. Instead, I am particularly interested in asking what queer theory can teach us about the foreskin and how the foreskin can participate in ongoing debates within that field.

---

Marie Fox and Michael Thomson, "Short Changed? The Law and Ethics of Male Circumcision," *The International Journal of Children's Rights* 13 (2006): 161; and Joseph Zoske, "Male Circumcision: A Gender Perspective," *The Journal of Men's Studies* 6, no. 2 (1998): 189.

23    Morris, "Why Circumcision Is a Biomedical Imperative," 1147.

Travis Wisdom, for instance, writes, "it is estimated that less than seventeen percent of the world's men are circumcised."[24] While this claim is echoed by Dunsmuir and Gordon,[25] Morris contends that 25 percent of men are circumcised,[26] a figure supported by Updegrove, who reports that "globally one in four infant males are circumcised."[27] While estimates clearly vary, what remains certain is that an overwhelming majority of men globally are not circumcised. The case of the United States, where the vast majority of men appear to be circumcised, presents another story. As Daniel M. Harrison explains, "in 1870 only 5 percent of American males were circumcised. By 1940 the rate was 55 percent, increasing to 85 percent of American boys some four decades later."[28] This rapid increase in circumcision rates was due, in large part, to the medicalization of circumcision.[29] More recently,

> the National Health and Nutrition Examination Survey from 1999 to 2004 found that a total of 79% of US males were circumcised, with 88% of whites, 73% of blacks, 42% of Mexican Americans, and 50% of "others" reporting that they were circumcised.[30]

It is certainly true that the "rate of circumcision appears to be declining" in the United States. The reasons for this decline range from cultural shifts and increased immigration to varying scientific opinions (for instance, those of the American Academy of Pediat-

---

24   Travis Wisdom, "Questioning Circumcisionism: Feminism, Gender Equity, and Human Rights," *Righting Wrongs: A Journal of Human Rights* 2, no. 1 (2012): 2.

25   W.D. Dunsmuir and E.M. Gordon, "The History of Circumcision," *BJU International* 83, suppl. 1 (1999): 1.

26   Morris, "Why Circumcision Is a Biomedical Imperative," 1147.

27   Updegrove, "An Evidence-Based Approach to Male Circumcision," 415.

28   Harrison, "Rethinking Circumcision," 302.

29   See, for instance, Robert Darby, *A Surgical Temptation: The Demonization of the Foreskin and the Rise of Circumcision in Britain* (Chicago: University of Chicago Press, 2005).

30   Zachary T. Androus, "Critiquing Circumcision: In Search of a New Paradigm for Conceptualizing Genital Modification," in *Circumcision, Public Health, Genital Autonomy, and Cultural Rights*, eds. Matthew Johnson and Megan O'Branski (London and New York: Routledge, 2014), 63.

rics) and insurance programs willing to fund the procedure. And yet it must also be admitted that the "most recent data estimates between 50% and 60% of newborn males are circumcised."[31] In the case of the United States, then, to be uncircumcised is to exist outside of the realm of the presumably normative and hegemonic.[32]

In 2003, Sarah E. Waldeck observed that "circumcision is consistent with American notions of good parenting"[33]—that is, once more, circumcision has become a part of, if not essential to, American identity. This claim is echoed by Adam Henerey, who notes that "circumcision is a practice performed by the masses of America."[34] And, in thinking about why circumcision continues as part of the American ethos, Mary E. Buie writes, "tradition continues to influence the practice of circumcision in the United States."[35] Circumcision, though often framed and understood as a religious ritual, is central to the American spirit. As Harrison notes, "relative to other nations, the popularity of male circumcision in the USA is highly anomalous, especially given the societal absence of a strong religious imperative toward the procedure."[36] One might be tempted to go so far as to argue that circumcision has become a part of the American civic religion and perhaps, above all, that circumcision is another element of American exceptionalism.

For Zachary T. Androus, "circumcision is afforded *exceptional* status in scientific medicine, especially in the United States."[37] Circumcision has become an integral part of national identity, so much so that Buie speaks of it in terms of American values, including tradition, equity, and fraternity.[38] We know that routine neonatal circumcision (RNC) is a "routine medical practice in the U.S." and that the "European medical establishment considers RNC an

31  Ibid.
32  I recognize the complexity of the language at play here, as surely the "intactivists" would note that what is non-normative is circumcision itself.
33  Waldeck, "Social Norm Theory and Male Circumcision," 57.
34  Adam Henerey, "Evolution of Male Circumcision as Normative Control," *The Journal of Men's Studies* 12, no. 3 (2004): 266.
35  Buie, "Circumcision," 103.
36  Harrison, "Rethinking Circumcision," 302.
37  Androus, "Critiquing Circumcision," 68 (emphasis added).
38  Buie, "Circumcision," 103.

unnecessary surgical procedure."[39] Nevertheless, the American medical establishment continues to suggest, unlike that of other countries, that circumcision is beneficial and perhaps even necessary because the foreskin is dirty, a "magnet for HIV,"[40] and so on. The American context has ensured that circumcision comes to symbolize proper hygiene, cleanliness, discipline, and order. Indeed, circumcision becomes a part of American sexual exceptionalism insofar as it "signals distinction from (to be unlike, dissimilar) as well as excellent (imminence, superiority)"[41] in relation to seemingly unexceptional subjects. It hardly stretches the imagination to understand how male circumcision becomes a site of exceptionalism that renders the American male "distinct" from others (for instance, Europeans) while assuring him of his "excellence," at least at the level of health (and, perhaps, sexuality). The default idea that the circumcision is a biomedical imperative suggests that the uncircumcised penis has failed to live up to the demands of hygiene. We often find references in the literature to the circumcised penis as cleaner and therefore healthier. Such an understanding, of course, depends upon how one engages with the available scientific material, wherein the debates are murky at best. Another side of this, in terms of sexuality, is that "the culturally dominant aesthetics of the penis . . . continue to value circumcision,"[42] at least in the twentieth century.[43]

At this point, I wish to return to Morris's argument that "those not circumcised are mainly immigrants from cultures in which circumcision is supposedly unfamiliar."[44] Even if the "facts" of this statement are true, the prose itself reveals a great deal about the

---

39   Wim Dekkers, "Routine (Non-Religious) Neonatal Circumcision and Bodily Integrity: A Transatlantic Dialogue," *Kennedy Institute of Ethics Journal* 19, no. 2 (2009): 125.

40   Seppa, "Better-Off Circumcised," 213.

41   Jasbir K. Puar, *Terrorist Assemblages: Homonationalism in Queer Times* (Durham, NC: Duke University Press, 2007), 2.

42   Amanda Kennedy, "Masculinity and Embodiment in the Practice of Foreskin Restoration," *International Journal of Men's Health* 14, no. 1 (2015): 46.

43   For a larger discussion of aesthetics and the foreskin, see Jonathan A. Allan, "The Foreskin Aesthetic or Ugliness Reconsidered," *Men and Masculinities* (2018), https://doi.org/10.1177/1097184X17753038.

44   Morris, "Why Circumcision Is a Biomedical Imperative," 1147.

politics of circumcision, particularly as they relate to the question of citizenship and the nation. In his study, Morris bluntly labels circumcision as a biomedical imperative; however, what lurks behind his prose is, in a sense, a kind of national security project wherein good, naturalized Americans have embraced the biomedical imperative, while the supposed "bad" Americans—immigrants (legal and non-status) and nonconforming Americans—have chosen not to follow or adhere to that imperative. For Morris, the foreskin becomes an affront to the biomedical security of the nation, and this security threat comes not from within the American border but from beyond it, "from cultures in which circumcision is unfamiliar."[45] For queer theorists, it is crucial to think carefully about how the foreskin and circumcision are being framed, and not just in terms of biomedical security but also the ways in which circumcision becomes exceptionalized and, above all, complicit in a project that seeks to presumably free American heterosexual bodies from fears of HIV/AIDS while not explicitly concerning itself with non-heterosexual bodies and immigrants. If we read through the language closely, we recognize that the critical question might become, is the foreskin, like the rectum, a grave?[46] Put another way, what does the foreskin do beyond providing a "reservoir for infection"?[47]

For Leo Bersani, the answer might well be obvious enough. Bersani, while not speaking about circumcision and the foreskin, does provide a useful phrase: "heterosexual anxiety." This particular manifestation of heterosexual anxiety binds the presumed proximity of HIV/AIDS to the foreskin and, of course, to sexuality itself. Consider what the biomedical imperative might really be about: the protection of heterosexuality and its (re)productive potential. Moreover, circumcision appears to be a visible, recognizable, signifying marking of the body that "shows" to anyone who sees the

---

45   Ibid.
46   Leo Bersani, "Is the Rectum a Grave?," in *Is the Rectum a Grave? And Other Essays* (Chicago: University of Chicago Press, 2010), 3.
47   Fox and Thomson, "Foreskin Is a Feminist Issue," 204.

cut penis that the circumcised person is presumably aware of the risks of the foreskin and has acted accordingly.[48]

Referring to media representations of HIV/AIDS during the early days of the crisis, Bersani writes,

> Instead of giving us sharp investigative reporting—on, say, *60 Minutes*—on research inefficiently divided among various uncoordinated and frequently competing private and public centers and agencies, or on the interests of pharmaceutical companies in helping to make available (to helping to keep unavailable) new antiviral treatments and in furthering or delaying the development of vaccine, TV treats us to nauseating processions of yuppie women announcing to the world that they will no longer put out for their yuppie boyfriends unless these boyfriends agree to use a condom.[49]

In this account, HIV/AIDS has less to do with gay men than it does with "yuppie women" and their "yuppie boyfriends," which is to say that Bersani observed that this was clearly about heterosexuality. We note that circumcision, like HIV/AIDS, is represented in terms of heterosexuality and the protection of heterosexual bodies. That is, in framing the discourse around protecting heterosexual bodies from HIV/AIDS, queer, gay, and other non-heterosexual bodies—and even non-sexual bodies such as virginal bodies, asexual bodies, or celibate bodies, all of which are non-sexual for a variety of reasons—are excluded from the analysis. As Bersani noted, this is about heterosexuality more than anything else, and so much of the research on male circumcision is about HIV/AIDS and how it might affect heterosexuality. In the same essay, Bersani further illuminated how heterosexual anxiety plays out and how others were expected to identify with this anxiety:

---

48    There is much to be said here about routine neonatal circumcision and the idea of compulsory heterosexuality, or, really, compulsory sexuality. If circumcision is imagined as a prophylactic measure, this also imagines that all bodies will become sexually active bodies (in relation to other people). I attend to this argument in my forthcoming book, *Uncut: A Cultural Analysis of the Foreskin*.

49    Bersani, "Is the Rectum a Grave?," 7–8.

Thus hundreds of thousands of gay men and IV drug users, who have reason to think that they may be infected with HIV, or who know that they are (and who therefore live in daily terror that one of the familiar symptoms will show up), or who are already suffering from an AIDS-related illness, or who are dying from one of these illnesses, are asked to sympathize with all those yuppettes agonizing over whether they're going to risk losing a good fuck by taking the "unfeminine" initiative of interrupting the invading male in order to insist that he practice safe sex.[50]

It is perhaps a surprising realization that in Bersani's essay HIV/AIDS is so deeply attached—literally and figuratively—to the penis (and not the rectum, despite the title of the canonical essay). In many ways, this appears to conform to and affirm the position of the World Health Organization, the United Nations, and nearly every example highlighted thus far in this chapter as part of what I have referred to as a kind of "sexual exceptionalism" that advocates male circumcision as a "natural condom." Bonner notes that "most of the epidemiological work done on male circumcision and HIV risk has looked at female-to-male transmission."[51] The United Nations, for this reason, advocates "male circumcision as a way to prevent HIV infection in *heterosexual* men."[52] Likewise, the World Health Organization and UNAIDS recommend "promoting circumcision . . . as an additional, important strategy for the prevention of *heterosexually acquired* HIV infection in men."[53] These organizations are fundamentally concerned with *heterosexual* male bodies that contribute to the growth and production of the nation, unlike homosexual and queer bodies, which are supposedly framed as having, in Lee Edelman's

---

50   Ibid., 8.
51   Bonner, "Male Circumcision," 149.
52   MacInnis, "U.N. Recommends Male Circumcision."
53   World Health Organization, "New Data on Male Circumcision and HIV Prevention: Policy and Programme Implications," last modified March 9, 2007, http://www.who.int/hiv/pub/malecircumcision/research_implications/en/.

provocative phrase, "no future."[54] To a certain extent, the World Health Organization and the United Nations seem to be framing HIV/AIDS as a "heterosexual crisis," which it surely can be as well but which also appears to conform to Bersani's theory regarding "heterosexual anxieties" about "homosexual" practices.

That is, if we were to consider in more depth the scene of "yuppie women" being afraid of contracting HIV/AIDS from their "yuppie boyfriends," we would quickly realize that "heterosexual anxiety" is deeply informed by homophobia. The greatest heterosexual anxiety may well be that one's partner is homosexual or engages in same-sex sexual practices. While one might read this as being about women's fear that their sexual partners will not be faithful to them, it can also reflect a fear that these partners are not being faithful to the very idea of monogamous coupling and to heterosexuality in general. In other words, all men are potential queers who might infect their "yuppie women," and thus these "yuppie women" must "tak[e] the 'unfeminine' initiative of interrupting the invading male in order to insist that he practice safe sex."[55] We should not be afraid to think carefully and critically about the ways in which the desire to protect heterosexual bodies is complicit in a project—the eradication of HIV/AIDS—that is informed by homophobia, however benevolent that project itself might appear. The question, then, becomes who gets left out?

If we accept Bersani's claim that "TV doesn't make the family, but it makes the family *mean* . . . a certain way,"[56] then we must consider that these studies and descriptions of the foreskin surely make *meaning* for and out of the foreskin. These meanings are affectively charged by their near-constant affiliation with disease and illness. The negotiation that Bersani deploys is the difference between "representation" and "reflection" that Stuart Hall considered in his work. In other words, there is the biological unit and the cultural identity that Bersani explores in thinking about the

---

54    Lee Edelman, *No Future: Queer Theory and the Death Drive* (Durham, NC: Duke University Press, 2004).

55    Bersani, "Is the Rectum a Grave?," 8.

56    Ibid., 8–9.

representation of the family on television. For Bersani, "the family identity produced on American television is much more likely to include your dog than your homosexual brother or sister."[57] In a similar fashion, research about the foreskin and its relation to HIV/AIDS is more likely, it seems, to be about heterosexual males than about homosexual, bisexual, or queer-identified males (to be clear, I am not making a quantitative argument here). I do not wish to negate the importance of this research, but we do have to ask about the implications of these studies for queer bodies.

In his analysis of the AIDS crisis, Bersani discusses "innocent victims" of HIV/AIDS, particularly in relation to the "persecut[ion] of children or of heterosexuals."[58] These "innocent victims," unlike gay men, are not supposed to acquire the virus, and thus, in many ways, to speak about the "innocent victims" is to create a sentimental space in which we can think about HIV/AIDS without thinking about, accepting, or affirming homosexual and queer sexualities. In a similar vein, the same kind of logic underpins so much of the language surrounding the foreskin and circumcision, as it becomes evident that it is about protecting heterosexual bodies. And so the language around circumcision, as we are coming to recognize it, is about protecting particular bodies. As queer theorists, we have to be aware of how these debates unfold politically. Again, in perhaps a strange way, it is about the proximity of sexual exceptionalism to national security, wherein circumcision becomes both prophylactic and protectionist, both of which form part of a national-sexual ethic that privileges discipline and control.

Of course historically, at least in the American context, routine circumcision has seemingly always been about discipline and control, whether it was disciplining the pleasure-seeking body or controlling illness and disease. For example, "the roots of circumcision in the US can be traced back to 1870 when Dr. John Lewis A. Sayre, an orthopedic surgeon, discovered the (now questionable) merits of circumcision in curing paralysis among male children suffering

---

57    Ibid., 9.
58    Ibid., 16.

from phymosis."[59] And, as David Gollaher has suggested, "not only orthopedic problems, but epilepsy, hernia, and even lunacy appeared to respond" to circumcision.[60] Circumcision has long been thought to be aligned with protection from certain forms of illness and disease, from epilepsy, a disease recorded as early as 2000 BCE, through to HIV/AIDS.

The other side of this—namely the question of pleasure—is equally complicated, for it was also assumed that the removal of the foreskin would reduce male masturbation. Mels van Driel notes that "the idea was that it would not only prevent masturbation, but would also combat sexually transmitted diseases or sexual neurasthenia, urinary tract infections and cervical cancer,"[61] all of which continues to conform to the production of heterosexual anxiety. Still, as is becoming clear, circumcision has long been about discipline and control: whether it be at the level of sexual pleasure or at the level of health.

Circumcision becomes part of a heterosexual anxiety about healthy and normal sexualities. In all of these gestures and phrases, then, for the American, the foreskin becomes the site of everything that is to be rejected, despised, removed, abstracted, and cut off. A good American—one who worries about biomedical security (of himself, his partners, his nation), one who worries about mental health, and one who remains "master of his domain"—would embrace the biomedical imperative. It would seem that circumcision is imagined in such a context as being essential to American masculinity.

But what about all of those men who refuse circumcision, or those who weren't circumcised? What about those bodies that are "marked" by their lack of marking, those bodies that are understood to be non-normative, if not "reservoirs for infection" and "magnets for the virus"? How does queer theory go about theorizing the foreskin in those cases?

---

59    Harrison, "Rethinking Circumcision," 303.
60    David L. Gollaher, "From Ritual to Science: The Medical Transformation of Circumcision in America," *Journal of Social History* 28, no. 1 (1994): 8.
61    Mels van Driel, *With the Hand: A Cultural History of Masturbation*, trans. Paul Vincent (London: Reaktion Books, 2012), 115.

Juliet Richters argues that, while "every time someone makes a claim about sex we need to test it against evidence, to examine its logic, to see what else it predicts," we also must "ask, 'Who is making this claim and who benefits from it?' This is politics. The answer to the second question cannot tell us whether the claim is right or wrong, but it can raise our suspicions."[62] In this fashion, while we may be skeptical of circumcision and its efficacy in combatting HIV/AIDS, we must ask about what we are skeptical of. Who, for instance, might benefit from making a claim that circumcision is a biomedical imperative and that the foreskin is primitive, prehistoric, and so on?

Robert Darby has framed the calls for universal circumcision as "voodoo science and medical imperialism."[63] For Darby, then, circumcision is complicit in a strategy that experiments on racialized bodies:

> In the nineteenth century English doctors keen to introduce circumcision assured people that it provided protection against syphilis—then as incurable and even less treatable than AIDS is now. Instead of innocent Africans they used innocent Jews to prove their case, claiming that Jewish men were highly resistant to syphilis (if not immune) because their foreskins had been removed.[64]

To be fair, Darby's argument *against* circumcision is, like arguments *for* circumcision, implicated within a political project. However, the similarities between "then" and "now" are surely telling, and once more "other" bodies are used to "prove" the scientific merit of circumcision. However, what remains consistent over two centuries is that the foreskin is always already prone to infection and must be removed for the biomedical security of the nation.

---

62 Juliet Richters, "Bodies, Pleasure and Displeasure," *Culture, Health & Sexuality: An International Journal for Research, Intervention, and Care* 11, no. 3 (2009): 234.

63 Robert Darby, "Been There, Done That: Thoughts on the Proposition that Yet More Circumcision Can Save the World from AIDS," *Australian Quarterly* 74, no. 5 (2002): 28.

64 Ibid, 29.

The foreskin, as seen in much of the literature, is deeply linked to heterosexual anxiety, which I have suggested is informed by—if not participating in—a homophobic project. So much of the work on circumcision has been pre-emptive, as in concerning protective measures taken with the future in mind—for instance, circumcising infants as a protective measure from humiliation in the locker room (the one kid with a foreskin being picked out from the crowd and possibly bullied) or as protection from future exposure to disease. D.W. Winnicott, however, in a brief letter to the editor of the *British Medical Journal*, remarks that "it is surely a queer indication for an operation [circumcision] on a baby that *he may one day be liable to venereal disease!*" He continues:

> When I am looking at a baby and contemplating the infinite complexity of his immediate and prospective physical and emotional development, I do not find myself being anxious about the possibility of his contracting syphilis or gonorrhea in twenty years' time.[65]

Winnicott's "queer indication" is, in many ways, precisely what is at the heart of so many arguments about the infant's foreskin, the biomedical imperative, the "sponge" or the "magnet" of the virus. It is a "queer indication" that *perhaps, at some point in the future, decades from now,* the infant's penis might come into contact with a venereal disease. That is, in the immediacy of the present, the circumcision is a future-oriented decision about the sexuality of the infant, the sexuality he might have, the sexualities he might participate in, and the utter conviction that the child has already been and will always be relationally sexually oriented.

And, for at least one critic, the aforementioned Daniel Harrison, "routinized circumcision might subtly reinforce what Judith Butler has referred to as the 'cultural field of gender hierarchy and the heterosexual imperative.' "[66] The circumcision of the penis therefore

---

65    D.W. Winnicott, "Circumcision," *The British Medical Journal* 1, no. 4071 (1939): 86 (emphasis added).
66    Harrison, "Rethinking Circumcision," 311.

orients the boy toward a future sexuality, and for Harrison this is about a heterosexual imperative. As such, he explains,

> If all men were circumcised, none would be tempted to dock—it would be a physical impossibility. Docking represents one of the many bodily permeabilities unsanctioned by the hegemonic order, and by learning to dock (or otherwise making erotic use out of the foreskin), uncircumcised males force common representations of the prepuce into a "demanding resignification."[67]

Is there an argument, however, to be made here about the queerness of the foreskin as a rejection of institutionalized heterosexuality—for instance, the heterosexuality of American exceptionalism? I am not certain how prevalent "docking" is in gay male sexuality, but what is certain is that the foreskin is privileged here, and by extension so is the presumed possibility of infection—even though "docking" is, as Darby and Cox suggest, a "fairly safe" form of sexual pleasure.[68] Robert Szabo and Roger Short have recently gone so far as to argue that

> It may also be time to re-think the definition of "safe sex." Since the penis is the probable site of viral entry, neither infected semen nor vaginal secretions should be allowed to come in contact with the penis, particularly in uncircumcised males. Thus, mutual male masturbation during which a penis is exposed to the potentially infected semen of another male should be regarded as risky sexual behaviour.[69]

It is imperative to note that "re-think[ing] the definition of 'safe sex'" has been under way from a range of perspectives for some

---

67   Ibid.

68   Robert Darby and Laurence Cox, "Objections of a Sentimental Character: The Subjective Dimensions of Foreskin Loss," *Matatu: Journal for African Culture and Society* 37, no. 1 (2008): 148.

69   Robert Szabo and Roger V. Short, "How Does Male Circumcision Protect Against HIV Infection?," *BMJ: British Medical Journal* 320, no. 7249 (2000): 1593–94.

time. Nevertheless, if previously "safe" sexual behaviours, such as mutual masturbation, are now deemed to be "risky," then surely we must add docking to that list of risky behaviours. But what is particularly telling about Szabo and Short's example is how quickly heterosexuality turns into homosexuality. The argument opens with recognition of how "neither infected semen nor vaginal secretions should be allowed to come in contact with the penis," but ultimately it concludes by discussing, as an example, "mutual male masturbation." How, then, can we, as critics, not see this as yet another indication of latent homophobia while advancing an argument about protecting heterosexual bodies?

Recent scholarship, notably Aaron T. Norton's work,[70] has begun to think about the "molecular politics of risk" with regard to the foreskin. This "risk" should hardly be surprising given the ways in which the foreskin has been spoken about: after all, it is a "sponge for the virus," we are told.[71] The foreskin becomes a hiding place for molecular risk and politics—much of the language coming out of circumcision campaigns is about the prophylactic value of circumcision. What, then, we might ask, does the foreskin mean in the context of barebacking?

Barebacking, as we well know, has long been theorized in relation to the virus. But what has yet to be considered, to my knowledge, is the place of the foreskin in these discussions. Does the uncut man become "interesting" in the context of barebacking? Does his foreskin signify him as being potentially riskier than those who are circumcised? Certainly, research has sought to ask, for instance, "are circumcised men safer sex partners?"[72] Another study, from Colombia, found that "beliefs that circumcision can minimize one's risk of acquiring an STI or HIV were not widespread"—indeed, according to that study, "approximately one third of survey participants did not know whether being circumcised or uncircumcised made it easier to get STIs (34%) or HIV (32%) and approximately half believed that

---

70   See Norton, "Foreskin and the Molecular Politics of Risk," *Social Studies of Science* 47, no. 5 (2017): 655–80.

71   Andriette, "Cocks Aquiver," 69.

72   Molly S. Rosenberg et al., "Are Circumcised Men Safer Sex Partners? Findings from the HAALSI Cohort in Rural South Africa," *PloS One* 13, no. 8 (2018): 1–10.

circumcision would not make a difference in STI (42%) or HIV (53%) risk."[73] In one of the few studies to take place in the Global North, the authors found that "circumcision is unlikely to be an effective strategy for HIV prevention among MSM [men who have sex with men] in Britain."[74] Certainly, these scholarly studies would seem to offer us some evidence that circumcision makes little difference epidemiologically and perhaps socially, but more research is needed. Indeed, what barebacking looks like in the United States may well look quite a bit different in other locales, and perhaps desire and disgust—common themes surrounding the foreskin—will function differently in a given context. Many questions remain, especially those that move toward considerations of desire and pleasure, a point Richters has noted.[75]

It is hard not to become paranoid when reading through the various reports and analyses of circumcision. While I am generally anxious about embracing a "paranoid reading,"[76] it does seem worthwhile to ask some of these paranoid questions, if only to produce more critical work on the politics of the foreskin. And while this chapter has hardly answered every question it has asked, my hope is that readers will consider the place of the foreskin in queer theory. The foreskin is a site of significant debate, passion, and curiosity, and what remains true across all studies—the one thing on which nearly all critics, scientists, and theorists agree—is that work remains to be done. And perhaps queer theorists might have a role in these debates, especially in an age in which circumcision is being "tested" in previously colonized regions, and in which pronouncements regarding circumcision avoid the queer, homosexual, and gay body, and thus become oriented toward compulsory

73    Felisa A. Gonzáles et al., "Popular Perceptions of Circumcision among Colombian Men Who Have Sex with Men," *Culture, Health & Sexuality* 14, no. 9 (2012): 1000.

74    Rita Doerner et al., "Circumcision and HIV Infection among Men Who Have Sex with Men in Britain: The Insertive Sexual Role," *Archives of Sexual Behavior* 42 (2013): 1319.

75    Richters, "Bodies, Pleasure, and Displeasure."

76    Eve Kosofsky Sedgwick, "Paranoid Reading and Reparative Reading; Or, You're So Paranoid, You Probably Think This Introduction Is about You," in *Touching Feeling: Affect, Pedagogy, Performativity* (Durham, NC: Duke University Press, 2003), 123–52.

heterosexuality. Certain questions remain, though: Why are so many studies devoted to reducing HIV/AIDS? Where circumcision might fit into that endeavour, why are such studies only interested in heterosexual males (and, by extension, their female partners)? Is routine circumcision complicit in the construction of hegemonic forms of masculinity? What are we not talking about when we are not talking about the foreskin?

## REFERENCES

Allan, Jonathan A. "The Foreskin Aesthetic, or Ugliness Reconsidered." *Men and Masculinities* (March 2018). https://doi.org/10.1177/1097184X17753038.

Andriette, Bill. "Cocks Aquiver." *The Guide* 27, no. 3 (2007): 69–70.

Androus, Zachary T. "Critiquing Circumcision: In Search of a New Paradigm for Conceptualizing Genital Modification." In *Circumcision, Public Health, Genital Autonomy, and Cultural Rights*, edited by Matthew Johnson and Megan O'Branski, 56–70. London and New York: Routledge, 2014.

Bersani, Leo. *Is the Rectum a Grave? And Other Essays.* Chicago: University of Chicago Press, 2010.

Bonner, Kate. "Male Circumcision as an HIV Control Strategy: Not a 'Natural Condom.'" *Reproductive Health Matters* 9, no. 18 (November 2001): 143–55.

Boon, James. *Verging on Extra-Vagance: Anthropology, History, Religion, Literature, Arts . . . Showbiz.* Princeton, NJ: Princeton University Press, 1999.

Buie, Mary E. "Circumcision: The Good, the Bad, and American Values." *American Journal of Health Education* 36, no. 2 (February 2005): 102–08.

Cuckow, Peter, and Pierre Mouriquand. "Saving the Normal Foreskin." *BMJ: British Medical Journal* 306, no. 6875 (February 1993): 459–60.

Darby, Robert. "Been There, Done That: Thoughts on the Proposition that Yet More Circumcision Can Save the World from AIDS." *Australian Quarterly* 74, no. 5 (September–October 2002): 26–35.

———. *A Surgical Temptation: The Demonization of the Foreskin and the Rise of Circumcision in Britain.* Chicago, University of Chicago Press, 2005.

Darby, Robert, and Laurence Cox. "Objections of a Sentimental Character: The Subjective Dimensions of Foreskin Loss." *Matatu: Journal of African Culture and Society* 37, no. 1 (2008): 145–68.

Dekkers, Wim. "Routine (Non-Religious) Neonatal Circumcision and Bodily Integrity: A Transatlantic Dialogue." *Kennedy Institute of Ethics Journal* 19, no. 2 (June 2009): 125–46.

Doerner, Rita, Eamonn McKeown, Simon Nelson, Jane Anderson, Nicola Low, and Jonathan Elford. "Circumcision and HIV Infection among

Men Who Have Sex with Men in Britain: The Insertive Sexual Role." *Archives of Sexual Behavior* 42 (January 2013): 1319–26.

Dritsas, Lawrence S. "Below the Belt: Doctors, Debate, and the Ongoing American Discussion of Routine Neonatal Male Circumcision." *Bulletin of Science, Technology & Society* 21, no. 4 (August 2001): 297–311.

Dunsmuir, W.D., and E.M. Gordon. "The History of Circumcision." Supplement, *BJU International* 83, no. 1 (January 1999): 1–12.

Edelman, Lee. *No Future: Queer Theory and the Death Drive*. Durham, NC: Duke University Press, 2004.

Fox, Marie, and Michael Thomson. "Foreskin Is a Feminist Issue." *Australian Feminist Studies* 24, no. 60 (May 2009): 195–210.

———. "The New Politics of Male Circumcision: HIV/AIDS, Health Law, and Social Justice." *Legal Studies* 32, no. 2 (June 2012): 255–81.

———. "Short Changed? The Law and Ethics of Male Circumcision." *The International Journal of Children's Rights* 13 (February 2006): 161–81.

Gollaher, David L. "From Ritual to Science: The Medical Transformation of Circumcision in America." *Journal of Social History* 28, no. 1 (Autumn 1994): 5–36.

Gonzales, Felisa A., Maria Cecilia Zea, Carol A. Reisen, Fernanda T. Bianchi, Carlos Fabian Betancourt Rodríguez, Marcela Aguilar Pardo, and Paul J. Poppen. "Popular Perceptions of Circumcision among Colombian Men Who Have Sex with Men." *Culture, Health & Sexuality* 14, no. 9 (August 2012): 991–1005.

Harrison, Daniel M. "Rethinking Circumcision and Sexuality in the United States." *Sexualities* 5, no. 3 (August 2002): 300–16.

Henerey, Adam. "Evolution of Male Circumcision as Normative Control." *The Journal of Men's Studies* 12, no. 3 (June 2004): 265–76.

Hirshberg, Charles. "Should All Males Be Circumcised?" *Men's Health*, January 28, 2009. https://www.menshealth.com/health/a19531693/debate-over-circumcision/.

Kennedy, Amanda. "Masculinity and Embodiment in the Practice of Foreskin Restoration." *International Journal of Men's Health* 14, no. 1 (Spring 2015): 38–54.

MacInnis, Laura. "U.N. Recommends Male Circumcision to Prevent HIV." *Reuters*, March 28, 2007. https://www.reuters.com/article/us-aids-un-idUSL2862367220070328.

Morris, Brian J. "Why Circumcision Is a Biomedical Imperative for the 21st Century." *BioEssays* 29, no. 11 (2007): 1147–58.

Norton, Aaron T. "Foreskin and the Molecular Politics of Risk." *Social Studies of Science* 47, no. 5 (2017): 655–80.

Puar, Jasbir K. *Terrorist Assemblages: Homonationalism in Queer Times*. Durham, NC: Duke University Press, 2007.

Richters, Juliet. "Bodies, Pleasure, and Displeasure." *Culture, Health &Sexuality: An International Journal for Research, Intervention, and Care* 11, no. 3 (March 2009): 225–36.

Rosenberg, Molly S., Francesc X. Gómez-Olivé, Julia K. Rohr, Kathleen Kahn, and Till W. Bärnighausen. "Are Circumcised Men Safer Sex Partners? Findings from HAALSI Cohort in Rural South Africa." *PLoS One* 13, no. 8 (2018): 1–10.

Sedgwick, Eve Kosofsky. "Paranoid Reading and Reparative Reading; Or, You're So Paranoid, You Probably Think This Introduction Is about You." In *Touching Feeling: Affect, Pedagogy, Performativity*, 123–52. Durham, NC: Duke University Press, 2003.

Seppa, Nathan. "Better-Off Circumcised? Foreskin May Permit HIV Entry, Infection." *Science News*, March 31, 2004. https://www.sciencenews.org/article/better-circumcised-foreskin-may-permit-hiv-entry-infection.

Sontag, Susan. *Illness as Metaphor and AIDS and Its Metaphors*. New York: Picador, 1990.

Stewart, William, and Emily Hamer. "Cut." In *Cassell's Queer Companion: A Dictionary of Lesbian and Gay LIfe and Culture*, 62. London: Continuum International Publishing Group, 1995.

Szabo, Robert, and Roger V. Short. "How Does Male Circumcision Protect Against HIV Infection?" *BMJ: British Medical Journal* 320, no. 7249 (June 2000): 1592–94.

Updegrove, Kimberly K. "An Evidence-Based Approach to Male Circumcision: What Do We Know?" *Journal of Midwifery & Women's Health* 46, no. 6 (January–February 2001): 415–22.

van Driel, Mels. *With the Hand: A Cultural History of Masturbation*. Translated by Paul Vincent. London: Reaktion Books, 2012.

Waldeck, Sarah E. "Social Norm Theory and Male Circumcision: Why Parents Circumcise." *The American Journal of Bioethics* 3, no. 2 (2003): 56–57.

Winnicott, D.W. "Circumcision." *British Medical Journal* 1, no. 4071 (1939): 86–87.

Wisdom, Travis. "Questioning Circumcisionism: Feminism, Gender Equity, and Human Rights." *Righting Wrongs: A Journal of Human Rights* 2, no. 1 (May 2012): 1–32.

World Health Organization. "New Data on Male Circumcision and HIV Prevention: Policy and Programme Implications." Last modified March 9, 2007. http://www.who.int/hiv/pub/malecircumcision/research_implications/en/.

Zoske, Jospeh. "Male Circumcision: A Gender Perspective." *The Journal of Men's Studies* 6, no. 2 (March 1998): 189–208.

# CHAPTER 2

# HIV PRE-EXPOSURE PROPHYLAXIS (PrEP), "THE TRUVADA WHORE," AND THE NEW GAY SEXUAL REVOLUTION

## Octavio R. González

**1**

My first point in this chapter is that in sex panics about HIV, barebacking, and "bugchasing," we continue to be haunted by the original trauma of AIDS. We cycle through passionate debates about the moral and behavioural risks of HIV transmission and queer sex that recapitulate the original "gay men's health crisis."[1] As many know, once AIDS was linked to sexual transmission, a sex panic set in. Community leaders advocated shutting down bathhouses, promoting safer sex, and ending promiscuity.[2] And so, the beginning of the AIDS crisis

---

1   Octavio R. González, "Tracking the Bugchaser: Giving the Gift of HIV/AIDS," *Cultural Critique* 75 (Spring 2010): 82–113.

2   The shift was to cultivating, among gay men, more "intimate and long term relationships." As Aviva Leber writes, "the dangers of AIDS necessitated an examination of the cause and validity of [promiscuous sexual] attitudes. At the first AIDS forum in Boston in 1983, gay panelists began to question [the gay male] promiscuous lifestyle and disregard for the spread of STDs. : . . The loneliness of this lifestyle was also exposed and examined. From these ideas a new acceptance and respect grew within the gay community, for intimate and long term relationships. In addition, for those who desired a more promiscuous lifestyle, there was a new and important emphasis on respect for yourself and your partners by engaging in safe sex." Aviva Leber, "AIDS: A Catalyst of

meant the end of gay sexual liberation. HIV/AIDS transformed the meaning of homosexual promiscuity from a form of queer kinship to irresponsible, unsafe sexual behaviour. Among men who have sex with men (MSM), having anal sex without condoms became a relic of the pre-AIDS era, replaced by the condom code.[3] Preventing the exchange of bodily fluids became not only a public-health mandate but also a categorical imperative, as evinced by an article by David L. Chambers from the early days of the crisis, in which Chambers summarizes the mass behavioural shift toward condom use among MSM:

> For sexually active people, and for gay men in particular, the answer to the epidemic, our "magic bullet," is the condom, a thin layer of latex to shield us from infection and death. AIDS organizations run largely by gay men announce a message that sex is fine, and that anal sex is fine—so long as a condom is used. These organizations imbue the directive about condoms with the force of a moral code. Not wearing a condom is not simply unwise; it is wrong. Not wearing a condom violates obligations to other gay men and, in the views of some, obligations to a larger gay community.[4]

Chambers adds that the moral directive was largely successful: "Men who have sex with other men . . . made huge changes in their sexual behaviour, changes that researchers in public health regard as among the most profound they have ever observed."[5]

However, with the advent of the protease inhibitor and combination therapy in the late 1990s, the staggering number of AIDS-related deaths and the urgency of AIDS activism began to subside in

---

Change for the Gay Community," University of Ottawa, Summer 2005, https://web.archive.org/web/20160625085357.

3    I use the terms "men who have sex with men" and "MSM" to indicate not only MSM, but also trans men and women who have sex with men. In the interest of readability, these populations are included in the "MSM" label used throughout this essay.

4    David L. Chambers, "Gay Men, AIDS, and the Code of the Condom," *Harvard Civil Rights–Civil Liberties Review* 29, no. 2 (1994): 353.

5    Ibid., 354.

the United States.[6] Around the same time, the term "barebacking" entered the gay cultural lexicon: memorably, on the February 1999 cover of *Poz Magazine*.[7] *Poz* situated barebacking as an underground sexual practice, denoting anal sex without condoms, in defiance of the norm.[8] The accompanying article involved AIDS activist Stephen Gendin interviewing Tony Valenzuela, whom Gendin described as "the Poster Boy of Unsafe Sex." Valenzuela discussed how he became a "pariah of the movement" once he "confessed to loving anal sex without condoms" to a "crowd of 2,000 gay and lesbian honchos." Valenzuela became a "sacrificial lamb at the altar of AIDS angst and anger," Gendin added, in the "community sex wars" instigated by public confessions of barebacking by AIDS activists. This 1999 *Poz* issue signalled that, by the end of the decade, the condom code was quietly suspended in what Tim Dean astutely dubs barebacking subculture.[9] As Dean suggests, the practice of

---

6    A side effect of this shift in AIDS prognoses, from death sentence to medical condition, was that HIV and AIDS became less visible in US culture more broadly. The ongoing realities of continued infections and diagnoses—both here and abroad—became less visible to the mainstream public. For instance, in the United States, the CDC reports that an average of fifty thousand people are diagnosed with HIV every year. This figure has not budged since the beginning of the epidemic. Of those annual new infections, 18 percent don't know they are infected. See "HIV in the United States: At a Glance," Centers for Disease Control and Prevention, last modified August 6, 2018, http://www.cdc.gov/hiv/statistics/overview/ataglance.html.

7    I use the term "poz" to denote self-identified MSM who are openly HIV-positive and belong to communities that draw strength and solidarity from developing a "poz" cultural identity. See González, "Tracking the Bugchaser."

8    The cover headline reads "Bareback" in a large font, and above it is a photo of HIV-positive AIDS activist Tony Valenzuela riding a horse without saddle, a neat visual way to connect the term's original meaning with the new one: anal sex without condoms between men. Stephen Gendin, "They Shoot Barebackers, Don't They?" *Poz Magazine*, February 1999, https://www.poz.com/article/They-Shoot-Barebackers-Don-t-They-1459-4936. But note that the next article in the issue involves an "HIV-negative prevention activist" who "goes through the latex looking glass to discover who's doing it raw, and why." So the slippage of "barebacking" from only seropositive to seronegative MSM is foreshadowed by this exposé. See Michael Scarce, "A Ride on the Wild Side," *Poz Magazine*, February 1999, https://www.poz.com/article/A-Ride-on-the-Wild-Side-1460-8374.

9    Tim Dean, *Unlimited Intimacy: Reflections on the Subculture of Barebacking* (Chicago: University of Chicago Press, 2009).

barebacking was more prevalent among HIV-positive MSM.[10] Dean claims that barebacking later became "organized" as a subculture: "After two decades of safe-sex education, erotic risk among gay men has become organized and deliberate, not just accidental."[11] But same-status barebacking was a mode of risk reduction. Those already infected had little to lose if they only had sex with others of the same serostatus; the data about reinfection, or so-called superinfection, were inconclusive, Dean adds.[12] By the mid-2000s, as barebacking became more prevalent in gay porn, it exceeded the original bounds of the subculture and then became more visible, if not more widespread, among MSM. For example, in my years as an HIV-prevention counsellor in AIDS research, there was collective hand-wringing about communal norms sliding toward condomless sex among all MSM.[13]

Today, this shifting of sexual norms away from the condom code looks very different given new biomedical tools for controlling and preventing HIV. The first breakthrough was "treatment-as-prevention," or TasP, which became a way to lower transmission rates by treating HIV-positive individuals to lower their infectiousness. The more recent development is using one of these antiretroviral medicines—called pre-exposure prophylaxis or PrEP—to prevent infection with HIV.[14] Many studies have shown the efficacy of PrEP

---

10  Ibid., 13n19.

11  Ibid., ix.

12  Ibid., 13n20.

13  Not least, by the mid-2000s, barebacking—mitigated by serosorting—was advocated as a form of harm reduction by some community leaders. For more on serosorting, see Dean, *Unlimited Intimacy*, 12–15.

14  *Post*-exposure prophylaxis, or PEP, precedes PrEP, but follows the same logic of a pre-emptive strike against possible risk of infection. The PEP regimen is almost superseded by PrEP, which is a protocol that follows a daily schedule regardless of possible risk of infection. For now, the FDA-approved protocol for PrEP takes the form of a once-daily dose of Truvada, an antiretroviral originally used for treating HIV infection. Intermittent dosing, as in the iPERGAY trial, is not yet approved by the FDA or other health authorities like the CDC. According to the "PrEP Facts" Facebook group, at least seven days' worth of daily Truvada is required to develop the necessary level of emtricitabine and tenofovir to be protected against HIV through sexual contact. This evidence of ersatz, community-based circulation of knowledge about PrEP is consistent with how PrEP is viewed by many activists, as empowering those who are relatively disempowered,

in preventing transmission between, say, serodiscordant partners where one has HIV and the other does not. The level of protection from Truvada (still the only FDA-approved regimen for PrEP) can be as high as 96 to 99 percent if the pill is taken daily.[15]

These new biomedical treatments have profoundly changed how individuals calculate sexual risk. Savvy early adopters among MSM are turning to Truvada as PrEP, and some are barebacking with little, if any, fear of seroconversion. (Among them is Damon Jacobs, the world's first PrEP activist, and founder of the Facebook group PrEP Facts, which has almost 22,000 members.[16]) So, now, if you go on gay dating apps or websites, you will see a proliferation of HIV statuses—from "undetectable" to "HIV-negative, on PrEP."

**2**

This proliferation of labels for "new" HIV serostatuses, along with the rise in barebacking, points to my central claim: we are entering a new era in the history of sexuality, a new gay sexual revolution, based on the widespread uptake of PrEP primarily among gay and bisexual men. This new era began in similar fashion to the barebacking phenomenon, sketched by *Poz Magazine* and the "Poster Boy for Unsafe Sex" in 1999. As with the origins of barebacking, the advent of PrEP has elicited a cultural backlash, the predictable

---

non-experts or non-insertive partners in particular: non-medically-trained community members are learning about pharmacokinetics and clinical-trial data, and sexually receptive partners in anal or vaginal intercourse no longer need to rely on the "tops" to use a condom. The long history of the AIDS crisis is, of course, based on the militant activism of the AIDS Coalition to Unleash Power (Act Up), which spearheaded this democratization of scientific discourse, to empower communities and add tremendous urgency to sluggish efforts made toward finding a cure or toward developing better treatments.

15    See, for example, the CDC's "HIV basics" page on PrEP, last modified August 23, 2018, http://www.cdc.gov/hiv/basics/prep.html.

16    PrEP Facts, "Rethinking HIV Prevention and Sex," Facebook, accessed October 23, 2018, https://www.facebook.com/groups/PrEPFacts/members/. There is another Facebook "PrEP Facts" group for women, which, by contrast, numbers just over five hundred members. See PrEP Facts, "Women's Sexuality and HIV Prevention," Facebook, October 23, 2018, https://www.facebook.com/groups/PrEP4Women/.

panic response from leaders in the community and certain legacy AIDS activists.

It is important to note that these related sex panics—barebacking and, more recently, PrEP—are based on a rethinking of what counts as "protection" or as "safer sex." "Safer sex" used to refer to wearing a condom for anal sex. But this new normal of individuals on PrEP—or those on TasP, who are undetectable—now challenges this legacy notion. Many of these individuals bareback while insisting that they are practising "safer sex." PrEP's early adopters thus increasingly seem to be turning away from condoms, a trend already established among HIV-positive or "poz" men almost two decades ago.

And so, with the advent of PrEP, a new gay sex panic has arisen. Again, this new panic echoes earlier fears about queer cultures of promiscuity that date back to the original "gay men's health crisis." And these fears turn on the persistent cultural notion that "the rectum [is] a grave," in Leo Bersani's memorable phrase.[17] As Priscilla Wald shows, the AIDS crisis was seen as a "contagion narrative," which is the way an epidemic is rhetorically framed for the public.[18] Wald claims that these narratives share certain features. Randy Shilts's influential account, *And the Band Played On*, turns on the mythic stereotyping of Gaëtan Dugas, infamously reduced to that hoary figure from homophobic imagination, the flat character we know as the "promiscuous gay flight attendant."[19] Shilts represents Dugas as "Patient Zero" or the individual case that introduced HIV to North America. Even early on, scientists disputed this origin myth. But the science isn't the point: the cultural logic of "contagion," of "the rectum [as] a grave," is. This cultural logic continues to attach itself to other figures who occupy the same mythic role of "disease carrier." And so, if we are never far from reliving the original trauma of the AIDS crisis, then any substantive transformation in the sexual behaviour of MSM inspires a new moral panic,

---

17    Leo Bersani, "Is the Rectum a Grave?" *October* 43 (1987): 197–222.

18    Priscilla Wald, *Contagious: Cultures, Carriers, and the Outbreak Narrative* (Durham, NC: Duke University Press, 2008). See especially Wald's chapter on HIV, " 'The Columbus of AIDS': The Invention of 'Patient Zero.' "

19    Randy Shilts, *And the Band Played On: Politics, People, and the AIDS Epidemic* (New York: St. Martin's Press, 1987).

invoking the latest spectre of gay male promiscuity. In short, with the advent of PrEP, we invoke a new villain, with a new name, but the song remains the same.

Indeed, since Gaëtan Dugas, there have been a series of AIDS "panic icons"—a long list of Patient Zeroes.[20] First, there was the 4-H group, the "high-risk group" of homosexuals, Haitians, heroin users, and hemophiliacs. With developments in treatment and prevention, the late 1990s and early 2000s saw the advent of new sex panics,[21] this time about the rise of condomless (or "unprotected") anal sex between men. New panics produced new panic icons: that of the barebacker, who intentionally has unprotected sex; the bugchaser, who intentionally seeks to become HIV-infected; the giftgiver, who intentionally infects the bugchaser with HIV, perversely viewing the virus as a "gift"; and the down-low figure, who has sex with men and women and thus infects unsuspecting, "innocent" wives and girlfriends.[22]

As we saw with the dubious construct of Patient Zero, science is no barrier to the cultural logic that pathologizes queer sexuality. And so, the profound shift in sexual risk and public health that PrEP represents does not come without a moral backlash. The PrEP backlash has been led primarily by Michael Weinstein of the AIDS Healthcare Foundation: our generation's own Randy Shilts, you might say.

In brief, the homophobic cultural logic that "the rectum is a grave," which animates the trope of "Patient Zero," persists. But before I discuss the latest version of the HIV/AIDS panic icon—the

---

20  Wald speaks of the "heirs to Patient Zero" as figures drawn from newer outbreaks, such as SARS (217). But she does not address the "heirs" that are themselves part of the ongoing HIV/AIDS "contagion narrative" or moral panic, as I do in this essay.

21  These gay "panic icons," in the words of Barry Adam, originally symbolized the existential threat HIV infection posed for uninfected people. Barry D. Adam, "Infectious Behaviour: Imputing Subjectivity to HIV Transmission," *Social Theory and Health* 4, no. 2 (2006): 168–79.

22  The latter two "panic icons"—men on the down low and gift-givers—are not only pathologized, but also racialized and criminalized, because they threaten the social quarantine of HIV/AIDS among communities of colour and the poor, who bear the brunt of the pandemic in the United States.

so-called Truvada whore—I should emphasize that these panic icons are constructed and mobilized for an HIV-negative audience, in the context of protecting public health and, by extension, the public interest. That is to say, these sex panics are meant to ideologically discipline the uninfected, to encourage them to continue protecting themselves from HIV. Panic icons promote the idea of "good" subjects—in this case, "good gays."[23]

## 3

And yet, my point that PrEP represents a new normal, a new gay sexual revolution, is based on the scientific fact that Truvada disrupts the link between unprotected sex and HIV risk. What PrEP does is remove the transgression from barebacking. In a sense, the condom code precipitated the barebacking transgression that is now being remoulded because of PrEP. It is that very notion—that barebacking is transgressive because it is dangerous from a public-health perspective—that PrEP threatens to disrupt. As Dean claims, PrEP seems to "licence enjoyment without limits": Truvada shows

---

23   For the statistics on how HIV largely impacts populations of colour—MSM and trans women, as well as cis women—see Centers for Disease Control and Prevention, "HIV Among African Americans," last modified July 5, 2018, https://www.cdc.gov/hiv/group/racialethnic/africanamericans/index.html. On the rates and risks among trans women, the CDC has this to say: "the highest percentage of newly identified HIV-positive test results was among transgender people (2.1%). For comparison, the lowest percentages of newly identified HIV-positive test results were among females (0.4%), followed by males (1.2%). Among transgender people in 2010, the highest percentages of newly identified HIV-positive test results were among racial and ethnic minorities: Blacks/African Americans comprised 4.1% of newly identified HIV-positive test results, followed by Latinos (3.0%), American Indians/Alaska Natives and Native Hawaiians/Other Pacific Islanders (both 2.0%), and whites (1.0%). In New York City (2007–2011), there were 191 new diagnoses of HIV infection among transgender people, 99% of which were among transgender women. The racial/ethnic disparities were large: approximately 90% of transgender women newly diagnosed with HIV infection were Blacks/African Americans or Latinas. Over half (52%) of newly diagnosed transgender women were in their twenties. Also, among newly diagnosed people, 51% of transgender women had documentation in their medical records of substance use, commercial sex work, homelessness, incarceration, and/or sexual abuse as compared with 31% of other people who were not transgender."

"what worry-free sex between men in the 21st century might be."[24] He adds, "it is this idea that has provoked such strong and opposing reactions. . . . While some observers fear that Truvada [as PrEP] will finish off the dwindling commitment to condoms altogether, others celebrate the paradoxical possibilities of risk-reduced bareback."[25]

This new PrEP-mediated cultural and sexual landscape inspires fantasies on both sides of AIDS activism. Some celebrate the advent of "worry-free" bareback sex, because barebacking itself can now be a form of "protected" sex more effective than even latex. But old-guard activists like Weinstein denounce Truvada as just another "party drug," akin to crystal methamphetamine, used to "party and play"—that is, getting high and having lots of bareback sex.[26] Weinstein argues that PrEP entails not the end of AIDS but rather the opposite: large-scale PrEP use will promote increases in sexually transmitted infections (STIs), and even in HIV transmission rates, the reason being that PrEP promises to, in Dean's words, "finish off the dwindling commitment to condoms altogether."[27] With PrEP, the choice to use condoms becomes an individual choice, one that speaks to an individual's autonomy in balancing the desire for sexual intimacy and for risk reduction. The latex condom is no longer the "magic bullet"—but as the rise of barebacking shows, it had already ceased to be.[28]

---

24 Tim Dean, "Mediated Intimacies: Raw Sex, Truvada, and the Biopolitics of Chemoprophylaxis," *Sexualities* 18, no. 1–2 (2015): 229.

25 Ibid.

26 I discuss the subculture of "party and play" (or PnP) in more detail below.

27 Dean, "Mediated Intimacies," 229.

28 An earlier version of this sentence contained the question: "So why use condoms at all?" To which my friend and colleague Philip Longo responds: "It occurs to me that the reasons are: 1) other STDs; 2) as a way to manage intimacy—it seems that [condom use] allows [for a certain] level of intimacy—e.g., 'I only [bareback] with special partners'; and 3) 'I'm not one of those slutty bottoms.'" Philip Longo, communication with author, March 15, 2016. The last point, *pace* Longo, buys in to the "Truvada whore" mentality that is the problem with the rhetorical persistence of the "whore"/"slut" trope around queer male sexuality. This slut-shaming rhetoric is fundamentally a bottom-shaming rhetoric. The persistence of the shame and stigma attaching to the "bottom" or anal-receptive position returns us to the main point of Bersani's essay: choosing to be penetrated is a "lawless" desire equated with the radical loss of masculinity and its attendant privileges of self, including self-control. (The "law" here being the patriarchal law, the Law

**4**

Intriguingly, the PrEP backlash is blind to this shift in community norms or blind to its life-affirming dimension. While PrEP may remove the notion and function of transgression from barebacking, the larger cultural logic remains fixed in an earlier era. And so, I see the figure of the Truvada whore within the genealogy of AIDS panic iconography. But this particular icon, as a metonym for PrEP, can also stand for a "new normal" in the history of sexuality—newly liberated queer eroticism. Now, with the advances of PrEP, one might argue that *the rectum is no longer a grave.*

It is in this sense that biomedical developments such as PrEP and TasP can weaken the climate of fear and paranoia surrounding AIDS. And so, in my view, TasP and PrEP are developments that rehabilitate queer sex. These biomedical developments restore to queer sex its pride of place as a historically important form of queer kinship and sociality. PrEP—which is, ironically, a biomedical breakthrough—liberates sex between men from the medical model of HIV/AIDS: the public-health paradigm of sexual behaviour, the contagion narrative, and the culture of panic over condomless anal sex.[29]

of the Father.) In this context, the social norm of toxic masculinity projects a sexually licentious "femininity" and its queer avatar, the "slutty bottom," both predicated on the emasculating desire to be penetrated by the valourized male member. Equating bottoming with emasculation creates a powerful cultural stigma against the "bottom," itself based on pervasive patriarchal misogyny. The "Truvada whore" label shows how this phobic rhetoric is recapitulated in public-health discourse about HIV risk-taking, which recycles the cultural stigma surrounding bottoming, or being "feminized," even in LGBTQ communities. For more on the cultural position of bottoming as a site of resistance, see Katherine Bond Stockton, *Beautiful Bottom, Beautiful Shame: Where Black Meets Queer* (Durham, NC: Duke University Press, 2006). For more on the racialization and stigmatization of bottoming, especially for Asian-American queers, see Tan Hoang Nguyen, *A View from the Bottom: Asian American Masculinity and Sexual Representation* (Durham, NC: Duke University Press, 2014). For a recent discussion of "bottom-shaming" in contemporary culture, see J. Bryan Lowder on the Shonda Rhimes television procedural *How to Get Away with Murder* (which had a PrEP storyline involving one of the main characters), "What's with All the Bottom Shaming in *How to Get Away with Murder?*," *Slate.com*, October 28, 2014, https://slate.com/human-interest/2014/10/why-are-how-to-get-away-with-murders-gay-sex-scenes-full-of-bottom-shame.html.

29  Again, included in this phrasing is the less readable but more accurate "(anal) sex between men and trans people."

**5**

Enter the Truvada whore, a figure for supposed drug-fuelled gay male promiscuity. As I have already suggested, this figure is only the latest in the long line of queer monsters. The Truvada whore icon was invented to contain the revolutionary potential of PrEP. Such an icon revitalizes an old narrative, which insists that the rectum is still a grave, that anal sex between men is still, first and foremost, a matter of HIV, STIs, and sexual risk—queer eroticism contained within the HIV/AIDS "contagion narrative," as it has been for over thirty-five years.

As I see it, the cultural discourse surrounding Truvada as PrEP has fallen under two main categories, the Truvada whore and the Truvada wars.[30] This chapter focuses on the first. The term "Truvada whore" was coined by a journalist, David Duran, writing in late 2012 for the *Huffington Post*.[31] "Truvada whore" was the title of Duran's piece, and the label has since taken on a life of its own, becoming a hashtag (#TruvadaWhore) and even an ironic T-shirt. In fact, since Duran's stigmatizing piece on PrEP, some queers have reclaimed the "Truvada whore" and "PrEP whore" labels as badges of honour, much like the label "queer" was reappropriated. These activists wear the scarlet letter in defiance of the slut-shaming implied in the epithet "whore."

It is important to note, however, that in the evolution of the PrEP "whore" rhetoric, Duran publicly rescinded his initial opposition to PrEP, and he openly regrets inventing the stigmatizing label.[32] In this about-face, Duran sees the problem with his original tactic: that of deploying a moral discourse via a gay panic icon, which trades on AIDS stigma to promote "safer sex." Promoting fear about

---

30    The phobia around PrEP is dissipating, as is the "whore" rhetoric. See note below.
31    The second is encapsulated in the phrase "Truvada Wars," a military metaphor that signifies the virulence of the debate in favour of or opposed to PrEP. "The Truvada Wars" is even the title of a scholarly article about this heated debate within the scientific community. See David Duran, "Truvada Whores?" *Huffington Post*, November 12, 2012, updated February 2, 2016, https://www.huffpost.com/ entry/truvada-whores_b_2113588. But make sure to see Duran's follow-up piece, "An Evolved Opinion on Truvada," *Huffington Post*, March 27. 2014, updated December 6, 2017, https://www.huffpost.com/entry/truvadawhore-an-evolved-o_b_5030285.
32    Duran, "An Evolved Opinion on Truvada."

HIV/AIDS is, as we have seen, a public-health strategy developed in response to knowledge about viral transmission. And yet, such strategies have always been divisive, prioritizing the uninfected and pathologizing those already infected. The latter are framed as "fallen" figures or, as we have seen, as monstrous icons in their own right. A recent ad campaign from Weinstein's AIDS Healthcare Foundation illustrates this divisive tactic, which disciplines the body politic by sowing fear and perpetuating the stigma of HIV/AIDS. The rhetoric and logic of such prevention campaigns compete against the logic of sexual intimacy itself, by focusing on the individual as the paranoid protector of a vulnerable body. Sexual intimacy, as Bersani's body of work argues,[33] is based on an openness to the other that can take many forms but that carries many risks—HIV risk being only one of many, including the emotional vulnerability inherent in laying bare one's erotic fantasies and desires. Embodied sexual openness, by abandoning the latex barrier, is a key feature of carnal intimacy in the age of AIDS. And, as this ad illustrates, such an appeal to self-protection against potential contamination serves to divide the community, one couple at a time. The now much-mocked advertisement features a cisgendered male couple in bed. One is shown hugging the pillow in the foreground, his face positioned toward the camera, but his eyes averted, with his back to his lover. The other hovers behind him in the background, looking in his lover's direction, frowning, with a suspicious look. The tag line is "Trust Him?" which refers, in this context, to the possibility that someone might be lying about his HIV status. The ad lets the secrecy and paranoia over HIV/AIDS hover over both men, neither of whom is rendered trustworthy. The couple are thus together physically but apart psychically. The ad implicitly challenges MSM not to trust their partners, insofar as this trust can be exploited as the basis for condomless sex. Indeed, eschewing condoms as a

---

33　Bersani is associated with modes of "self-shattering," or ways of attenuating the aggrandized subject, which includes the barebacker. See Leo Bersani and Adam Phillips, *Intimacies* (Chicago: University of Chicago Press, 2008). Lauren Berlant speaks against the notion of sovereign subjectivity and its propping up of an unequal social field under the guise of proper civil citizenship in "Slow Death (Sovereignty, Obesity, Lateral Agency)," *Critical Inquiry* 33 (2007): 754–80.

sign of romantic trust or sexual intimacy—notably in the context of a stable monogamous relationship—is often the Achilles heel of risk reduction.[34] This ad warns gay men not to fall for that "trap," warning them that it isn't safe to have unprotected sex with your partner, since you don't know what he's hiding about his HIV status. And so the ad impels its intended gay male viewer to trust it over and against one's own partner—get tested, get verified, and keep him at bay sexually. Don't give up on condoms, with anyone, the ad suggests—HIV risk means every man for himself.

As in the rhetoric of the bugchaser and giftgiver, the Truvada whore trades on the persistence of HIV/AIDS stigma: the public imperative to avoid the virus by minimizing contact with the HIV-positive or persons with AIDS (PWAs) or those suspected as such (which could virtually be any and every sexual partner). More specifically, the Truvada whore rhetoric trades on "slut-shaming," as well as "bottom-shaming." For to be a Truvada whore means to be wanton about wanting to bottom bareback, for multitudes of men, as though wanting to star in one's own porn film. As Duran wrote in his original piece, for "legit couples who are in monogamous relationships, [PrEP] might be something to consider. But for men who engage in unsafe sex with other men, this is just an excuse to continue to be irresponsible." Duran's original article targets PrEP users as "irresponsible" for promoting barebacking, because such behaviour erodes safer-sex norms and because of the risk of STIs (which PrEP does not prevent).[35] The idea that anal intercourse

---

34  See some of the pornographic work of Michael Lucas, who for the longest time was opposed to showcasing bareback sex in his films. When he finally succumbed, possibly to market demands, he did so under the pretense of wanting to show real-life couples in monogamous relationships relinquishing the condom for the sake of intimate sex. My thanks to Ricky Varghese for this insight.

35  Predictably, there is now porn with titles like "Teenage Truvada Whore." See, for instance, "Secrets of a Truvada Whore" on Tumblr, http://truvadawhore.tumblr. com/. The blog archive dates back to April 2015, and the tag line is "Darkest and dirtiest desires. Messages and recommendation welcome. Run by a 23-year-old PrEPared bottom." This suggests the evolution of the PrEP discourse of the "Truvada whore," to the discourse's pharmacopornofication, to borrow a term from Paul B. Preciado. According to Preciado, our contemporary era is defined by a "pharmacopornographic" bio-political consumer-capitalist economy, in which erotic desires are mediated and regulated by what you might call an erotic-

without condoms is only "legit" for "monogamous" "couples" is telling here, as it signals the moralism inherent in shaming those who want other kinds of sexual pleasure, other kinds of sexual partnerships.[36] Along with Duran, however, other initial opponents of PrEP have similarly changed their minds, including ACT UP founders Peter Staley and Larry Kramer, who now see the transformative effect PrEP could have on the stubbornly high rates of infection among vulnerable populations, especially younger men and women of colour. By calling Truvada a "party drug,"[37] Weinstein animates the discourse of decadent male homosexuality.

Ironically, the rhetoric of the Truvada whore inspired a provocative public-service advertisement for PrEP. This PSA targets a specific subculture—those who, as the tag line goes, "like to party"—a population considered resistant to HIV-prevention messaging.

---

industrial system that incites and shapes sexual desires through pornographic-cum-pharmaceutical modes of production and consumption. Modes of mediation include pornography, such as "barebacking" (and now "Truvada whore") porn like that produced by Paul Morris and Treasure Island Media, and erotically enhancing pharmaceuticals like Cialis, and even testosterone for cis- and transgender men. (See Dean's *Unlimited Intimacy* for more on bareback pornography as a subculture, and Treasure Island Media as its privileged content creator.) These erotically enhancing drugs now include Truvada as PrEP andnewer erectile-dysfunction pharmaceuticals, including the new "female Viagra," recently approved by the FDA, as well as illicit drugs such as "Tina" (crystal methamphetamine) or "Molly" (MDMA). But there is precedent here, and more evidence to support Preciado's argument: the entire class of HIV antiretrovirals, well before PrEP, was eroticized early on—note the term "drug cocktail" from the late 1990s and early 2000s to describe early combination treatment. See Paul B. Preciado, *Testo Junkie: Sex, Drugs, and Biopolitics in the Pharmacopornographic Era*, trans. Bruce Benderson (New York: Feminist Press, 2013).

36  The stigma surrounding the original label of "Truvada whore" has inspired ever-multiplying, often less-stigmatizing monikers, developed by PrEP activists and members of the general queer community: PrEP Whore, PrEP Warrior, PrEPster, PrEPpie, and even being PrEPared (as in the "Secrets of a Truvada Whore" *Tumblr* blog with the "PrEPared" tag line; see note above). The evolution in this discourse represents a departure from the thirty-five-year-old cycle of "sex panic" iconography related to HIV risk, and the queer burden of representation that consistently filters the epidemic through the lens of "gay male sex" in the public imaginary.

37  See "Divide Over HIV Prevention Drug Truvada Persists," *USA Today*, April 6, 2014, http://www.usatoday.com/story/news/nation/2014/04/06/gay-men-divided-over-use-of-hiv-prevention-drug/7390879/.

**6**

I will conclude with an examination of that PSA, which appeared online in 2015. The video segment is entitled "I Like to Party."[38] As mentioned, "I Like to Party" seems inspired by the moralizing rhetoric about PrEP. The PSA also seems to trade on this discourse by being centred on a personified Truvada whore. The goal of the PSA is to reach the population of MSM that does recreational drugs or engages in party and play. (Tina, or "T," puts the capital *T* in "ParTy and Play.") In so doing, the PSA ironically presents an aspirational Truvada whore figure, incarnated as the popular twink porn star J.D. Phoenix. The public-service announcement thus leverages the Truvada whore discourse, turning the panic icon into a provocative yet ultimately conformist figure for "responsible" party and play.

There is a moment in the video that seems to crystallize the outrage over the ad (no pun intended). J.D. Phoenix is shown in close-up, topless, dancing in a nightclub. Facing the camera, he says, "I like to party," moving his head and torso to the beat, while his expression implies a devil-may-care attitude—a half-shrug meaning I like to party, and I make no apologies for it. Phoenix's character is unapologetic about liking to "party." The subculture targeted by the ad understands "liking to party" as a subcultural reference to barebacking while using crystal meth. LGBT community members were appalled that an ad crafted to prevent HIV transmission seems to glamorize or advocate "partying," given the substantial data showing crystal meth's impact on health outcomes for HIV-infected and uninfected communities alike.[39]

---

38  The PSA is short and can be found on YouTube; see Kenny Shults, "I Like to Party," video, 0:37, November 4, 2015, https://youtu.be/FXZcoBsoGBY.

39  For an overview, see Perry N. Halkitis, "The Impact of Crystal Methamphetamine Use on HIV-Positive Individuals," *GMHC Treatment Issues* (June 2009): 1–3. There is also a segment on PrEP in this edition of the *GHMC Treatment Issues* newsletter, by Cassandra Willyard ("The Promise of Pre-Exposure Prophylaxis," 3–5). The health risk is not solely in terms of crystal meth fuelling bareback sex among MSM. Halkitis warns that, for HIV-positive individuals, "methamphetamine may have even more severe effects. In addition to exacerbating the potential for the transmission of HIV to sexual partners, the substance itself has significant effects on the biological system of seropositive individuals, including neurological complications and associated increase in viral replication" (2). There is a large body of research on the community-wide impact of crystal methamphetamine

The director of the PSA, Kenny Shults, openly admits that he "wanted to find the ideal incarnation of [Michael] Weinstein's 'Truvada Whore.'"[40] Shults adds that he chose the porn actor J.D. Phoenix because Phoenix "makes no apologies for his work in porn or love of sex." That Phoenix "makes no apologies" for being a porn star and "lov[ing] sex" is thus crucial to his being cast as "the ideal incarnation" of the Truvada whore. The target audience, similarly, is imagined as an unapologetic member of party-and-play subculture, whom Phoenix is meant to represent. Someone who, like Phoenix, could claim "I like to party—and I like to be safe."

The choice of conjunction seems deliberate and canny. In adding "and" between "I like to party" and "I like to be safe," the PSA implicitly adopts a harm-reduction approach to HIV risk reduction: one that perceives "partying" and HIV prevention as not mutually exclusive. Rather than take the typical injunction to use condoms, or the abstinence-only approach, Shults admits that the "harm-reduction" strategy was intentional. He wanted to reach a subculture that is already barebacking and "partying" but whose risk would be greatly reduced if they went on PrEP. This is in fact the population that PrEP would benefit the most. Ironically, by exploiting the trope of the Truvada whore to reach the party-and-play subculture, the PSA implicitly reinforces Weinstein's condemnation of Truvada as a "party drug" but with an added twist. The harm-reduction model belies the equation of PrEP with "irresponsible" or condom-free sexual behaviour and that of condom-free with "unsafe" sex. Phoenix clearly insists on both: he wants to have his party and his cake; he does not want to seroconvert.

The ad begins with Phoenix saying, "When straight guys have a lot of sex, they're called studs. But when gay guys have a lot of sex, they're called sluts." The opening frames the message as a critique of the slut-shaming inherent in the Truvada whore rhetoric by

on queer subcultures of barebacking. Halkitis has been at the forefront of this research for some time.

40    See "Meet the Man Behind the Controversial 'I Like to Party' Gay HIV Campaign," *HIVPlus Magazine*, November 30, 2015, http://www.hivplusmag.com/stigma/2015/11/30/meet-man-behind-controversial-i-party-gay-hiv-campaign (emphasis added).

reminding viewers that there exists a sexual double standard that shames gay and bisexual men (and, implicitly, women) for being promiscuous but not straight men for doing the same. The opening line signals that the ad is against the rhetorical slut-shaming of those who choose PrEP and those who party and play. Beforehand, we see a shot of Phoenix's keys, some condoms, and a small sachet of pills, presumably a mix of licit and illicit drugs. He takes these before he goes out to the club. These accoutrements signal Phoenix's mixed intention to both party and be safe before he says it outright: he brings condoms along, which speaks to his "responsible" approach to sex, an approach qualified by the drugs he also carries. And so, toward the end of the ad, we see a shot of Phoenix's Grindr profile with a reminder: "Time to PrEP!" It ends with Phoenix opening a daily-reminder pillbox, from which he draws out a tablet of Truvada, which he then holds up as positive proof of his good intentions to party and play and to play safe.[41]

Shults admits that "using drugs and having unprotected sex is risky—everyone is clear on that. But it is our job to bring those men into the fold and meet them where they are, not kick them off the island and suggest that they get what they deserve. . . . No one deserves to get a disease because of the way they experience intimacy."[42] He admits to leveraging the Truvada whore figure not to instill fear, or focus blame, or perpetuate AIDS stigma, but rather to show that it is possible to party and have sex without being "kicked off the island" as an "irresponsible" queer and without the

---

41   As of October 23, 2018, the PSA is attributed to Public Health Solutions and is "supported by funding from" Gilead Sciences, the maker of Truvada, which makes its de-stigmatizing of "Truvada whore" iconography problematic in certain important ways. But the reality of PrEP is that it is only the latest iteration of the successful treatment and containment of HIV in those already infected, as I mention at the beginning of this chapter. If we expand PrEP, we should also expand access to HIV/AIDS antiretroviral treatment, especially among the uninsured or underinsured, who tend to be people of colour. Promoting PrEP also entails promoting the expansion of access to STI and HIV testing and medical follow-up, again particularly among less-capitalized-upon community members, or those members (belonging to the PnP subculture) normally ignored by traditional public-health campaigns. The side benefit of PrEP, of course, is that it requires just this kind of regular testing and treatment for STIs and HIV, as needed.

42   Shults, "Meet the Man Behind the Controversial 'I Like to Party' Gay HIV Campaign."

existential fear of acquiring HIV. This fear has been the status quo; now, it may be the status quo ante. This PSA repurposes a new panic icon at this late stage of the AIDS pandemic: the Truvada whore. But he is a figure that just might predict the demise of the culture of stigma and fear that arose as a way to combat the epidemic. The biomedical advances in treatment, and, now, prevention, may mean that the end of AIDS is near. Or, at least, the end of the moral panic surrounding "outlaw" forms of queer sexuality.[43]

Yet I do not underestimate the sexual moralism that disciplines the body politic in light of unregulated experiments or transformations in sexual practice. Taking the long view, these transformations include the original sexual revolution and the accompanying moral backlash against the birth control pill. What I am calling the "gay sexual revolution" is also instigated by a pill—often analogized to *the* pill, even in official epidemiological discourse. This analogy is rife with complications—too many to address here. However, by way of conclusion, the analogy between one sexual revolution and another bears some examination.

The condom code instituted at the beginning of the AIDS crisis is still the dominant socio-sexual form for most of us worried about HIV transmission—which is to say almost everyone.[44] The advent of PrEP—as well as PEP and TasP, and any future breakthroughs in controlling HIV—promises a potentially revolutionary transformation in the grim calculus of sexual risk. But, in tandem with these developments, epidemiologists warn that STIs continue to rise among MSM. As a media report from the 2016 Conference on

---

43  In a witty parallelism, Dean talks about barebackers as "queer outlaws" emerging as a sexual subculture around the same time as the "gay in-laws" of marriage equality and the mainstream LGBTQ movement's assimilationist agenda. For more, see Dean, *Unlimited Intimacy*.

44  In Chambers's 1994 essay, cited at the beginning of this chapter, he makes a point of comparing condom usage among heterosexuals to that of gay men. He notes that one study found that among heterosexuals "with a 'risk factor' (most commonly multiple sexual partners) only 19% who said they practiced anal intercourse claimed always to use condoms; 71% claimed never to have used them" (353n3). Chambers adds: "The proportion of gay men who say they always use condoms varies across studies, but most studies find that the proportion has risen from almost none prior to the epidemic to at least 60% in recent years" (Ibid.).

Retroviruses and Opportunistic Infections (CROI) indicates, "one of the most common concerns surrounding PrEP is the high rate of STIs seen among users." And yet, cultural rhetoric to the contrary notwithstanding, the writer reports that there "is *little evidence* that PrEP *actually causes* an increase in STIs," as "gay and bisexual men at risk for HIV already have high STI rates, and many PrEP users are likely to be already having, or wish to have, sex without condoms."[45] This refreshingly temperate line of thinking points to a paradox brought about by this new normal in the age of AIDS, where barebacking and HIV are no longer intimately linked, in both senses of the phrase. And that paradox is that condomless anal sex persisted before PrEP and persists after it. The epidemiological risk surrounding HIV is almost neutralized by PrEP, but the moral hazard remains an open question, disregarding, for a moment, the predictable cultural hysteria occasioned by the advent of PrEP and the predictable personification of this panic in the genesis of the Truvada whore. As I write this, PrEP is becoming increasingly normalized, as the 2016 report on the CROI suggests. It is no longer scandalous from a public-health or subcultural perspective. Like the original sexual revolution, the PrEP revolution is no panacea. It may in fact be a poison pill, one that "actually causes an increase in STIs." But, in the words of a PrEP investigator, even if "the pre-existing trajectory of rising STIs [among MSM] is carrying on," PrEP means "HIV doesn't have to rise too."

The existential fear—and, at times, erotic *frisson*—that HIV has continually provoked is fading. And, today, the moral panic against PrEP seems to be fading as well. This new sexual revolution may not appear revolutionary, in the wider public sphere, but it is slowly changing the queer cultural landscape. Already, the revolution has been televised in mainstream network programs.[46] Perhaps the promise of PrEP will be dimmed by a rising cultural conservatism, like that which, during the Reagan years—the original context of

---

45  Liz Highleyman, "High Sexually Transmitted Infection Rates among Men on PrEP Supports More Frequent Monitoring," *AIDS Map*, March 16, 2016, http://www.aidsmap.com/High-sexually-transmitted-infection-rates-among-men-on-PrEP-supports-more-frequent-monitoring/page/3043557/. Emphasis added.

46  In HBO's (now cancelled) *Looking* and ABC's *How to Get Away with Murder*.

the AIDS crisis—reversed the gains of the sexual revolution. But there are many ways to make queer sex *risky*—in culturally positive as well as negative senses—after the spectre of HIV, personified in panic icons like the Truvada whore, is laid to rest. PrEP allows us to envision a future without AIDS: a vision that is truly revolutionary.[47]

## REFERENCES

Adam, Barry. "Infectious Behaviour: Imputing Subjectivity to HIV Transmission." *Social Theory and Health* 4, no. 2 (April 2006): 168–79.

Berlant, Lauren. "Slow Death (Sovereignty, Obesity, Lateral Agency)." *Critical Inquiry* 33 (Summer 2007): 754–80.

Bersani, Leo. "Is the Rectum a Grave?" *October* 43 (Winter 1987): 197–222.

Bersani, Leo, and Adam Phillips. *Intimacies.* Chicago, University of Chicago Press, 2008.

Centers for Disease Control and Prevention. "HIV among African Americans." Last modified July 5, 2018. http://www.cdc.gov/hiv/group/racialethnic/africanamericans/.

——. "HIV among Trans People." Last modified April 23, 2018. http://www.cdc.gov/hiv/group/gender/transgender/.

——. "HIV in the United States: At a Glance." Last modified August 6, 2018. http://www.cdc.gov/hiv/statistics/overview/ataglance.html.

——. "PrEP." Last modified August 23, 2018. https://www.cdc.gov/hiv/basics/prep.html.

Chambers, David L. "Gay Men, AIDS, and the Code of the Condom." *Harvard Civil Rights–Civil Liberties Review* 29, no. 2 (1994): 353–85.

Dean, Tim. "Mediated Intimacies: Raw Sex, Truvada, and the Biopolitics of Chemoprophylaxis." *Sexualities* 18, nos. 1–2 (April 2015): 224–46.

——. *Unlimited Intimacy: Reflections on the Subculture of Barebacking.* Chicago: University of Chicago Press, 2009.

"Divide Over HIV Prevention Drug Truvada Persists." *USA Today*, April 6, 2014. http://www.usatoday.com/story/news/nation/2014/04/06/gay-men-divided-over-use-of-hiv-prevention-drug/7390879/.

Duran, David. "An Evolved Opinion on Truvada." *Huffington Post*, March 27, 2014. http://www.huffingtonpost.com/david-duran/truvadawhore-an-evolved-o_b_5030285.html.

47   My thanks to Ricky Varghese, Philip Longo, David Kurnick, Tim Dean, my partner Brian Fuss, and my co-participants in the 2016 American Comparative Literature Conference seminar, "AIDS at 35," at which I presented an earlier version of this chapter: Dean Albritton, Michael Buso, Julie Minich, Kevin Regan-Maglione, Roshaya Rodness, and Stephanie Youngblood.

———. "Truvada Whores?" *Huffington Post*, November 12, 2012. http://www.huffingtonpost.com/david-duran/truvada-whores_b_2113588.html.

Gendin, Stephen. "They Shoot Barebackers, Don't They?" *Poz Magazine*, February 1 1990. https://www.poz.com/article/They-Shoot-Barebackers-Dont-They-1459-4936.

González, Octavio R. "Tracking the Bugchaser: Giving the Gift of HIV/AIDS." *Cultural Critique* 75 (Spring 2010): 82–113.

Halkitis, Perry N. "The Impact of Crystal Methamphetamine Use on HIV-Positive Individuals." *GMHC Treatment Issues* (June 2009): 1–3.

Highleyman, Liz. "High Sexually Transmitted Infection Rates among Men on PrEP Supports More Frequent Monitoring." *AIDS Map*, March 16, 2016. http://www.aidsmap.com/High-sexually-transmitted-infection-rates-among-men-on-PrEP-supports-more-frequent-monitoring/page/3043557/.

Leber, Aviva. "AIDS: A Catalyst of Change for the Gay Community." University of Ottawa, Summer 2005. https://web.archive.org/web/20160625085357/http://www.med.uottawa.ca/historyofmedicine/hetenyi/leber.html.

Lowder, J. Bryan. "What's with All the Bottom Shaming in *How to Get Away with Murder*?" *Slate.com*, October 28, 2014. http://www.slate.com/blogs/outward/2014/10/28/why_are_how_to_get_away_with_murder_s_gay_sex_scenes_full_of_bottom_shame.html.

"Meet the Man behind the Controversial 'I Like to Party' Gay HIV Campaign." *HIVPlus Magazine*, November 30, 2015. http://www.hivplusmag.com/stigma/2015/11/30/meet-man-behind-controversial-i-party-gay-hiv-campaign.

Nguyen, Tan Hoang. *A View from the Bottom: Asian American Masculinity and Sexual Representation*. Durham, NC: Duke University Press, 2014.

Preciado, Paul. *Testo Junkie: Sex, Drugs, and Biopolitics in the Pharmacopornographic Era*. Translated by Bruce Benderson. New York: The Feminist Press, 2013.

PrEP Facts. "Rethinking HIV Prevention and Sex." Facebook, June 30, 2013. https://www.facebook.com/groups/PrEPFacts/.

———. "Women's Sexuality and HIV Prevention." Facebook, March 28, 2016. https://www.facebook.com/groups/PrEP4Women/.

Scarce, Michael. "A Ride on the Wild Side: An HIV-Prevention Activist Goes through the Looking Glass to Discover Who's Doing It Raw, and Why." *Poz Magazine*, February 1, 1999. https://www.poz.com/article/A-Ride-on-the-Wild-Side-1460-8374.

Shilts, Randy. *And the Band Played On: Politics, People, and the AIDS Epidemic*. New York: St. Martin's Press, 1987.

Shults, Kenny. "I Like to Party." YouTube video, 0:37. Posted by Public Health Solutions, November 4, 2015. https://youtu.be/FXZc0Bs0GBY.

Stockton, Katherine Bond. *Beautiful Bottom, Beautiful Shame: Where Black Meets Queer*. Durham, NC: Duke University Press, 2006.

Wald, Priscilla. *Contagious: Cultures, Carriers, and the Outbreak Narrative.* Durham, NC: Duke University Press, 2008.

Willyard, Cassandra. "The Promise of Pre-Exposure Prophylaxis." *GMHC Treatment Issues* (June 2009): 3–5.

# CHAPTER 3

# HETEROSEXUALITY, MEN, AND NARRATIVES OF VIRILITY AND VIRALITY

## Frank G. Karioris

### INTRODUCTION

**"I**t just doesn't feel as good with a condom." This refrain—as a figurative "shot heard round the world"—is a statement that the conditions for barebacking, while not universal, are frequently a large part of heterosexual sex. Though the term "barebacking" has generally referred to unprotected[1] anal sex between men who have sex with men, this chapter will show the importance in linking theorizing on this concept to heterosexual practices that similarly reject, abandon, or do not include condoms (be they oral, anal, or vaginal). As such, from the beginning, it is important to note that this chapter contests a limiting suggestion that barebacking is related strictly to unprotected anal sex between gay men. Part of the purview of this chapter will be to explore barebacking as any and all penetrative forms of sex that occur without a condom and how this opens up new avenues for understanding both the concept and, more broadly, the sets of sexual relations at play. Tim Dean

---

1    Throughout this chapter, I use the term "unprotected" to clearly indicate the physical state of the situation. This does not seek to excessively pathologize the act, occurrence, or otherwise.

has himself begun opening this avenue for further exploration.[2] In fact, unprotected sex for heterosexual men can be thought of not just as anxiety-provoking but also, on occasion, as contrarily more exciting and tied to notions of virility. This element of excitement and eroticism is contained within the conceptualization of barebacking itself, as "barebacking represents a conscious, firm decision to forgo condoms and, despite the dangers, unapologetically revel in the pleasure of doing it raw."[3] This chapter, focusing on the twenty-first century, will explore narratives surrounding barebacking and its relation to virility and virality—having, contracting, or enacting a state of living with the viral—and how they come into play through and within these discussions. This focus stems from both the historical background and the important changes that took place at the end of the twentieth century and the beginning of the twenty-first. This entwining movement between virility and virality will work as a key theoretical question throughout this exploration. Virality will be put in relation to Dean's statement that "subcultural membership [in barebacking] does not depend on race, class, age, serostatus, or even sexuality but simply on one's willingness to embrace risk, to give and to take semen. In this respect, bareback culture is *unusually democratic*."[4] This chapter is not in opposition to Dean's argument but complicates it through expansion with a recognition that gender imbalances lay on top of the passing, presenting, and pushing forth of the unidentified viral.

Through a consideration of the novel *Jack Holmes and His Friend*, in conjunction with an examination of the controversies surrounding James Deen, this chapter will open up the conversation on barebacking to a more sustained discussion surrounding heterosexual sex and the distinct ways that the specifically heterosexual uptake of barebacking is often founded on a masculine enactment and understanding of virility and virality. In their own respective ways,

---

2    Tim Dean, *Unlimited Intimacy* (Chicago: University of Chicago Press, 2009), 1–2.
3    Michael Scarce, "A Ride on the Wild Side: An HIV-Prevention Activist Goes Through the Latex Looking Glass to Discover Who's Doing It Raw, and Why," *Poz*, February 1, 1999, https://www.poz.com/article/A-Ride-on-the-Wild-Side-1460-8374.
4    Dean, *Unlimited Intimacy*, 40–1 (emphasis added).

these two case studies open up not only the forms that barebacking might take in heterosexual intercourse but also more importantly, the dichotomous elements that link virality to virility. Whereas *Jack Holmes* shows the ways by which admissions of need may be combined with virality, Deen's case showcases the impasse that can root itself in the connectivity between virility and virality. As such, it is not that these examples were simply the only ones at hand; rather, they were chosen as a way to elaborate the groundwork itself. After considering them, this chapter will conclude by looking at the two De(e)[a]ns (Dean and Deen) to further explore the ways by which this superimposing of bareback sex upon heterosexual sex acts challenges simplistic narratives about protection and barebacking as seemingly only related to homosexual sex acts, while recognizing the necessarily complex modes by which men and women engage in sex without condoms.

## BAREBACKING, VIRILITY, AND VIRALITY

While barebacking has been thought of as related to homosexual anal sex, no inherent quality stops it from referring to heterosexual sex (anal or otherwise). In this, then, it is surprising how little discussion has focused on the ways that bareback sex functions in hetero sex. This is not to flatten differences between the acts of homo and hetero sex but, in fact, to highlight the differences that remain even when the conditions of lack of protection remain the same. Dean states that, "after two decades of safe-sex education, erotic risk among gay men has become organized and deliberate, not just accidental."[5] In much the same way, this chapter will showcase the ways that erotic risk, related to virality, is similarly deliberate in hetero sex. The purpose, though, is substantially different. It is not, as with barebacking in homosexual sex, about community or kinship but far more closely related to articulations of gender relations and virility as connected to virality. Dean's original work and profound research focused on bugchasers seeking out HIV/AIDS, which puts barebacking in conversation with what in this chapter is

5    Ibid., ix.

called virality. That said, unprotected hetero sex can contain some of the wild abandon of homo sex and certainly still holds a form of appeal as "more intimate."

In thinking through bareback sex and relating it to heterosexuality and its particular relationship to virility, it is important to think back to what Sigmund Freud said in his consideration of *coitus interruptus*. Consistent with Freud's thinking, David Friedman has suggested it "not only signified the male pulling out before ejaculation but conventional intercourse with condoms."[6] In this we see the long-standing connection between virility—here fulfilled, in part, by the culmination of the sex act—and virality. This connection will be explored throughout this chapter. This is not to indict Freud—a common anti-psychoanalytic sentiment since his death to blame him for anything and everything—but to point to the way by which, through the linguistic pairing of virility/virality, one arrives at a new way of exploring the practice of sex without condoms. It is important to note that this connection is not in itself new or unique to this particular context of heterosexual sex.

The Janus-faced experience of virility and virality opens up a way of thinking about men's sexuality that casts a wide net over violence, the virile, and the viral. I aim to utilize this *Janus* not as a dichotomous placeholder or creation but as a methodological tool for exploration, situating it more as a stand-in rather than a concrete splitting or dichotomy. In brief, virility is meant here as a placeholder for supposed manliness, the perceived strong or powerful elements of masculinity, the sense of a risk-taking drive. It is a word oddly absent from Dean's monograph on the topic, though the idea is certainly present throughout much of that book. As discussed briefly below, the virile is a constituent characteristic of the heterosexual man, and, as will be shown in this chapter, it is folded in with the viral.

This connected pairing of virility/virality assists in asking of barebacking and heterosexuality such questions as: Who is risking what?

---

6    David M. Friedman, *A Mind of Its Own: A Cultural History of the Penis* (New York: The Free Press, 2001), 165–66.

Who takes on this risk? In what ways does heterosexuality require or mobilize narratives of the virus to move beyond HIV/AIDS and sexually transmitted infections (STIs) and address pregnancy? How can theorizing on barebacking address power imbalances between men and women that might not exist in the same way in homosexual sex?[7] Without disowning and/or disavowing women's agency, how are aspects of hetero barebacking masculine and constitutive of risk-taking? What does it mean to be a sexually active heterosexual man having condomless (hetero) sex in an age of HIV? It is in this particular dialogue that bridging and explicitly linking the ways that virility and virality work together finds productive ground. It does this, to a degree, against the notional position of vitality, seeking, through exploring the linkages between virility and virality, to showcase, rather, the pushing away from the always-thought-of vital or life.

Situated in the present United States, this chapter explores the ways in which masculinity's pursuit of virility simultaneously entails or flirts with a state of virality. In considering virality and masculinity, I explore discourses of condomless sex (for example, one report says that on average women are engaging in more unprotected anal sex than gay men).[8] Acknowledging the rhetoric of male risk-taking, I suggest that the risks being taken are linked to an imposing/imposed virility and a sense of control precisely understood as the absence of control. I then move from this scene of virality to examine the role of pornography in this trend; in particular, I will examine the role (or lack thereof) of condoms in the representation of sex. I will also explore the controversies involving the male porn star James Deen, utilizing these to demonstrate the connection between virility and virality and the necessity of thinking through heterosexual sex in relation to notions of barebacking.

---

7    This is not to say that there are no power imbalances in same-sex sexual situations, but to explicitly state that such power imbalances that may exist between gay men (or lesbians) within these sexual scenarios are distinct from those that may exist between heterosexual women and men.

8    Nina Liss-Schultz, "Worried about the Planet? These Condoms Are Your Ticket to Guilt-Free Sex," *Mother Jones*, November 29, 2015, https://www.motherjones.com/environment/2015/11/condoms-sustain-natural-environmentally-friendly-green/.

## THE UNTHOUGHT/UNTHINKING BAREBACKER

In Edmund White's novel *Jack Holmes and His Friend*, a story about a gay man (Jack) and his friendship with a straight man (Will), we see how some of the quintessential ignorance of sexual diseases operates, but more importantly we are given a tale of the almost desirous seeking out of disease and risk. Straight Will, having left his wife and kids, moves in with the single and gay Jack and begins taking on lovers and attending swinger parties and orgies. In his second orgy, he "participates" with three women—"Good ones, lusty ones."[9] A few days later, Will comes into Jack's room and, we are told, "unbelievably [for Jack]" pulls down his underwear and shows "a drop of white puss gathering at the slit [of his penis]."[10] Jack reacts by calmingly telling him that he has the clap, and Will's reaction is a simple "But how on earth?" In a mocking fashion, as a response, Jack retorts, "It's the spoils of gallantry . . . the white badge of courage. Today, my son, you are a man."[11] One should note that, in this turnaround, it is the gay male figure crying out and proclaiming the formation/making of a man. In many instances, homosexuality has been disallowed to claim the mantle of masculinity; yet here Jack is able to not only claim it for himself but also simultaneously validate Will's masculinity. Put another way, Jack opens the door of masculinity for Will—in terms of sex, in terms of disease, in terms not of risk, violence, or the like but of virality. Here, we see Jack, who is impossibly un-virile as a gay man (his "gayness" is presumed to steal away from him his capacity to be fully virile), not crowning Will as a man with virility, but placing on him a badge of virality. Will is ignorant of the cause, the issue, and the solution. He is, for all intents and purposes, uneducated. The suggestion is that this ignorance comes not from lack of experience but almost directly from his heterosexuality—a heterosexuality that, conjoined with his masculinity, has risked without refutation or loss. Heterosexuality allows Will to wilfully choose to be ignorant—the privilege of ignorance is granted as part of his heterosexuality. His virile show

---

9    Edmund White, *Jack Holmes and His Friend* (London: Bloomsbury, 2012), 369.
10   Ibid., 375.
11   Ibid., 375–6.

of strength—and, in this case, sexual prowess—prevails over an as yet uncovered and latent viral possibility and soon-to-be reality.

Will, surprisingly in light of notions of manliness in the United States that posit men's general refusal to go to the doctor or admit weakness, visits a doctor—though he goes downtown to the "gay doctor" rather than his usual one. While at the doctor's, Will is told about the new disease GRID (gay-related immune deficiency), the early name for HIV/AIDS. Taking this as his cue—for change, for a notion of "life," and for "survival"—Will moves back in with his wife and kids; he leaves a note for Jack, suggesting that Jack "find one person who's clear and hunker down with him for the duration. Our libertine days are over."[12] The "our" here is not simply epistolary but a statement of togetherness for Will and Jack; yet this "our" can be read to mean men more broadly construed. Nothing is said here of condoms or even the illusion of "protection"—a lack that is true of much of literature, including popular romance novels.[13] This scene is not simply about the lack of understanding or experience demonstrated by Will's heterosexuality but the way that he is able to mobilize Jack's supposed "gay knowledge" of STIs in much the same way as Lauren Berlant and Michael Warner's friends seek to ply them with questions about sex toys. Berlant and Warner tell us of a straight couple they know whose "reproductivity governs their lives . . . [and] their relations to everyone and everything else."[14] The couple had done some "mail order shopping" for sex toys and tell them "you're the only people we can talk to about this; to all of our straight friends, this would make us perverts."[15] Just as the friends

---

12    Ibid., 379.

13    Susan Quilliam, " 'He Seized Her in His Manly Arms and Bent His Lips to Hers . . .': The Surprising Impact That Romantic Novels Have on Our Work," *Journal of Family Planning and Reproductive Health Care* 37, no. 3 (2011): 179–81; A. Dana Ménard and Christine Cabrera, " 'Whatever the Approach, Tab B Still Fits into Slot A': Twenty Years of Sex Scripts in Romance Novels," *Sexuality & Culture* 15, no. 3 (September 2011): 240–55; Jackie C. Horne, "Romancing the Condom: Contraception Use in Romance Novels," *Romance Novels for Feminists*, January 15, 2013, http://romancenovelsforfeminists.blogspot.com/2013/01/romancing-condom-contraception-use-in.html.

14    Lauren Berlant and Michael Warner, "Sex in Public," in *Publics and Counterpublics*, ed. Michael Warner (New York: Zone Books, 2002), 206.

15    Ibid.

had to "make *us* [Berlant and Warner] into a kind of sex public,"[16] so too must Will make Jack not only his sex public but his queer companion in viral sex. Jack is seen not as a bearer of virility, and yet he bears the mark of virality in such a way that he knows not merely the cause but the solution to the infection. The act—of swinging, of participating in orgies—is not the problem, in the sense that the risk itself does not come under scrutiny; it is simply the STI that is the problem to be solved. In this way, it is the behaviour built on risk and left unconstrained or attached to virility and detached from the viral that itself needs to be cured. These episodic moments for Will—the sex parties, rather than the supposedly more quotidian sex between couples—signify that which is often left unsaid about heterosexuality, such as the presumption of the absence or lack of risk by virtue of being a heterosexual man.

## CONDOMLESS PORN AND VIRALITY: THE ULTIMATE VIRILITY?

James Deen has been the poster boy for a new image of pornography and has been hailed as a "feminist."[17] This has occurred even though he explicitly stated he was "absolutely not [a feminist]" in a 2014 interview with the *Observer*.[18] In addition to being declared a feminist in some circles,[19] he also gained widespread notoriety in the public eye by performing in the mainstream Hollywood movie *The Canyons* in 2013. This is merely one of his performances; on the Internet Movie Database, he has 1,356 credited performances as

---

16  Ibid.

17  Mandie Williams, "This Angry Feminist's Open Letter to James Deen," *TheGloss.com*, November 15, 2013, https://www.huffingtonpost.com/2013/11/15/feminist-open-letter-jame_n_4280715.html; Katie J.M. Baker, "James Deen: Feminist Hero or 'Lady Porn' Star?" *Jezebel*, March 14, 2012, https://jezebel.com/5892942/james-deen-feminist-hero-or-lady-porn-star.

18  Jordyn Taylor, "Here's Why James Deen is the Bob Dylan of Porn," *Observer*, October 21, 2014, http://observer.com/2014/10/heres-why-james-deen-is-the-bob-dylan-of-porn/.

19  Cheryl Wischover, "James Deen on Feminism, His Fans, and Why He's So Damn Popular," *Elle*, August 3, 2015, https://www.elle.com/culture/movies-tv/a29631/feminism-with-james-deen/.

an actor.[20] Deen has even been referred to as the "Ryan Gosling of porn"[21]—a clear reference to the "good guy" persona of Ryan Gosling (who has been the subject of a series of popular feminist theory memes made from photographs circulating on the Internet and who has, as well, linked himself to feminism multiple times).[22] All of this has deep import when examining the recent spate of allegations against Deen and broader conceptions about condoms and bareback sex in the context of heterosexuality and its relationship to virility and virality.

Before moving further, one must contextualize Deen's position within the broader context of the porn industry in the United States. For instance, it is fascinating to note that the pornographic website Straight Guys for Gay Eyes states explicitly that "[almost] all hardcore scenes are shot without condoms because all models are tested through the Adult Industry Medical Clinic which is the standard testing service for straight porn studios. So come in and watch real straight guys having real straight sex, but shot with the gay man in mind."[23] This pornographic twist can also be seen through the comments made by many of those discussing heterosexual and gay porn. One comment about heterosexual bareback porn reads, "It looks like they fucked bareback? Thank goodness straight women can't carry AIDS!"[24] An unidentified woman tells us, "as a female, I couldn't possibly care less if the male performer is bisexual or supposedly 100% straight. I care about them giving a good performance. As for condoms, if the content is good enough, I can overlook them. But if the content is subpar to begin with,

---

20   "James Deen," *Internet Movie Database*, last modified 2018, http://www.imdb.com/name/nm1776976/.

21   Sanjiv Bhattacharya, "James Deen Interview: The Ryan Gosling of Porn," *Esquire*, July 26, 2013, https://www.esquire.com/uk/culture/film/news/a4447/james-deen-interview-the-ryan-gosling-of-porn/.

22   Sarah A. Harvard, "Saint Ryan Gosling Says Women Are Stronger Than Men,'" *Mic*, June 2, 2016, https://mic.com/articles/145178/saint-ryan-gosling-says-women-are-stronger-than-men.

23   "About Straight Guys for Gay Eyes," *Straight Guys for Gay Eyes*, last modified 2018, http://www.sg4ge.com/general/about.php.

24   Zachary Sire, "John Magnum Fucked a Fat Chick," *The Sword*, September 30, 2010, http://thesword.com/john-magnum-fucked-a-fat-girl.html.

condoms are a deal-breaker."[25] These comments, and the *modus operandi* of Straight Guys for Gay Eyes, provide insight into both the current climate of bareback sex in porn and the context within which Deen operates.

In recent times, the state of California has sought to challenge the norm in heterosexual porn, which is that sex is performed condomless. Los Angeles, where a significant amount of porn in the United States is produced, attempted to pass a city ordinance requiring actors to wear condoms while performing.[26] Unlike gay porn—where, more often than not, the use of condoms is an unmarked territory, a territory with a history behind it as such, and where condomless porn has, at one point, been considered a subgenre or marked category—heterosexual porn has almost entirely been a condomless space. A 2014 study by researchers at UCLA, for instance, found that "two-thirds (69 percent) [of porn stars] said they never used condoms on the job, despite city and county laws mandating them for porn in most of Los Angeles beginning in 2013."[27] Conversely, only 6.3 percent always wore a condom while on set.[28] This study, 75 percent of whose respondents were female, found that 60 percent "had done scenes including vaginal or anal ejaculation" and that 13 percent said "they ended up doing something on set that they did not want to do."[29] Condomless sex, or barebacking, has been particularly linked to gay communities and is oft-times connected to bug chasing and the contraction of HIV/AIDS. As such, barebacking is more often than not a referent for a practice to which either a passive or an active viral component is ascribed.

25  Sachetorte, "Which is a Bigger Turn Off: Gay Guys in Straight Porn or Condoms," *MikeSouth.com*, August 27, 2013, http://www.mikesouth.com/uncategorized/which-is-a-bigger-turn-off-gay-guys-in-straight-porn-or-condoms-8171/.

26  Christina Salvo, "LA Porn Condom Ordinance Goes into Effect," *ABC7 Eyewitness News*, March 5, 2012, http://abc7.com/archive/8568659/.

27  Dennis Romero, "1 in 4 Porn Stars Has Had Gonorrhea or Chlamydia, UCLA Study Says," *LA Weekly*, June 10, 2014, https://www.laweekly.com/news/1-in-4-porn-stars-has-had-gonorrhea-or-chlamydia-ucla-study-says-4778033.

28  Marjan Javanbakht, Pamina Gorbach, M. Claire Dillavou, Robert W. Rigg Jr., Sixto Pacheco, and Peter R. Kerndt, "Adult Film Performers Transmission Behaviors and STI Prevalence," (paper presented at 2014 National STD Prevention Conference, Atlanta, GA, June 9–12, 2014).

29  Romero, "1 in 4 Porn Stars."

In this way, one might suggest, tentatively, that barebacking can be seen as a form of virality *par excellence* in that its roots aim at the active uptake of a virus. Bareback virality within the gay community, though, is often disinterred—a word stemming from "inter," related to the placing in a grave or tomb—from the virile and virility as it is connected to homosexuality.

With this in mind, it is worth considering that, not only is barebacking in heterosexual porn a norm, but also "many pornographic movie producers have complained that using condoms in their films may turn viewers away because they bring real-life worries of pregnancy and disease into the fantasy of the film."[30] This shows not only the motives behind the porn industry but also the fact that viewers of porn—and consider that Pornhub has stated that 76 percent of its viewers in 2015 were men[31]—are looking to look beyond illness. One is forced, then, to ask how this fantasy of the illness's absence is recreated in practice and action. The "real life" implicated here, though, should not be left abstracted from the image and the actions of the actors themselves.

In setting up this discussion, it is important to look at the elements of the allegations against Deen that are not simply about barebacking, but which speak to the broader sets of implications related to virility, as well as the responses his actions have garnered. At the end of November 2015, James Deen was accused by his former girlfriend and fellow porn star Stoya of "holding her down and raping her."[32] Following this, Tori Lux published an essay in which she said that Deen "pinned her down and hit her in the face on set at a porn studio in June 2011."[33] These allegations were followed by various other alleged examples of violent sexual

30    Dana Dovey, "Porn Stars Must Now Use Condoms If They Want to Work in Los Angeles, Much to the Chagrin of Actors and Producers," *Medical Daily*, December 16, 2014, https://www.medicaldaily.com/porn-stars-must-now-use-condoms-if-they-want-work-los-angeles-much-chagrin-actors-and-314592.

31    "2015 Year in Review," *Pornhub.com*, last modified January 6, 2016, http://www.pornhub.com/insights/pornhub-2015-year-in-review.

32    Emanuella Grinberg, "Porn Star James Deen Accused by Women of Rape, Assault," *CNN*, December 2, 2015, https://www.cnn.com/2015/12/01/entertainment/james-deen-rape-assault-allegations-feat/index.html.

33    Ibid.

behaviour by Deen, often on set for a video shoot. This violence was not in front of the camera but alleged to have occurred, in multiple cases, outside of the film rolling. In the case of Kora Peters, Deen allegedly "ignored her refusal to perform anal sex and did so forcibly, after which the crew 'all high-fived him.' "[34] These allegations have resulted in Deen's dismissal from various contracts, websites, and a sex column he wrote for the *Frisky*, an online women's blog. In discussing her termination of Deen's relationship to the website, Editor-in-Chief Amelia McDonell-Parry said, "I liked his emphasis on communication, honesty and, most of all, CONSENT."[35] Deen responded to these allegations via Twitter, stating that "I want to assure my friends, fans and colleagues that these allegations are both false and defamatory" and that "I respect women and I know and respect limits both professionally and privately."[36] With the repeated allegations of serious sexual misconduct, it is difficult not to see Deen's response as a reflection of his own boundaries rather than those of the performers he was partnered with.

These broken boundaries were compounded by health and safety issues related to his company, James Deen Productions. In March 2016, it was brought to light that Deen and his company were facing fines for failing to use condoms on set and to have proper health precautions. His company was issued with "a total of nine violations, including four that were serious enough that 'death or serious harm could result from the actual hazardous condition,' according to the state [of California]."[37] These infractions speak to a serious lack of consideration for one's employees, firstly, and more broadly to a notion of sexual risk that could lead to oneself and others possibly becoming infected. Deen, in response to the

---

34  Itay Hod and Beatrice Verhoeven, "James Deen's Porn Company Faces Stiff Fines for Failing to Use Condoms on Set," *The Wrap*, March 9, 2016, https://www.thewrap.com/james-deens-porn-company-faces-stiff-fines-for-failing-to-use-condoms-on-set/.

35  Grinberg, "Porn Star."

36  Ibid.

37  Sam Levin, "Controversial Porn Actor James Deen Faces $77,875 Fine for Condom Violation," *Guardian*, March 9, 2016, https://www.theguardian.com/culture/2016/mar/09/james-deen-porn-sex-actor-fine-condom-violation-california.

fines and the citations, stated, "[none] of the citations issued by Cal/OSHA even allege that there was any actual injury or illness that occurred. The vast majority of the $77,875.00 in fines was for potential exposure, not actual injuries or even an actual exposure to any illness."[38] For Deen, "potential exposure" should not itself be an issue; the viral opening itself needs to remain virile and strong, even uncontested.

When combined with the above-mentioned allegations of sexual violence, one might see this as a blatant joining of virility's use of strength and power (not to mention [supposed] sex drive) with virality's ignoring of risk, health issues, or physical concerns. Together they demonstrate a more fleshed-out and pronounced dominance that sets out not simply to physically control (women) but also to expose oneself to risk as a way to maintain and obtain an access to virility. It is not random that many of the violations were related to condomless sex and the exposure of workers—most of whom are women—to infection. In this way, barebacking is tied intimately to these fines and, as suggested earlier, to the broader porn industry's perspectives on viral exposure. We see—for instance, in the high-fiving mentioned after the assault on Kora Peters—the rejoinder to and of those around him: not only is this a demonstration of a homo-sociality premised on sexual violence toward women,[39] but also we are able to see the building of a form of virility through the enactment of virality, a virality that is not simply individualized, but that is externalized onto others (in this case, onto Kora Peters and those who witnessed what had taken place). The lack of acceptance of the possibility or potentiality of risk in Deen's response further builds upon the idea that the risk is, to some extent, in the consequences themselves; that until the consequences come into being or present themselves, the risk is presumed to be not risky enough to be addressed.

38    Itay Hod, "James Deen 'Vigorously Denies' Endangering Porn Stars in Condom Scandal," *The Wrap*, March 10, 2016, https://www.thewrap.com/james-deen-vigorously-denies-endangering-porn-stars-in-condom-scandal/.

39    Michael Flood, "Men, Sex, and Homosociality: How Bonds between Men Shape Their Sexual Relations with Women," *Men and Masculinities* 10, no. 3 (April 2008): 339–59.

## THE RISKS INVOLVED: BEYOND HIV/AIDS

What we are able to see in James Deen's actions is not simply the intersection between virility and virality, but the conjoined—in both its form or format, and in popular discourse—of the notions of manliness and virility that were once seen as distinct from one another. In ancient Rome, virility was explicitly a sense of virtue, and of control over one's desires, whereas manliness was seen as beneath virility and premised more on brute strength.[40] James Deen's virility is built on and intertwined with what might be called *viral carnage*—opening up a play on the word "carnage" that both retains its notion of violence while maintaining, more than just semantically, its *carnal* element. This violent element is brought out by actual violence and through a turning of the carnal moment into one of viral risk and, more to the point, of putting another at risk. It is, in part, this "another" or "other" that further cements the distance between this virility and that which stood in line with virtue rather than violence; and, in the move away from virtue, it explicitly attaches itself to the viral here. By positioning the condomless man in connection with virility/virality, one might suggest that the condomed man then risks finding himself exposed as less than a man; for the present conditional (always open to contest) position of virility bears down heavily and expresses a necessity for full compliance, even in the face of conditionals. In this sense, then, the condomless man, exposed to the conditions of virality, is made immune from loss of the connected form of virility and its affixed power.

The case of James Deen represents a singular avenue within which one is able to see the condomless man outside of the intimacy that Dean linked to epidemiological descriptions of barebacking.[41] Deen's escalated use of risk as a form of virility sees barebacking move away from intimacy and closer to virality. While Dean acknowledges the viral element—stating that barebacking "combines

---

40    Joshua Rothman, "When Men Wanted to be Virile," *New Yorker*, April 14, 2016, https://www.newyorker.com/culture/cultural-comment/when-men-wanted-to-be-virile; Alain Corbin, Jean-Jacques Courtine, and Georges Vigarello, eds., *A History of Virility* (New York: Columbia University Press, 2016).

41    Dean, *Unlimited Intimacy*, 11.

a desire for unprotected sex with a desire to contain HIV"[42]—the viral component in heterosexual coupling, while not necessarily taking precedence over other elements, assumes a different tint than for gay men. In particular, as is alluded to through Dean's use of kinship, marriage, and "breeding,"[43] heterosexual sex frequently includes the possibility of pregnancy. As such, it moves barebacking beyond simply the contraction of STIs toward the practicality and actuality of pregnancy.

The risk of pregnancy, much like the transmission of HIV, is more present for one partner than the other. Siri, an adult film star and owner of the porn site Abby Winters, says, "basically, it's up to each individual female performer to protect herself from unwanted pregnancies." Continuing, she says that, "when it comes to birth control (or lack thereof) in adult films, it's every girl for herself."[44] Heather Corinna, a sex activist and writer, confirms this position, saying, "there are no industry standards around birth control."[45] In this sense, one is able to see here that James Deen, via his role as the owner of a porn company, puts the ownership of the risk of pregnancy upon the women in the relationship.[46] By installing women as managers of their own risks in a situation that is not completely manageable, one sees, again, that the risk undertaken is not simply wished for—as in the case of gay male bugchasers—but necessitated by the position they are put in. What can be seen in this and the gestures described above is a dismissal of the *feminine* through risk-taking practices that capitalize on a masculine virility, through the implementation of a virality that constitutes a form of intimacy that is at its origin disjointed vis-à-vis a reproduction of imbalanced gender relations.

---

42    Ibid., 12.

43    Tim Dean, "Breeding Culture: Barebacking, Bugchasing, Giftgiving," *The Massachusetts Review* 49, no. 1/2 (Spring-Summer 2008): 80.

44    Siri, "How Do You Deal With the Worry of Pregnancy in Adult Entertainment?" *Quora.com*, October 21, 2014, https://www.quora.com/How-do-you-deal-with-the-worry-of-pregnancy-in-adult-entertainment.

45    Heather Corinna, "Birth Control in the Sex Industry." *Scarleteen*, March 28, 2014, http://www.scarleteen.com/article/gender/why_is_birth_control_always_the_womans_responsibility.

46    There is limited information regarding male porn stars' use of vasectomies, so it is hard to comment on the prevalence of the procedure.

## CONCLUSION: TWO DE(E)[A]NS

What I hope to have explored through this chapter are the ways by which barebacking in heterosexual sex is not the experimenting with "kinship relations by way of viral consanguinity"[47] that it is for gay men, but is in fact weighed down by a variety of complicated, gendered relations that both utilize barebacking to further these gender disparities and further make use of these gendered relations as part of the practice of barebacking itself. This is not to suggest that women may not be interested in bugchasing and virality, and the attached risks. The subject of women's agentic desire for bareback sex is one that this chapter has alluded to, but could not provide an answer for because it is beyond the scope of this specific discussion. In fact, many reports suggest that the use of the pull-out method—rather than condoms, birth control, or intrauterine devices—is on the rise among women.[48] In this sense, one could potentially argue that women are taking on their own agency more in relation to bareback sex in the scene of heterosexual intercourse.

Rather than postulating the sorts of reasoning for the practice of bareback sex either by men or women, this chapter sought to open up both the diffuse and distinct implications that the practice itself has in the context of heterosexuality, and the relation that it has specifically to notions of masculinity, virility, and the intertwined substance of risk and virality. In this sense, James Deen is not a stand-in for men writ large, but rather the demonstrative exemplar of the narrative and narrated masculine leitmotifs.

By extending the conceptual notion of barebacking toward heterosexual sex, one discovers the interstices that underlie the practice and perhaps showcase its less democratic implications. While Dean has sought to demonstrate that gay men's practise of barebacking is

---

47    Tim Dean, "Bareback Time," in *Queer Times, Queer Becomings*, eds. E.L. McCallum and Mikko Tuhkanen (Albany: SUNY Press, 2011), 76.

48    Catherine Pearson, "Why So Many Young Women Love the 'Pull-Out Method,'" *Huffington Post*, April 27, 2016, https://www.huffingtonpost.com/entry/why-so-many-young-women-love-the-pull-out-method_us_5718f1f0e4b024dae4f14305; Marissa Gold, "Why Is the Pull-Out Method Making a Comeback among Grown Women?" *Women's Health*, July 20, 2016, https://www.womenshealthmag.com/sex-and-love/a19998449/does-the-pull-out-method-work-0/.

an affirmation of "a community of outlaws,"[49] this chapter suggests that sometimes such outlaws include bystanders whose desire to be outlaws is not always taken into full consideration and that sometimes outlaws, while robbing the bank as a form of resistance and as a form of demonstrating their outlaw status, enact a demeanour to convince others to go along with them. In a way, James Deen is thus the Jesse James to Tim Dean's Robin Hood. Whereas Robin Hood stole from the rich and was part of the community, James took only for himself and represented disenfranchised white men from the post–Civil War era.[50]

What remains open for inquiry is, thus, how bareback sex might be lived out in real (as in non-pornographic) heterosexual sexual encounters. We know it happens frequently; what is important to explore are the pressures faced by those who engage in these encounters, and how much the practice is chosen versus implicitly constituted via a single party involved. This is not to suggest a simplistic narrative regarding consent, nor to suggest some blunted version of "peer pressure," but to state openly that sexual relations are always conflictual, and that to ignore that fact, and the necessary impact that heteronormative gender orders have on them, will find us failing to understand the true consequences and experiences involved in these situations.

I have attempted to demonstrate here that not only is heterosexual barebacking distinct from the subculture described by Dean and others, but that the implications—viral and otherwise—of the sex itself are imbricated in masculinity's pursuit of a virile selfhood constituted through risk and virality. Unlike bareback subcultures where "unprotected sex may entail as great a sense of responsibility as getting married and having children,"[51] for Deen it appears to be simply a chance to gain from his outlaw status rather than an act of taking up responsibility for or toward others.

---

49    Dean, "Breeding Culture," 82.

50    Will Haygood, "A Story of Myth, Fame, Jesse James," *Seattle Times*, September 17, 2007, https://www.seattletimes.com/life/lifestyle/a-story-of-myth-fame-jesse-james/.

51    Dean, "Breeding Culture," 92.

## REFERENCES

Baker, Katie J.M. "James Deen: Feminist Hero or 'Lady Porn' Star?" *Jezebel*, March 14, 2012. http://jezebel.com/5892942/james-deen-feminist-hero-or-lady-porn-star.

Berlant, Lauren, and Michael Warner. "Sex in Public." In *Publics and Counter-Publics*, edited by Michael Warner, 187–208. New York: Zone Books, 2002.

Bhattacharya, Sanjiv. "James Deen Interview: The Ryan Gosling of Porn." *Esquire*, July 27, 2013. http://www.esquire.co.uk/culture/film/news/a4447/james-deen-interview-the-ryan-gosling-of-porn/.

Corbin, Alain, Jean-Jacques Courtine, and Georges Vigarello, eds. *A History of Virility*. New York: Columbia University Press, 2016.

Corinna, Heather. "Birth Control in the Sex Industry." *Scarleteen*, March 28, 2014. http://www.scarleteen.com/cgi-bin/forum/ultimatebb.cgi?ubb=get_topic;f=20;t=000313;p=0.

Dean, Tim. "Bareback Time." In *Queer Times, Queer Becomings*, edited by E.L. McCallum and Mikko Tuhkanen, 75–100. Albany: SUNY Press, 2011.

——. "Breeding Culture: Barebacking, Bugchasing, Giftgiving." *The Massachusetts Review* 49, nos. 1–2 (Spring-Summer 2008): 80–94.

——. *Unlimited Intimacy: Reflections on the Subculture of Barebacking*. Chicago: University of Chicago Press, 2009.

Dovey, Dana. "Porn Stars Must Now Use Condoms If They Want to Work in Los Angeles, Much to the Chagrin of Actors and Producers." *Medical Daily*, December 16, 2014. http://www.medicaldaily.com/porn-stars-must-now-use-condoms-if-they-want-work-los-angeles-much-chagrin-actors-and-314592.

Flood, Michael. "Men, Sex, and Homosociality: How Bonds between Men Shape Their Sexual Relations with Women." *Men and Masculinities* 10, no. 3 (April 2008): 339–59.

Friedman, David M. *A Mind of Its Own: A Cultural History of the Penis*. New York: Free Press, 2001.

Gold, Marissa. "Why Is the Pull-Out Method Making a Comeback among Grown Women?" *Women's Health*, July 20, 2016. http://www.womenshealthmag.com/sex-and-love/does-the-pull-out-method-work.

Grinberg, Emanuella. "Porn Star James Deen Accused by Women of Rape, Assault." *CNN*, December 2, 2015. http://edition.cnn.com/2015/12/01/entertainment/james-deen-rape-assault-allegations-feat/.

Halperin, David. *What Do Gay Men Want? An Essay on Sex, Risk, and Subjectivity*. Minneapolis: University of Minnesota Press, 2008.

Harvard, Sarah A. "Saint Ryan Gosling Says Women Are Stronger than Men." *Mic*, June 2, 2016. https://mic.com/articles/145178/saint-ryan-gosling-says-women-are-stronger-than-men.

Haygood, Will. "A Story of Myth, Fame, Jesse James." *Seattle Times*, September 17, 2007. http://www.seattletimes.com/life/lifestyle/a-story-of-myth-fame-jesse-james/.

Hod, Itay. "James Deen 'Vigorously Denies' Endangering Porn Stars in Condom Scandal." *The Wrap*, March 10, 2016. http://www.thewrap.com/james-deen-vigorously-denies-endangering-porn-stars-in-condom-scandal/.

Hod, Itay, and Beatrice Verhoeven. "James Deen's Porn Company Faces Stiff Fines for Failing to Use Condoms on Set." *The Wrap*, March 9, 2016. http://www.thewrap.com/james-deens-porn-company-faces-stiff-fines-for-failing-to-use-condoms-on-set/.

Horne, Jackie C. "Romancing the Condom: Contraception Use in Romance Novels." *Romance Novels for Feminists*, January 15, 2013. http://romancenovelsforfeminists.blogspot.com/2013/01/romancing-condom-contraception-use-in.html.

Internet Movie Database. "James Deen." Last modified 2018. https://www.imdb.com/name/nm1776976/.

Javanbakht, Marjan, Pamina Gorbach, M. Claire Dillavou, Robert W. Rigg Jr., Sixto Pacheco, and Peter R. Kerndt. "Adult Film Performers Transmission Behaviors and STI Prevalence." Paper presented at the 2014 National STD Prevention Conference, Atlanta, GA, June 9–12, 2014.

Levin, Sam. "Controversial Porn Actor James Deen Faces $77,875 Fine for Condom Violation." *Guardian*, March 9, 2016. http://www.theguardian.com/culture/2016/mar/09/james-deen-porn-sex-actor-fine-condom-violation-california.

Liss-Schultz, Nina. "Worried about the Planet? These Condoms Are Your Ticket to Guilt-Free Sex." *Mother Jones*, November 29, 2015. http://www.motherjones.com/environment/2015/11/condoms-sustain-natural-environmentally-friendly-green.

Ménard, A. Dana, and Christine Cabrera. " 'Whatever the Approach, Tab B Still Fits into Slot A': Twenty Years of Sex Scripts in Romance Novels." *Sexuality and Culture* 15, no. 3 (September 2011): 240–55.

Pearson, Catherine. "Why So Many Young Women Love the 'Pull-Out Method.' " *Huffington Post*, April 27, 2016. http://www.huffingtonpost.com/entry/why-so-many-young-women-love-the-pull-out-method_us_5718f1f0e4b024dae4f14305.

Pornhub.com. "2015 Year in Review." Last modified January 16, 2016. http://www.pornhub.com/insights/pornhub-2015-year-in-review.

Quilliam, Susan, " 'He Seized Her in His Manly Arms and Bent His Lips to Hers . . .': The Surprising Impact that Romantic Novels Have on Our Work." *BMJ Sexual and Reproductive Health* 37, no. 3 (June 2011): 179–81.

Romero, Dennis. "1 in 4 Porn Stars Has Had Gonorrhea or Chlamydia, UCLA Study Says." *LA Weekly*, June 10, 2014. http://www.laweekly.com/

news/1-in-4-porn-stars-has-had-gonorrhea-or-chlamydia-ucla-study-says-4778033.

Rothman, Joshua. "When Men Wanted to Be Virile." *New Yorker*, April 14, 2016. https://www.newyorker.com/culture/cultural-comment/when-men-wanted-to-be-virile.

Salvo, Christina, "LA Porn Condom Ordinance Goes into Effect." *ABC7 Eyewitness News*, March 5, 2012. http://abc7.com/archive/8568659/.

Scarce, Michael. "A Ride on the Wild Side: An HIV-Prevention Activist Goes through the Latex Looking Glass to Discover Who's Doing It Raw, and Why." *Poz*, February 1, 1999. https://www.poz.com/article/A-Ride-on-the-Wild-Side-1460-8374.

Sire, Zachary. "John Magnum Fucked a Fat Chick." *The Sword*, September 30, 2010. https://www.thesword.com/john-magnum-fucked-a-fat-girl.html.

Straight Guys for Gay Eyes. "About Straight Guys for Gay Eyes." Last modified 2018. http://www.sg4ge.com/general/about.php.

Taylor, Jordyn. "Here's Why James Deen Is the Bob Dylan of Porn." *Observer*, October 21, 2014. http://observer.com/2014/10/heres-why-james-deen-is-the-bob-dylan-of-porn/.

White, Edmund. *Jack Holmes and His Friend*. London: Bloomsbury, 2012.

Williams, Mandie. "This Angry Feminist's Open Letter to James Deen." *TheGloss.com*, November 15, 2013. https://www.huffingtonpost.com/2013/11/15/feminist-open-letter-jame_n_4280715.html.

Wischover, Cheryl. "James Deen on Feminism, His Fans, and Why He's So Damn Popular." *Elle*, August 3, 2015. http://www.elle.com/culture/movies-tv/a29631/feminism-with-james-deen/.

# BODILY
# LIMITS

CHAPTER 4

# BLACK CUMJOY: PLEASURE AND A RACIST VIRUS [1]

## Rinaldo Walcott


*Nothing can bring back the hygienic shields of colonial boundaries.*
*The age of globalization is the age of universal contagion.* [2]

*No, I regret nothing*
*Of the gay life I've led . . .* [3]


I t is worth continually recalling that HIV/AIDS began in a moment of profound anti-Blackness. The origins of the syndrome were first linked to Haiti, and then to Africa. In each moment, the link was meant to demonstrate some idea that African practices

---

1    Sections of the chapter have been published as "Black Queer Studies, Freedom, and Other Human Possibilities," in *Understanding Blackness Through Performance: Contemporary Arts and the Representation of Identity*, eds. Anne Crémeieux, Xavier Lemoine, and Jean-Paul Rocchi (New York: Palgrave-Macmillan, 2013), 143–57. Permission has been granted by the publisher to reprint these sections.

2    Antonio Negri and Michael Hardt, *Empire* (Cambridge: Harvard University Press, 2000), 136.

3    Assoto Saint performing David Frechette's poem " 'Non, Je Ne Regrette Rien.' " See Assoto Saint in *Non, Je ne regrette rien (No Regret)*, directed by Marlon Riggs (San Francisco: California Newsreel, 1992). Frecheet's poem first appeared in *PWA Coalition Newsline*, no. 56 (June 1990) and was reprinted in *Brother to Brother: New Writings by Black Gay Men*, ed. Essex Hemphill (Boston: Alyson Publications, 1991), 119–20.

and behaviours caused a species jump, ushering HIV and thus AIDS into the world. One cannot help but notice that even the idea and language of species jump drags along with it the idea that Black and African people are outside of the human, and thus remain susceptible to breaching the divide between human and non-human, bringing with them contaminants and pollutants for human beings.

Thus, even with the "identification" of Patient Zero, Africa remained a central figure in the origins of HIV/AIDS. In the contemporary moment, where the idea of the species jump has taken centre stage as a more legitimate way of explaining the origins of the virus, Africa and its practices still remain central, even if the "scientific" claim is that no blame should be accorded to the continent. Indeed, given the vilification that Haitians experienced in the United States of America and in some parts of the Caribbean at the initial moment of the virus's recognition, it seems to me legitimate to ask: Can a virus be racist? I ask the question because I hope to demonstrate that, in some ways, the racist articulation of HIV/AIDS as a Black people's "invention" is not yet behind us.

It feels clear in the context of safer-sex discourse that if a Black man fucks you, you will die. This chapter's brief recalling of the history of the origin of HIV to ask if a virus can be racist is necessary to understand that hygienic practices, practices of health and sexual well-being in the modern West, are premised on Black bodily pollution for the rest. With such a concern in mind, then, I attempt here to think of the joys and pleasures of cum—what I will call "Black cumjoy"—as constitutive of post-HIV Black queer sexualities. Indeed, what I call Black sex is central to the issue of concern here. I hope to attempt a consideration of the ways in which Black queers are positioned in conversations concerning what is euphemistically called "safer sex," but can really only be about one thing for "the Black": death. I make use of the typological term "the Black" to distinguish the racialogical dimensions of Black life from those of a racial imaginary that renders Black people less than human in many ways. Our imagined Black death conditions your cumjoy. Let me say that my thinking here is characterized by an ongoing conversation with the down low, as well as with cross-racial sex. The former is more explicitly addressed here than the latter.

I transmogrified my notion of Black cumjoy from Ishmael Reed's notion of "Black pleasure."[4] While Reed makes an argument for an understanding of Black pleasure as embedded in the cultural retentions of transatlantic slavery and the deep memories of that trauma, he is also explicitly aware of the dangers of articulating such an idea as Black pleasure. Reed's desire in articulating a notion of Black pleasure is to try to rescue and perhaps resuscitate a moment of Africanity in the Americas, and more specifically the United States, that might allow for a making sense of how and why African-American cultural practices like music, dance, and style have been so dominant in the imaginations of this nation, and now globally. My transmogrification is more ambivalent than Reed's. I want to limn the contradictions of Black cumjoy or Black sex—both its stereotypes and its pleasures. In short, I am, in some moments, after the pleasure of stereotype. To be frank, then, Black sex might be even more profane than other types of sex when the pleasure of stereotype is accounted for, especially if our cum can kill you.

Black sex is not unique to homo-sex; Black sex is, in many ways, a much larger phenomenon that concerns the ways in which transatlantic slavery and African colonialism and their reproductive regimes remade gender and sex for those who were enslaved and colonized, and their descendants. But significantly, for my purposes, Black sex is a large element of any urban homo-space in the white-dominated Western metropolis. Additionally, Black sex has a much larger historical, social, and cultural significance. In this chapter, however, I will limit myself to what is understood to be homo-sex, even though in the context of Black sex, homo-sex is in fact the link to the broader configurations of "racist sex." I will hold off giving any more definitional clarity for what I mean by Black sex, and instead, if I succeed, Black sex will unfold as a kind of phenomena and practice that is situational, imaginary, and yet very real, and always assumed and fantasized to bring death with it.

---

4    Ishmael Reed, "Black Pleasure: An Oxymoron," in *Soul: Black Power, Politics and Pleasure*, eds. Monique Guillory and Richard C. Green (New York: New York University Press, 1998), 169–71.

As I indicated before, Black sex has a long history that might be said to begin with the sexualized nature of transatlantic slavery and plantation life in the Americas. Transatlantic slavery produced an immediate collusion of race and sex for the enslaved Black person. In the context of the plantation Americas, the production of the buck, the jezebel, the sapphire, and the belly-warmer (the plantation owner's male or female sexual "play-thing") all function to bring Black sex into being through discourses that work to render Black people's sex and sexualities profane and disgusting both for white and Black alike, and it marks Black people as outside the category of the human. The aberrations of plantation slavery that give rise to Black sex in its ambiguous and ambivalent manifestations are numerous and many. Those moments have been well plotted in Black diasporic literature and in film, which seek to struggle and come to terms with the multiple traumas of transatlantic slavery, and its aftermath of anti-Black imaginaries.

However, let me limit my discussion to the post–Black Power era and the post-Stonewall moment, a time closer to what I would argue is the full emergence of Black sex as a type of sex in which public-sphere conversations and representations about its circulation and travel are forced to happen more openly, even if without calling those conversations "Black sex conversations." Indeed, a significant body of scholarship has emerged to think of this problem of Black sex. Often these conversations are accomplished by centring HIV/AIDS since Black sex is usually conceived as a dangerous kind of sexual activity. The work of Marlon Bailey, Jeffery McCune, and C. Riley Snorton stand out in this realm. Each of them tackles the concern from a place of rebuffing Black people's sexualities and their sexual practices as pathological. Snorton conceives of a glass closet that proposes to both know or see Black sexualities and simultaneously confine them. McCune tackles the "down low" as a way to clear some ground for Black queer masculinities to have authority over their sexual practices. Finally, Bailey offers an ethnographic account of how Black queer and gender-non-conforming people respond to HIV/AIDS as a community-making project through ballroom culture. In each of these works, scholars tackle Black sex as a problematic working at the edges of racist pathology, but also, importantly, pushing itself into autonomous forms of Black pleasure and joy.

Such scholarship helps us to better conceptualize where Black cumjoy for others and never "the Black" becomes a problem, both as a bodily threat but also as a deadly sought-after pleasure. Here, specifically, I think of the Blaxploitation film period and its aftermath, and the conditions of sexual liberation brought into being in the eventful moment of the post-Stonewall era with regard to Black men in particular. It is not coincidental, then, that Reed coins his phrase "Black pleasure" in a collection of essays organized around the notion of soul and Black popular culture of the 1970s. Black sex reaches its nadir in that decade, but since then it has been everywhere and nowhere all at once, bringing with it its pleasurable, polluted, and deadly cum.

Take for example the enormously popular conversation of the down low concerning Black queer sexual relations and practices. The down low conversation threatens to tell us something about sex, but it never seems to get there. Instead it tells us a story about Black men and the lies some of us might tell and do tell, but it says nothing about cumjoy; it does, however, warn of cumdeath. While revealing lies can be a morally pleasurable game, one would think that, in the case of the down low, sex talk would be more apt. Indeed, instead we get talk of death, of which I will say more later.

Many years ago, in the midst of the HIV/AIDS pandemic, Samuel Delany wrote an essay called "Street Talk/Straight Talk" in which he began to make a distinction between those two types of talk in an attempt to clear some ground for thinking about how various folks might characterize and name their sexual practices in a moment when judgment and moral claims concerning queer sexualities were particularly vicious. Delany was attempting to get at the difficult and dangerous knowledge of what safe sex practices and naming one's sexual practices might mean in the context of claims to identity around those various practices. He begins this exploration by analyzing a letter to the *New England Journal of Medicine*, which made the claim that a woman had contracted the virus from her husband through oral sex. Delany asked us to consider in that moment whether a man who was married and still with his wife thirty years later would admit to homosexuality or intravenous drug use at that time, or rather claim heterosexuality.[5] Put another way, he would have to admit to how his cum came to be "bad." What identities and practices are men who engage in sex with other men willing to lay claim to? What is the truth of Black male sexualities? What are the textual, cultural, social, political, and economic claims that can be made on Black sexuality's behalf? What is Black sex, and how do Black gay men practise or not practise it? What is the Black sex claim to truth, and can it even have a claim to truth?

The presence of HIV/AIDS among Black people in North America is cause for a melancholic response, but such a response would have to account for the ethicality of relations to at least two imagined communities it is assumed one naturally belongs to (queer and Black), and those that it is assumed one does not belong to. As Cathy Cohen argued in *The Boundaries of Blackness: AIDS and the Breakdown of Black Politics*, Black elites who headed Black organizations mounted an inadequate response during the eventful first days of HIV/AIDS.[6] This neglect has no doubt had a massive impact on the spread of the virus and efforts to combat it, both at the beginning and even now in the midst of the continuing pandemic. As Cohen astutely argues, what was at stake in this neglect was a difficult mixture of stigma, class desires and aspirations, homophobia, religious belief, and a feeling of racial embattlement on many other fronts, all struggled over by those organizations in an attempt to retain and articulate the boundaries of Black community. Put another way, "epistemological respectability" concerning the Black community was at stake in terms of how Black elites made sense of what would be an acceptable representation of the community, and thus Black humanity, to Euro-America. In other words, the Haitian origin still loomed.

The ensuing consequences have no doubt been devastating, as HIV/AIDS has ravaged Black communities, and indeed continues to

---

5   Samuel Delany, "Street Talk/Straight Talk," *Differences: A Journal of Feminist Cultural Studies* 3, no. 1 (Summer 1991): 21–38.

6   Cathy Cohen, *The Boundaries of Blackness: AIDS and the Breakdown of Black Politics* (Chicago: University of Chicago Press, 1999).

do so. This occurs right alongside Euro–North American efforts that have produced dramatic results for gay men in the midst of the pandemic, coterminous with a partial and sometimes effusive mainstream acceptance of gay and lesbian identity claims. Thus, the time of HIV/AIDS is not synchronous across North America or, furthermore, the globe; and that is why we must think it and think with it in our scholarship again, especially its anti-Black origins.

The problems of sex, Black cum, and pleasure are foreclosed and require conversation in queer theory and LGBT studies in a way that has only now begun to occur. Significantly, the loss of numerous Black queer voices to HIV/AIDS in the 1990s means that conversations concerning, for example, the down low have been sorely impoverished. The down low came into US and global consciousness in 2001. That year, the Centers for Disease Control released a study demonstrating that African-American and Latino men between eighteen and twenty-four years of age suffered the fastest growing HIV infection rate of any segment of the US population. A part of the explanation was that many of these men posed risks to communities of which they were members—queer and heterosexual alike. The *Village Voice* was among the first news outlets to run a story on these new figures, and there the central concern about the inability to reach Black gay and other men of colour who are non-heterosexual through traditional safe sex messaging was revealed as a significant problem for safer-sex education. In Canada, Pride Vision TV (the former lesbian and gay cable channel, now called Out TV), which had been recently launched, ran a segment on the new statistics and the language of the down low. Shortly thereafter, the phrase "down low" proliferated and infected all of our lives, making Black gay men disappear from view, and instead ushering in to Black sex yet another threat and villain. What this moment confirmed was that "the Black" always comes bearing death. Thus, "the Black" might murder you or "the Black" might fuck you to death. It is always death nonetheless.

Samuel Delany's 1994 novel *The Mad Man* begins as follows:

I do not have AIDS. I am surprised that I don't. I have had sex with men weekly, sometimes daily—without condoms—

since my teens, though true, it's been oral not anal. My adventures with homosexuality started in the early-middle seventies, in the men's room of the terminal on the island side of the Staten Island Ferry; a guy at least thirty years older than I, clearly scared to death someone might walk in, pulled his small, uncircumcised dick out of my mouth the moment he came, stuffed himself back in his fly, leaving semen tracks on his sharkskin pants, grunted a perfunctory ". . . thanks," fingered through his red hair, and pushed out the door as a bored policeman walked in.[7]

Delany has been a constant commentator on questions of sex within queer theory since its inception. His essays and novels have pushed the boundaries of sex talk in ways that bring us to "the brink of intelligibility," as William Haver puts it.[8] *The Mad Man* is a novel about sex, knowledge (philosophy), the academy, and race and pleasure. But, more precisely, it follows the pursuits of John Marr, a middle-class African-American gay man who is a PhD student researching the life of the philosopher Timothy Hasler. Marr's investigation into Hasler's life unfolds against the backdrop of Marr's own descent into a world of sexual experimentation in the midst of the HIV/AIDS pandemic, including encounters with homeless men in his neighbourhood, which tends to mirror Hasler's life in an earlier time. The novel is a harsh, profane portrayal of sex, desire, and the continuing viciousness of the modern and the postmodern for those concerned with the excesses of our times. I won't go into much more of the details of the novel here because I am after something else altogether. I want to pose the question of queer theory's failure to think Black sexuality—in particular, Black queer sexualities—in any sustained way as a project of its research. And by so doing, I make use of Delany's *The Mad Man* as a segue to one of his most cogent interlocutors: William Haver.

---

7    Samuel Delany, *The Mad Man* (New York: Masquerade Books, 1994), 7.
8    William Haver, "Of Mad Men Who Practice Invention to the Brink of Intelligibility," in *Queer Theory in Education*, ed. William Pinar (Mahwah, NJ: Lawrence Elbaum Associates, 1998).

Haver has written two essays on queer research and pedagogy that are useful for my purposes. In "Of Mad Men Who Practice Invention to the Brink of Intelligibility," he makes use of *The Mad Man* to ask a series of questions concerning queer pedagogy, AIDS, and death. There, Haver stages the unteachability of *The Mad Man* as "the incompletion of subjectivity, [which] is not itself without relation to what a queer pedagogy might be."[9] In this way, then, queer pedagogy is an interruption that might refashion the body as more than just a boundary for protection, as Haver reads the erotics of excess and the erotics of bodily excrement in Delany's *The Mad Man*.

In the second essay, "Queer Research; Or, How to Practise Invention to the Brink of Intelligibility," Haver begins with a series of questions that trouble the current terms and conditions, the very epistemology of queer research. He asks—and I identify with his question—"What if, therefore, queer research was to actively refuse epistemological respectability, to refuse to constitute that wounded identity as an epistemological object such as would define, institute, and thus institutionalize a disciplinary field?"[10] Haver asked, Is it possible for queer research to think the "social field" as more than mere plurality rather as an uncontainable multiplicity, and therefore to refuse the academic desire to manage and control?[11] (But he goes further still, and asks, What if queer research "refuses intellectual hegemony, to provide a better explanation of the world?"[12]) These are not easy or facile questions for Haver. He queries, "What if queer research were not merely undertaken in the interest of action (by providing a new and improved theory or interpretation of the world according to which we would act) but were itself an active intervention, a provocation: an interruption rather than a reproduction?"[13] Haver's questions actually help us to understand why conversations concerning actual sex and Black men would

---

9    Haver, "Of Mad Men," 364.

10   William Haver, "Queer Research; Or, How to Practise Invention to the Brink of Intelligibility," in *The Eight Technologies of Otherness*, ed. Sue Golding (London and New York: Routledge, 1997), 278.

11   Ibid.

12   Ibid.

13   Ibid.

help to disappear Black queer men, especially those who refused identity on the basis of sexual practice. Again, something like the down low promises to give a better explanation of the world and as much as we might want to read the period of 1985 to 1995 as one of identity affirmation for Black queers, I would argue that it was something more. Commenting on the period, Cheryl Clarke signals that "something more" like this:

> Black gay masculinity has often meant living on a continu-
> um of multiple identities that are deployed like strategies
> to enable one to do one's work, as Marlon Riggs asserted
> in "Reflections of a SNAP! Queen." Most often the vexing
> of black macho has meant knowing where the danger is
> and going there anyway.[14]

Clarke's comments beg me to misread them as almost another way of talking about condomless sex. In this way, then, the various necessary moves that both produced Black gay male identity in the affirmative and worked to simultaneously question white dominance functioned to disappear those same bodies in the eventful moment of the institutionalization of gay and lesbian studies and queer theory in the academy and the wider culture. The failure of queer theory and that of its cousin, gay and lesbian studies, have functioned in part to produce the more comforting conversation of the down low. That I would come to this conclusion at this time is telling, for it reveals that, despite or in spite of the many books and articles of queer theory and gay and lesbian studies by queers of colour, its theoretical institution still retains a normative whiteness for which Black sex poses a fundamental problem. There is no actual pleasure in Black cum, but Black people can have cumjoy nonetheless. In this instance, cumjoy exceeds the sexual as much as it is embedded in the sexual. Let me now turn to Marlon Riggs's filmic work as a further example of my thinking here. In much of the work on Riggs,

---

14    Cheryl Clarke, "The Failure to Transform: Homophobia in the Black Community,"
      in *Dangerous Liaisons: Blacks, Gays, and the Struggle for Equality*, ed. Eric Brandt
      (New York: New Press, 1999), 8, 31–44.

as much as we mark his dying, we refuse to mark that his dying in turn marks his sexual practice. We arrive at Riggs's identity without thinking his identity's relationship to cum and cumjoy.

## MARLON RIGGS'S LESSON ON DYING

Picture this: he lies dying on a bed, his body decaying right before our eyes. As viewers we get to witness his death in action, only because friends and colleagues complete his last will and testament to the idea that "Black is Black ain't." Marlon Riggs decays before us, dying in the frame of the camera as he unites life and death—his life, our coming deaths—in a filmic text that requires viewers to engage the ethics and desires of seeing and witnessing. Riggs's *Black Is . . . Black Ain't*, then, is obviously a film about life and its intimate relationship to death. In Riggs's final statement on Black ontology/ies, he positions both desire and ethics as central to late-modern articulations of Black being, and the politics of the gaze that frames, shapes, and fashions our encounters with Black subjects. *Black Is . . . Black Ain't*, then, is a film that moves fluidly from the singular to the plural in its insistence on singularity as the force through which the difficulties of community might become possible, and how we might gaze on HIV/AIDS, the disease, and his dying body as it disintegrates before our eyes. His disintegration beckons to our own coming deaths, and simultaneously requires us to command an ethics of, and for, living life.

In Michele Wallace's obituary of Marlon Riggs, she honestly revealed that she often asked herself why his flame was turned up so high. In retrospect, Wallace acknowledged that she did not immediately realize the urgency in and of Riggs's work at that point. In a film like *No Regret*, Riggs dealt with death in a fashion that required viewers to think about how Black dying and death is different. The film features lips, hands, teeth, and even fruit-themed poetry as a way to encapsulate the humanity of Black gay men, men dying, decaying, from HIV/AIDS. The work of the film offers a different kind of Black embodiment. It is an embodiment in which history, struggle, and defiance mark the sites of Black queer possibility in the face of racist homophobia from white queer communities and

Black homophobic communities. Made at the height of the pandemic, *No Regret* is a film in and with death as a frame for Black humanness and freedom. As Assotto Saint declares at the end of the film, "I did it all, and I have no regrets." The film asks viewers to engage how our livability is conditioned by the deaths of others. Riggs's lesson for living, then, requires us to engage an ethics of mutual political responsibility in which queer sexualities are not other to a normative hetero-Blackness.

Death is a marker of Black diasporic life. It is indeed a kind of poetics of diasporic subjecthood across a range of conditions, expressions, and desires, and thus foundational to our histories. The crossing of the Atlantic inaugurates our intimate relation to death in a fashion that I believe is different from many human others. As Barbara Christian reminds us in "Fixing Methodologies," Black diasporic people have never been able to put their dead to rest in ways that honour them, and thus we/they are continually haunted by the inability to do so, which makes the notion/experience of living with our dead a much more immediate and intimate living.[15] Their deaths—our dead, that is—became our lives, their deaths our troubles and our desires to set them free, and thus our freedom is tied to them as well. Such histories condition our relationship to dying and death, and such conditions fashion our desires for witnessing, and indeed for engaging an ethics of care conditioned through the move toward death as central to Black being. Nonetheless, I am going to suggest, through Riggs, that what he offers us in our encounters with his dying and death is an ethics of life and living. More significantly, I am suggesting that Black (gay) artists have inherited from their ancestors—or, put another way, simply from their pasts—a poetics of care of the self that frames how some contemporary Black artists engage the "dark and lovely" subject of the Black image.[16] The ethics of life and living that we inherit from Riggs is one that requires us to think about the ways in which

---

15    Barbara Christian, "Fixing Methodologies: Beloved," *Cultural Critique* 24 (Spring 1993): 5–15.

16    See Kobena Mercer, "Dark and Lovely: Black Gay Image-Making," in *Welcome to the Jungle: New Positions in Black Cultural Studies* (London and New York: Routledge, 1994.).

contemporary conversations about the Black queer—especially, but not limited to, Black queer men—can limit one's life and thus to attend to such limits.

In Dagmawi Woubshet's *The Calendar of Loss*, he argues that his own work turns away from AIDS "as metaphor, spectacle, and signification—*The Calendar of Loss* turns away from the kind of critical work and instead begins to contemplate the forms and uses of grief for early AIDS mourners."[17] He further states, "[this] shift in emphasis—from a study of AIDS discourse to a study of AIDS mourning—reconstructs the early history of AIDS not from the dominant discourse of AIDS but from the vantage point of the bereaved facing their own mortality."[18] In the reading I am offering, it is exactly the position of "the bereaved facing their own mortality" that Riggs's film asks us to contend with. The vantage point of Riggs's coming death from AIDS as captured in the film exceeds the celluloid, requiring us to think differently about how to make or remake a world where such forms of death might register differently. My argument is that such ethical accounting cannot be without a grappling with Black sex, cumjoy, and the multiple frames of Black sexualities and sexual practices.

The thinking or thought of this chapter, alas, is about what I call the homopoetics of Black death. This idea of homopoetics comes to me through engagements with the work of the late Édouard Glissant. He wrote, "I define as a free or natural poetics any collective yearning for expression that is not opposed to itself either at the level of what it wishes to express or at the level of the language that it puts into practice."[19] Glissant begins to formulate a notion of poetics that I find useful for beginning the work of thinking a Black diasporic homopoetics within the Americas. I am interested in the ways in which theories and studies of queerness, discourses of sexuality—especially gay, lesbian, bisexual, and trans—work within the Afro-Americas to constitute conversations that work at the level

---

17    Dagmawi Woubshet, *The Calendar of Loss: Race, Sexuality, and Mourning in the Early Era of AIDS* (Baltimore: Johns Hopkins University Press, 2015), 25.

18    Ibid.

19    Édouard Glissant, *Caribbean Discourse: Selected Essays*, trans. J. Michael Dash (Charlottesville: University of Virginia Press, 1989), 120.

of the ephemeral to produce communities of sharing and political identifications across a range of local, national, and international boundaries of desire and sex, but are all brought together through and by death and dying. It is, in part, my argument that queer image-making contributes significantly to such identifications. I am thus similarly interested in the bodies that circulate across and within the Atlantic and Caribbean zones of the Americas and the places and spaces those bodies occupy, imaginary and otherwise. This interest in thinking "the Black homosexual of the Americas," or what I call, following Glissant, "the homopoetics of relation," is particularly urgent and sensitive as HIV/AIDS continues to be a significant defining feature of the Afro-American region, alongside an alleged "Black homophobia" that these days is often exemplified by claims of a "violent Caribbean homophobia," an exaggerated homophobia, as evidenced in Jamaican dancehall's global reach.[20]

Glissant is interested in movement, as am I. The idea is not to queer Glissant; instead, I work with his already rather queer theories and insistences to make links, if only ephemeral, of the relation of non-relation of thought, as an exercise of making the political appear. In such fashion, Riggs's insistence on requiring us to think death through witnessing his own is analogous to Glissant's poetics of relation, in that they both ask us—indeed, require us—to think relation and singularity as the condition of plurality, and thought as the act of non-relation producing relation and proximity, as formations and foundations for an ethics of living together. In part what I am suggesting, influenced by Barbara Christian, is that what is at stake are different conceptions of time, memory, and the past in which each condition is lived intimately in the present. The intimacy of putting one's dead to rest, or not doing so, is also a way to live

---

20   "Hated to Death: Homophobia, Violence and Jamaica's HIV/AIDS Epidemic," Human Rights Watch, last modified November 16, 2004, https://www.hrw.org/report/2004/11/15/hated-death/homophobia-violence-and-jamaicas-hiv/aids-epidemic; Tim Padgett, "The Most Homophobic Place On Earth?" *Time Magazine*, April 12, 2006, http://content.time.com/time/world/article/0,8599,1182991,00.html. It must be noted that, on matters of sexuality, Jamaica often comes to stand in for the entire Anglo-Caribbean outside the region of the Caribbean, erasing the differences concerning the regulation of sexuality across the other island nation-states.

in the present. Such living can be either a troubled living or one in which some kind of reparation is made to the dead.

I am suggesting that the homopoetics of relation and of Black queer death(s) requires us to think filmic and photographic representations differently, to think them as acts of thought, thought that produces relation as new modes of communication with community, with life, and with the ethics of living. But I am also suggesting that Black queer film and photography ask that we think death as an essential element of subjectivity too. I am further suggesting that the brilliance of Riggs's last will and testament—in particular, *No Regret* and *Black Is . . . Black Ain't*—bequeaths to us a set of ethical demands to attend to a care of the self as a care of and for community. These films ask viewers to come to terms with and to commit to practices for which the death-dealing horrors of modernity might be put to rest. Freedom, then, is central to these works—a notion of freedom that might remake what human possibility is, and thereby remake what the human is too. Thus, the ethical demands made by these works do more than just represent identity, and disrupt community and heteronormativity; these demands require us to think differently about the stakes of the present, and how our practices of sexuality produce modes of being human and less than human. It has been my argument that Black sex and Black cumjoy thematize these ethical dilemmas for all of us. Films like Riggs's require of us an encounter with the urgency of the present so that we might confront and re-signify the past in such a way that the present is experienced differently. These films are indeed about cumjoy beyond the sexual encounter.

Drawing on Freud and José Esteban Muñoz, Woubshet argues, "inconsolable mourning or melancholia can have productive uses for disprized groups."[21] Indeed, his insight is the doubled meaning of threat and pleasure that Black cumjoy instantiates. By this I mean that the ways in which Black men are generally disprized are not only epidermalized but also below the surface of their skin and, thus, in their cum as well. Black cumjoy asks us to think about Black cum fetish as central to the long history of Black non-humanness. But it also asks that we simultaneously notice the ways in which Black

---

21   Woubshet, *The Calendar of Loss*, 22.

queer men, especially artists, respond by plotting new or different modes of being together.

## CONCLUSION

In an earlier and shorter draft of this chapter, presented at a conference to honour the late Stuart Hall, I turned to one of his essays, "Cultural Studies and Its Theoretical Legacies,"[22] to crystallize what cultural studies might do concerning these questions. I often return to that essay as a kind of signpost for understanding the politics of intellectual work, rather than for its "story" of the emergence of cultural studies as a field. I also return to it as a caution against the fetish of what we used to call "theory." I read the gut of that essay through the only example that Hall uses that remains with us still as a daunting politics of the material and the representational: that of AIDS. In his long paragraph on AIDS, Hall asks us to think death, to think representation, and to think the work that cultural studies might do. In that paragraph, he writes about cultural studies and the work it might do in regard to AIDS as follows:

> Unless we operate in this tension, we don't know what cultural studies can do, can't, can never do; but also what it has to do, what it alone has a privileged capacity to do. It has to analyze certain things about the constitutive and political nature of representation itself, about its complexities, about the effects of language, about textuality as the site of life and death.[23]

Hall's insights into cultural studies, and that passionate passage, offer us a theory of mourning in scholarship that might guide us to grapple with the difficult questions that AIDS and Black sexualities throw up for us as thinkers.

---

22  Stuart Hall, "Cultural Studies and Its Theoretical Legacies," in *Stuart Hall: Critical Dialogues in Cultural Studies*, eds. Kuan-Hsing Chen and David Morley (London and New York: Routledge, 1996), 262–75.

23  Ibid., 272–73.

In the period from 1985 to 1995, Black gay men launched an assault on white male homo-culture. Much of that assault was fought out in the racial battlegrounds of the US political scene. Central to these political contestations was the issue of naming. Naming—in this case, naming the down low—has come back to haunt Black gay men. One name that Black gay men coined for themselves was "same-gender-loving," a term that was popularized largely by Black queers on the West Coast. This term did not catch on in any significant way, but I think its presence needs to be carefully thought. Same-gender-loving offered a possibility to think about Black queer sex and love outside of the identity categories of gay and lesbian, and thus to evade a particular kind of Euro-American naming of Black cultural forms. As many of us know, one of the central conceits of Black diasporic resistant forms is to refuse the continual naming of Black forms by Euro-Americans. Much lies in the story of the emergence of the down low as a term that concerns itself with Black men having sex with Black and other men: as the category of same-gender-loving receded to the historical background as a term for naming Black queer sex and love, by 2001, the down low morphed from heterosexual infidelity to emerge as Black male same-sex pathology, specifically at such a moment when the men who had forged the debate on Euro-American LGBT racism had disappeared as a result of AIDS. This moment, then, demands we think Black sex again along with its complicated pleasures. Thus, Essex Hemphill asks us in his poem "Now We Think,"

*Now we think*
 as we fuck
 this nut
 might kill us.
 There might be
 a pin-sized hole
 in the condom.
 A lethal leak.[24]

---

24  Essex Hemphill, *Ceremonies: Prose and Poetry* (New York: Plume, 1992), 155. Copyright © Essex Hemphill. Reprinted by permission of The Frances Goldin Literary Agency.

Hemphill's poem is one moment of recognizing the trauma of HIV/ AIDS while still seeking sexual pleasure for Black gay men. The notion that the Black body always carries death with it is crucial for any analysis that seeks to give it life. Indeed, Hemphill's poetry was enmeshed with his efforts to give the Black queer subject life, and a life of pleasure too. Black cumjoy and its link to death remain in his poem as important reminders of how Black life is conditioned by forces beyond our control. It reminds us that in every narration of Black life and joy, another narration seeks to make it disappear. Black sex, then, is continually positioned in relation to anti-Blackness and white supremacy in which Black selfhood is in constant negotiation. Or, put another way, Black cumjoy is positioned between the attempt at self-authorship and the cross-racial sexual moment of the sticky, sweet pleasure of being asked by a non-Black sexual partner "What do you eat? That Black cum is so tasty." But for whom is the joy?

**REFERENCES**

Bailey, Marlon. *Butch Queens Up in Pumps: Gender, Performance, and Ballroom Culture in Detroit*. Ann Arbor: University of Michigan Press, 2013.

Christian, Barbara. "Fixing Methodologies: Beloved." *Cultural Critique* no. 24 (Spring 1993): 5–15.

Clarke, Cheryl. "The Failure to Transform: Homophobia in the Black Community." In *Dangerous Liaisons: Blacks, Gays, and the Struggle for Equality*, edited by Eric Brandt, 31–44. New York: New Press, 1999.

Cohen, Cathy. *The Boundaries of Blackness: AIDS and the Breakdown of Black Politics*. Chicago: University of Chicago Press, 1999.

Delany, Samuel. *The Mad Man*. New York: Masquerade Books, 1994.

———. "Street Talk/Straight Talk." *Differences: A Journal of Feminist Cultural Studies* 3, no. 1 (Summer 1991): 21–38.

Glissant, Édouard. *Caribbean Discourse: Selected Essays*. Translated by J. Michael Dash. Charlottesville: University of Virginia Press, 1989.

Hall, Stuart. "Cultural Studies and Its Theoretical Legacies." In *Stuart Hall: Critical Dialogues in Cultural Studies*, edited by Kuan-Hsing Chen and David Morley, 262–75. London and New York: Routledge, 1996.

Haver, William. "Of Mad Men Who Practice Invention to the Brink of Intelligibility." In *Queer Theory in Education*, edited by William Pinar, 349–64. Mahwah, NJ: Lawrence Erlbaum Associates, 1998.

———. "Queer Research; Or, How to Practise Invention to the Brink of Intelligibility." In *The Eight Technologies of Otherness*, edited by Sue Golding, 277–92. London and New York: Routledge, 1997.

Hemphill, Essex. *Ceremonies: Prose and Poetry*. New York: Plume, 1992.

Human Rights Watch. "Hated to Death: Homophobia, Violence, and Jamaica's HIV/AIDS Epidemic." Last modified November 16, 2004. https://www.hrw.org/report/2004/11/15/hated-death/homophobia-violence-and-jamaicas-hiv/aids-epidemic.

McCune, Jeffrey Q. *Sexual Discretion: Black Masculinity and the Politics of Passing*. Chicago: University of Chicago Press, 2014.

Mercer, Kobena. "Dark and Lovely: Black Gay Image-Making." In *Welcome to the Jungle: New Positions in Black Cultural Studies*, 221–32. London and New York: Routledge, 1994.

Negri, Antonio, and Michael Hardt. *Empire*. Cambridge, MA: Harvard University Press, 2000.

Padgett, Tim. "The Most Homophobic Place on Earth?" *Time Magazine*, April 12, 2006. http://content.time.com/time/world/article/0,8599,1182991,00.html.

Reed, Ishmael. "Black Pleasure: An Oxymoron." In *Soul: Black Power, Politics, and Pleasure*, edited by Monique Guillory and Richard C. Green, 169–71. New York: New York University Press, 1998.

———. "Black Is ... Black Ain't (1994)." Vimeo video, 1:27:00. Posted by California Newsreel, February 7, 2019.

Riggs, Marlon. "Non, Je ne regrette rien (No Regret) (1992)." Vimeo video, 38:05. Posted by California Newsreel, June 28, 2018. https://vimeo.com/ondemand/riggs/.

Snorton, C. Riley. *Nobody Is Supposed to Know: Black Sexuality on the Down Low*. Minneapolis: University of Minnesota Press, 2014.

Walcott, Rinaldo. "Homopoetics: Queer Space and the Black Queer Diaspora." In *Black Geographies and the Politics of Place*, edited by Katherine McKittrick and Clyde Woods, 233–46. Toronto: Between the Lines Books, 2007.

Wallace, Michele. *Dark Designs and Visual Cultures*. Durham, NC: Duke University Press, 2004.

Woubshet, Dagmawi. *The Calendar of Loss: Race, Sexuality, and Mourning in the Early Era of AIDS*. Baltimore, MD: Johns Hopkins University Press, 2015.

# CHAPTER 5

# "YOUR BLOOD DAZZLES M/E": READING BLOOD, SEX, AND INTIMACY IN MONIQUE WITTIG AND PATRICK CALIFIA

Elliot Evans

> *your blood dazzles m/e, your pallor plunges m/e into confusion distraction ecstasy. . . . Each drop of your blood each spurt from your arteries striking m/y arteries vibrates throughout m/e. . . . I tremble before the bright red efflux.*[1]

> *The sight of someone else's blood, my own blood, makes me shake with excitement. It is life. Shedding it and sharing it is the ultimate violation and intimacy for me. . . . My own blood has no taste.*[2]

What can be made of an erotics bound up with the need to go beyond the imagined limits of the body, to make contact with what lies beneath another's skin? What do we mean when we suggest someone has "gotten under our skin"? In this chapter, I ask how the transgression of barriers of skin or latex—the breach of bodily

---

1   Monique Wittig, *The Lesbian Body*, trans. David Le Vay (New York: William Morrow and Company, 1975), 21.

2   Patrick Califia, "Slipping," in *Melting Point: Short Stories* (Boston: Alyson Publications, 1993), 222.

or prophylactic limits—is eroticized in two authors whose writing is concerned with lesbian sex: French lesbian activist, poet, and essayist Monique Wittig, and the former lesbian separatist, infamous pornographer, and transgender and BDSM activist Patrick Califia. Both authors' works express a desire for the fluids of another's body found beyond these limits—whether blood, sweat, or cum. What is at stake in this desire to incorporate part of another's body? What are the implications for the relation between subject and other, and what kind of intimacy might be sought in such an exchange?

My reading of Wittig's work alongside Califia's is in many ways political: Wittig's essays and literary work set the foundations for much of queer theory, contributing in particular to Judith Butler's groundbreaking *Gender Trouble*. As a result, contemporary readings of Wittig's seminal work often employ a queer theoretical lens. Yet queer theory's peculiar habit of downplaying sex has meant that such readings often overlook accounts of sex and sexuality in her work. Juxtaposing these two authors is an attempt to redress this, a way to explore how readings invested in queer theory might emphasize queer sex. Best known as co-founder of Samois, the San Francisco–based lesbian BDSM collective,[3] and as author of *Macho Sluts*, Califia's intelligent and unerringly provocative pornographic writing often displays a certain intimacy in sharing bodily fluids, whether through bareback sex or via sadomasochistic practices of blood exchange. I read a number of Califia's works alongside fantasies of bleeding, bodily permeability, and invasion in Wittig's genre-defying *Le Corps lesbien* (*The Lesbian Body*).[4] Reading these texts together allows for a greater understanding of Wittig's previously overlooked consideration of sex and intimacy in relation to the transgression of both bodily and relational limits. I hope to

---

3    Samois published *Coming to Power*, the ground-breaking collection of lesbian BDSM writing, in 1981, and *The Second Coming* in 1996. The group encountered significant opposition to BDSM and leatherdyke culture from both mainstream and feminist groups. See Samois, ed., *Coming to Power: Writing and Graphics on Lesbian S/M* (Boston: Alyson Publications, 1981), and Patrick Califia and Robin Sweeney, *The Second Coming: A Leatherdyke Reader* (Los Angeles and New York: Alyson Publications, 1996).

4    Originally written in French and published as *Le Corps lesbien* in 1973, this chapter will refer to the subsequent English edition; see Wittig, *The Lesbian Body*.

demonstrate that Wittig's understanding of subjectivity is unavoid-
ably grounded in sexual desires and practices.

\* \* \* \* \* \* \* \* \* \* \* \* \* \*

*It is striking how quickly the intractable materiality of sex drops
out of the discourses of queer critique, in favour of other issues.*[5]

*Queer intellectuals are curiously reticent about
the sexuality they claim to celebrate.*[6]

Monique Wittig's collected essays, *The Straight Mind*,[7] have been
hugely influential in contemporary queer discourse. They include
the diagnosis of a "heterosexual contract" that dictates and forms
societal relations between men and women. Wittig's thinking in
this respect, alongside Adrienne Rich's concept of compulsory
heterosexuality, marked a key contribution to the development
of the concept of heteronormativity, and to Butler's "heterosexual
matrix," as outlined in *Gender Trouble*. As well as her essays, Wittig produced astonishing and innovative literary works, including
*L'Opoponax* (a recipient of the Prix Médicis), *Les Guérillères*, and
*The Lesbian Body*, with the latter two best known through Butler's
reading of them in *Gender Trouble*.

*The Lesbian Body*, which I focus on in this essay, is an entirely
unique work of lyric poetry. The text is composed of a number of
short fragments or scenes staging a series of violent, carnal, and
erotic meetings between its protagonists, "j/e" and "tu." These are
not distinct or coherent characters; rather, they always appear in
relation to the other, engaging in increasingly inventive, reciprocal
acts of bodily dismemberment: eating each other bone by bone,
lifting the other's skin layer by layer, licking their internal organs,
and devouring flesh. The writing is undoubtedly erotic, and Wittig

---

5    Tim Dean, "Queer Theory without Names," *Paragraph* 35, no. 2 (2012): 430.
6    Leo Bersani and Adam Phillips, *Intimacies* (Chicago: University of Chicago Press,
     2008), 31.
7    Monique Wittig, *The Straight Mind and Other Essays* (London: Beacon Press, 1992).

notes a range of works and authors famed for their eroticism as inspiration for her verse. These include the Song of Songs, Jean Genet, and, especially, the poems of Sappho. In Wittig's text, the singular first-person pronouns "je" and "mon" are always split by a bar (e.g., "j/e" and "m/on" or "m/a"), and this is translated by David Le Vay into English as an italicized "*I*" and a barred "m/y."[8] The bar denotes a kind of subjectivity that is never impermeable or self-contained, but always permeated and infected by alterity. This is repeatedly performed in the scenes where one figure incorporates, ingests, or invades the other in the graphic descriptions of bodily disintegration and reconstruction inflicted by "j/e" and "tu" upon one another.

The carnal violence of the text is immense, and it is impossible to describe here partly due to the fact that its force is rendered even more powerful by the unrelenting repetition of various and increasingly inventive grisly dismemberments. To give some idea, in one particularly gruesome scene, "*I*" pulls out "you's" teeth, probes the wounds with her tongue and teeth, receives the ensuing blood flow in her hands and mouth, and uses the blood to draw on "you's" body.[9] There are frequent descriptions of the blood, bodily fluids, or organs of both protagonists spilling beyond their skins and merging with one another. These scenes are unerringly erotic in their description of violence, blood, and dismemberment, and it is this erotic charge that I fear has been overlooked previously. I want to emphasize this violent erotics as entirely underpinning and fuelling Wittig's conclusions regarding relationality and subjectivity drawn on by thinkers such as Butler.

Wittig's work is no less sexual for either the strangeness or the violence of the erotic fantasies she presents. In fact, her use of both fantasy and violence is integral to the erotics of the piece. Her protagonists morph into creatures and objects, including wolves, writhing snakes, a single cell, a stretched-out, exsanguinated human

---

8    The second-person singular pronoun "tu" (and its related possessive pronouns, ton/ta/tes) is not barred in the original French, and is therefore translated by Le Vay simply as "you" (and "your").

9    Wittig, *The Lesbian Body*, 127.

pelt, or biting swarms of spiders; but so too do Califia's. In "Blood and Silver," Califia's protagonists become wolves in a retelling of "Little Red Riding Hood" as a lesbian tale of sex-worker vengeance.[10] In the short story "The Vampire," from *Macho Sluts*, Califia's rendering of his eponymous protagonist as non-human allowed him to portray a fantastic amount of blood exchange in a BDSM context by circumventing his publisher's policy against including descriptions of high-risk sexual practices, including fluid exchange.[11] Califia's work also features werewolves ("The Wolf Is My Shepherd, I Shall Not Want"[12]) and mermen ("Swimmer's Body"[13]), and some pieces could be described as works of science fiction, pieces such as "Skinned Alive,"[14] a bareback fantasy set in a future dystopia so obsessed with sterility that the only way to have sex legally is to be separated entirely by a sheet of poly film.

Another reason to place Wittig's work alongside Califia's is *The Lesbian Body*'s clearly eroticized writing on violence. This work certainly does not explore the complex codes of BDSM subculture as Califia's does, but it nevertheless includes references to blindfolds, bondage, gags, whips, flagellation, bloodletting, and the erotic pleasure of submission and domination. Consider the following line:

> *I* am the plaited whip that flagellates the skin, *I* am the gag that gags the mouth, *I* am the bandage that hides the eyes, *I* am the bonds that tie the hands, *I* am the mad tormentor galvanized by torture and your cries intoxicate m/e.[15]

Another scene offers the fantastic image of cilia (the protuberances from a cell's surface, such as those that line the trachea or lungs)

---

10 Patrick Califia, "Blood and Silver," in *No Mercy* (Los Angeles and New York: Alyson Publications, 2000), 110–25.

11 Califia, "The Vampire," in *Macho Sluts* (Boston: Alyson Publications, 1988), 243–62.

12 Califia, "The Wolf Is My Shepherd, I Shall Not Want," in *Hard Men* (Los Angeles and New York: Alyson Publications, 2004), 96–110.

13 Califia, "Swimmer's Body," in *Hard Men*, 17–36.

14 Califia, "Skinned Alive," in *No Mercy*, 74–89.

15 Wittig, *The Lesbian Body*, 16.

upon the surface of "you," monstrously magnified and flagellating
"*I*'s" shoulders with a "brutal" force:

> You agitate the collectivity of your vibratile cilia all over
> your surface. *I* approach your flagella, m/y palms barely
> come into contact with them and withdraw. A violent
> movement traverses you. All your whips retract and begin
> to whirl, *I* do not flinch when at the next moment they fall
> brutally on m/y shoulders. . . . The silk of your cilia make
> m/e shiver from head to feet.[16]

Wittig was not so naive as to have been unaware of the connotations of her lines, and to suggest so would reinforce myths regarding
the supposed innocence of lesbian sexuality. Her work *Lesbian Peoples:
Materials for a Dictionary*,[17] co-written with her partner Sandé Zeig,
contains a number of tongue-in-cheek dictionary definitions for
terms in an imagined future lesbian society. These include entries on
lesbian staples such as chickpeas, cats, and vegetarianism, but also
on leather, which is described as a predilection for many lesbians
(referred to as "amazons" in the text). Another entry describes an
annual day on which it is customary to wear traditional lesbian
attire: apparently tuxedos, as well as leather jackets and straps. Of
course, not every fragment of *The Lesbian Body* is quite as overt as
those cited above, but each one ceaselessly maintains this erotically
charged violence. Not one reading of Wittig, however, takes such
connotations into account. Butler's reading of *The Lesbian Body* in
*Gender Trouble* considers Wittig's exploration of universal and particular or minoritarian subjectivity in her use of barred pronouns,
while barely mentioning its grounding in sexuality.[18] Similarly,

---

16   Ibid., 45. The original French uses the verb *frissoner*, which has more overtly sexual
     connotations than Le Vay's translation, which uses "shiver." For comparison, see
     Monique Wittig, *Le Corps lesbien* (Paris: Éditions de Minuit, 1973), 36.

17   Monique Wittig and Sandé Zeig, *Lesbian Peoples: Materials for a Dictionary* (London:
     Virago, 1980). Originally published in French as *Brouillon pour un dictionnaire des
     amantes* (Paris: Grasset, 1976).

18   Butler's singular reference to sex in an extended reading of Wittig is as follows:
     "In *The Lesbian Body*, the act of love-making literally tears the bodies of its partners
     apart. As lesbian sexuality, this set of acts outside of the reproductive matrix

Butler diagnoses the extraordinary violence in Wittig's text as a way to subvert expectations of women and femininity without any mention of its eroticism.[19]

In contrast, Sue-Ellen Case has hinted at a reading of Wittig that emphasizes lesbian sexuality, suggesting that Wittig's coupling of "*I*" and "you" may be understood as a "coupled self" linked to butch-femme practices:

> The butch-femme as subject is reminiscent of Monique Wittig's "j/e," or coupled self, in her novel *The Lesbian Body*. These are not split subjects, suffering the torments of dominant ideology. They are coupled ones who do not impale themselves on the poles of sexual difference or meta-physical values, but constantly seduce the sign system through flirtation and inconstancy into the light fondle of artifice, replacing the Lacanian slash with a lesbian bar.[20]

Such a reading is only suggested by Case (these are the full extent of Case's comments on Wittig published in this essay), but even in these few lines she notes lesbian sexuality, practices, and even bar culture. Intriguingly, in her article "Sexual Indifference and Lesbian Representation," Teresa de Lauretis cites an earlier, unpublished version of Case's essay:

---

produces the body itself as an incoherent center of attributes, gestures, and desires." See Judith Butler, *Gender Trouble: Feminism and the Subversion of Identity* (London and New York: Routledge, 1990), 160.

19    Butler writes that "Wittig's texts have been criticized for this use of violence and force—notions that on the surface seem antithetical to feminist aims. But note that Wittig's narrative strategy is not to identify the feminine through a strategy of differentiation or exclusion from the masculine. . . . [Rather,] Wittig offers a strategy of reappropriation and subversive redeployment of precisely those 'values' that originally appeared to belong to the masculine domain." See Butler, *Gender Trouble*, 160–61.

20    Sue-Ellen Case, "Towards a Butch-Femme Aesthetic," *Discourse* 11, no. 1 (1988–89): 56–57. The French psychoanalyst Jacques Lacan considered the subject not as unified but rather as always divided. From 1957 onwards, he used the algebraic symbol "S" split by a slash or bar ( \$ )to describe this split subject. Wittig herself was no fan of psychoanalysis but was well aware of Lacan's line of thinking.

The butch-femme couple, like Wittig's *j/e-tu* and like the s/m lesbian couple . . . propose a dual subject.[21]

Here, Case alludes to an understanding of subjectivity in Wittig's *The Lesbian Body* that is not only linked to lesbian sexuality and butch-femme identity, but also to BDSM. This line is redacted from the final, published version—perhaps simply due to a lack of space or a change of focus—yet there does appear to be a general reticence in acknowledging the violent lesbian sexuality in Wittig's work. Why *not* offer a reading of Wittig imagining each of her poetic fragments as BDSM scenes? Does a book of erotic lesbian poetry need to be placed alongside sufficiently "heavyweight" references (a Lacan or a Kristeva) in order to legitimize their inclusion in an academic essay? I do not for one moment suggest the approach I offer here is the *correct* way to read *The Lesbian Body*. I would argue, though, that when texts that are entirely permeated with queer sexuality are *desexualized* in their reading through a queer theoretical lens, something has gone awry. What is the benefit of queer theory if it fails to acknowledge queer sex, and even repeats the ways in which it is rendered invisible or illegitimate? In what follows, I offer a short reading of Wittig that emphasizes and voices queer sexuality rather than skipping over it, or using it as a means to deconstruct hegemonic norms rather than focusing on it as a valid object of study, in and of itself.

**BLOOD**

I *discover that your skin can be lifted layer by layer, I pull, it lifts off.*[22]

I *need what lies beyond the barrier.*[23]

Both Wittig and Califia eroticize the breakdown of barriers between bodies, whether these are figured as skin or as latex. Califia's writ-

---

21    Teresa de Lauretis, "Sexual Indifference and Lesbian Representation," *Theatre Journal* 40, no. 2 (1988): 168.
22    Wittig, *The Lesbian Body*, 17.
23    Califia, "Slipping," 219.

ing about lesbian sex before he transitioned in the late 1990s was permeated by a claustrophobic sense of a world becoming smaller and more inhibited due to the AIDS crisis. In what is perhaps his most personal work, "Slipping," Califia writes of the deaths of his gay male friends—as well as bisexual and lesbian women, including former partners—from AIDS-related illness. What was known about HIV/AIDS was very limited at this point, and Califia rails against the lack of concern from health officials for the sexual health of lesbians—Califia reports one such official telling him that "lesbians don't have much sex"[24]—and the assumptions from within the lesbian community that "real lesbians don't shoot drugs, share needles, or play sex games that expose them to somebody else's blood."[25] Califia's world involved intravenous drug use, sex with gay men, non-monogamy, BDSM, and blood play, and he and others were terrified at the lack of knowledge regarding the risks involved in sexual acts, especially those involving blood and fluid exchange.

In both his fiction and safer-sex guides for lesbians engaging in BDSM,[26] Califia's writing addresses these taboos head-on, as well as the racism and classism contributing to the endemic hypocrisy over who should be considered more "risky" as a sexual partner.[27] Despite the pressure he feels to have "safe sex" (something of an unknown) with his partners, Califia expresses a distaste for barriers:

> By my bed, I keep bottles of water-based lubricant, a box of rubber gloves, and Trojans. . . . The rule is that I will always use latex barriers with tricks. I will have unsafe sex only with my lovers, and then only if we both test HIV-negative.[28]

---

24  "Dr. Charles Schable of the Centers for Disease Control told a reporter at *Visibilities* that 'Lesbians don't have much sex' " (Califia, "Slipping," 216).

25  Ibid., 210.

26  Califia's writing on safer sex for lesbians include *Sapphistry: The Book of Lesbian Sexuality* (Kansas City, MO: Naiad Press, 1980) and *The Lesbian S/M Safety Manual* (Boston: Lace Publications, 1988).

27  These themes are treated especially in Patrick Califia's "Unsafe Sex," in *Melting Point: Short Stories* (Boston: Alyson Publications, 1993), 121–27, and in *Hard Men*, 87–95.

28  Califia, "Slipping," 216–17.

While he knows that "safer sex is not a form of prudery . . . based on hatred of the body, on aversion to bodily fluids," something in him cannot accept this:

> I tell myself and I tell myself, but my tongue does not believe what my brain believes. My hand does not believe what my brain believes. I need what lies beyond the barrier.[29]

Despite Califia's aversion to latex, he is unable to write about fluid exchange in some of his fictional work due to the aforementioned policy held by Alyson Publications, an LGBT publishing house, against publishing descriptions of high-risk sexual practices. He thus had to "go back and write . . . out" each instance of fluid exchange in *Macho Sluts*.[30] The way Califia works within these restrictions on his writing is fascinating. Although he fears that the introduction of prophylaxes in his work will dilute the "highly charged emotional content" of "cum touching taste buds or mucous membranes,"[31] Califia doesn't so much write *out* sexual fluids as write *in* prophylaxes, in ways that often result in actually emphasizing what lies beyond them. In one scene, he writes that the "prophylactic outlined and exaggerated every wrinkle and vein" of the penis it covered.[32] In another, a protagonist takes off a "doused condom, tie[s] a knot in it, and tuck[s] it down the front of her jeans. It was still warm."[33] Even when he is unable to write about fluid exchange, the presence of bodily fluids is still felt, and the latex barrier is transgressed, if only by the warmth exuded by the semen it contains.

Here and elsewhere, the possibility of sharing bodily fluids is eroticized. It is not only latex barriers that are breached, but those of skin as well. Despite the climate created by the AIDS crisis, Califia wants blood. In his poems, he writes of "want[ing] to take you

---

29   Ibid., 219.
30   Califia, *Macho Sluts*, 17.
31   Ibid.
32   Califia, "The Surprise Party," in *Macho Sluts*, 218.
33   Ibid., 220.

into an alley, and fuck you until your ears bleed."[34] In one story, he describes a character who wants to "take that motherfucking whip in both hands and . . . bring it down as hard as I can until the walls are spattered with blood."[35] And again in "Slipping" he writes,

> I have someone stretched underneath me. Her hands are tied. I have cut her back, and I suppose I could pretend that I don't intend to put my mouth on the wound I've just made. But this is not an ornamental cut. . . . It is utilitarian, two short lines that cross each other at right angles. It delays the clotting of blood, which wells up thick as tar, a bead of perfect scarlet. Any second now, it will break and run. It will be wasted. . . . I put my face down to her back and bite the skin around the cut so the blood spurts into my mouth. . . . The sight of someone else's blood, my own blood, makes me shake with excitement. It is life. Shedding it and sharing it is the ultimate violation and intimacy for me. . . . My own blood has no taste. . . . If I get sick tomorrow, will you feel any compassion for me?[36]

For Califia, his blood *alone* "has no taste." It is only when it is shared with another's that it comes to represent "the ultimate violation and intimacy" for him: that is, a fantasy representing the violation of discrete subjectivity. Sharing blood not only signifies the violation of a membrane, but also of personhood, and indeed demonstrates that subjectivity may be formed *through* such an act of violation.

Both Wittig and Califia go much further than a simple desire for sex without latex. There is a desire to traverse the barrier of skin as well, in order to touch—even consume—what lies beneath, whether eroticized bodily fluids (blood, bile, vomit, piss) or body parts. In *The Lesbian Body*, Wittig's protagonists rip off each other's skin, perforate membranes, and chew through bone to reach the

---

34  Califa, "Canada," in *High Risk: An Anthology of Forbidden Writings*, eds. Amy Scholder and Ira Silverberg (London: Serpent's Tail, 1991), 55.
35  Califia, "Daddy," in *Melting Pot*, 84.
36  Califia, "Slipping," 221–22.

interior of the other's body. Her fragments continually describe skin as permeated, perforated, or ruptured: "the bandage keeps m/y eyes closed. . . . Suddenly *I* am perforated by bites."[37] In another scene, the presence of blood is eroticized: "you part your lips m/y mutilated one over your bloodstained gums, *I* insert m/y tongue into each socket in succession, *I* probe your wounds, m/y lips m/y fingers receive your blood."[38] Even further, Wittig's protagonists display an erotic fascination with bodily interiority:

> you take the heart in your mouth, you lick it for a long time, your tongue playing with the coronary arteries [you are] covered with liquids acids chewed digested nourishment, you full of juices corroded in an odour of dung and urine crawl up to m/y carotid in order to sever it. Glory.[39]

This is not simply a scopic desire to witness the inside of bodies, but also to touch, lick, and consume them.

In Wittig's fragments, the rupture and perforation of skin is not always inflicted on one character by the other but is often mutual: "Perforations occur in your body and in m/y body joined together."[40] Here, perforation of the body's border—the skin—results in a kind of commingling and confusion of bodily fluids and parts. Skin is imagined as the barrier separating an absolute material synthesis of two bodies in a single organism: "The orifices multiply over our two bodies causing m/y skin and your skin to burst alike. . . . There is nothing else to do but to attempt to insinuate ourselves one into the other . . . our two bodies which now constitute a single organism."[41] Likewise, in an incredible fantasy of exsanguination, Wittig writes,

> It is not the gentle sound of rain that *I* hear just now, but your blood falling on the metal, it spurts from the seven

---

37  Wittig, *The Lesbian Body*, 78.
38  Ibid., 127.
39  Ibid., 86.
40  Ibid., 108.
41  Ibid., 109.

openings, the temporal arteries are severed, the carotid is cut through, the iliac arteries the radials are holed, *I* am spattered from top to toe. Your blood deserts its circuits. *I* am inundated, glory.[42]

Not content with receiving "you's" blood, or being "inundated" by it, the fragment continues with "*I*" opening her own arteries: "*I* follow you in your journey, the blood spurts from m/y badly sectioned arteries, *I* become impatient, *I* cut m/yself to pieces in m/y haste."[43] She goes on:

> *I* come m/y adored one *I* follow you *I* come to you *I* draw near you . . . m/y blood mingles with yours inundating you entirely, the inwards of our arms finding and pressing each other, ultimately desire finds us, we move towards each other in great travail.[44]

As in Califia's work, sharing blood results in movement toward one another—a closeness or intimacy—to the extent that an utter confusion between the propriety and identity of their two bodies results, disrupting any notion of them as discrete entities.

**SEX**

> *I have swallowed your arm. . . . Your fingers form a*
> *fan in m/y oesophagus. . . . I am penetrated endlessly*
> *by you, you thrust into m/e/, you impale m/e.*[45]

> *I want to suck your arm into my ass, I want to*
> *eat you alive in little bloody chunks.*[46]

---

42 Ibid., 90.
43 Ibid.
44 Ibid., 91.
45 Ibid., 58.
46 Califia, "What Girls Are Made Of," in *Melting Point*, 191–92.

The transgression of bodily limits extends beyond incisions into the surface of the skin and the eroticization of "interior" bodily fluids: both Califia and Wittig include references to fisting in their work, which again impacts upon the way that subjectivity is understood. In the lines cited above, Wittig presents penetration by another's hand as a violent invasion, "impalement." Conversely, Califia's words juxtapose the desire to "suck your arm into my ass" with a desire to consume the other: this is not so much an invasion by another, but the *absorption* of that other. Both of these lines could be read profitably alongside psychoanalytic descriptions of incorporation. Incorporation has been described as a fantasy whereby an object penetrates a body and is retained therein. According to Laplanche and Pontalis, it possesses multiple meanings: "to obtain pleasure by making an object penetrate oneself; . . . to destroy this object; and . . . by keeping it within oneself . . . to appropriate the object's qualities."[47] Incorporation is part identificatory insofar as one displays a desire to take on qualities admired in another, part violent impulse to destroy (indeed, identification is also always violent ambivalence), and it is at root erotic—Freud originally described it in his *Three Essays on the Theory of Sexuality* as a confusion of erotic and life-preserving drives. Although Freud initially linked incorporation to the oral phase of development—and to fantasies of eating or swallowing—it is also imagined as occurring via "erotogenic zones . . . skin, respiration, sight, hearing," or via genital and/or anal incorporation.[48] Mária Török and Nicolas Abraham built on Freud's work to distinguish between the notions of incorporation and introjection. Török describes introjection as a gradual process of normal psychic development whereby objects (or their loss) are named, articulated in language with the effect of enriching the ego. In contrast, incorporation describes a fantasy of unmediated access to the object: it is "instantaneous and magical," sometimes

---

47 Jean Laplanche and Jean-Bertrand Pontalis, *The Language of Psychoanalysis*, trans. Donald Nicholson-Smith (London: Karnac Books, 1988), 212.

48 Ibid.

even "hallucinatory."[49] For Török, incorporation occurs when introjection is prevented through some linguistic block (something unspeakable or unacknowledged), and represents an immediate *fantasy* of unmediated union with another: "Because our mouth is unable to say certain words and unable to formulate certain sentences, we fantasize . . . that we are actually taking into our mouth the unnameable, the object itself."[50] For this reason, they describe incorporation as deceptive: while total bodily intimacy is *imagined*, the gap between subject and other remains intact, being bridged only in fantasy.

Wittig's and Califia's works are full of fantasies of incorporation: fantasies that frequently explore violence, and which are bound up with questions of subjectivity and eroticism. As fantasies of incorporation, the kinds of relationality and the implications for subjectivity they provoke are thus inseparable from questions of sexuality. In one instance of such a fantasy, Wittig writes that "M/y clitoris m/y labia are touched by your hands. Through m/y vagina and m/y uterus you insert yourself breaking the membrane up to my intestines."[51] Again, one body is "inserted" within another. Elsewhere she writes,

> you are m/yself you are m/yself (aid m/e Sappho) you are m/yself, *I* die enveloped girdled supported impregnated by your hands infiltrated suave flux infiltrated by the rays of your fingers.[52]

Wittig's protagonist "*I*" is again invaded ("impregnated," "enveloped," and twice "infiltrated"),[53] and as a result there is a total disruption and confusion between self and other: "you are m/yself," she repeats,

---

49  Maria Török and Nicolas Abraham, *The Shell and the Kernel: Renewals of Psychoanalysis*, trans. Nicholas T. Rand (Chicago: University of Chicago Press, 1994), 113–14.

50  Ibid., 128.

51  Wittig, *The Lesbian Body*, 37.

52  Ibid., 50.

53  The original French uses *infiltrer* and *imprégner* with the same effect (Wittig, *Le Corps lesbien*, 42).

until eventually "*I*" dies quite literally by the hands of the other. Tim Dean's understanding of the implications for subjectivity resulting from the practice of fisting in *Unlimited Intimacy* seems to resonate acutely with Wittig's writing here:

> The sexual act of fisting brings one man so far inside another as to temporarily obliterate the boundaries that conventionally separate persons. By occupying exactly the same physical space simultaneously, the men in this fantasy have become in some sense identical, beyond individuation. Here sexual contact shades into communion.[54]

The "communion" of sexual contact in Wittig and Califia is not only imagined through the sharing of blood, but also by reaching inside another's body. The term "communion" here resonates with Wittig's confusion of bodily borders, and is in fact exactly how Califia describes the experience of fisting in "Holes." His partner becomes "joined to [him] like a Siamese twin," and Califia comments, "I wanted to share this communion with him."[55] The term of course also contains religious signification. In the Eucharist, taking communion is an act of remembrance, of summoning the presence of an entire body (the body of Christ), and of incorporating that body into one's own through drinking his blood and eating his body (or a symbol of that body, depending on one's views on transubstantiation).[56] The Christian act of "communion"—and I do not say this simply to provoke—is very similar to Califia's and Wittig's approach to incorporating the body of another into their own through acts that seek to verify the other's presence, that retain this other within their own body, and that represent a fantasy of intimacy. Indeed, in *Totem and Taboo*, Freud linked Christian

54    Tim Dean, *Unlimited Intimacy: Reflections on the Subculture of Barebacking* (Chicago: University of Chicago Press, 2009), 46.
55    Califia, "Holes," in *Hard Men*, 253.
56    The four Apostles, as well as Saint Paul in Corinthians, all describe Jesus's command to his disciples at the Last Supper to eat his body and drink his blood: "do this in remembrance of me," he tells them.

communion to the oedipal desire to kill the father, and, in eating this father, to ideas of incorporation.[57]

\* \* \* \* \* \* \* \* \* \* \* \* \* \*

*I absorb you m/y very precious one, I retain you within m/e.*[58]

*My obsession . . . to have what he had. To be part of him. To carry him with me, inside of me, forever.*[59]

In addition to the subjective implications of fisting, both writers' work expresses the desire to incorporate the body of another within oneself through eating another's body, or through being sexually infected and transformed by another. "I eat m/y fill of you m/y so delectable one," Wittig writes, and in this fragment "*I*" devours "you," expulsing her in a fit of vomiting and then eating her again, "lick[ing] the last scraps on your belly, *I* get rid of the traces of blood."[60] Ingesting the other's body, as in the Eucharist, is a way to absorb and retain the other: "*I* absorb you m/y very precious one, *I* retain you within m/e." While Wittig's work precedes HIV/AIDS, one line from *The Lesbian Body* could well have been written by a bugchaser: "*I* catch your sickness, you know it *I* am so sick from you that *I* am extremely happy."[61] What is at stake in this line is not just the ability to touch another's skin free from latex, or even ingesting a part of the other, but the notion of being infected by another in a way that renders oneself transformed.

Califia's work frequently deals with HIV/AIDS, as well as bareback sex. In addition to his fiction, he also wrote as an agony uncle for

---

57 Sigmund Freud, *Totem and Taboo*, trans. James Strachey (London and New York: Routledge, 2001), 179.

58 Wittig, *The Lesbian Body*, 24.

59 Califia, "Skinned Alive," 85.

60 Wittig, *The Lesbian Body*, 122.

61 Ibid., 135. "Bugchaser" is a term used predominantly by gay men who engage in bareback sex to refer to those who actively seek out unprotected sex with HIV-positive individuals in order to contract the virus. For an exploration of this language, see Tim Dean, "Breeding Culture: Barebacking, Bugchasing, Giftgiving," *Massachusetts Review* 48, nos. 1–2 (2008): 80–94.

Poz.com, a website for people living with or affected by HIV. One of his stories in *Hard Men*, "Swimmer's Body," was written before the AIDS crisis, but still deals with the idea of the consensual "merging [of] internal ecosystems"[62] through the exchange of semen. "Skinned Alive" deals explicitly with barebacking, and recounts a bugchasing fantasy set in a dystopian future where full body suits are worn at all times, sex must be performed by partners separated entirely by a sheet of poly film, and babies are birthed through plastic chutes to protect them from their mother's internal biology. Califia's protagonist feels "allergic to the film," is "left completely limp" by having his "mouth penetrated by a poly-coated tongue."[63] Not only does he seek out skin contact without the film, but also sexual contact with those infected with a deadly disease known as the "purple plague," contact that will result in his death.[64] During sex without the poly film, he imagines his skin perforated, "nipples drilling into my gloriously bare body,"[65] as well as eating his partner: "I chewed on beards. I put toes in my mouth. . . . Gnawed on necks."[66] This character desires his sexual partner's virus—"I wanted what he carried, invisibly circulating in his body fluids and tissues"[67]—writing of his semen that "to me, the thick, salty cream was an emblem of generosity and freedom, nothing to be terrified about."[68] Califia's protagonist understands breeding as an act of generosity.[69] What appears to be at stake is sharing something of oneself with another, the generosity of opening one's bodily and subjective borders to another, and to *otherness*. Indeed, in "Holes," Califia is "amazed . . . by the power and generosity"[70] of those he has topped or fisted, of how they are able to "let go and invite me into their psyche and their

62   Califia, *Hard Men*, xiii.
63   Califia, "Skinned Alive," 78.
64   Ibid., 77.
65   Ibid., 81.
66   Ibid., 80.
67   Ibid., 84.
68   Ibid., 80.
69   Dean notes that "much bareback discourse uses metaphors of insemination, pregnancy, and paternity" (Dean, "Breeding Culture," 86). This includes the description of sex with the aim of HIV transmission as "breeding."
70   Califia, "Holes," 249.

orifices."[71] Califia is well aware of the implications for subjectivity these practices can symbolize.

## INTIMACY

> *Some of us know what we should do, we do it most of the time, and sometimes we slip. We slip because the condition of being aroused creates moisture. Hazardous footing. Melts boundaries. Makes the edges fuzzy.* [72]

> *Your skin splits from throat to pubis, m/ine in turn from below upwards, I spill m/yself into you, you mingle with m/e m/y mouth fastened on your mouth. . . . I feel our intestines uncoiling gliding among themselves.*[73]

Tim Dean's *Unlimited Intimacy* notes that while barebacking among gay men should be understood in its own specific context (the material facts surrounding HIV/AIDS, the visual culture, technologies, and discourses that create and sustain that subculture), "barebacking concerns an experience of unfettered intimacy, of overcoming the boundaries between persons, that is far from exclusive to this subculture or, indeed, to queer sexuality."[74] It is the desire, the need, for an "experience of unfettered intimacy" that I have identified in Wittig and in Califia through fantasies of breaching bodily borders, or through hosting another's limbs, blood, or cum inside one's body. Both Dean's *Unlimited Intimacy* and Bersani and Phillips's *Intimacies* reflect on the "openness to alterity" they locate in barebacking practices.[75] For Dean, "barebacking allegorizes such openness through its acceptance of risk and its willingness to dispense with barriers."[76] For Bersani and Phillips, barebacking represents a relational model of "impersonal intimacy" in becoming biologically linked with an

---

71   Ibid., 250.
72   Califia, "Slipping," 223.
73   Wittig, *The Lesbian Body*, 51–52.
74   Dean, *Unlimited Intimacy*, 2.
75   Ibid., 30.
76   Ibid.

HIV-positive sexual partner who may be a total stranger.[77] They describe this as "the ascesis of an ego-divesting discipline,"[78] where "the subject allows himself to be penetrated, even replaced, by an unknowable otherness."[79] Just as with "communion," the religious language used here—an "ascetic" practice that allows for "unknowable otherness" to enter the self—underlines the ritual and the symbolization involved in such sexual practices.

Both Wittig's and Califia's writing explores this openness to otherness fuelled by erotic desire. While bodies temporarily join—blood mingles, arms are swallowed by various orifices—they do not become self-identical. Otherness is *preserved*. The subject is infected by it, sometimes materially as well as metaphorically. Alterity is not only presented as desirable in these texts, but also as repulsive. Wittig's characters often waver between desire and revulsion—sometimes quite literal nausea: "*I* am suddenly revolted, *I* vomit you up."[80] Califia writes, "There is always a little nausea for me in the second before my mouth makes contact with somebody else's sex. But the urge forward is greater than whatever qualms I have about safe sex or sodomy."[81] Revulsion, and the protagonists' openness to being revolted by another, appears to be as much a part of intimacy as attraction.

The scenes I have presented from Califia's and Wittig's work amount to repeated imagery of fantastic incorporation of the other (even where that incorporation of bodily fluids is "real," it still undoubtedly also—perhaps primarily—operates on the level of fantasy). I suggest that such examples offer a new perspective on the value of fantasies of incorporation, and what kind of relation to otherness they represent. For Török, the positive aspect of introjection exists in the process of strengthening the ego by replacing an object with language—that is, naming the object, the other. And yet, the effects of articulating an object are to pull it into one's own sphere of reference, rendering this object the linguistic property of

---

77    Bersani and Phillips, *Intimacies*, 53.
78    Ibid., 35.
79    Ibid., 53.
80    Wittig, *The Lesbian Body*, 122.
81    Califia, *No Mercy*, 137.

the subject, and therefore as no longer *other*. Incorporation, on the other hand, refuses to enact the linguistic violence of naming the *other*, allowing otherness to persist. Incorporation acknowledges that the bridge between self and other can *only* be crossed in the structure of fantasy. Alterity remains intact despite the fantasy of incorporation: it remains "something strange to me, although it is at the heart of me."[82]

Perversely, fantasies of incorporation, of ingestion and bodily union, can express an intimacy that may actually preserve distance and alterity, a kind of intimacy that can accommodate alterity, eat it whole, and vomit it out again.[83] To me, this can express something more like Bersani and Phillips's "impersonal intimacy," a kind of relationality that respects alterity rather than seeking to render it knowable. A fantasy of eating another does not render that other identical to oneself—in fact it does nothing to disrupt alterity but simply allows it within, inevitably unsettling one's own subjectivity. From both Wittig and Califia, we may learn that erotic encounters with alterity are often bruising and bloody, tearing apart the subject while leaving otherness intact. Incorporation is positively Levinasian in its refusal to co-opt otherness: when faced with the other, one should peel the skin from its face; chew through its ears into its brain; let its ears bleed; vomit it out.

In her concept of a "coupled" or "dual" subject, Case noted that the subjectivity presented by Wittig in *The Lesbian Body* is never discrete but always relational, always understood in relation to the other. The short excerpt from Wittig in my title—"your blood dazzles m/e"—encapsulates this. The subject, "m/e," is "dazzled" by another, by an erotic communion with that other through the material presence of her blood. This subject can no longer be understood as isolated, coherent, or self-contained, its infection by otherness represented by the slash that divides the pronoun "m/e." Indeed, the subject is formed and re-formed through its relation with the other and otherness. The account of subjectivity, as well as the

---

82  Jacques Lacan, *The Ethics of Psychoanalysis 1959–1960*, vol. 7, trans. Dennis Porter (New York and London: W.W. Norton & Company, 1992), 71.

83  With thanks to Bex Williams for discussions on this subject.

relation between subject and other, offered by Wittig's work is not separable from the erotic. Eroticism fuels this ambivalent relation to otherness, drives it to the point where the subject is infiltrated, invaded, and fundamentally divided.

The lines from Wittig and Califia above demonstrate the violent ambivalence of eroticism. Desire splits skin open, and internal organs glide together. Desire, indeed, makes us slip, removing material barriers as well as those between self and other. Califia wants to taste alterity, to locate it on his tongue: while his "own blood has no taste,"[84] latex doesn't either. "The bland skin of the condom"[85] is impersonal: "I am the kind of girl who prefers to swallow it. It is affirmation and salvation. Sex without that salty taste makes me lonely."[86] The loneliness of a lack of contact with others he feels resulting from prophylaxis is returned to again and again, most dramatically in "Skinned Alive," with its stifled, permanently poly-suited characters. Califia commented on the piece: "I wrote 'Skinned Alive' in a deep sense of grief, trying to communicate what it has meant to me to be isolated from other men because of fear of infection."[87]

"Skinned Alive" was also written for Tony Valenzuela, a gay activist pilloried by the gay and mainstream press for speaking about his desire for bareback sex. Califia wrote the story "to humanize [him], because the harsh truth is that a lot of us have made the same decisions that he made; we just don't admit to it in public."[88] This hypocrisy about who experiences prohibited desires extends beyond the gay community: while gay men are burdened with pathologization for their desire for prophylactic-free sex, these desires are shared, as I have shown, by heterosexuals and lesbians alike. "Horror," "fetishization," "anxiety," and "need" are some of the words Califia uses to describe his reactions to bareback sex, and it is important to voice these reactions.[89] He writes of the safe

---

84  Califia, "Slipping," 222.
85  Califia, "The Surprise Party," 219.
86  Califia, "Slipping," 219.
87  Califia, *Hard Men*, xvi.
88  Ibid.
89  Ibid.

sex campaigns that have "made it damn hard for us to talk or even think about what we give up when we stop sharing come."[90] Queer theory emerged in response to the AIDS crisis in the United States at a time when shame surrounded the illness. It has always been, at its heart, invested in the need to speak the unspeakable, to consider the unacceptable aspects of sexuality. It must, I believe, attempt to voice what has been silenced about queer sexuality, whether that is lesbian sexuality, BDSM, or the desire to fuck bareback. As a theory of sexuality, queer analysis must be able to talk about sex and, above all, must be able to talk about queer sex.

## REFERENCES

Bersani, Leo, and Adam Phillips. *Intimacies*. Chicago: University of Chicago Press, 2008.

Butler, Judith. *Gender Trouble: Feminism and the Subversion of Identity*. London and New York: Routledge, 1990.

Califia, Patrick. "Canada." In *High Risk: An Anthology of Forbidden Writings*, edited by Amy Scholder and Ira Silverberg, 55–59. London: Serpent's Tail, 1991.

———. *Hard Men*. Los Angeles: Alyson Publications, 2004.

———. *The Lesbian S/M Safety Manual*. Boston: Lace Publications, 1988.

———. *Macho Sluts*. Boston: Alyson Publications, 1988.

———. *Melting Point: Short Stories*. Boston: Alyson Publications, 1993.

———. *No Mercy*. New York: Alyson Publications, 2000.

———. *Sapphistry: The Book of Lesbian Sexuality*. Kansas City, MO: Naiad Press, 1980.

Califia, Patrick, and Robin Sweeney. *The Second Coming: A Leatherdyke Reader*. New York: Alyson Publications, 1996.

Case, Sue-Ellen. "Towards a Butch-Femme Aesthetic." *Discourse* 11, no. 1 (Fall–Winter 1988–89): 55–73.

Dean, Tim. "Breeding Culture: Barebacking, Bugchasing, Giftgiving." *Massachusetts Review* 49, nos. 1–2 (Spring–Summer 2008): 80–94.

———. "Mediated Intimacies: Raw Sex, Truvada, and the Biopolitics of Chemoprophylaxis." *Sexualities* 18, nos. 1–2 (April 2015): 224–46.

———. "Queer Theory without Names: A Response to *Queer Theory's Return to France*, edited by Oliver Davis and Hector Kollias." *Paragraph* 35, no. 2 (July 2012): 421–34.

———. *Unlimited Intimacy: Reflections on the Subculture of Barebacking*. Chicago: University of Chicago Press, 2009.

90    Ibid.

Freud, Sigmund. *Totem and Taboo*. Translated by James Strachey. London and New York: Routledge, 2001.

Lacan, Jacques. *The Ethics of Psychoanalysis 1959–1960: The Seminar of Jacques Lacan*, vol. 7. Translated by Dennis Porter. New York: W.W. Norton, 1992.

Laplanche, Jean, and Jean-Bertrand Pontalis. *The Language of Psychoanalysis*. Translated by Donald Nicholson-Smith. London: Karnac Books, 1988.

de Lauretis, Teresa. "Sexual Indifference and Lesbian Representation." *Theatre Journal* 40, no. 2 (May 1988): 155–77.

Samois (organization), ed. *Coming to Power: Writing and Graphics on Lesbian S/M*. Boston: Alyson Publications, 1981.

Torok, Maria, and Nicolas Abraham. *The Shell and the Kernel: Renewals of Psychoanalysis*. Translated by Nicholas T. Rand. Chicago,: University of Chicago Press, 1994.

Wittig, Monique. *Le Corps lesbien*. Paris: Éditions de Minuit, 1973.

——. *Les Guérillères*. Paris: Éditions de Minuit, 1969.

——. *Les Guérillères*. Translated by David Le Vay. Chicago: University of Illinois Press, 2007.

——. *The Lesbian Body*. Translated by David Le Vay. New York: William Morrow and Company, 1975.

——. *L'Opoponax*. Paris: Éditions de Minuit, 1964.

——. *The Straight Mind and Other Essays*. London: Beacon Press, 1992.

Wittig, Monique, and Sandé Zeig. *Brouillon pour un dictionnaire des amantes*. Paris: Grasset, 1976.

——. *Lesbian Peoples: Materials for a Dictionary*. London: Virago, 1980.

# PORNO-
# GRAPHIC
# LIMITS

# CHAPTER 6

# THE RETURN OF THE REPRESSED: VISUALIZING SEX WITHOUT CONDOMS[1]

## Evangelos Tziallas

### BAREBACKING'S RETURN

The normalization of condom use throughout the nineties went hand-in-hand with the liberal mainstreaming of gay identity. Behaviour considered less than savoury, such as sex without condoms, was stigmatized and pushed both underground and out of the spotlight to ensure that narratives and representations of gay sexuality remained commensurate with meta-narratives concerning healthy, responsible, and productive citizenship. Explicit representation became a site of intervention, one targeted by health advocates and used by AIDS activists to promote safer sex among gay men.[2] After years of mounting pressure, the gay male porn industry capitulated to this new reality and

---

1    This chapter is largely derived from my doctoral thesis, "Between the Gothic and Surveillance: Gay (Male) Identity, Fiction Film, and Pornography (1970–2015)" (PhD diss., Concordia University, 2015). My analysis of *Focus/Refocus* is taken from chapter 6.

2    See Cindy Patton, *Inventing AIDS* (London and New York: Routledge, 1990); Cindy Patton, "Safe Sex and the Pornographic Vernacular," in *How Do I Look?: Queer Film and Video*, ed. Bad Object-Choices (Seattle: Bay Press, 1991); and Richard Fung, "Shortcomings: Questions about Pornography as Pedagogy," in *Queer Looks: Perspectives on Lesbian and Gay Film and Video*, eds. Martha Gever, John Greyson, and Pratibha Parmar (Toronto: Between the Lines Books, 1993).

adopted a self-regulating system that mandated uniform condom use, tacitly becoming the face (and body politic) of a widespread safer-sex campaign aimed at gay men.[3]

A subculture of barebacking once nurtured by privacy proliferated onscreen throughout the new millennium's first decade, spearheaded in large part by the exponential popularity of bareback porn companies like Treasure Island Media (TIM), Dark Alley Media, Raw Fuck Club, Jake Cruise, and Maverick Men. These production companies have proliferated in the digital era, pushing studios that were once committed to condom use (for example, Lucas Entertainment, Sean Cody, and Corbin Fisher) to "go bareback," and leaving those who remain committed to condom use struggling to attract the gaze. Furthermore, since the publication of Tim Dean's groundbreaking auto-ethnographic study *Unlimited Intimacy: Reflections on the Subculture of Barebacking*, TIM and barebacking have become key focal points in queer and porn discourse.[4] Significant attention has been paid to questions concerning intimacy, identity, sociality, and the correlations between representation and reality. Still, there appears to be a dearth of research focusing on the industrial pressures the commercial gay male porn industry faces in relation to changes in aesthetic categories and the evolution of twenty-first-century gay male sensibility. It is this connective thread I wish to flesh out in this chapter.

It is not coincidental that TIM's success also coincides with the growing demand for explicit amateur content, with the studio often relying on an amateur style of shooting itself. Indeed, TIM's success is inextricably linked not only to new modes of distribution that have allowed the studio to supersede imposed limitations and taboos, but also to new modes of production that evolve the aesthetics of pornography and, by extension, its affective registers.[5]

Writing recently about the HIV-prevention medication Truvada, Dean observes that the term "barebacking" has recently given way

---

3    Jeffrey Escoffier, *Bigger Than Life: The History of Gay Porn Cinema from Beefcake to Hard Core* (Philadelphia: Running Press, 2009).
4    Chris Ashford, "Bareback Sex, Queer Legal Theory, and Evolving Socio-Legal Contexts," *Sexualities* 18, no. 1/2 (2015): 195–209.
5    Susanna Paasonen, *Carnal Resonance: Affect and Online Pornography* (Cambridge, MA: MIT Press, 2011).

to the notion of "raw" sex. Raw sex is the fantasy of transcending mediation, even though "there can be no sexual experience that remains unmediated by social conceptions of what sex is or should be."[6] Because gay men's sex lives are "more heavily mediated than most," they are "particularly susceptible to the fantasy that 'raw sex' represents."[7] Raw is associated with "real," "natural," and "authentic,"[8] as captured, for instance, by the title of a recent symposium on barebacking held in May 2014 at the University of Toronto—"From Raw to Real." It is this precise question of the real, of reality, of realness, that fuses barebacking with new forms of unfettered amateurism. Condomless sex and its visual incarnation are inextricably woven into the fantasy of returning to something "real," of effacing mediation and intervention.

Although the politics of "raw sex" is newly emergent, it remains firmly rooted in the desire to liberate oneself from the antiseptic politics associated with regimes of intervention—to return to a period before governmental and bio-political interventions introduced sex to a system of regimentation, calculation, and surveillance—even if Truvada, at least according to Dean, is a stealthy mixture of both. Because condomless sex is predicated on the presumed (or imagined) anti-normative impulse of promiscuity, it is, then, also inextricable from the sexual minority revolution that organized sex into a political movement, that of gay liberation. To fuck without condoms is to embody the fantasies and potentialities of gay liberation, to relive the period before the split between safe and unsafe and, by extension, before the split between the past and the present became erected and sheathed with latex.

To be clear, there was no "barebacking" before the AIDS crisis;[9] barebacking does not exist outside the regime of uniform condom

---

6      Tim Dean, "Mediated Intimacies: Raw Sex, Truvada, and the Biopolitics of Chemoprophylaxis," *Sexualities* 18, nos. 1–2 (2015): 224.

7      Ibid., 224–25.

8      Ruth Barcan, "In the Raw: 'Home-Made' Porn and Reality Genres," *Journal of Mundane Behaviour* 3, no. 1 (2002): 87–109.

9      Tim Dean, *Unlimited Intimacy: Reflections on the Subculture of Barebacking* (Chicago: University of Chicago Press, 2009).

use instituted in the early nineties.[10] The condom instantiated a metaphoric break in time, erecting a barrier between a past that needs to be continually "unremembered,"[11] and the normalized present that must remain secured for a healthy and productive future in which subjects are meant to flourish.[12] If barebacking is not a new practice, then the removal of the condom in porn (and in the bedroom) opens a rupture that collapses the queer past and the queer present.[13] Barebacking partially returns gay culture to its pre-condom roots. It also brings the past into the present, re-embodying behaviour and ideals that were repressed by the condom. It is, in a manner of speaking, the return of the repressed.

The condom hasn't just acted as a semen barrier, but also one that has blocked the memories of a tumultuous and optimistic past (of gay liberation), as well as a horrifying one (the AIDS crisis), from flooding and unsettling the present.[14] "The condom is built into barebacking," writes Stuart Scott, arguing that "the memory of the condom appears also to extend backwards in that it exists symbolically when and where it never existed physically."[15] Although not explicitly mentioned, it is difficult not to identify gay liberation as the "when" and "where" to which he refers. Scott observes that "gay pornography can be categorized into three broad, overlapping genres and time periods: in reverse chronological order, they are Bareback, Condom, and Pre-condom."[16] Scott argues that "it is this pre-condom, prelapsarian state that much bareback pornography harks back to": the utopia of unfettered sex.[17]

---

10     Stuart Scott, "The Condomlessness of Bareback Sex: Responses to the Unrepresentability of HIV in Treasure Island Media's *Plantin' Seed* and *Slammed*," *Sexualities* 18, nos. 1–2 (2015): 210–23.

11     Christopher Castiglia and Christopher Reed, *If Memory Serves: Gay Men, AIDS and the Promise of the Queer Past* (Minneapolis: University of Minnesota Press, 2011).

12     Lee Edelman, *No Future: Queer Theory and the Death Drive*. Durham, NC: Duke University Press, 2004.

13     Tim Dean, "Bareback Time," in *Queer Times, Queer Becomings*, eds. E.L. McCallum and Mikko Tuhkanen (Albany: SUNY Press, 2011), 75–99.

14     Castiglia and Reed, *If Memory Serves*.

15     Scott, "The Condomlessness of Bareback Sex," 222.

16     Ibid., 220.

17     Ibid.

Bareback pornography, especially that produced by TIM, and amateur pornography have presented sustained challenges to the commercial gay porn industry's commitment to uniform condom use, threatening not only its profits, but also its unofficial status as gay male culture's ambassador and epicentre. Through an in-depth textual analysis of Raging Stallion Studio's (RSS) two-part opus *Focus/Refocus* (2009), I examine the ongoing industrial, representational, and political battles taking place in the gay porn industry as a microcosm for the various ruptures and reformations taking place off-screen.

If uniform condom use ultimately led to the repression of a culture of promiscuity and ushered in a normative one, I argue that reframing barebacking as the threatening monstrous other that has returned from the past—from its repression—to thwart normal stasis provides a new conceptual framework for thinking through bareback porn's disruptive affective registers. Bareback pornography is ultimately a destabilizing agent that seeks to undo the inextricable link between condom use and liberal-normative culture: a system of social disciplining that posits good liberal gays at the top of the hierarchy and at the centre of the spotlight, and the undisciplined at the bottom and/or on the margins. *Focus/Refocus* not only visualizes the anxiety barebacking poses to liberal-normative gay culture and the commercial porn industry, but also bespeaks the contentious debates about Truvada that ensued in the following decade.

## SEX AND/AS NARRATIVE

In the new millennium, explicit sex returned to narrative cinema. Hardcore arthouse film was mostly a European phenomenon, although films like John Cameron Mitchell's *Shortbus* (2006), Larry Clark's (banned) *Ken Park* (2002), Vincent Gallo's *Brown Bunny* (2003), and Travis Mathews's *I Want Your Love* (initially released as a short film in 2010 and then as a feature length in 2012) ensured that American cinema wasn't left out of the trend. While narrative fictions were exploring the boundary between arthouse sex and pornography, narrative commercial pornography—such as *Focus/Refocus*, along with several other studio productions—was doing likewise, but from the other side of the divide. Narrative fiction filmmakers looked to explicit sex to explore the limits of storytelling, sexuality, and subjectivity, and the affective potentials of the cinematic form.[18] Returning to their porn-chic roots, commercial studio productions turned to higher production values, extended storytelling, character development, and cinematic aesthetics. Hoping to close the gap between porn and film, porn makers adopted cinematic strategies to bring back viewers they were losing to free amateur content (found on sites such as Xtube), "professional amateur" (pro-am) porn starring the likes of Sean Cody and Corbin Fisher, and bareback studio productions (like TIM). In the millennium's first decade, a battle over the control of the pornographic gaze emerged within the gay male porn industry.

In addition to facilitating the "do-it-yourself"/amateur porn revolution, the apparent democratizing capabilities of digital technology allowed a new generation of ambitious tech-savvy entrepreneurs to start their own porn companies.[19] Online studios such as Sean Cody and Corbin Fisher tended to adopt an amateur aesthetic, and favoured shooting individual scenes rather than entire movies. By forgoing a narrative structure, these studios were able to cut production costs to a bare minimum. And, by selling their content over the Internet, they were able to sell subscriptions to their online repositories, giving subscribers access to all of their videos for a weekly, monthly, or yearly fee. "Pre-digital" studios such as RSS and Falcon Studios continued to sell physical copies of their products on VHS, DVD, and later Blu-ray, using narrative as a way to string together a standardized four or six sex scenes to sell a discrete product. Digital studios, on the other hand, embraced a "compilation format," suturing together scenes according to content or theme rather than a storyline, and the lucrative potential of perpetual "renting" over ownership.

The demand for amateur and pro-am content presented the non-digital-based commercial gay male porn industry with some challenges—challenges that were only exacerbated by the demand

---

18    Linda Williams, *Screening Sex* (Durham, NC: Duke University Press, 2008).

19    Susanna Paasonen, *Carnal Resonance.*

for porn without condoms. Shooting paid professional models with an amateur aesthetic became a booming enterprise, satisfying people's desire for something real but with better production values than free amateur content. Bareback companies such as TIM initiated and capitalized on this trend, selling professionally produced porn that mimicked the homemade porn a viewer might find on amateur-centred platforms such as Xtube.[20] Realism became defined by both aesthetic choices and a lack of a central organizing plot. Indeed, bareback studios tend to adopt amateur aesthetics and reject both the condom and the narrative. Narrative is seen as the purview of commercial safe sex productions, and a hindrance to the real.[21] The effect of the demand for greater amounts of realism in porn cannot be understated, but it is important to stress how distribution practices have also had an impact on content as well as style, especially in the case of bareback pornography.[22]

What developed during the early years of the new millennium was an ideological shift that manifested itself across formal, aesthetic, and economic lines, largely contingent on the presence or absence of the condom. We see a number of discursive and aesthetic changes that come with the condom's removal from the scene of pornographic production.

## PORN AND GAY CULTURE

The Internet made porn more popular and mainstream than ever before,[23] but in the process it also "killed" the industry.[24] Pirating

---

20   Byron Lee, "It's a Question of Breeding: Visualizing Queer Masculinity in Bareback Pornography," *Sexualities* 17, nos. 1–2 (2014): 100–20.

21   Paul Morris and Susanna Paasonen, "Risk and Utopia: A Dialogue on Pornography," *GLQ: A Journal of Lesbian and Gay Studies* 20, no. 3 (2014): 215–39.

22   Sharif Mowlabocus, "Porn 2.0? Technology, Social Practice, and the New Online Porn Industry," in *Porn.com: Making Sense of Online Pornography*, ed. Feona Attwood (New York: Peter Lang, 2010), 69–87.

23   Linda Williams, "Porn Studies: Proliferating Pornographies On/Scene: An Introduction," in *Porn Studies*, ed. Linda Williams (Durham, NC: Duke University Press, 2004), 1–23.

24   Mike Stabile, "End of the Porn Golden Age," *Salon*, March 2, 2012, http://www.salon.com/2012/03/03/life_after_the_golden_age_of_porn/.

and porn tube sites (video-sharing/streaming websites whose history is rooted in cable television[25]) allowed consumers access to content for free,[26] while live webcamming offered new interactive ways to engage sexually with images onscreen.[27] Since the early nineties, along with safe sex campaigns and AIDS service organizations, the commercial gay male porn industry has acted as one of the ambassadors for safer sex and (Western) gay male culture.[28] Indeed, safe sex advocates were able to instill their vision precisely because, by the mid-eighties, a "small group" of companies dominated the production of gay male pornography,"[29] anchored in large part by Falcon Studio, Colt Studio, and Catalina and HIS video. But with pornography's "onscenity"—the shift from off-screen ("obscene") to onscreen ("onscene")[30]—came the loss of control. A re-cut, non-explicit retail version of *Focus/Refocus* was released as *Focus/Refocus: When Porn Kills*. The porn in question, though, is not commercial pornography, but amateur pornography.

Amateur pornography in *Focus/Refocus* is a stand-in for the Internet and barebacking, both of which the film indicts for "killing" the commercial porn industry. *Focus/Refocus* very clearly condemns what Brian McNair calls the "democratization of desire"[31] and, along with it, the democratizing capabilities of digital technology for robbing the studio industry's control over the cultural artifacts that heavily shaped the contours of gay culture. The gay male porn

---

25  Luke Stadel, "Cable, Pornography, and the Reinvention of Television, 1982–1989," *Cinema Journal* 53, no. 3 (2014): 52–75.

26  Steven Brown, "Porn Piracy: An Overlooked Phenomenon in Need of Academic Investigation," *Porn Studies* 1, no. 3 (2014): 326–30.

27  Patrick Henze, "Porn 2.0 Utopias: Authenticity and Gay Masculinities on Cam4," *Networking Knowledge: Journal of MeCCSA Postgraduate Network* 6, no. 1 (2013): 48–62.

28  Sharif Mowlabocus, *Gaydar Culture: Gay Men, Technology, and Embodiment in the Digital Age* (Farnham, UK: Ashgate Publishing, 2010).

29  John Mercer, "Seeing is Believing: Constructions of Stardom and the Gay Porn Star in US Gay Video Pornography," in *Framing Celebrity: New Directions in Celebrity Culture*, eds. Su Holmes and Sean Redmond (London and New York: Routledge, 2006), 146.

30  Williams, "Porn Studies."

31  Brian McNair, *Striptease Culture: Sex, Media, and the Democratization of Desire* (London and New York: Routledge, 2002).

star has been a critical focal point for gay male culture.[32] But along with the gay male porn industry's expansion comes the decline of the figure of the porn superstar and the safe sex industry's control over this figurative ideal.[33] *Focus/Refocus* testifies to how gay male culture became inextricably linked to porn and pornographic representation. But *Focus/Refocus* isn't just cultural critique; it is also a critique of the industry at the pinnacle of a multi-pronged faceoff. The film (both its explicit and non-explicit versions) cannot be properly understood outside of its industrial context.

Regardless of its political dimensions, *Focus/Refocus* is still a porn movie, and as such it has certain expectations to fulfill—namely to turn viewers on and help them get off. Despite the industrial-cultural critique it offers, *Focus/Refocus* attempts to meet its audience halfway, blending together amateur- and professional-style shooting into a two-part, explicit neo-noir erotic thriller. The film's narrative revolves around the hunt for a serial killer attacking gay men in San Francisco's Castro neighbourhood. The plot bears resemblance to the gay classic *Cruising* (1980),[34] doubling as a densely layered investigation of contemporary gay male sexuality and subjectivity in the digital era. *Focus/Refocus* places significant emphasis on the amateur recording apparatus, framing it as a device that has contributed to bareback's onscenity, a conduit for the return of the repressed, condomless sex.

In a pivotal interrogation scene near the end of the movie, when the character Joe is asked by the detective why he decided to confront Eddie, his killer ex-boyfriend, on his own rather than calling on the police, Joe rhetorically asks the officer, "Why do you smoke? You know it's going to kill you one day. Why do people jump out of perfectly good airplanes, or why are guys having bareback sex?" He goes on to tell the detective that he'd had a taste of risk, *"real* risk," and liked it. "I mean, it was fucking exciting!" he exclaims, confessing

---

32    John R. Burger, *One-Handed Histories: The Eroto-Politics of Gay Male Video Pornography* (New York: Harrington Park Press, 1995).

33    Dean, *Unlimited Intimacy.*

34    Guy Davidson, 'Contagious Relations': Simulation, Paranoia, and the Postmodern Condition in William Friedkin's *Cruising* and Felice Picano's *The Lure*," *GLQ: A Journal of Lesbian and Gay Studies* 11, no. 1 (2005): 23–64.

that his ex, Eddie, saw and exploited an underlying thirst for risk in him. The decision to equate barebacking with cigarette smoking aligns sex without condoms not only with risky thrill-seeking, but also with addiction, illness, and death. Besides this singular reference to barebacking, HIV/AIDS isn't mentioned even once throughout *Focus/Refocus*, and yet, the allusion to AIDS permeates the entire narrative. From the attempt to insert the condom into an aesthetic regime that has been co-opted by barebacking (as in the case of certain forms of amateur porn), to the focus on risk, the film's dark tone and aesthetic choices, and of course the unusually large number of deaths for a porn movie, the spectre of barebacking and the AIDS crisis imbues every character and sexual encounter.

## FOCUS: DIGITAL RECORDING TECHNOLOGY AND THE RISE OF THE AMATEUR PORNOGRAPHER

The film begins with Joe being interrogated by a police detective. The officer records the interrogation with a small camcorder that sits on a tripod to his left and slightly behind him. It points diagonally at Joe from across the corner of the table, focusing entirely on him. The narrative is told through a series of flashbacks, and before transitioning into the first flashback, the interrogating officer asks Joe to "start from the beginning." Shot first from the corner of the room, the film cuts to Joe pointing at the camcorder and saying, "Okay, I'll start with one of those." The film then cuts to a close-up shot of the camcorder's screen. In the out-of-focus background, we see Joe pointing accusingly at the camcorder. On the camcorder's screen, however, we see Joe pointing directly at us, the viewer. His finger covers his mouth; his accusatory finger appears to say everything. From the very beginning, the film implicates the digital recording apparatus and interpellates the viewing subject; by strategically adopting the detective genre as its generic vehicle, the film codes the scenes of explicit sex as "evidence" to be examined. The opening scene's final image "refocuses" our attention to the digital recording apparatus, suggesting that this exploration of Joe's past will revolve around recording, revisiting recordings, shifting perceptions, and parallax views.

From the opening interrogation scene, we transition to a point-of-view (POV) shot of Eddie lying in his underwear in bed, staring up into Joe's camcorder. He asks Joe, "Is that thing in focus?" Joe responds by informing Eddie that "it's autofocus, no thinking necessary," with the latter playfully adding "or skill." Right from the beginning, there is a critique levelled against amateur productions: legitimate porn is imagined to require skill and thought, while amateur porn requires neither.[35] The film cuts back to the filmic camera (the invisible production camera through which we observe the narrative unfold) and shows Joe on top of Eddie, filming him. Eddie confesses that he's done this before. Surprised, Joe asks, "You did porn?" To which Eddie defensively responds, "No, no, nothing like that. It was a home video." Joe seems really into the idea, so Eddie decides to indulge his fantasy. The explicit home movie, however, will soon be uploaded to "Porn Tube," a fake amateur porn site, transforming it into a public entity whose circulation will come to have very real consequences, both inside and outside the bedroom.

What follows is a twenty-three-minute sex scene that plays with a variety of shots to blend together professional and amateur aesthetics. While the integration of amateur-style shooting acknowledges the target audience's demand for perceived realism and tries to meet them halfway, it also attempts to recode, if not recuperate, amateur aesthetics and realign them with safe sex practices. *Focus/Refocus* places heavy emphasis on condom use, and its first sex scene wants to assure us that, despite the scenes we may encounter online, gay men still use condoms. Before we see Joe sit on Eddie's erect penis, we are treated to a POV close-up of the former putting the condom on the latter and then giving the latex-sheathed penis a little kiss. Rather than a perceived barrier, here the condom becomes an ingrained part of the couple's intimacy.

*Focus/Refocus* co-opts the aesthetic of realism and the mundane to interpellate its viewer. The various shots throughout the first sequence tend to fall under three general categories that prioritize different emotional currents, the most prominent and out of character being the embodied POV shot. POV shooting is common in

---

35    Paasonen, *Carnal Resonance*.

amateur and pro-am porn, a style of shooting and sub-genre known as "gonzo," but less common in narrative commercial productions. Gonzo porn is intimately connected to reality, amateurism, and the domestic, and gonzo-style shooting tends to be featured outside typical narrative configurations.[36] The opening scene in particular comments on the degree to which pornography has shaped gay male sexuality,[37] as well as how amateur porn tends to efface the influence and inflections of professionally produced pornography[38]—as though it could ever divorce itself from prior and ongoing mediation.[39] But the first sex sequence also sets up an underlying critique of self-shooting as a form of intimacy, consciously aligning the amateur recording apparatus with the erosion of privacy.[40] The private home video will eventually be uploaded to the Internet and become a part of the public pornographic assemblage;[41] whatever is filmed for private purposes can easily be made public in the digital era, and the sexual objects often seen to beckon our gaze are those that were once private.[42]

The next sex scene discursively extends from the previous one and has Joe renting a video of his favourite porn star, Dario Stefano, and returning home to masturbate. Upon his return, Joe pops in the rented DVD and begins to masturbate to Dario's "solo" scene. In a bit of a generic twist, rather than voyeuristically spying on a character as he masturbates, Joe instead watches the object of his desire perform on his television screen. The intimate and affective relations between pornographic images and consumers are reflexively incorporated into the scene's layered mise-en-abyme structure: Joe mimics the behaviour displayed onscreen, and we, the audience, (presumably)

---

36  Ibid.
37  Mowlabocus, *Gaydar Culture*.
38  Niels Van Doorn, "Keeping It Real: User-Generated Pornography, Gender Reification, and Visual Pleasure," *Convergence: The International Journal of Research into New Media Technologies* 16, no. 4 (2010): 411–30.
39  Dean, "Mediated Intimacies."
40  Barcan, "In the Raw."
41  Brandon Arroyo, "Sexual Affects and Active Pornographic Space in the Networked Gay Village" *Porn Studies* 3, no. 1 (2016): 77–88.
42  Evangelos Tziallas, "Gamified Eroticism: Gay Male Social Networking Applications and Self-Pornography," *Sexuality and Culture* 19, no. 4 (2015): 759–75.

do likewise. We again see the directors actively trying to appease their viewers. If the previous scene played with gay pornography's tendency toward the reflexive to undermine barebacking's co-option of intimacy and realism, then this sequence incorporates reflexivity to stress as well as critique the mimetic relations between screens and bodies. Both porn and film are contingently mimetic, but porn, more so than film, requires mimesis not only to "succeed," but also to become ontologically "complete."[43] Porn is about mimicking—if not the activity, then at least the feelings of pleasure being simulated or projected through self-stimulation. You watch porn to feel what those onscreen feel.[44]

But what we see play out in this scene is Joe's over-identification with the pornographic image. He doesn't want to just merely feel what Dario feels or be with Dario. He wants to *become* Dario. The sequence is carefully shot to position Dario as Joe's televisual double, a symbol of who he desires to be and tries to become. It is not insignificant that Dario's last name, Stefano, is also that of gay porn legend Joey Stefano, who was diagnosed with HIV in 1990 and died of an overdose in 1994.[45] Joe is temporarily living out his porn star fantasy through mimetic fandom. By mimicking Dario, he is identifying with, and learning how to become, his desired image double. The sequence ends with Joe standing next to, and ejaculating onto, the television screen—a moment that recalls Max Renn's (played by James Woods) intimate relationship with his television in David Cronenberg's *Videodrome* (1983), a mainstream film about the intersection between recording technology and sexuality. By the end of his masturbatory session, Joe has been absorbed into the screen.

Narratively, this scene sets up the relationship between Joe and the soon-to-be-revealed *homme fatal* Dario. Conceptually, it sets up Joe's quest to make the fantasy world of pornography his reality. Emotionally, though, there is a lingering, ominous feeling

43    Magnus Ullén, "Pornography and Its Critical Reception: Toward a Theory of Masturbation," *Jump Cut: A Review of Contemporary Media* 51 (2009): http://www.ejumpcut.org/archive/jc51.2009/UllenPorn/text.html.

44    Paasonen, *Carnal Resonance*.

45    Christopher Isherwood, *Wonder Bread & Ecstasy: The Life and Death of Joey Stefano* (New York: Alyson Books, 1996).

that engenders extreme ambivalence. The proliferation of the manufactured gay male porn star coincides with the popularity of VHS in the late 1980s, when the gay male porn star became a vital ancillary to securing sales and profits.[46] Performers often signed exclusive contracts with studios, and many still do today—such as RRS "exclusive" Steve Cruz, who plays Dario—but the porn industry's evolution has also fundamentally altered its star system, as well as the porn star's identificatory currency.

The gay male porn star was a figure of idealized health.[47] His body not only reflected the turn toward the "gym body" gay men took up in the wake of the AIDS epidemic, but also helped to normalize that body and its masculine connotations as the ideal[48]—even the Czech studio Bel Ami, which debuted in 1993, succeeded in part by subtly promoting "health," allowing audiences to gaze at newly discovered, unalloyed, healthy, and young white bodies that had been kept hidden behind the Iron Curtain.[49] The gay male porn star was a crucial figure of identification that helped to mould gay male sexuality, becoming an important ancillary to safe sex campaigns.[50] Now anyone with a camcorder and a penchant for exhibitionism can become a porn star, decentralizing the controlled image of the commercial performer. Joe's journey from private citizen to wannabe porn star is a parable of the "dangers" of amateur pornography: the personal consequences of shedding one's privacy for visibility symbolizing the collective "threat" of allowing anyone with a camcorder to commandeer the pornographic gaze.

After Joe ejaculates onto the television screen, Eddie barges in and begins to scold him for uploading their private sex tape to the Internet: Joe likes the attention; Eddie doesn't. It turns out that the video has gone *viral*. Joe is now a porn star: his fantasy has become

---

46  Mercer, "Seeing is Believing."
47  Ibid.
48  Erick Alvarez, *Muscle Boys: Gay Gym Culture* (London and New York: Routledge, 2008).
49  Evangelos Tziallas, "The New 'Porn Wars': Representing Gay Male Sexuality in the Middle East," *Psychology and Sexuality* 6, no. 1 (2015): 93–110.
50  Michael Lucas, "On Gay Porn," *Yale Journal of Law and Feminism* 18, no. 2 (2006): 299–302.

a reality—foreshadowed by the image of his reflection on the television screen. Eddie is furious that his privacy has been violated, and storms out of the room. Turned on by his newfound visibility and popularity, Joe decides to indulge his desire for this type of public sex.

The remaining sex scenes further obfuscate the distinction between amateur and professional, and between real and creative performance. We first see Joe filming himself in gonzo style while performing oral sex on an anonymous stranger in a secluded public space. Like before, Joe decides to upload this private video to the Internet; and, like before, the video goes viral. It isn't long before Eddie catches wind of Joe's "indiscretion." And after a co-worker streams the filmed blow job on his phone for Eddie, he immediately rushes home and breaks up with Joe. No longer held back by his boyfriend, Joe fully embraces his predilection for filming. He secretly records two men he comes across having sex in an underground parking garage, and is even hired by an "A-list queen" to film a private gangbang scene. By the end of *Focus/Refocus*, Joe is an exhibitionist and a voyeur, a star and a director, blurring the lines between amateur and professional.

With respect to the anonymous, self-filmed blow job scene, we again see the film playing with and twisting the conventions and meanings of POV shooting and amateurism: Joe is both an actor and a director, but so is porn performer Cole Streets (who plays Joe). The porn performer in this instance is also a figurative *and* literal porn maker, collapsing the performer's and the character's body into a singular pro-am entity. If Joe/Cole is in control of the camera and decides how to film himself sucking cock, and how he wants to suck that cock, how does it differ from anyone else who does similarly and then uploads the video to a site like, for instance, Xtube? Insofar as the oral sequence cuts between the filmic and amateur lens, the scene is metaphorically pro-am. Even if the self-shot scene is part of a larger narrative script, the very act of self-filming demarcates those instances as actually amateur and not feigned amateurism. Indeed, if one were to cut out the professional shots and edit together the ones shot by Joe and by his anonymous partner, the video would look, and in many ways would be, no different from what one might find on Xtube.

The directors are making a concerted effort to obscure the division between narrative (representation) and reality in *Focus*, constructing a story with which many viewers can identify—less so in the case of *Refocus*, whose narrative revolves entirely around death. The majority of *Focus* remains grounded in reality, emulating and playing out scenarios that could be deemed typical of gay male experience: Joe has sex with his boyfriend; he masturbates to porn; he gives a random guy a blow job; he watches two guys have sex. There's nothing fantastical or entirely out of the ordinary going on here. And considering more than half of the film's sex scenes are shot with an amateur lens, primarily by Joe, the entirety of *Focus* verges on being a pro-am production, the irony of which the directors reflexively engage with in *Focus*'s final scene. After gaining enough experience on his own, Joe decides to take the next step of trying his hand at a semi-professional shoot. Joe and Eddie's video lands him a private filming gig starring, coincidentally, none other than Dario Stefano. When he arrives at the private residence, he finds four men preparing for their close-ups. Joe begins to record their warm-up, and a few moments later Dario walks in, disrobes, and joins the group.

The lengthy, forty-minute gangbang scene fulfills the obligatory "three-or-more" requirement of most commercially produced gay male porn videos, but it also allows for an extended visual and ideological play. Essentially, what we observe is a professionally choreographed scene that is supposed to appear like a "behind the scenes" making of a pornographic home movie—or amateur porn through a professional lens. As with earlier sequences, the camera cuts back and forth between POV shots of Joe's amateur recordings and the filmic camera, slowly blending the two gazes. The final group cum sequence has Joe masturbating over the video's patron, who temporarily takes over the filming duties and records Joe stroking himself to orgasm. Joe begins as a passive observer recording the action, but as the two gazes align, he becomes a full-fledged participant. This pivotal scene is where fantasy and reality collide. Joe has managed to insert himself into the pornographic image: he has become a real porn star, and Cole a real porn maker.

## REFOCUS: THE RETURN OF THE REPRESSED

In part two, we discover Eddie has a secret murderous past that refuses to stay in the past and a murderous instinct he just couldn't seem to suppress. The much darker sequel features as many murders as it does orgasms. We see several characters—a local bartender; a detective secretly following Joe; Joe's friend Barton, who works at a local San Francisco porn shop (Rock Hard); Dario and Eddie—get off and get killed off too. By the time we reach the narrative's dramatic reveal and duel, it is apparent that the entire film has revolved around not only the return of the repressed, but also its return through the personal recording apparatus—something made more apparent on *Focus/Refocus*'s retail cover than its explicit one. The personal recording apparatus becomes a conduit through which not only reality and fantasy literally and figuratively converge, but the past can return—crystallized in the final battle between Joe and Eddie.

Joe enters an abandoned theatre and sees his earlier sexual encounter with Dario, who was murdered post-coitus while Joe was showering in the next room, being projected on a big screen. He also sees the detective who's been watching him from afar with his throat slit sitting in the audience. Eddie enters from the shadows from the left and stands on stage in front of the big screen. In typical "bad guy" form, he makes a grand confession, detailing his lust for risk and admitting to sleeping with Dario and other risk-takers, indulging his "good and evil sides." Turns out Eddie is the voyeur who secretly filmed Dario and Joe, violating their privacy, giving Joe a taste of his own medicine. Eddie goes on to tell Joe that he wanted to find someone "normal" to show himself how "normal people live," but realized that deep down Joe was "just itching to go bad." The final sequence appropriates the generic good-versus-evil binary to juxtapose barebacking ("risky") with safer sex ("normal"). Even though we see Eddie use condoms when he has sex (RSS is a committed safe sex company), Eddie is coded as a barebacker, as the return of the repressed.

It is not insignificant that the final showdown is set in a movie theatre. The porn theatre was a social space where gay male culture and sexuality flourished.[51] The directors' decision to exhibit private amateur rather than commercial footage in this abandoned public space is indicative of the degree to which the real has become the spectacle we now seek—the spectacle of real sex has replaced the desire for artistic mediation. But the return to the pornographic theatre is also a return to one of gay identity's primal scenes, bringing post-Stonewall gay culture in the West back full circle and, in many ways, to a close: the space that brought us together, projected our desires, and validated our existence[52] has been replaced by privatized creation and consumption that mimic, while simultaneously chipping away at, gay pornography's original goals.

The theatre in *Focus/Refocus* is coded as a gothic space haunted by ghosts, symbolized by the dead detective in the audience and Dario's image onscreen—an ideal space for the repressed, Eddie's true persona, to return. After the villain's obligatory confession comes the obligatory final faceoff. But rather than battle it out with guns or fists, the two fight to the death with their cocks and assholes as their weapons of choice—*la petite mort* cum actual death. The final showdown begins with Eddie bending Joe over one of the theatre seats in the front row, pulling down his pants, and entering him from behind. Lacking the ubiquitous condom shot, it seems as though the two are engaging in unprotected sex. The first close-up, however, reveals Eddie is indeed wearing a condom. As he thrusts himself into Joe, the camera cuts between close-ups of penetration and medium long shots of the actors' bodies in the foreground and the amateur footage playing onscreen in the background. It appears that Eddie is going to fuck Joe to death, this *dénouement* symbolized by the projected home video that resulted in Dario's death.

As the scene progresses, Eddie and Joe pause momentarily; before making their way to the stage, the latter performs oral sex on the former. What is unique about this brief interlude is that Eddie

---

51  Rich Cante and Angelo Restivo, "The Cultural-Aesthetic Specificities of All-Male Moving-Image Pornography," in *Porn Studies*, ed. Linda Williams (Durham, NC: Duke University Press, 2004), 142–66; and José B. Campino, "Homologies of Space: Text and Spectatorship in All-Male Adult Theaters," *Cinema Journal* 45, no. 1 (2005): 50–65.

52  Burger, *One-Handed Histories*.

continues to wear a condom while Joe fellates him, something rarely seen in porn (let alone practised by gay men). Partly functional (lubricating his erection for reinsertion) and partly symbolic, the practice recalls earlier attempts to eroticize condom use in porn (such as in *On the Rocks* [1990], where a young man inserts a condom into his mouth and then rolls it down the head and shaft of Jeff Stryker's erection before intercourse).[53] The two then make their way to the stage for their final carnal tryst. Eddie lies on his back, while Joe is on top. Facing each other, they begin to strangle one another as they fuck, and right before Joe kills Eddie the latter removes the condom and orgasms. Although momentarily shocked by his actions, Joe continues to masturbate and ends the scene by ejaculating over his ex-lover's corpse. The film cuts back to Joe in the interrogation room, where he is formally charged with murder. The narrative comes full circle, and ends with Joe picking up the officer's cigarette and taking a drag.

The cigarette is a complex symbol that connotes not only risk and death, but also pleasure and defiance. And although the ending is ambivalent, leaving itself open to interpretation, within the context of the narrative smoking serves as a metaphor for barebacking and, quite possibly, HIV. Indeed, *Focus/Refocus*'s narrative appears to be an allegory for the return of the practice that brought about the AIDS crisis. A serial killer of gay men, Eddie seems to symbolically stand in for AIDS. Although Eddie has already killed before Joe uploads their private sex tape onto the Internet, it is only after the video has gone *viral* that he begins to kill at a more rapid rate. Rather than hinder or curtail his killing spree, the amateur recording apparatus aided its acceleration: visibility has failed to discipline and control what is perceived as the undesirable. Although Eddie is dead, his spirit lives on in Joe, who is now also a killer of gay men—the proverbial condom wasn't enough to protect our protagonist. Joe has figuratively been "infected" by Eddie, a past lover who has managed to get inside Joe in more ways than one—a past lover who will stay with Joe forever.

The spectre of AIDS haunts the narrative and sex scenes. The film is heavy with a sense of foreboding—ambivalent, perhaps, about

---

53  Burger, *One-Handed Histories.*

its own complacent appropriation of realist aesthetics, straddling the line between professional and pro-am. While lamenting, via the theatre, the past's passing, the film also displays a deep anxiety about the past's return through digital media technology. The prelapsarian past,[54] the period of unbridled lust and unfettered carnal pleasure, can never truly come into being in the present because it can never bypass the consequences that brought about its fall. Leo Bersani argues that "barebacking is a literalizing of the ontology of the sexual. As such, it also implicitly destroys the crucial psychoanalytic distinction between fantasy and reality."[55] If pornography is an inherently utopian genre[56] that manufactures a contained world filled with an abundance of pleasure that lacks real consequences, then *Focus/Refocus* reimagines pornography in terms of dystopia, one whose consequences are all too real.

## CONCLUSION

The condom is one of the emblematic icons of liberal-normative gay culture, and its abandonment may very well entail the return of previous cultural formations that lie in stark contrast to the mainstreamed one promoted over the last few decades. Liberal-normative culture is contingent upon the conservative ideals of life, health, security, and productivity,[57] whose ideological underpinnings were embodied by the condom.[58] *Focus/Refocus*, and the discourse of barebacking, reveal deep-seated anxieties about the future, but a future whose roots seem to stretch back to the late seventies. Legal rights and social acceptance were contingent upon building an idealized facade to appease a hostile, fearful majority spurred on by campaigns like Anita Bryant's "Save Our Children"

---

54 Scott, "The Condomlessness of Bareback Sex."

55 Leo Bersani, "Shame on You," in *After Sex? On Writing Since Queer Theory*, eds. Janet Halley and Andrew Parker (Durham, NC: Duke University Press, 2011), 107.

56 Linda Williams, *Hard Core: Power, Pleasure, and the "Frenzy of the Visible,"* 2nd ed. (Berkeley: University of California Press, 1999).

57 Lee Edelman, *No Future: Queer Theory and the Death Drive* (Durham, NC: Duke University Press, 2004).

58 Dean, *Unlimited Intimacy.*

and the AIDS crisis. Barebacking serves as a counterpoint not only to that manufactured idealized image, but also to the ideological and discursive circuitry on which that image has been built. The risk of contracting HIV and the tacit shaming of those living with the virus steered gay men toward modelling themselves after their heterosexual counterparts. More recently, however, with biomedical advances such as Truvada, the threat of HIV has diminished and along with it the strictures buttressed by that presumed threat.

The suppression and repression of gay liberation and the AIDS crisis cultivated normative culture, but at the same time maintained both eras as inextricable spectres. "A ghost, of course, haunts," observes David Oscar Harvey, and "a haunting instils a troublesome impression of its presence."[59] The past continues to haunt the queer imaginary, compelling pre-eminent French queer scholar Didier Eribon to proclaim that he has "always thought that gay lives are haunted lives."[60] "My life," he tenderly confesses, "is haunted by those whom the disease took away—by those, more precisely, whom I managed to survive."[61] And yet, a spiralling sensation that something is in the process of returning can be detected in the writings of prominent queer theorists, whose work over the last decade or so, taken collectively, has focused rather intently on memory,[62] time,[63] the uncanny,[64] and the future.[65]

As the condom era potentially comes to a close, so too might the reign of liberal-normative culture. The onscenity of barebacking and the continued obscenity of HIV/AIDS have rendered the

---

59  David Oscar Harvey, "Ghosts Caught in Our Throat: Of the Lack of Contemporary Representations of Gay/Bisexual Men and HIV," *Jump Cut: A Review of Contemporary Media* 55 (2013): http://www.ejumpcut.org/archive/jc55.2013/HarveyPoz/index.html.

60  Didier Eribon, "Haunted Lives: AIDS and the Future of Our Past," *Qui Parle: Critical Humanities and Social Sciences* 18, no. 2 (2010): 311.

61  Ibid., 310.

62  Castiglia and Reed, *If Memory Serves.*

63  Elizabeth Freeman, *Time Binds: Queer Temporalities, Queer Histories* (Durham, NC: Duke University Press, 2010).

64  Paulina Palmer, *The Queer Uncanny: New Perspectives on the Gothic* (Cardiff, UK: University of Wales Press, 2012).

65  José Esteban Muñoz, *Cruising Utopia: The Then and There of Queer Futurity* (New York: New York University Press, 2009).

HIV-positive subject ghostly[66] but perhaps not for too much longer. The horizon of queer futurity is unclear, but what is certain is that, for better or worse, the future will be shaped by the past and its incremental return.

## REFERENCES

Alvarez, Erick. *Muscle Boys: Gay Gym Culture*. London and New York: Routledge, 2008.

Arroyo, Brandon. "Sexual Affects and Active Pornographic Space in the Networked Gay Village." *Porn Studies* 3, no. 1 (March 2016): 77–88.

Ashford, Chris. "Bareback Sex, Queer Legal Theory, and Evolving Socio-Legal Contexts." *Sexualities* 18, nos. 1–2 (April 2015): 195–209.

Barcan, Ruth. "In the Raw: 'Home-Made' Porn and Reality Genres." *Journal of Mundane Behaviour* 3, no. 1 (2002): 87–109.

Bersani, Leo. "Shame on You." In *After Sex? On Writing since Queer Theory*, edited by Janet Halley and Andrew Parker, 91–109. Durham, NC: Duke University Press, 2011.

Brown, Steven. "Porn Piracy: An Overlooked Phenomenon in Need of Academic Investigation." *Porn Studies* 1, no. 3 (July 2014): 326–30.

Burger, John R. *One-Handed Histories: The Eroto-Politics of Gay Male Video Pornography*. New York: Harrington Park Press, 1995.

Campino, José B. "Homologies of Space: Text and Spectatorship in All-Male Adult Theaters." *Cinema Journal* 45, no. 1 (Fall 2005): 50–65.

Cante, Rich, and Angelo Restivo. "The Cultural-Aesthetic Specificities of All-Male Moving-Image Pornography." In *Porn Studies*, edited by Linda Williams, 142–66. Durham, NC: Duke University Press, 2004.

Castiglia, Christopher, and Christopher Reed. *If Memory Serves: Gay Men, AIDS, and the Promise of the Queer Past*. Minneapolis: University of Minnesota Press, 2011.

Davidson, Guy. "'Contagious Relations': Simulation, Paranoia, and the Postmodern Condition in William Friedkin's *Cruising* and Felice Picano's *The Lure*." *GLQ: A Journal of Lesbian and Gay Studies* 11, no. 1 (2005): 23–64.

Dean, Tim. "Bareback Time." In *Queer Times, Queer Becomings*, edited by E.L. McCallum and Mikko Tuhkanen, 75–99. Albany: SUNY Press, 2011.

——. "Mediated Intimacies: Raw Sex, Truvada, and the Biopolitics of Chemoprophylaxis." *Sexualities* 18, nos. 1–2 (April 2015): 224–46.

---

66  David Oscar Harvey, "Ghosts Caught in Out Throat: Of the Lack of Contemporary Representations of Gay/Bisexual Men and HIV," *Jump Cut: A Review of Contemporary Media* 55 (2013): http://www.ejumpcut.org/archive/jc55.2013/HarveyPoz/index.html.

————. *Unlimited Intimacy: Reflections on the Subculture of Barebacking.* Chicago: University of Chicago Press, 2009.

Dyer, Richard. "Idol Thoughts: Orgasm and Self-Reflexivity in Gay Pornography." In *More Dirty Looks: Gender, Pornography and Power* (2nd ed.), edited by Pamela Church Gibson, 102–09. London: British Film Institute Publishing, 2003.

Edelman, Lee. *No Future: Queer Theory and the Death Drive.* Durham, NC: Duke University Press, 2004.

Eribon, Didier. "Haunted Lives: AIDS and the Future of Our Past." *Qui Parle: Critical Humanities and Social Sciences* 18, no. 2 (Spring–Summer 2010): 309–21.

Escoffier, Jeffrey. *Bigger than Life: The History of Gay Porn Cinema from Beefcake to Hard Core.* Philadelphia: Running Press, 2009.

Freeman, Elizabeth. *Time Binds: Queer Temporalities, Queer Histories.* Durham, NC: Duke University Press, 2010.

Fung, Richard. "Shortcomings: Questions about Pornography as Pedagogy." In *Queer Looks: Perspectives on Lesbian and Gay Film and Video*, edited by Martha Gever, John Greyson, and Pratibha Parmar, 355–67. Toronto: Between the Lines Books, 1993.

Harvey, David Oscar. "Ghosts Caught in Our Throat: Of the Lack of Contemporary Representations of Gay/Bisexual Men and HIV." *Jump Cut: A Review of Contemporary Media* 55 (2013). http://www.ejumpcut.org/archive/jc55.2013/HarveyPoz/index.html.

Henze, Patrick. "Porn 2.0 Utopias: Authenticity and Gay Masculinities on Cam4." *Networking Knowledge: Journal of MeCCSA Postgraduate Network* 6, no. 1 (August 2013): 48–62.

Isherwood, Christopher. *Wonder Bread and Ecstasy: The Life and Death of Joey Stefano.* New York: Alyson Publications, 1996.

Lee, Byron. "It's a Question of Breeding: Visualizing Queer Masculinity in Bareback Pornography." *Sexualities* 17, nos. 1–2 (February 2014): 100–20.

Lucas, Michael. "On Gay Porn." *Yale Journal of Law and Feminism* 18, no. 1 (2006): 299–302.

McNair, Brian. *Striptease Culture: Sex, Media, and the Democratization of Desire.* London and New York: Routledge, 2002.

Mercer, John. "Seeing Is Believing: Constructions of Stardom and the Gay Porn Star in US Gay Video Pornography." In *Framing Celebrity: New Directions in Celebrity Culture*, edited by Su Holmes and Sean Redmond, 145–60. London and New York: Routledge, 2006.

Morris, Paul, and Susanna Paasonen. "Risk and Utopia: A Dialogue on Pornography." *GLQ: A Journal of Lesbian and Gay Studies* 20, no. 3 (June 2014): 215–39.

Mowlabocus, Sharif. *Gaydar Culture: Gay Men, Technology, and Embodiment in the Digital Age.* Farnham, UK: Ashgate Publishing, 2010.

——. "Porn 2.0? Technology, Social Practice, and the New Online Porn Industry." In *Porn.com: Making Sense of Online Pornography*, edited by Feona Attwood, 69–87. New York: Peter Lang, 2010.

Muñoz, José Esteban. *Cruising Utopia: The Then and There of Queer Futurity*. New York: New York University Press, 2009.

Paasonen, Susanna. *Carnal Resonance: Affect and Online Pornography*. Cambridge, MA: MIT Press, 2011.

Palmer, Paulina. *The Queer Uncanny: New Perspectives on the Gothic*. Cardiff, UK: University of Wales Press, 2012.

Patton, Cindy. *Inventing AIDS*. London and New York: Routledge, 1990.

——. "Safe Sex and the Pornographic Vernacular." In *How Do I Look? Queer Film and Video*, edited by Bad Object-Choices (organization), 31–51. Seattle: Bay Press, 1991.

Scott, Stuart. "The Condomlessness of Bareback Sex: Responses to the Unrepresentability of HIV in Treasure Island Media's *Plantin' Seed* and *Slammed*." *Sexualities* 18, nos. 1–2 (April 2015): 210–23.

Stabile, Mike. "End of the Porn Golden Age." *Salon*, March 2, 2012. http://www.salon.com/2012/03/03/life_after_the_golden_age_of_porn/.

Stadel, Luke. "Cable, Pornography, and the Reinvention of Television, 1982–1989." *Cinema Journal* 53, no. 3 (Spring 2014): 52–75.

Tziallas, Evangelos. "Between the Gothic and Surveillance: Gay (Male) Identity, Fiction Film, and Pornography (1970–2015)." PhD diss., Concordia University, 2015.

——. "Gamified Eroticism: Gay Male 'Social Networking' Applications and Self-Pornography." *Sexuality and Culture* 19, no. 4 (December 2015): 759–75.

——. "The New 'Porn Wars': Representing Gay Male Sexuality in the Middle East." *Psychology and Sexuality* 6, no. 1 (2015): 93–110.

Ullén, Magnus. "Pornography and Its Critical Reception: Toward a Theory of Masturbation." *Jump Cut: A Review of Contemporary Media* 51 (2009). http://www.ejumpcut.org/archive/jc51.2009/UllenPorn/text.html.

Van Doorn, Niels. "Keeping It Real: User-Generated Pornography, Gender Reification, and Visual Pleasure." *Convergence: The International Journal of Research into New Media Technologies* 16, no. 4 (November 2010): 411–30.

Williams, Linda. *Hard Core: Power, Pleasure, and the "Frenzy of the Visible"* (2nd ed.). Berkeley: University of California Press, 1999.

——. "Porn Studies: Proliferating Pornographies On/Scene: An Introduction." In *Porn Studies*, edited by Linda Williams, 1–23. Durham, NC: Duke University Press, 2004.

——. *Screening Sex*. Durham, NC: Duke University Press, 2008.

**FILMS DISCUSSED IN THIS CHAPTER**

Cronenberg, David, dir. *Videodrome*. Montreal FilmPlan International, 1983.
Clark, Larry and Ed Lachman, dirs. *Ken Park*. Paris: Marathon Media, 2002.
Gallo, Vincent, dir. *Brown Bunny*. Los Angeles: Gray Daisy Films, 2003.
Johnson, Chris Mason, dir. *Test*. San Francisco,: Serious Productions, 2013.
Mathews, Travis, dir. *I Want Your Love*. San Francisco: Naked Sword Studios, 2012.
Mitchell, John Cameron, dir. *Shortbus*. New York: THINKFilm, 2006.
Ward, Chris, and Tony DiMarco, dirs. *Focus/Refocus: When Porn Kills*. Philadelphia: Breaking Glass Pictures, 2010.
Ward, Chris, Ben Leon, and Tony DiMarco, dirs. *Focus/Refocus*. San Francisco: Raging Stallion Studios, 2009.

# CHAPTER 7

# STRANGE OPTIMISM: QUEER RAGE AS VISCERAL ETHICS

## Paul Morris and Susanna Paasonen

*There are a number of levels in effect here—*
*the two (or more) people having sex,*
*the videographer plus the men,*
*the company, a simulacrum of culture,*
*the porn industry as system of knowledge,*
*the socio-sexual culture,*
*the larger culture,*
*the epidemiological system.*

—PAUL MORRIS

This chapter is an exchange between Paul Morris, a pornographer who engages with and enjoys scholarship, and Susanna Paasonen, a feminist media studies scholar who researches and enjoys pornography. Building on our two previous co-authored texts on intensity, mediation, and the visceral appeal of porn,[1] it inquires after the ethical reverberations in the

---

1   Paul Morris and Susanna Paasonen, "Coming to Mind: Pornography and the Mediation of Intensity," in *The Oxford Handbook of Sound and Image in Digital Media*, eds. Carol Vernallis, Amy Herzog, and John Richardson (Oxford: Oxford

work of Morris and his production company, Treasure Island Media (TIM). In what follows, we examine the form and role of queer ethics in the production of subcultural pornography, building on the premise that scholarship on the topic has much to benefit from working with practitioners as co-producers of knowledge. In fact, we argue that such collaboration is pivotal in pushing debates regarding pornography, ethics, sex, and work from the level of generalized abstraction (of moral norms) toward questions of context and politics (the plane of ethics). Our exchange assumes no uniformity of opinion and produces no singular authorial voice. In order to separate the two voices within this text for clarity, that of the pornographer is presented in italics and indented from the unitalicized text, as composed by the academic. While the unitalicized text, grounded in more conventional academic delivery, forms the framework for the overall exchange, the text in indented italics takes flight in diverse directions toward considerations of queer sex, bareback porn, heteronormative culture, and the diverse politics connected to the virus.

Established in 1996 in San Francisco, TIM has identified itself primarily as a documentary project focusing on under-represented practices within the gay male community, from obsessive nipple play to unconsciousness, coprophagia, and smoking fetishism. The company's fame and notoriety, however, are owed largely to its production of extensive work that depicts oral and anal unprotected sex, often with and among HIV-positive men. TIM's barebacking titles are known for their excessive exchange of semen (e.g., *The 1,000-Load Fuck*), a spectacular eroticization of cum, and depictions of "seeding" and "breeding" the virus. Indeed, it was Morris who introduced the latter term into gay sexual parlance with the release of the 2002 film *Breeding Mike O'Neill*. TIM's productions, then, represent a stance that is diametrically opposed to the pedagogy of safe sex, as well as to the widespread use of condoms and the non-ingestion of semen in oral sex, in gay porn films since the outbreak of the HIV epidemic.[2]

University Press, 2013), 549–61; Morris and Paasonen, "Risk and Utopia: Dialogue on Pornography," *GLQ: A Journal of Lesbian and Gay Studies* 20, no. 3 (2014): 215–39.

2    Cindy Patton, "Visualizing Safe Sex: When Pedagogy and Pornography Collide," in *Inside/Out: Lesbian Theories, Gay Theories*, ed. Diane Fuss (London and New York: Routledge, 1991), 373–86.

Over the years, Morris and TIM have resisted attacks and sanctions against their work and the sexual practices depicted in them, and fought against their definition as harmful and unethical by state and private agencies. In 2014, California's Division of Occupational Safety and Health Appeals Board ruled against TIM for workplace safety violations on the grounds that there was a "substantial probability that employees would suffer serious exposure resulting in serious physical harm or death if violation occurred." According to the ruling, TIM was guilty of unethical conduct for causing its employees harm. This is predictable, given the degree to which discussions on porn work and ethics, general examinations of the ethics of pornography,[3] and guidelines on sexual ethics all revolve around—and foreground—bodily safety and the risk of harm.

Departing from binary divisions of right and wrong connected to health and harm, this chapter asks what kinds of queer ethics might be at play in the work of TIM in order to better understand its logics of operation. In other words, our exchange explores the ethical underpinnings and principles that stand within TIM's work as its unobserved, yet ever-present, skeletal support.

**UNREASONABLE ETHICS**

By "ethics," we refer—with something of an Aristotelian reverb—to context-specific principles of a good life. The notion of morals, while in practice arduous to detach from ethics, stands for the more abstract, general considerations of right and wrong. Since ethics encompasses that which is of importance to different constituent groups of society, it is of necessity a field of enmeshed and overlapping yet occasionally antithetical spheres of significance, meaning, and normativity. Ethics is concerned with the relative importance of conflicting principles and practices prior to and separate from the definition of behaviour, thought, or expression as moral, immoral, or amoral by social identities or groups. It is also fundamentally a matter of the freedom of action and its limits.

---

3   See for example Richard Vernon, "John Stuart Mill and Pornography: Beyond the Harm Principle," *Ethics* 106, no. 3 (1996): 621–32.

For his part, Morris defines his ethics as "based in the admixture of a loopy but real American optimism and a nearly insane degree of queer rage" in the context of heteronormative culture where queer identities and sexual practices have become entangled with the virus:

> What are the ethical considerations of a virus, seen from the viral point of view? What are the ethics of a pornographer who trades in virus-trafficking sex? What are the responsibilities of a pornographer who engages in the optimism of the West, of America in particular?
>
> Here's the heart of it: in a world defined and ruled by heterosexuality, the queer isn't human. The life of the queer is a composite, synthetic experience, something necessarily non-native and never belonging. All contemporary queer experience is defined in contrast to the heterosexual "real": as failure, as emulation, as irrational, as unhealthy, as lacking. The only hope for the queer to ever be more than ornamental to the hetero-imperative is the absolute reversal of the way things are. Queer sex is the primal experience from which identities develop. I suck dick, therefore I am. But to argue this requires that one be perfectly unreasonable from within the framing of life as being hetero-based.
>
> In a world that tells you that you are sick, dying, dead, how unreasonable is it to state with perfect assuredness that, far from being ancillary or mal-conceived, we are the centre of the world, our promiscuous and limitless sexual pleasure an endlessly creative and pure mine from which all else is derived and conditional.
>
> It's been my experience that pessimism and fear are tools of oppression perpetrated by power in order to maintain the status quo, particularly the distribution of wealth. This is a commonplace truth. Engaged and sustained optimism—particularly concerning the larger systems that include more life-types than the human—then becomes a real and effective blade to be used in cutting oneself away from the throttling status quo and moving willy-nilly toward a world of queer difference.
>
> In order to be optimistic—I'm not talking about happiness here—one must be unreasonable, literally.

Seen in this vein, the features of Morris's work that are con-sidered most ethically controversial or problematic in terms of workplace safety are politically and ethically the most central in their adamant, optimistic unreasonableness and refusal to adjust. This articulation of unreasonable ethics revolves around the queer politics of the virus. Obviously enough, it is in sharp conflict with the reproductive futurism tied to the institutions of heterosexuality, as well as with moral notions connected to so-called good sexuality as wholesome exchanges lacking in risk.[4] In Morris's unreasonable queer ethics, sex is front and centre; since sex not only matters but is primary, it is worth taking risks for. Although extensive editing is involved, TIM shoots sexual interactions as they unfold in sessions that are both improvised and based on the fantasies and practices of the participating men who share their life, and sex, with a virus.

*I think that if I can be said to have thoughts about ethics, these thoughts can best be either read through, or extrapolated from, the specificities of the pornography I've made. They are precise things for me. This might seem like an odd statement, since my mode of production heavily involves anti-professionalism, ineptitude, accident, the absence of overseeing directing, and so forth. But what I mean to say is that a precise prior idea or intent works against the possibility of documentary truth. So when I say that the porn is precise, the precision is in the sex. And if I have a feeling of behaving ethically or unethically, it's relative to the clarity with which the sex and the specific sexual improvisations of the men are presented.*

*Although there's an implicit narrative inherent in every porn scene, to approach shooting sex with a narrative beyond, say, "two men fuck," would reduce the session to "an idea produced" rather than "an event recorded." I don't like to compare sex to jazz, but in a very crude sense, a session is rather like asking the men if*

---

4    See also Gayle Rubin, "Thinking Sex," in *Pleasure and Danger: Exploring Female Sexuality,* ed. Carole S. Vance (London: Pandora, 1984), 267–319; Michael Warner, *The Trouble With Normal: Sex, Politics, and the Ethics of Queer Life* (Cambridge, MA: Harvard University Press, 2000).

*they'll perform a particular jazz chart for me. And in the same sense that a musician performs differently for different audiences, men who are having sex while being recorded will reveal completely different things depending on the nature of the person recording them. So rather than asking them to perform "for" me, I ask them to perform "with" me, meaning that the camera work has to be both sexual and distinct from the sex. What I like to think of as professional ineptitude—anti-technique—is a state of involvement that enables the constant interruption of my sense of purpose by the realities of the unfolding sex.*

As they energetically engage with each other's body, the men's palpable—albeit tacit—relationship with the virus is both ignored and celebrated. The festive abandon with which the men exchange and play with cum involves the pleasures and potentialities of bodies depicted through utopian vignettes of plentitude and satiation. While the virus is certainly more than gestured toward in the films' titles (for example, *Breeding Season 1* and *2*; *Plantin' Seed 1* and *2*) and in the participants' body art, which routinely involves tattoos of bio-hazard signs, its presence in the rhythms and scenes of sex is seldom explicated as such. The virus remains present as a post-human agent gifted with the semen, and an elementary component in the loops of desire and fantasy that the films compose. Setting out to capture the intensity of men having sex with men, the films balance documentary realism with the fantastic excess of bodies, lust, and cum. All this involves no small degree of reverence.

*I work with the creative medium of everyman: genitals, pleasure, the body, the alchemy of sleaze.*

*For me, the gravity of recorded sex overwhelms ethics. And when sex and porn have been impacted by a calamity such as the HIV epidemic, one has to think about the continuity of sexuality, queerness, and humanness. To extend Edelman's statement, I would say that male pornography secondarily humbles the intellect but primarily opens a space within which queer identity can recognize and remember itself. When terror runs in the blood, important things can be lost or forgotten. In order to remember the male sexual language of the body, everything that threatens the body has to be incorporated, digested, and assimilated into the sex. To say that my porn is unethical means that what men are is unethical.*

*Now, it's possible that the men, the acts, and the recording of the acts are all unethical from a modernist, bio-political vantage point. And a way to argue for these being ethical—in the sense of being socially responsible—is if we're thinking in terms of a promiscuous and interchangeable individual, a fragmented human-ish entity that fits with ease into multifarious and infinitely variable situations, something or someone that is lavishly and lovingly monstrous. It isn't that the acts and recordings are unethical, then; it's that they are working within an ethic that negates modernist identity. In this case, these acts simply go along with the process of post-human, anti-bio-political streamlining, and they insist unreasonably that the sex in this porn is of an importance equal to other "heroic" chance-taking practices.*

Writing on enchantment, political theorist Jane Bennett defines it as an experience of being "struck and shaken by the extraordinary that lives amid the familiar and the everyday." Enchantment is "a condition of exhilaration or acute sensory activity. To be simultaneously transfixed in wonder and transported by sense, to be both caught up and carried away—enchantment is marked by this odd combination of somatic effects."[5] In their combinations of the quotidian and the rapturous reverence of the male body, TIM's titles revolve around, and are driven by, such enchantment that firmly foregrounds visceral, material, and sensory intensities as ones that matter.

## THE CIRCUITS OF SEX AND MONEY

Since the 1970s, anti-porn activists have identified porn as harmful, immoral, and unethical in its production practices and cultural

---

5    Jane Bennett, *The Enchantment of Modern Life: Attachments, Crossings, and Ethics* (Princeton, NJ: Princeton University Press, 2001), 4, 5.

reverberations; these core arguments have remained similar despite the drastic transformations in the production, distribution, and consumption of pornography. Critiques of pornography are often mired in neo-Victorian images of sweatshops and slavery, of trafficking and non-agency on the part of the performers. In such scenes, the porn producer is cast in the role of exploiter, given the degree to which they build on static conceptions of what pornography is, why it is made, by whom it is made, and how it is made. As a necessary correlate to this unchanging vision of pornography, the very notion of the porn industry often remains vague and undefined as an assumedly singular point of reference.

According to some critics, freely produced and distributed (amateur) pornography is more ethical than commercial products.[6] For others, paying for porn is ethical in that it guarantees the performers and producers proper compensation for their work.[7] According to the latter argument, porn is work. According to the former argument, it is not work if performed outside the framework of commercial production and distribution. While both stances associate porn with positive and ethically "laudatory values and goals, including the freedom of expression, creativity, exploration of potential/new forms of sexuality,"[8] the former seems premised on the ethical unsustainability of commercial sex. According to this line of thinking, the relations of control and power—and the possibilities of exploitation connected to them—remain absent from pornography when money does not change hands in its production and when no financial value is extracted from it. At the same time, free labour is elementary to the operating principles of video aggregator sites on which current porn distribution is centralized. These platforms generate value from the video clips viewed, independent of how, or whether, their producers are compensated. Within this

---

6    See Susanna Paasonen, "Labors of Love: Netporn, Web 2.0, and the Meanings of Amateurism," *New Media and Society* 12, no. 8 (2010): 1297–1312.

7    See, for example, Jiz Lee, " 'Ethical Porn' Starts When We Pay for It," *Medium*, January 14, 2015, http://jizlee.com/ethical-porn-consumption-pay-for-porn-anti-piracy/; see also Heather Berg, "Labouring Porn Studies," *Porn Studies* 1, nos. 1–2 (2014): 75–9.

8    Charles Ess, *Digital Media Ethics* (Oxford: Polity Press, 2014), 174.

framework, considerations of ethics in the work of pornography are not reducible to binary divisions of paid versus unpaid. When further zooming in on the labour practices of commercial pornography, things grow equally complex.

> *There are three ways of using money in porn. One is to get people to do things that they usually wouldn't be caught dead doing. That's the idea behind two kinds of porn: "gay for pay," and what I call "prisoner of war" porn. "Gay for pay" porn is something everyone is familiar with. "Prisoner of war" porn is when pornographers pay very poor people in countries that have been destroyed by war to do things that they would rather not do, but, well, the family has to eat.*
>
> *The second way of using money in porn is to entice men into believing that they can make a living in porn by paying them a large initial fee, and getting them to sign a contract that locks them into working for only one studio. That studio then has them by the balls, as it were.*
>
> *The third way of using money in porn is to make porn that is precisely what the guys in it already do, what they long to do, what they live to do. When money is used in this way, the men are as often as not surprised that they're being paid to do what they would easily do for free. Almost universally, these men have professions outside of porn and are not depending on the income from porn for their sustenance or rent. When you use money like this in porn, it's not uncommon for men to sincerely offer to make porn with you for no money at all. This is because they're doing it for the sex, not the money. They want the sex much more than they want (or need) the money. This is how I use money in making porn. In this case, the men can't be used as interchangeable commodities. They can't be asked to do things that they would rather not do. There is no coercion, there are no contracts, there's no pretending, there are no starving families.*

TIM has, over the course of its two decades in operation, evolved into a highly recognizable company with a broad international fan base. As a "brand community," TIM is an active contributor to pornographic cultures through the titles it releases, the fan-generated animated GIFs it affords, and the broader resonances it evokes in terms of gay male sexual cultures. At the same time, Morris is careful to separate his perspective and practice from the denominator of the porn industry, possibly precisely due to the homogeneity that the term falsely implies.[9] Furthermore, while TIM is currently a commercial actor of some stature, Morris remains more attached to his early work of the late 1990s.

> *The only period of work that still really intrigues me is that which took place during the most controversial period, that during which death was as present as pleasure. These were the crudest videos I made, the ones in which I had absolutely no concern for technical expertise or "professionalism" precisely because what I was dealing with was so brimming with immediacy.*
>
> *I also felt very strongly that my refusal to learn how to do things professionally was not only emblematic of my loathing for the lies and shallow politics of the rest of gay porn at the time, but was also an acceptance on my part of an element of my own queer identity, that which argues through intentional ineptitude for the obverse of "straight." To bring this back to ethics, this was in every sense a violent argument on my part for the destruction of everything that repressed the queer world/identity.*
>
> *I won't say that this was a conscious element of the decisions—the choices—I made, but it is clear that one must either put oneself on the side of the ultimate right of individual pleasure, or on the side of the sort of world in which political torture becomes acceptable. That is, the world that I represented, especially in the earliest videos but certainly also the rest of them since then, is a world in which torture is impossible unless it is chosen as a path of realization by the individual receiving it. The locus of meaning is removed from the wider political entities, and placed squarely on the shoulders of those engaged in these specific acts.*

---

9    See also Shira Tarrant, *The Pornography Industry: What Everyone Needs to Know* (Oxford: Oxford University Press, 2016).

*I'm not being solipsistic or naive, I hope. Several queer groups (including Gay Shame SF) marched in protest of a jail-themed mega-party that was held at the production centre for Kink.com in San Francisco on June 27, 2014. The party coincided with gay pride celebrations. The queer protesters were incensed by what they perceived to be tacit support by Kink of the inequities of the US prison system, and several of them carried a banner that read, "There is no prison in a queer utopia." And I couldn't disagree more strongly. Obviously there would be prisons in a queer utopia built precisely for those who felt the deep need to be imprisoned or to imprison, to experience and undergo the state of abject powerlessness or absolute and freely eroticized power. I know many men who would choose this prison for a time. I wouldn't deny them their needs, nor would I judge their needs as an indication that correction or therapy or amelioration of any kind is called for. I would, rather, see it as evidence of self-awareness, playfulness, and growth.*

## FREEDOM, PLEASURE, AND POWER

Ethics can be considered as an issue of minor freedoms. For Foucault, "ethics is the considered form that freedom takes when it is informed by reflection."[10] In practices of everyday life, ethics, then, concerns the freedom of an individual to act in the world in relation to others, as well as the relationship one has with oneself.[11] The concern here is for an individual to construct himself or herself as a moral subject; it is a matter of moral subjectivation. A moral code, for Foucault, would be that which regulates individual and collective action as more abstract norms and principles, "a set of values and rules of action that are recommended to individuals through the intermediary of various prescriptive agencies such as the family (in one of its roles), educational institutions, churches, and so forth."[12]

---

10   Michel Foucault, *Ethics: Subjectivity and Truth* (New York: The New Press, 1997), 284.

11   Ibid., 300.

12   Michel Foucault, *The History of Sexuality, Volume 2: The Use of Pleasure*, trans. Robert Hurley (New York: Vintage, 1990), 25.

Seen in this vein, morals involve general prescriptions of a good life, whereas ethics is primarily a relationship that an individual has with himself. Morality, then, comprises both codes of behaviour and forms of subjectivation.

Following Foucault, ethical action does not simply involve following given rules of conduct. Rather, it necessitates both reflexivity and forms of self-discipline and is, as such, an issue of freedom. Defiant in terms of generalized prescriptions for action, Morris points out that "resisting an almost universal ethic may be wise if that by which you're motivated is the remote possibility of an existence lived according to one's nature." This call for living according to one's nature privileges the visceral intensities of sexuality—the enchanting experiences of "swervy vitality"[13] that add to and make up the very sense of aliveness. This, again, concerns both queer ethics and queer politics.

> *I think when you're dealing with work such as porn, it's inevitable and appropriate that ethics be approached from, on the one hand, a somewhat phenomenological sense, and on the other hand, from a vantage point that admits the complex "nested" nature of the work. If you accept the story in which your work participates, any of these various categories [the list from the beginning of this chapter], then tentative and variously appropriate ethical and unethical positions will be made obvious.*
>
> *In Sex, or the Unbearable,[14] Berlant and Edelman speak of the roles, possibilities, and the strictures of "story" itself. They disagree on "story"—Edelman taking a stance derived from his allegiance to Lacanian psychoanalysis, Berlant finding favour in the middle stage of each story (that is, when the inevitable drive of the story itself is at its weakest and the affective attachments of the various constituent parts are most tangled, chaotic, and "free").*
>
> *But story, like ethics, is written into the native programming of that which is human—we perceive story in a sentence, an*

---

13  Bennett, *The Enchantment of Modern Life*, 105.

14  Lauren Berlant and Lee Edelman, *Sex, or the Unbearable* (Durham, NC: Duke University Press, 2014).

*intimation, a glance, a sigh, a cloud, a word, a letter, and so on, in all directions infinitely extended in all stages of scale.*

*Each political, social, or historical epoch is sustained and organized precisely by these stories: stories of value, the story that is money, stories of emotion, denigration, ambition, relative human intelligence and worth, and so on. In each system, there are those identities that are expected and required to assume roles for which they are neither suited nor that will provide them with a way of existing as conscious humans that is satisfactory according to their needs. That is, there is societal dissonance, inequity, suffering. The dominant system will, in times of change, allow exaggerated and harmless roles for the oppressed in order both to show them how harmless and ineffective they are . . . and, more to the point, to act as inoculations for the system against the possibility that the native and subverted stories of those identity groups might organize, and recognize themselves for who they are, and create either a relative destabilization or an existential threat to the system.*

*Now, in this situation, those in the less-powerful role have a few precarious options. One, of course, is to accede to the dictates of the dominant order, and "fit in" as best one can. Buy a home (or rent from a bank, until one is dead). Get married, and define yourself via the "normal" stories of life deferred through service to that which Edelman has been most accurate and most eloquent about: the infinite linear prison of heteronormative futurity.[15] However, in such a narrative, one becomes exceptionally vulnerable to the ever-changing whims of the dominants. One really cannot say with any firm certitude that in five years faggots will be free to express publicly (in whatever modality "public" might manifest at that time) their desires, their nature, their actual stories. In particular, given the ever-increasing reach of web-driven power, the freedom of the queer will be a fragile thing indeed.*

*So I'm thinking now, in this time of radical control and ever-increasing surveillance, of how I would actually approach*

---

15  Lee Edelman, *No Future: Queer Theory and the Death Drive* (Durham, NC: Duke University Press, 2004).

*the question of ethics from my own very queer nature. It's an old notion that language is a virus, but one has to be careful. As the words are written you feel the various levels of control and story. So navigating the sea of social existence using consensus-reality sentences while trying to be precisely true to the queer nature is hard.*

Understood as a form of queer resistance that both captures the intensities of men having sex with men and further fuels them in the scenarios they generate, TIM's films involve a utopian impulse. The queer ethics that can be seen as emerging from them need to be decoupled from any normative, generalized notions of what constitutes a so-called good life. The glimpses of the good life that the films offer involve the enchantment and plentitude of bodily pleasures, intensities, and proximities within queer communities of men. Their spaces of sex are connected to, yet momentarily cut loose from, broader spatial and cultural contexts as cocoons of a kind for celebrating the complex liveliness of bodies in ways that do not foreclose awareness of their finitude. Their emergent, queer figure of the good life is therefore uncoupled from linear narratives of intimate relationships, partnerships, or family formations, and, indeed, from notions of futurity external to the immediacy of the sexual exchanges themselves.

*Queer agency is both under the thumb of and in excess of straight agency. The conditional nature of queer agency in the straight world requires the translation into the imaginary: play, fantasy, make-believe. Desire is a sign that moves one toward being, but desire is rendered conditional by being violently framed by the terroristic rigours of baby-making, child-rearing. The common-place message produced by straights and their gay quislings is that no pleasure and no love compares to that of parent for genetic offspring. It's held as the ontological grail.*

*What this means, I think, is that we don't have a clue as to what queer agency is. Like a boat tacking against a powerful headwind, the queer moves toward its own authenticity necessarily in an endless series of calculated errors, of conditional approximations. I can't emphasize this strongly enough: we live in a world that is not ours, not of, by, or for us. Because we aren't a racial or genetically obvious people, we create our invisible skin through, for want of a better word, our style.*

Foucault's late work, in *History of Sexuality* and elsewhere, has been critiqued for its individualistic embrace of freedom and technologies of the self. Jan Rehmann, for example, argues that he failed "to grasp the potentials of collective agency and self-determination. It is at this point that Foucault's 'care of the self' merges with the ideological conjuncture of neoliberalism."[16] Seeing the matter differently, Bennett points out that, for Foucault, freedom is not defined "in opposition to a system of external constraints; freedom is rather a reflective heteronomy" as possibilities of moving beyond the limits that have been imposed.[17] Bennett notes that "it is the recognition of one's implication in a web of social and physical relations within which reside vital opportunities for self-direction."[18] Exhilarating moments of experiencing freedom do not, in this framework, transcend power, but involve "tentative explorations of the outer edges of the current regime of subjectivity."[19]

Considered in this vein, the queer ethic of TIM firmly emerges in relation to forms of bio-power regulating sexuality as non-risky, wholesome, and intertwined with the circuits of procreation while aiming to convey different planes of bodily intensity. On the level of prescribed morality, the imperative of safety becomes framed as the sexually ethical. Morris, again, associates the conflation of safety and sex with late-capitalist commodity formation connected to HIV:

*It's not an overstatement to say that, in the burgeoning mechanics of pharma, disease is very much a function of capital. Not only in the sense that late capitalism requires its inhabitants to be as*

---

16    Jan Rehmann, "The Unfulfilled Promise of the Late Foucault and Foucauldian 'Governmentality Studies,' " in *Foucault and Neoliberalism*, eds. Daniel Zamora and Michael C. Behrent (Oxford: Polity Press, 2016), 136.

17    Bennett, *The Enchantment of Modern Life*, 146.

18    Ibid.

19    Ibid.

*"safe" and as "productive" as possible for the longest possible life duration, but also in the sense that disease and the apparatus of medicine is owned and developed as any other capitalist industry is owned and developed.*

*Perhaps more than any other company, Gilead Sciences (a California Bay Area biopharmaceutical corporation) has spearheaded successful and controversial anti-HIV medical strategies, particularly with their development, promotion, and sole ownership of Truvada. At the same time, their corporate behaviour and immense profits have been directed by board members (and principal shareholders) such as Donald Rumsfeld and George Shultz, arch-conservative Republicans whose careers in politics and commerce are ethically questionable. To the extent that HIV can be considered a commercial opportunity, Gilead Sciences and its shareholders reap immense profit from it.*

*How, then, does one identify being ethical with being sexually "safe" by using their HIV infection prevention and from HIV infection?*

Subscribing to safety may then come at the cost of subscribing to a political economy that works against one's own best interests. TIM is fundamentally embedded in late-capitalist commodity formation as a commercial production studio trading in pornography, but without being reducible to its operations. This is not merely a matter of privileging the intensities of sex among men, but one involving bareback culture as a sexual public with its specific political concerns that rub against normative notions of intimacy, individual productivity, and social reproduction alike. The work of pornography centred on physical pleasure is, in this instance, also an issue of queer ethics as the discovery of minoritarian forms of being and acting in the world. Sex can be understood as an autotelic practice where the pleasure of the activity is an end in and of itself: there is no other purpose, instrumentality, or function beyond that.[20] In this sense, sex is productive of pleasure as bodily intensity but

---

20   Elizabeth Grosz, "Animal Sex," in *Sexy Bodies: The Strange Carnalities of Feminism*, eds. Elizabeth Grosz and Elspeth Probyn (London and New York: Routledge,

hardly productive in the sense of fitting in with the productivity mandates connected to individuality within consumer capitalism.

*From the standpoint of the straight organization—of thought, of people, of anything—queer sex is the most ornamental and least utilitarian of all forms of expression. And that's purely because it's seen from the inevitable standpoint of procreation. But from the queer point of view—that is, from the point of view of a way of knowing that takes abstraction and renders it physical—our sex is the highest form of creation and communication. This is the root of the difference between male/female porn and male porn. The former is using the extravagance of the genre to escape the limits of bourgeois physical identity (that is, to erase the function of procreation entirely), whereas the latter is using every aspect of the genre to prove the eloquence and actuality of the individual male body. There's the core of it.*

## ANXIOUS, VISCERAL ETHICS

Pornography both taps into the dominant regimes of sexuality, gender, and economy, and disturbs them with the primacy it places on lust and orgasmic pleasure as aims and purposes in and of themselves. As we have suggested in a previous dialogue, TIM both exists in the confines of the status quo and provides means for escaping it by showing what a utopia feels like.[21] Morris's films can be seen as coining spaces of resistance by turning "inward" from the social world of public protest, and moving toward visceral sexual encounters that nevertheless, in their mediated circulation and cultural presence, are "public in the sense of accessible."[22] These unreasonable heterotopias (or sexual publics), dwelling in fleshy intensities, rub up against the primacy placed on the rational, socially and economically productive, subjectivity.

---

1995); Susanna Paasonen, *Many Splendored Things: Thinking Sex and Play* (London: Goldsmiths Press, 2018).

21 See Morris and Paasonen, "Risk and Utopia."
22 Lauren Berlant and Michael Warner, "Sex in Public," in *Intimacy*, ed. Lauren Berlant (Chicago: University of Chicago Press, 2000), 326.

In her work on affect and ethics, Bennett foregrounds enchantment as sensations of captivation involving "experimentally cultivated responsiveness to others."[23] Residing between "a striking reality and the stricken body," sensibility is "a refinement or new assemblage of sensible primordia" that is "culturally encoded and temperamentally delimited" yet still, to a degree, educable. Foregrounding the sensory and the affective in conceptualizations of the good life—and hence helping to outline an affective ethics of sex—Bennett's ethics of aliveness thinks beyond the divides of the individual and the social, the immediate and the mediated, and the affective and the reflexive in ways that resonate with TIM's utopian tendencies in its emphasis on corporeal enchantment. Bennett's work is also helpful in broadening Foucault's discussion of ethics and care of the self from an individual level to a more collective, queer project. Sketched out in this vein, the queer ethic emerging from the work of TIM is one adamantly emphasizing visceral bodily intensities and their connections with identities, communities, and political attachments. Here, care, any more than ethics, is not a matter of safety but one of identity tied in with subcultural sexual practice and community formation. The issue of health again takes post-human forms in the entanglements of the human and the viral that TIM's films so minutely display and enthusiastically embrace.

> Years ago, I wrote that the dilemma of being queer in this historical period was in being an identity that replicated through the same processes that enabled this virus to flourish. I no longer think this, particularly in that the relationships between that which is human and that which is viral are more clearly understood today as being necessarily tangled, complex, and involving a "health" that takes the more-than-human into account.
>
> This is to say that, above all, ethics must be anxious. That is, it must be an endeavour that looks into the dark depths of nature, and with necessary anxiety and terror considers the difference between the human and the queer. And opens itself up to what,

---

*from the simplistic standpoint of an obsolete bourgeois identity, will seem irrational, unreasonable, monstrous, unspeakable.*

**REFERENCES**

Bennett, Jane. *The Enchantment of Modern Life: Attachments, Crossings, and Ethics.* Princeton, NJ: Princeton University Press, 2001.

Berg, Heather. "Labouring Porn Studies." *Porn Studies* 1, nos. 1–2 (March 2014): 75–79.

Berlant, Lauren, and Lee Edelman. *Sex, or the Unbearable.* Durham, NC: Duke University Press, 2014.

Berlant, Lauren, and Michael Warner. "Sex in Public." In *Intimacy*, edited by Lauren Berlant, 311–30. Chicago: University of Chicago Press, 2000.

Edelman, Lee. *No Future: Queer Theory and the Death Drive.* Durham, NC: Duke University Press, 2004.

Ess, Charles. *Digital Media Ethics.* Oxford: Polity Press, 2014.

Foucault, Michel. *Ethics: Subjectivity and Truth.* New York: New Press, 1997.

——. *The History of Sexuality, Volume 2: The Use of Pleasure.* Translated by Robert Hurley. New York: Random House, 1990.

Grosz, Elizabeth. "Animal Sex." In *Sexy Bodies: The Strange Carnalities of Feminism*, edited by Elizabeth Grosz and Elspeth Probyn, 278–99. London and New York: Routledge, 1995.

Lee, Jiz. " 'Ethical Porn' Starts When We Pay for It." *Medium*, January 14, 2015. http://jizlee.com/ethical-porn-consumption-pay-for-porn-anti-piracy/.

Morris, Paul, and Susanna Paasonen. "Coming to Mind: Pornography and the Mediation of Intensity." In *The Oxford Handbook of Sound and Image in Digital Media*, edited by Carol Vernallis, Amy Herzog, and John Richardson, 549–61. Oxford: Oxford University Press, 2013.

——. "Risk and Utopia: A Dialogue on Pornography." *GLQ: A Journal of Lesbian and Gay Studies* 20, no. 3 (June 2014): 215–39.

Paasonen, Susanna. "Labors of Love: Netporn, Web 2.0, and the Meanings of Amateurism." *New Media and Society* 12, no. 8 (June 2010): 1297–1312.

——. *Many Splendored Things: Thinking Sex and Play.* London: Goldsmiths Press, 2018.

Patton, Cindy. "Visualizing Safe Sex: When Pedagogy and Pornography Collide." In *Inside/Out: Lesbian Theories, Gay Theories*, edited by Diane Fuss, 373–86. London and New York: Routledge, 1991.

Rehmann, Jan. "The Unfulfilled Promise of the Late Foucault and Foucauldian 'Governmentality Studies.' " In *Foucault and Neoliberalism*, edited by Daniel Zamora and Michael C. Behrent, 134–58. Oxford: Polity Press, 2016.

Rubin, Gayle. "Thinking Sex." In *Pleasure and Danger: Exploring Female Sexuality*, edited by Carole S. Vance, 267–319. London: Pandora Press, 1984.

Tarrant, Shira. *The Pornography Industry: What Everyone Needs to Know*. Oxford: Oxford University Press, 2016.

Vernon, Richard. "John Stuart Mill and Pornography: Beyond the Harm Principle." *Ethics* 106, no. 3 (April 1996): 621–32.

Warner, Michael. *The Trouble with Normal: Sex, Politics, and the Ethics of Queer Life*. Cambridge, MA: Harvard University Press, 2000.

# CHAPTER 8

# "BODIES THAT SPLUTTER": THEORIZING *JOUISSANCE* IN BAREBACK AND CHEMSEX PORN[1]

## Gareth Longstaff

### INTRODUCTION

The pornographic work of UK-based director Liam Cole, and increasingly popular and visible websites such as RawFuckClub.com, belong to a specific genre of cis-gendered gay male porn predominantly identified as bareback. Recent work examining this genre of pornography emphasizes the increasing complexity and paradox involved in both its production as pornography and its critical discussion within the emergent and interdisciplinary arena of porn studies.[2] However, the potentials of aligning it to psychoanalytic theory have yet to be fully developed. This chapter aims to explore these potentials and, in so doing, explore how problems of phallocentric *jouissance* for gay male bodies that attempt to lay claim to the

---

1   This essay first appeared in *Porn Studies* 6, no. 1 (2019). Reprinted here with permission from the publisher.

2   See Chris Ashford, "Bareback Sex, Queer Legal Theory, and Evolving Socio-Legal Contexts," *Sexualities* 18, nos. 1–2 (2015): 195–209; Stuart Scott, "The Condomlessness of Bareback Sex: Responses to the Unrepresentability of HIV in Treasure Island Media's *Plantin' Seed* and *Slammed*," *Sexualities* 18, nos. 1–2 (2015): 210–23; and John Mercer, *Gay Pornography: Representations of Sexuality and Masculinity* (London: I.B. Tauris, 2017).

phallus on Lacanian terms may energize other perspectives on *jouissance* and pornography.

In the psychoanalytic context, *jouissance* is often aligned with Jacques Lacan's register of the Real and understood as a phallic, pre-symbolic, orgasmic, and ejaculatory form of pleasure, yet it can also find a symbolic genus in non-phallic expression, most famously explored in Lacan's theory of feminine *jouissance* in *Seminar XX Encore: On Feminine Sexuality, The Limits of Love and Knowledge*.[3] While many aspects of Lacanian *jouissance* may be heavily reliant on a cis-normative and gender-binary understanding of pleasure/desire mapped onto the phallus, Lacan also offers up a form of "*jouissance* [that is] wrapped in its own contiguity"[4] to "offer momentary respite from the severity of signifying law"[5] while concurrently remaining an effect of the signifier. The possibility of aligning *jouissance* with the visual politics of bareback and chemsex porn drives it toward an ideological, political, and subjective limit, and, in this way, it is stripped—just like the pornographic representations it haunts—of its enigmatic flexibility and resilience to interpretation and analysis. This wrench between *jouissance* and language,[6] between identity and desire,[7] and between a "drift from 'pleasure' to 'bliss' [that] indicates queer theoretical values and investments"[8] also underpins its power as "provocatively sexy, intimate, scandalous and bodily."[9] Alongside the work of Lacan, other key theoretical interventions and accounts of *jouissance*, such as Roland Barthes's *The Pleasure of the*

---

3  Jacques Lacan, *On Feminine Sexuality, The Limits of Love and Knowledge, 1972–73* (New York: W.W. Norton, 1999).

4  Malcolm Bowie, *Lacan* (London: Fontana Press, 1991), 149.

5  Ibid., 202.

6  Bruce Fink, *The Lacanian Subject: Between Language and Jouissance* (Princeton, NJ: Princeton University Press, 1995).

7  Tim Dean, *Beyond Sexuality* (Chicago: University of Chicago Press, 2000); and Tim Dean, *Unlimited Intimacy: Reflections on the Subculture of Barebacking* (Chicago: University of Chicago Press, 2009).

8  Kathryn Bond Stockton, "*Jouissance*, the Gash of Bliss," in *Clinical Encounters in Sexuality: Psychoanalytic Practice and Queer Theory*, eds. Noreen Giffney and Eve Watson (New York: Punctum Books, 2017), 104.

9  Ibid., 102.

*Text* (1975), position *jouissance* liminally between forms of language and desire that simultaneously "wound or seduce me."[10]

Furthermore, much of the power that *jouissance* yields is located through this seductive wounding. It has ideological, political, and subjective interpretations and, in this way, remains difficult and unruly. Just as it is often discussed through the signification of the phallus and phallic *jouissance*, it is also here that it begins to resist definition or representation, and the subsequent ways in which it is theorized call into question the critical nature of what *jouissance* may be in relation to desire. It is worth noting here that the use of "phallic" has often been misconstrued as something that pertains to distinctly masculine, patriarchal, and dominant tropes. In fact, the critical point that Lacan was striving to emphasize was that the phallic and the phallus are fragile and fallible. As Bruce Fink observes, "one cannot take the failure out of the phallus,"[11] so that when this notion is plugged into how the signifier and *jouissance* are both theorized and articulated in terms of cis gay male bareback and chemsex porn, something like the provisional and intersectional nature of a phallic "cis gay male bareback and chemsex" ontology is exposed. To say that *jouissance* is only phallic is to foreclose and confine its locality only to a phallic imaginary. Lacan suggests that the *objet a*—or that signifier that causes *jouissance*, rather than that which attempts to sustain it—has its most obvious or explicit grounding in a materiality connected to *jouissance*'s cause: in other words, a pleasure that reaches a particular point, but a point that ultimately brings *jouissance* to an end. In this way, "the signifier is what brings *jouissance* to a halt."[12] Here, and in an attempt to express it *as* a pornographic *jouissance*, we find an erratic tension at work in this structure, one that locates *jouissance* as both a cause or spur to desire and a stop or terminator of that desire.

---

10  Roland Barthes, *The Pleasure of the Text*, trans. Richard Miller (New York: Hill and Wang, 1975), 38.

11  Bruce Fink, "Knowledge and *Jouissance*," in *Reading Seminar XX: Lacan's Major Work on Love, Knowledge, and Feminine Sexuality*, eds. Suzanne Barnard and Bruce Fink (Albany: SUNY Press, 2002), 39.

12  Lacan, *On Feminine Sexuality*, 24.

In light of these tensions, there may be challenges within bare-back porn that arise due to its distinctly phallic formation of *jouissance*. Tim Dean's *Unlimited Intimacy: Reflections on the Subculture of Barebacking* is regarded as perhaps the seminal text on barebacking practices, and its critical steer is toward axioms of queer theory and ethnography. Articles that employ psychoanalytic frameworks, such as Christien Garcia's "Limited Intimacy: Barebacking and the imaginary," explore "the subjective tensions between experience and representation,"[13] but do not move beyond the Lacanian frameworks of Imaginary narcissism and fantasy. Perhaps more provocatively, Leo Bersani and Adam Phillips suggest that barebacking is analo-gous to psychoanalytic notions of "sexual desire as indifferent to personal identity, antagonistic to ego requirements and regulations . . . and inferences about the unconscious,"[14] which in turn begin to energize considerations of barebacking and pornography, and the potentials of linking them to *jouissance*. *Jouissance* as something more specifically allied to barebacking and chemsex is something that they (vis-à-vis Dean) assimilate and recognize. Here, the malevolent dismissal of barebacking as "mindless fucking" bound to the ethi-cal, legal, and medical discourses (and inherent dangers and risks) of HIV and AIDS is also "deeply invested with meaning . . . [that] signals profound changes in the social organization of kinship and relationality," and how desire might be invoked and expressed.[15]

Furthermore, in recent work such as *Gay Pornography: Representa-tions of Sexuality and Masculinity*, John Mercer places emphasis on the representational and visual politics of bareback and chemsex porn. Here, tensions between an aesthetics of realism, authenticity, and documentary "truth" are traversed by "the extraordinary, the extreme and the excessive aspects of sexual play."[16] Like *jouissance*, there is an ethical implication to the drug- and cum-fuelled orgies where endless pleasures seem to take place; and, in this way, barebacking differs

---

13    Christien Garcia, "Limited Intimacy: Barebacking and the Imaginary," *Textual Practice* 27, no. 6 (2013): 1031.

14    Leo Bersani and Adam Phillips, *Intimacies* (Chicago: University of Chicago Press, 2008), 43.

15    Ibid., 46.

16    Mercer, *Gay Pornography*, 141.

from earlier iterations of practices of sex between gay men without the use of condoms. From the mid- to late nineties, the shift away from practices of "unprotected anal sex"[17] between cis gay men toward practices of "condomless" sex[18] developed to construct bareback sex. This is sex that relies upon the transmission and abjectly pleasurable ejaculation and/or "breeding" of semen (also variously referred to as "cum," "seed," "load," "dump," and "juice") to fortify and enhance a "heightened erotic charge, cultural cachet and recklessness," also problematically underpinned by the practices of "men transmitting HIV at its heart."[19] As a way to buttress these key epistemological and ontological features of barebacking and chemsex, it is clear that both inside and outside of this genre of gay pornography this " 'transmission' of seminal fluid from one partner to another not only deposits genetic material, but serves to breach the membrane of hygiene and 'good gay' sex that the homonormative and contemporary sex education seeks to prescribe."[20] Here, porn inflected by barebacking and chemsex also fosters a mediated "site where the taxonomy of objective/subjective representation collapses in on itself,"[21] and it goes some way toward capturing the "visual conflation of reality and fantasy"[22] in a range of ideological, political, and aesthetic ways.

Greteman also argues that the barebacker (in porn) exists within "a contested 'empirical reality' "[23] that forces cis gay men—and, perhaps more pertinently, queer theory and the range of non-cisgenders and sexualities it overarches—to reposition the tensions between sexual regulation, assimilation, and normality. This forges an ambiguous kind of crossing point or schism in which the tripartite of

---

17    Eric Rofes, *Dry Bones Breathe: Gay Men Creating Post-AIDS Identities and Cultures* (Binghamton, NY: Haworth Press, 1998), 196.

18    Scott, "The Condomlessness of Bareback Sex."

19    Ashford, "Bareback Sex," 195.

20    Ibid., 196.

21    Garcia, "Limited Intimacy," 1038.

22    Michael McNamara, "Cumming to Terms: Bareback Pornography, Homonormativity, and Queer Survival in the Time of HIV/AIDS," in *The Moral Panics of Sexuality*, eds. Breanne Fahs, Mary L. Dudy, and Sarah Stage (London: Palgrave Macmillan, 2013), 233.

23    Adam J. Greteman, "Fashioning a Bareback Pedagogy: Towards a Theory of Risky (Sex) Education," *Sex Education* 13, suppl. 1 (2013): s22.

barebacking-chemsex-HIV/AIDS might offer "a particular promise of a queer lifestyle"[24] in response to "the pale of bourgeois respectability"[25] that phallocentric gay masculinity, same-sex marriage, and the commodification of gay culture have led us to. In other words, there may also be scope to suggest that by reorganizing and/or renegotiating the phallic, moral, ethical, and political implications of barebacking-chemsex-HIV/AIDS, an alternative and transgressive configuration of kinship, bonding, and affirmation may be possible. In sync with *jouissance*, barebacking is difficult to define. In his introduction to a special issue of the journal *Sexualities*, "Bareback Sex and Queer Theory across Three National Contexts," Oliver Davis positioned barebacking "in its most minimal acceptance" as "anal sex between men without using condoms and in cognizance of HIV/AIDS."[26] More specifically, in this chapter, this cognizance situates this shifting epistemology of barebacking to chemsex and cis gay masculine pornographic representation.[27] By also aligning this to the psychoanalytic concept of *jouissance*, it aims to identify some of the tensions aligned with our knowledge of bareback sex and pornography in both theoretical and ideological frames. To do this in relation to *jouissance* requires that the affective and representational spaces of the body in porn are addressed. In the next section, this is positioned through a consideration of the discursive limits of bodies and sex via bodies that have performatively "mattered" and unconsciously "muttered," so they might be reconceptualized so that they also "splutter."

## BODIES THAT MATTER, BODIES THAT MUTTER, BODIES THAT SPLUTTER

Tim Dean states that, in her "rhetoricalist" account of psychoanalysis, Judith Butler fails to see how *jouissance* and the subject are always

---

24  Ibid., 25.
25  Dean, *Unlimited Intimacy*, 84–85.
26  Oliver Davis, "A Special Issue of *Sexualities*: Bareback Sex and Queer Theory across Three National Contexts (France, UK, USA)," *Sexualities* 18, nos. 1–2 (2015): 120.
27  Rigmor C. Berg, "Barebacking: A Review of the Literature," *Archives of Sexual Behavior* 38, no. 5 (2009): 754–64.

underpinned by a "desire [that] is predicated on the incommensurability of [that] body and subject."[28] In this way, Dean suggests that Butler misconstrues the unconscious ego as a "bodily ego" aligned with conscious, anatomical, and biological sexual difference, and, as a result, fails to develop how egos "occlude—rather than manifest—desire."[29] Using this contention, he renovates Butler's concepts allied to bodies that performatively "matter" into bodies that now unconsciously "mutter."[30] Dean's muttering body is one demarcated by a limitless *jouissance* because it cannot be rationalized or demarcated through an ego or a body that "matters." Also central to Dean's critique of Butler is the restrictive ways in which we, as desiring subjects, misapprehend and, in many ways, misrepresent desire in terms of an imaginary, identifiable, personalized, and bodily "other," as opposed to one riven through Lacan's conceptual registers of the symbolic Other and the Real.

Here, the body is one that is mindful of its "mattering" and materiality but unaware of the "muttering" possibility of desire. Or, in other words, the mattering body is one that accounts for "subjects of the signifier and not subjects of desire."[31] From the confines of the imaginary signifier, the mattering body fails to recognize desire, and more so *jouissance*, beyond the constraints of the ego and the materiality of that ego. For instance, the imaginary cis gay male body that is represented, read, looked at, and thus embodied through bareback and chemsex porn can only be re-represented, reread, and reinterpreted through its own disembodiment that mutters as a form of diffuse and disruptive *jouissance*. This muttering body also serves to emphasize the failures and limits of a cis gay male ego that "obscures the subject of desire," to formulate that, "while the ego matters, the body mutters."[32] While Dean conveys this in terms of an imaginary ego that matters and a Real body that mutters, it is also within this formulation that the notion of a symbolic body that splutters is, on the one hand, neglected and, on the other,

---

28    Dean, *Beyond Sexuality*, 200.
29    Ibid.
30    Ibid., 202–05.
31    Ibid., 187.
32    Ibid., 202.

beckoned in. If this is the case, the alignment of "mattering" and "muttering" could be realigned to suggest that when the cis gay male body operates through *jouissance*, and is excessively signified in pornography, it symbolically splutters. This spluttering relies upon the symbolic Other and a cultural signifier (the body, an object, an image, a series of images), but also follows Dean's claim that "the difference between muttering and speaking [mattering] concerns the distinction involved in the notion of desire as something in language but not itself linguistic."[33] Spluttering occurs in this gap between mattering and muttering. Here, bodies must splutter through the force and peril of the symbolic Other before they can capture and relinquish the notions of "mattering" or "muttering" through *jouissance*.

Building on both Butler and Dean, this new construction of spluttering, which in this instance is aligned to cis gay masculinity in porn, forms a "contingent foundation"[34] of how to read *jouissance*, in that it locates this gay male spluttering body and its precarious phallic *jouissance* between bodies that matter and mutter. While muttering is "struggling to be heard,"[35] the "spluttering" bodies in bareback/chemsex porn are not necessarily struggling. They are repetitively activating desire *through* the process of spluttering—here, the spluttering body produces a symbolic form of anxious phallic *jouissance* that will only splutter because it is torn between a body that matters and a body that mutters. In this case, the gay male pornographic subject of the symbolic is spluttered, a subject who is both alert to and naive about the constraints and the limits of imaginary and Real modes of *jouissance*. This body that splutters is located between the mattering and muttering self, and the spluttering that is activated in this space is done so intensely, indeterminately, and repetitively, like the process of bareback penetration and ejaculation it awkwardly underpins. In this setting, spluttering is continuously realized retroactively through a gap, an excess, or a slippage between mattering and muttering. This spluttering

---

33   Ibid., 203.
34   Ibid., 205.
35   Ibid., 203.

involves processes of bodily and egotistical expulsion that falter, stumble, and hesitate to express the nature of phallic *jouissance*, and simultaneously undermine and distress the pornographic signifier. In any pornographic image, subjects can only express themselves through a series of representational constructions that rely upon impersonal and metonymic contiguity; and, in so doing, they begin their own practices of spluttering. Through this process, the ego and the associations that it has with an imaginary Other fail to articulate desire so that the potentiality of how *jouissance* can be realized is relocated to the symbolic and the Real.

### JOUISSANCE, BAREBACKING, AND CHEMSEX

It is clear that *jouissance* is a psychoanalytic concept that deliberately resists and subverts; it does not clearly translate from French into an English definition or word, and, as a result, it is balanced on the inscrutable threshold of its own perplexing signification and meaning. Yet Jacques Lacan first elaborates on the concept of particularly phallic *jouissance* in "The Subversion of the Subject and the Dialectic of Desire in the Freudian Unconscious" by stating that "the erectile organ comes to symbolize the place of *jouissance*, not in itself or even in the form of an image, but as a part lacking in the desired image."[36] This lack riven into the phallus is relevant to *jouissance* and how it is (and ultimately *is not*) expressed and represented in bareback and chemsex porn that relies upon both phallic and anal desire to express this lack *as jouissance*. In its resistance to definition or representation, the critical nature of what *jouissance* may be in relation to the disruptive tensions between pleasure and lack also forms a conundrum between the politics of bareback and chemsex representations within cis gay male porn and the practise of each outside and beyond porn. Potentially in all pornographic representation, *jouissance* is circumscribed as a form of visual and textual desire that shifts and sways between pleasures, excesses,

---

36    Jacques Lacan, "The Subversion of the Subject and the Dialectic of Desire in the Freudian Unconscious," in *Écrits: A Selection* (London and New York: Routledge, 2003), 353.

and, ultimately, barriers to itself. Here, the attempts that pornography makes at citing and fulfilling *jouissance* always destabilize that *jouissance*; more so in sexual practices allied to barebacking and/or chemsex, this works in a double bind or even deadlock. On the one hand, it invigorates how "sex can function as an arena in which the most basic of barriers—including those of disgust and shame—may be negotiated or overcome."[37] Yet it also remains vulnerable to the potentially reductive and "pernicious ideology of safety" and stigma allied to key discourses of disease, risk, and shame around HIV and AIDS.[38]

Here, the UK director Liam Cole's attempts to authenticate and visualize *jouissance* as it might be understood through the combination of barebacking and chemsex demand some attention. His work with Paul Morris's Treasure Island Media (TIM) has become synonymous with pornography that is inscribed with the spontaneity, rawness, and urgency of pure documentary film, yet it is also clear that this technique is still structurally and ideologically contained as a pornographic mode of production. Rather than an authentic way to represent the complex movements and intersections between the bodily and subjective states that barebacking and chemsex catalyze and inhabit, Cole aligns them to a performatively inscribed discourse of hyper-masculine barebacking and chemsex that controls what these practices might be or could be as *jouissance*. In porn, this discursive naming and citing of signifiers is somehow inevitable in that the imaginary and the symbolic orders "need to be named via the Other, or otherwise no subjectivity is possible,"[39] but in this way—and through the pornographic reproduction of barebacking and chemsex—we find that "the attempts to define something undefinable show us how radically we are cut off from it."[40] For instance, as Cole exploits "the 'real' settings of the apartment/sex club/hotel chain," he also forces them to "operate as liminal

---

37 Dean, *Unlimited Intimacy*, 137.
38 Ibid., 211.
39 Abe Geldhof and Paul Verhaeghe, "Queer as a New Shelter from Castration," in *Clinical Encounters in Sexuality: Psychoanalytic Practice and Queer Theory*, eds. Noreen Giffney and Eve Watson (New York: Punctum Books, 2017), 212–13.
40 Ibid., 215.

spaces due to their banality and anonymity,"[41] thereby miscarrying the "real" veracity of what barebacking and chemsex might be. In this way, and when the mutability of *jouissance* (phallic or not) is attached to the pornographic signifier, it unfetters the consumer and viewer of porn from the stimulating risks, traumas, and transgressions that barebacking and chemsex actually contain. Porn sanitizes and regulates these practices so that Cole's strategically amateurish and documentary aesthetic functions as an attempt to connect *jouissance* to a symbolic order that cannot contain it.

Still, in Cole's work this paradox is visualized to such an extent that the excessive practices of drug taking and unprotected sex between cis gay men sublimate and reposition the trauma of HIV/AIDS and/or crystal meth addiction into affirming and transformative practices. Here, pornographic subjects are neither on the side of objectification nor on the side of subjectification; rather, they and the practices aligned with their (dis)embodied states of desire "splutter *jouissance*" so that the subject/object bifurcation unravels toward, but never attains, *jouissance*. Here, the ejaculatory climax (and purpose) of cumming in the anus, which is enmeshed in breeding, seeding, spreading, and gifting, relies on an "erotic pleasure [that] can be gained by means of retention and release"[42] clustered around the risky potentials of sharing fluids, drugs, and, ultimately, HIV, so that within "a simultaneously lateral and vertical kin relation"[43] the possibilities of subverting and relocating discourses of phallocentrism, hetero- and homonormative conception, and marriage in a queer frame are also articulated.

The attempt to splutter and embark on a re-evaluation of kinship in which cis gay men volitionally and deliberately transmit and infect other men with HIV moves these practices toward a queer mode of desire, explored by Dean in the following ways:

[The] man whom one infects with HIV becomes his sibling in the "bug brotherhood" at the same time that one be-

---

41    Mercer, *Gay Pornography*, 141.
42    Jean Arundale, *Identity, Narcissism, and the Other: Object Relations and Their Obstacles* (London: Karnac Books, 2017), 78.
43    Dean, *Unlimited Intimacy*, 85.

comes his parent or "Daddy," having fathered his virus. If this man also happens to be one's partner or lover, then by "breeding" him one has transformed what anthropologists call a relational affine into a consanguine; one's "husband" has become one's "brother" via a shared bodily substance.[44]

Here, the conflation of impersonal sex with brothers, with husbands, and the queer potentials that might come from renegotiating these kernels of sexual and bodily pleasure and exchange, fit into both the discursive and psychoanalytical conflations of the virus (and its correlation to disease and death), drug use, *jouissance*, and the communion of "a piece of himself inside of me; his cum, like the sex itself, [that] has a psychological value far beyond anything physical."[45] However, it is also these affective urgencies, intensive thrills, and extreme levels of sexual and bodily arousal that extinguish *jouissance*. The phallic and cisgendered gay porn scene simultaneously facilitates and undercuts the mattering body, and, in so doing, urges it toward a muttering one to renegotiate and search for spaces in which a *doxa* of barebacking and chemsex that has been cultivated by figures such as Cole also splutters.

While this amalgamation of men phallically impregnating one another's anuses is "invested with woman's power to conceive . . . [whereby] the rectum becomes the procreative womb," it is also (and as Bersani famously asserts) here that the "barebacker's rectum is a grave."[46] Through this act, the potential for a queer inversion of reproductive sex as the giver of life into the non-reproductive transmission of a potential death allows the cis gay male barebackers to move toward a form of *jouissance* that comes close to the "essential insanity"[47] of barebacking and chemsex that Bersani, Dean, and Cole all recognize on their own conceptual and representational terms. More so and *as* pornography the subversive and transgressive potentials of *jouissance* are obscured if not obliterated in an

---

44 Ibid., 85–6.
45 Dean, *Unlimited Intimacy*, 87, citing Scott O'Hara, "Viral Communion: There's Life Beyond Condoms," *Poz*, November 1997, 69.
46 Bersani and Phillips, *Intimacies*, 45.
47 Ibid.

attempt to contain them within the signifying chain of tendencies that might be more broadly situated through neoliberalist and late-capitalist consumerism.

In *Homosexual Desire*, Guy Hocquenghem uses the notion of the sublimated anus to claim that "sublimation is exercised on the anus as on no other organ."[48] Writing in an era that preceded HIV and AIDS by almost a decade, and one that might now be regarded as a historical moment allied to gay liberation, Hocquenghem sees both the anus's function and its desirability as primarily private and personal. Barebacking, and more so the commodified value and power of Liam Cole's pornography in work such as *Slammed* (2012), *Overload* (2013), *Hard Cuts I* (2014), and *Hard Cuts II* (2015), transform, invert, and reroute this sublimation of the anus into an unstintingly visual politics of anal visibility and accessibility. The cum-drenched anus so central to Cole's work functions as an impersonally public and open space of desire cleaved and "gashed by bliss."[49] In paradoxical contrast to the technical scrutiny allowed by the close-up of the wet, gaping, and convulsing asshole in this genre of pornography, Hocquenghem's claim—that "there is no anal pornography . . . [because] the anus is over-invested individually because its investment is withdrawn socially"[50]—is upturned. The exposure and parting of the anus for anyone and everyone to enter force us to re-engage and re-evaluate how the anus that "forms the division between society and the individual"[51] is transposed so that the anus becomes a communal site. To rephrase Hocquenghem's claim that "the anus is overinvested *individually* because its investment is withdrawn *socially*," the anus is overinvested *socially* because its investment is withdrawn from the *individual*—a modulation that brings us closer to its potential as a space whereby the cis gay male subject productively embraces both desire and anxiety in parallel toward a queer model of *jouissance* that splutters between phallic and anal intersubjectivity.

---

48    Guy Hocquenghem, *Homosexual Desire* (Durham, NC: Duke University Press, 1993), 96.
49    Stockton, "*Jouissance*, the Gash of Bliss."
50    Hocquenghem, *Homosexual Desire*, 95.
51    Ibid.

Both inside and outside of Liam Cole's pornographic textuality, Bersani and Phillips's claim that "the community engendered by barebacking is completely nonviable socially and politically"[52] also resonates. This is precisely because it is increasingly commodified and trapped between the possibilities of anti-egoistical acts of self-subordination and affirmative impersonality, while always being anchored to a rhetorical politics of "hypermasculinized ego, the grotesquely distorted apeing of reproductive values, [and] the all-too-visible appeal of an eroticized militarism which in turn positions it as a perpetuation of homo and heterosexual hegemonic and dominant masculine values."[53] In barebacking and chemsex, the spluttering cis gay male subject attempts to connect, implicate, and haunt the other, but he is still barred from the *jouissance* of his own subjective experience. Barebacking and chemsex, and more so the signification and expression of how it "feels" in porn, could be seen as a queer attempt to renegotiate this barrier or limit. Here, the tensions between a psychoanalytic identification that fails overlap with queer identifications that partially connect the subject with the other through a complex milieu of sex, death, risk, regulation, and transgression. Through these practices and their situational intent, the impersonality of the self and the repositioning of what the narcissistic possibilities of that impersonality may be are where the truly affirmative and genuine possibilities of *jouissance* are located: a non-representational politics that moves beyond the bodily politics and archetypes of gay porn actors and the partiality of the visual signifiers that are all too familiar. In a search for *jouissance* outside identity politics and ideological networks of mediated desire, it may be that the politics of bareback and chemsex lie beyond the pornographically mediated and/or liminal spaces of the orgy or gangbang, as well as the porn actors who continue to maintain and repeat an embodied rhetoric of hyper-male, phallic, and cisgendered gay male signifiers such as tattoos, cropped and shaved hairstyles, piercings, jockstraps, and military jackboots. Porn of this type paradoxically undermines and confines the potential

---

52    Bersani and Phillips, *Intimacies*, 49.
53    Ibid., 51.

of the subject's diffuse, joyous, unconscious *jouissance*, and how it might relate to the stimulating epistemological and ontological potentials of spluttering bodies and the self-led shattering of the subject's own narcissistic ego.

## THE PROBLEM WITH NARCISSISM! SHATTERED, SUAVE, AND SPLUTTERING BODIES

A concept like bodies that splutter may also allow the cis gay male, and potentially all queer subjects and subjectivities, to get closer to a form of *jouissance* that is both sustained and disavowed by the symbolic in language. These faltering and spluttered significations are the ones that can only be partially expressed via the symbolic and *jouissance*. They also form the splutters that position the aimless, random, and obtuse ejaculations into the anus that "come/cum" close to how *jouissance* can only be incompletely expressed both metonymically and impersonally in bareback and chemsex porn. This approach to *jouissance* as expression of the impersonality of identity and ego can also be found in the critical reconsiderations of the narcissistic cis gay man in Lee Edelman's concept of "narci-schism"[54] and Leo Bersani's enduring exploration of impersonal narcissism,[55] which push cisgendered gay masculinity toward practices of narcissism outside of the gay male ego and its imaginary other.

For instance, Edelman understands that there is an imaginary relation between the narcissistic gay subject and the mirror as constitutive of gay male subjectivity, and, in turn, gay desire. Yet, as Edelman argues, this is also the foundation for an alternative notion of gay subjectivity or activism that would involve a self-disciplined depersonalization of narcissism as "narci-schism," so that "the luxurious 'passivity' derided as 'narcissism,' that signifies the erotic indulgence of the [cisgendered gay male] self that always

---

54    Lee Edelman, *Homographesis: Essays in Gay Literary and Cultural Theory* (London and New York: Routledge, 1994).

55    Leo Bersani, "Is the Rectum a Grave?," *October* 43 (1987): 197–222; Leo Bersani, *Homos* (Cambridge, MA: Harvard University Press, 1995); Bersani and Phillips, *Intimacies*.

threatens to undo the 'self'"[56] is either undermined or removed. In this instance, "narci-schism," which is assimilated from the "erotic mode of the dominant subject"[57] as self-disciplinary, has the potential to simultaneously reposition the gay male narcissist and his capacity as a "mirror bound narcissist reviled for a passivity"[58] as a "narci-schisist." That is, the subject who moves beyond his imaginary ego and the metaphors of gay identity toward a way of expressing his subjectivity (and *jouissance*) symbolically and impersonally.

In this way, the potential ruptures that the "narci-schisist" and "narci-schism" impart can also contribute to considerations allied to narcissism and the imaginary subject of desire seen in Bersani's theory of a "self-shattering" of the ego and subjectivity.[59] This shattering can be understood as a conceptualization of the "self" that Bersani and Phillips recognize via Freud's assertions that the narcissistic "sexualizing of the ego is identical to the shattering of the ego."[60] By aligning a shattering of the ego with a spluttering of the body in bareback and chemsex porn, it is also useful to think about how Bersani used shattering as a device to imagine gay masculinity "in which . . . the self is exuberantly discarded."[61] It is through the self-shattering of the ego, and through the ego's own struggles with narcissistic and "narci-schisistic" desire, that something Bersani constitutes as " 'impersonal narcissism' begins to make its own insensible sense."[62] On one hand, this stands if we literalize and invest in the pornographic images on the basis of an identifiable "bareback/chemsex culture" and "bareback/chemsex gay male subject" existing through personalizing, inclusive, and tangible forms of desire and identity. Yet, on the other, if we approach these images as traces of the depersonalized, exclusionary, and intangible desires they endlessly reproduce, we also begin to see them as close to a queer combination of "narci-schisistic" and shattered *jouissance*.

---

56  Edelman, *Homographesis*, 10.
57  Ibid.
58  Ibid., 108.
59  Bersani, "Is the Rectum a Grave?," 222.
60  Bersani and Phillips, *Intimacies*, 66.
61  Bersani, "Is the Rectum a Grave?," 217–18.
62  Bersani and Phillips, *Intimacies*, 92.

This connects to a spluttering body that also relies upon the conflicts rather than the failure "to distinguish others from Others"[63] in its search for *jouissance*. In pornography that claims to capture and represent bareback and chemsex practices, this can only be a vulnerably phallic body that splutters, a body that Dean might also position as "suave."[64] This "suave body" is situated as the body that has been rehearsed, smoothed over, repetitively copied, and "so completely rhetoricalized" that it is effectively "devoid of desire."[65] This is the body as a pornographic text whose devolution of desire is desire itself, a desire activated by its own loss of desire. On RawFuckClub.com, this intersection of spluttering and suaveness facilitates a form of phallic *jouissance* that is always strategized, constructed, and manipulated, and "not in any way liberated or liberating,"[66] so that the "suaveness" becomes an indicative part of how phallic *jouissance* as spluttering is expressed. For instance, in several gangbang scenes, such as *Alex Mason's Birthday Gang Bang* (2016), the close-up representations of bareback sex and/or the allusions to chemsex present us with a spluttering and suave subject who can only be identified through the limits of cisgendered gay masculinity and its alliance to the pornographic text. Here, the enigmatic nature of this spluttering underpins *and* undermines the discursive bodies "mattering" because of its pornographic representation *as* suave. This allows the performatively phallic and mattering body's imaginary ego from within the explicit porn image to fall into impersonal modes of sexual representation that symbolically splutter and strive toward *jouissance* because they are suave.

More problematically, we also see that the sexual pleasures of the suavely spluttering subject are embedded in a level of phallic power that is lacking, missing, or that remains frustratingly disavowed in both the imaginary and the symbolic. Through the Real, a muttering body is inaudible, while a spluttering body is one that can be partially understood. For example, if we consider the notion that

---

63    Dean, *Beyond Sexuality*, 187.
64    Ibid.
65    Ibid.
66    Ibid.

bareback bottoms such as Alex Mason possess an imaginary ego that "matters," we see that bareback pornography does something to position that subject as a subject. In the tagline for this particular scene, the viewer-as-consumer is told that "Alex Mason gets the gangbang of his life when six studs tear the slutty bottom apart. They fuck, double fuck and breed his hungry hole . . . all in real time! This is as close as you're gonna get to being there."[67] The cis gay male identity, personality, and sexual desire remain tethered to symbolic "meaning as a substitute for sexuality"[68] that disproportionately splutters. Yet, in turn, this is configured through the metonymic potential of a *jouissance* that splutters, and the stimulating impossibility and impersonality of a pornographically mediated "body that splutters" as a substitute for that meaning. While *the Real* body of Alex Mason that mutters may be the limit and the actual place of *jouissance*, we also see in signification, and via the signifier, that because the symbolic "Other is lacking,"[69] the subject's phallic *jouissance* is most powerfully realized as a form of spluttering.

In pornographic representations such as this, which could be aligned with barebacking and chemsex as "mainstreaming and normalizing," the mattering body "eroticizes the performance of hypermasculinity through sex acts that foreground danger, risk and abandonment."[70] Here, the potential of phallic *jouissance* is always obscured by the pornographic signifier, unwittingly and negligently limiting *jouissance* to imaginary othering. This pornographic subject of the signifier is tethered to a mattering body that is locked into a materiality by the signification of a bodily ego or, as Dean claims, one restrained by the imaginary (and always to an extent the symbolic) registers. It is clear that websites such as RawFuckClub.com produce a regulated and commodified representational space where egotistical "bodies that matter" attempt, yet also fail, to capture and release the inherent anxiety tethered to desire, the phallus, and *jouissance*. Yet it is within this failure

67   "Alex Mason's Birthday Gang Bang," Raw Fuck Club, last modified May 13, 2016, https://www.rawfuckclub.com/vod/RFC/watch.php?video=R326.
68   Dean, *Beyond Sexuality*, 188.
69   Ibid., 205.
70   Mercer, *Gay Pornography*, 139.

to express *jouissance* that the body begins to splutter, so that the imprudent preservation of gay male narcissism instilled through an imaginary Other gives way to a cisgendered gay subject that is both controlled and restricted by the symbolic Other while remaining aroused and exasperated by *jouissance*.

## CONCLUSION

To grasp *jouissance* and/or compound it to bodies that splutter, one must perhaps understand that "it is [the] barriers or limits to *jouissance* that 'permit the full spectrum of desire.' "[71] In terms of the cis gay male subjects or bodies that we see in bareback and chemsex porn, it is through the practices themselves and their attempts to superficially allow "unlimited access to *jouissance* that permits desire to flourish."[72] Yet it seems that to begin to articulate something— indeed anything—of *jouissance* and its inference in bareback and chemsex porn, we must connect to how language always instills a limit to the subject's *jouissance* as an unconscious pleasure, and also allows us to access and gain (temporary) pleasure from it. In light of this, what phallic *jouissance* alerts us to are the gap(s) (*faille[s]*) that Lacan claims exist between self and Other. These gaps can be identified as a form of desire that demands—that is, as a desire that is never exacting or sufficient but, rather, one that acts as a ceaseless and selfish cathexis, never giving up on its *jouissance* or, as Lacan states, "demanding it (*ne cesse pas*)."[73]

Bruce Fink suggests that it is precisely because desire and pleasure are inadequate that our "knowledge begins with a deficiency of *jouissance*."[74] A lot like the amplification of sexual pleasure and arousal that is represented in bareback and chemsex porn, this leaves both the spectator/consumer as well as the porn actors/barebackers wanting more. We/he/they want to see or take another dick deep in a raw, widened, and pulsating hole, and then "we/he/they" want it

---

71   Dean, *Beyond Sexuality*, 91.
72   Ibid.
73   Lacan, *On Feminine Sexuality*, 5.
74   Bruce Fink, *Lacan to the Letter: Reading* Écrits *Closely* (Minneapolis: University of Minnesota Press, 2004), 155.

again, and again, and again. This endlessness and this transgressive level of phallic pleasure also seem to locate barebacking, pornography, and, indeed, *jouissance* close to Lacan's ideas about the *objet a* or the "object as *cause* of desire."[75] This object of desire as its cause will never fulfill desire, and it meanders through formations of *jouissance* that endlessly cause "aporias, paradoxes and conundrums."[76] Just as the bodies that splutter do so because of the symbolic, they also splutter in response to a *jouissance* that perpetually "upsets the smooth functioning of structures, systems, and axiomatic fields" to form "another kind of pleasure," which (is) where the failure of signification to express this cause of desire is always "decompleted by the alterity or heterogeneity it contains within itself."[77]

In this way, it may be beyond the restrictions of market-driven pornography, and through self-representational and non-cisgendered modes of sexual desire, where the new possibilities of barebacking and chemsex can be situated. The self-representations that have emerged through "selfie culture," and which encompass a far more amateurish, objective, and raw representation of these practices, may be where we next need to relocate our emphasis. The ethnographic processes and "real" practices that Cole attempts to capture, that RawFuckClub.com commodifies, and that Dean narrates have been remediated onto vast, limitless, and potentially queer social media platforms. Here, and through processes of self-production and self-representation, the barebacking and chemsex so prevalent on Tumblr blogs, Grindr and Gaydar profiles, and in Snapchat and WhatsApp groups suggest that there is another layer of representation emerging to reposition the subjective and unconscious vectors of *jouissance* and bodies that splutter their *jouissance* through barebacking and chemsex.

A lot like the pursuit of *jouissance*, the production and use of pornography is a search for something transgressive and affirmative. Barebacking and chemsex *as* porn may be responses to the assimilatory and morally repressive discourses of cisgendered gay

---

75   Fink, *The Lacanian Subject*, xiii.
76   Ibid.
77   Ibid.

men as acceptable others, less marginalized, and now commodified. More so, and when compounded, these mattering, spluttering, and muttering potentials may also subvert legal, moral, and ethical discourses. Pornographies of barebacking, and more explicitly its convergent nature in the work of someone like Liam Cole, open up the possibilities that modes of phallic *jouissance* and bodies that splutter may contain in their capacity to splutter. Reconsidering what cis gay male pornography might be in light of *jouissance* may also allow for new forms of spluttered *jouissance* to exist as states of productive incoherence and excitement. At once instantaneous and ejaculatory, abject and enigmatic, the spluttering body and the *jouissance* through which it is torn apart seem to splutter together as impersonal traces of one another.

**REFERENCES**

Arundale, Jean. *Identity, Narcissism, and the Other: Object Relations and Their Obstacles.* London: Karnac Books, 2017.

Ashford, Chris. "Bareback Sex, Queer Legal Theory, and Evolving Socio-Legal Contexts." *Sexualities* 18, nos. 1-2 (April 2015): 195–209.

Barthes, Roland. *The Pleasure of the Text.* Translated by Richard Miller. New York: Hill and Wang, 1975.

Berg, Rigmor C. "Barebacking: A Review of the Literature." *Archives of Sexual Behavior* 38, no. 5 (January 2009): 754–64.

Bersani, Leo. *Homos.* Cambridge, MA: Harvard University Press, 1995.

———. "Is the Rectum a Grave?" *October* 43 (Winter 1987): 197–222.

Bersani, Leo, and Adam Phillips. *Intimacies.* Chicago: University of Chicago Press, 2008.

Bowie, Malcolm. *Lacan.* London: Fontana Press, 1991.

Butler, Judith. *Bodies that Matter: On the Discursive Limits of "Sex."* London and New York: Routledge, 1993.

Davis, Oliver. "A Special Issue of *Sexualities*: Bareback Sex and Queer Theory across Three National Contexts (France, UK, USA)." *Sexualities* 18, nos. 1–2 (April 2015): 120–26.

Dean, Tim. *Beyond Sexuality.* Chicago, University of Chicago Press, 2000.

———. *Unlimited Intimacy: Reflections on the Subculture of Barebacking.* Chicago: University of Chicago Press, 2009.

Edelman, Lee. *Homographesis: Essays in Gay Literary and Cultural Theory.* London and New York: Routledge, 1994.

Fink, Bruce. "Knowledge and *Jouissance*." In *Reading Seminar XX: Lacan's Major Work on Love, Knowledge, and Feminine Sexuality*, edited by Suzanne Barnard and Bruce Fink, 21–46. Albany: SUNY Press, 2002.

——. *Lacan to the Letter: Reading "Écrits" Closely*. Minneapolis: University of Minnesota Press, 2004.

——. *The Lacanian Subject: Between Language and Jouissance*. Princeton, NJ: Princeton University Press, 1995.

Garcia, Christien. "Limited Intimacy: Barebacking and the Imaginary." *Textual Practice* 27, no. 6 (2013): 1031–51.

Geldhof, Abe, and Paul Verhaeghe. "Queer as a New Shelter from Castration." In *Clinical Encounters in Sexuality: Psychoanalytic Practice and Queer Theory*, edited by Noreen Giffney and Eve Watson, 211–21. New York: Punctum Books, 2017.

Greteman, Adam J. "Fashioning a Bareback Pedagogy: Towards a Theory of Risky (Sex) Education." Supplement, *Sex Education* 13, no. 1 (February 2013): S20–S31.

Hocquenghem, Guy. *Homosexual Desire*. Durham, NC: Duke University Press, 1993.

Lacan, Jacques. *On Feminine Sexuality: The Limits of Love and Knowledge*. New York: W.W. Norton, 1999.

——. "The Subversion of the Subject and the Dialectic of Desire in the Freudian Unconscious." In *Écrits: A Selection*, 323–60. London and New York: Routledge, 2003.

McNamara, Michael. "Cumming to Terms: Bareback Pornography, Homonormativity, and Queer Survival in the Time of HIV/AIDS." In *The Moral Panics of Sexuality*, edited by Breanne Fahs, Mary L. Dudy, and Sarah Stage, 226–44. London: Palgrave Macmillan, 2013.

Mercer, John. *Gay Pornography: Representations of Sexuality and Masculinity*. London: I.B. Tauris, 2017.

Rofes, Eric. *Dry Bones Breathe: Gay Men Creating Post-AIDS Identities and Cultures*. Binghamton, NY: Haworth Press, 1998.

Scott, Stuart. "The Condomlessness of Bareback Sex: Responses to the Unrepresentability of HIV in Treasure Island Media's *Plantin' Seed* and *Slammed*." *Sexualities* 18, nos. 1–2 (April 2015): 210–23.

Stockton, Kathryn Bond. "Jouissance, the Gash of Bliss." In *Clinical Encounters in Sexuality: Psychoanalytic Practice and Queer Theory*, edited by Noreen Giffney and Eve Watson, 101–22. New York: Punctum Books, 2017.

# PSYCHO-
# ANALYTIC
# AND
# PEDA-
# GOGICAL
# LIMITS

# CHAPTER 9

# CROSS-DRESSING VIOLENCE: BAREBACKING AS SYMBOLIC DRAG[1]

## Diego Semerene

> *I consist of an artificial bitterness,*
> *Faithful to I don't know what idea.*
> *Like a make-believe courtesan, I don*
> *Majestic robes in which I exist*
> *For the artificial presence of the king.*
>
> *Yes, all I am and want are but dreams.*
>
> —FERNANDO PESSOA

### ANOINT ME: THE FORGING OF AN EQUATION

If the majority of early barebacking scholarship has assumed it to be a subcultural practice, a homosexual question, or solely an epidemiological concern, we can say without great risk that, in considering the practice, Jacques Lacan would know to not only *listen* to the barebacking subject as a subject *tout court*, but would simultaneously refuse to take him at his word. To consider barebacking from a Lacanian perspective is to thus choose a certain

---

1    Sections of this essay previously appeared in Diego Semerene, "Playing Dead: On Part-time Transvestism, Digital Semblance, and Drag Feminism," *Revista Periódicus* 5, no. 1 (2016): 235–53. Used here by permission of the publisher.

blindness where science sees tangible matter, epidemiologists see numbers, and queer theorists who tend to distance themselves from psychoanalysis see all sorts of things, except desire.

My intervention into barebacking utilizes the language of Lacanian psychoanalysis to speak of desire while borrowing from a queer theory that isn't so eager to change the world in the present juncture such that it forgets to analyze the very libidinal geography that structures, and rigs, that world. As in philosopher Paul B. Preciado's theory of the self as *de rigueur* channel, container, and filter through which all else flows, my analysis highlights the analyst in(side) the contaminating scene of analysis as an active and sexually implicated participant.[2] This is an inevitable condition of the text if its author, and readers, are willing to pay the price of avowal, of speaking.

Due to the application of testosterone and the subsequent questions surrounding what kind of feminist he then becomes, or wants to be, Preciado speaks of accepting the changes in his own body as operating as "the mutation of an epoch." Through a pharmacological self-remixing of sorts, he recognizes and challenges, among other things, the regulatory model of Foucault's panopticon as it plays itself out upon women's contraceptive pillboxes, both in their design and in their ominous effects. The pill, for Preciado, is formed out of the accumulated effects of a history of "social orthopedics" attempting to keep the subject from *growing sideways*.[3] The pill has replaced the control tower. A system of oral self-administration has replaced the whip. Its daily intake also reminds us of the new PrEP regimens, which eerily link gay men, trans people, and bio women[4]

---

2    This includes the subject's desire to be "infiltrated, absorbed and completely occupied" by power. Beatriz Preciado, *Testo Junkie: Sexe, drogue et biopolitique* (Paris: Grasset and Fasquelle, 2008), 162.

3    Preciado, *Testo Junkie*, 21, 159; my translation. While Kathryn Bond Stockton deploys her concept of sideways growth mostly as an effect of a particularly queer child's inability to grow according to the dicta provided by the normative moulds/modes of growing, I think of this non-vertical growth as signaling that which a heterosexist system stunts, to various degrees, in the human subject more broadly. Stockton, *The Queer Child, or Growing Sideways in the Twentieth Century* (Durham, NC: Duke University Press, 2009).

4    My utilization of the term "bio woman/women" is derived from Preciado's own usage of the term in his book, which I assume to mean "biologically constructed," or women whose gender identity matches the sex that they were assigned at birth.

in an invisible, symbolic kin-making coup. Gender, or womanhood anyway, is here exposed not as a genital matter, but as a question of pharmacology, toxicity, repetition, and juggling between invisible labour (the taking of the pill, contraceptive, or prophylaxis, as a private and anxious, if not shameful, affair) and the hyper-visible effects of that labour in (re)structuring behaviour and practices.

In this manner, the assigning of gender is a precarious affair marred by anxiety precisely because it depends on so much maintenance. Gendering is never done, as it must be projected—again, and again, and again—by the iterations that will make it legible and coherent to the point of confluence. That is, that illusion of seamlessness through visual trickery whereby gender's repetitions will be (mis)read as one single flow, and thus as a natural given.[5] Making sure gender sticks is, from the beginning, a dangerous business, as it risks coming undone if the repetition of, for instance, sartorial, performative, or prophylactic practice comes to a halt.

If the pill has served as a fundamental tool to build and manage the modern bio woman—not so "bio" after all: Preciado speaks of *bio-drag*, or somatic-political transvestism—how has the condom been used to build and manage the figure of the *gay man*[6] in the late twentieth century, and then been resignified as fetish so pervasively in the early twenty-first century? If the pill has, as the story goes, given bio women sexual freedom, or its illusion, while also being a vehicle for their subjection (of reproduction, sex, and gender identity), can we situate the condom similarly, "from ablation to reconstruction," from a repressively sartorial repetition (something

---

5   J.C. Flugel defines confluence in vestimentary terms, when "the mind fails to distinguish two things which under other circumstances are easily kept apart" and fuses them "into a unity." Here, too, confluence is under the threat of dissolution, "failing to undergo the necessary steps of incorporation." In the case that a garment is too large to seem like an extension of the self, for instance, or a particular fabric appears to have a will of its own, refusing "to become a part of an organic whole," then the body will look troublesomely foreign instead. J.C. Flugel, *The Psychology of Clothes* (London: Hogarth Press, 1930), 36–37.

6   I utilize *gay man* in italics throughout this chapter to stress the fact that this is a symbolic figure, not necessarily a gay man proper. I italicize *straight man* for the same reason. If I do not do the same for "gay men," it is because in those moments I am speaking of a group and, thus, the non-coincidence between the category and the individual should go without saying.

the *gay man* puts on) to a contra-sartorial one (something the *gay man* peels off)?[7] Can the forgoing of the condom as an identity-making device—condoms as prerequisite for the *gay man's* acting out *gay man*-ness—be the subject's attempt to *rename* himself, and thus to excavate an otherwise ungrantable access to a symbolic system where his desire is recognizable, at best, as a desire for others like him, for *gay man*-ness? By this set of questions I mean to suggest that the fantasy that gay men desire one another (not the *straight man* of the Symbolic), which has achieved its epitome in relentless quests for marriage equality, may break down at the level of (sexual) practice through barebacking. Here, the *gay man*, who is supposed to desire another *gay man*, may resort to the uncloaking of a prophylaxis (and equalizing) cover that has worked to turn him into someone who desires others like him, as a way to refuse such an equation (the *gay man* desires the *gay man*). If fights for marriage equality and subscriptions to a "born this way" mentality support the presumption of this fictitious equality at the level of desire (the *gay man* desires the *gay man*), the *gay man's* bodily practices may be saying otherwise. Barebacking appears, in this logic, as a way for the body to rebel against such fictions of equality, a way for the body to articulate the unwelcome desire's unwelcome truths into an equation that could say the awfully non-progressive "*gay man* desires *straight man*." In what follows, I shall explain why barebacking may amount to the bodily articulation—a horny speech act—of such an equation, where the *gay man* attempts to forge access to the *straight man* of the Symbolic—that is, the phallus proper, and not its queer double.

For psychoanalyst Sol Aparicio, naming is an operation of the Father, a symbolic figure, as construed within psychoanalysis, structured around castration, frustration, and privation. Naming, as a process involving the production of different signifiers, produces holes: if X isn't Y, then we now have something—a hole—that separates X from Y. The name itself, then, comes out of a hole. The name is put in place of a hole, like the phallus, to cover up a perceived absence. A hole spits out the name. Although this line of

---

7    Preciado, *Testo Junkie*, 164.

thought may seem puzzling, we would do well to bask in the sheer power of the metaphor, which is rendered particularly canny by Aparicio's linking of the hole to the prohibition of incest when she says that a "hole is always needed for a knot to be possible."[8] That is, the spatial absence that the hole represents can be a rather fecund one, spawning steady links (knots) and scripting subjects (naming): even if that fecundity is phantasmatic, as it is in the language of barebacking, where the *gay man* can be *bred*. The hole may even illustrate the hopeful gap between one iteration and the next, one of the most fertile arguments in Judith Butler's oeuvre, which we find in the economy of any repetition—the very gap that enables queer kinds of derailing, dissidence, and rogueness.

Does barebacking, then, led by the numbing repetitiveness of cruising—which ends up rendering inept every object that dares to interrupt its course—literalize an attempt to poke a hole in the Symbolic, a hole that may grant the *gay man* access to its many, even if fictitious, promises (of fertility, of reparation)? It seems that barebacking, in its irrational—that is, unconscious—insistence, works as a response to symbolic alienation. A response that is at once subversive and reactionary, as it cracks the Symbolic in order to claim it. Barebacking, I am arguing, dramatizes the new—or newly *express* ("easy and undetectable")—ability or demand for a borderlessness between the categories—*names*—that have historically inscribed the *gay man* onto a botched equation where he is supposed to desire (an)other *gay man*.[9] Social gains have been won through this equation, but subversive sexual practices that "defy the logic," such as barebacking, point to a body that longs for something else altogether. If this something else altogether can't be gained at the level of the flesh, it may be produced through a phantasmatic enactment of its presence. Namely, the all-powerful phallus, the *straight man*'s, irresistibly capable of wielding death and illness while never succumbing to either. Barebacking stages a relationship between

---

8    Sol Aparicio, "The Names of the Father and Fathers" (presentation, Research Group of Clinical Formations of the Lacanian Field seminar, Paris, July 6, 2013).

9    Preciado speaks of "pop control" and "pop microfascism." Preciado, *Testo Junkie*, 160, 162. My translation.

bodies that makes this phallus, this phallus that isn't mine and which, under "normal" conditions does not want me (or even see me), appear before me, flood me, destroy me, repair me, anoint me.

## AGAINST MOVEMENT: UNDER THE AEGIS OF THE SYMPTOM

Preciado's pharmacopornography may come in the micro-prosthesis of a pill, an app, or, for those left to wonder how to sexually inhabit/penetrate/contaminate/cum with the Symbolic, wrapping and yanking of the condom, which, in its unused state also resembles the regulatory circularity of the contraceptive pillbox, as well as the anal rim and the harmonious circularity of the symptom, whose movement buoys its stillness. The death drive, an often interpellated concept in analyzing so-called risky behaviour in general and in barebacking in particular, is not just a push toward (self-)destruction, but a soothingly rhythmic repetition (regular, circular, constant), the interruption of which represents death of an obnoxious and unaccounted-for kind: not the death courted, or even swallowed, through risk, but the unwanted death *qua* death that catches the subject off guard, dismantling any sense of mastery completely.

A close reading of the movement of images online—that is, within pharmacopornographic sexual economies—suggests that despite the widely available technology of moving images, the digital subject chooses the still image as a mode of self-representation. The pharmacological also cuts through such an economy, with pills that grant the body a sense of keeping up with the priapistic fantasy of an Other who is readily available, and a self who is always performing well enough not to be rejected by such an Other. Who hasn't been buzz-killed by the perfectly masculine still photograph of a potential hookup who subsequently dared to speak, to move, or to material-ize before our eyes? Is it not precisely because movement operates through a collection of gestures through time (analog cinema is the perfect literalization of this) *making sprocket holes*, as the case may be, that it is deemed too risky of a technology for self-presentation? When images move, holes are formed, threatening the confluence that otherwise guarantees the aura of unity surrounding the object of desire. Disenchantment lurks where these lacunae emerge. Clinging to the safety of the still image, the subject reveals, and exploits, its potential for seizing what the moving image leaks (its surplus beyond the Subject's control) in the same way the notion of the category contains, or maims, the excessive queerness of desire (its inherent perverseness).[10] And, perhaps, in the way philosopher Gerhard Richter argued for the anti-fascist properties of the human face, with its too many muscles and nuances, and which digital self-displays that use movement (for instance, video selfies) are wont to blur under the veil of filters: the truth of the face is revealed precisely when it does not remain what it is. It assumes its proper self most fully in the moment in which it is shifting toward something else, another face, another identity. This moment of the shift *is* the proper self of the face. The language of truth, as it is staged upon the scene of its face, is always already traversed by its other.[11]

No wonder, then, that within a new-media cruising economy of pledged bodies (forever-announced digital visitors that either never arrive or appear dead upon arrival, as in killed by disenchantment) we find the consistent withholding of the human face, even from the still images put forth in hookup apps such as Grindr. In the name of discretion, the faceless subject withholds not only his identity but that "shifting toward something else" that could expose the dissymmetry between phantasmatic representation and corporeal actuality.[12] The cruising subject withholds the face while making desperate demands to see the face of the Other, creating a tension

---

10   There has been a lot of debate around perversion as a proper *name* of a psychic structure in psychoanalysis (along with neurosis and psychosis), since we could say that desire writ large abides by a perverse structure, which I argue to be what makes desire itself *queer*—that is, unstable, excessive, and nebulous. Perversion as the very fabric and condition of desire is, Joan Copjec argues, a putatively universal non-coincidence between all subjects and their statements, the "democratic" opacity, anti-normativity, and unverifiability of desire. Discussed in James Penny, *The World of Perversion: Psychoanalysis and the Impossible Absolute of Desire* (SUNY Press, 2006).

11   Gerhard Richter, "Benjamin's Face: Defacing Fascism," in *Walter Benjamin and the Corpus of Autobiography* (Detroit: Wayne State University Press, 2002), 109.

12   It isn't without irony that we can locate the facial menace of Richter's "shifting toward something else" in Judith Butler's lacuna between gender-making repetitions—a hopeful space pregnant with off-script possibilities for the Subject.

that delays the still images of bodies from becoming bodies in motion subjected to the unaccounted-for properties that human contact warrants. This kind of cruising taps into the lacuna between contacts, prolonging the nothingness between iterations in ways that recall the current duration of HIV's own time of incubation, or its fantasy: forever. The tug-of-war maintains the stillness of the death drive, a sense of immobility fabricated through the regularity of rhythmic movement, and buys the Subject time before the shifts toward something else become inevitable, spoiling the image, halting the fantasy, and disrupting the cruising. The demand for the face of the Other in digital cruising can only be compared, in frequency and intensity, to the demand for masculinity (in the Other), both of which are contingent on an anticipated face and the masculinity of the self—one becoming the presumed guarantor of the other. This is the face as the ultimate giveaway or seal of approval for a masculinity that seems to always be elsewhere—in the (*straight man's*) Symbolic. If all faces were voluntarily on display, all addresses promptly brought forth, all availability clearly cited, and all sexual demands legitimately listed (and *read*), instead of the stillness through the rhythmic movement of the death drive, the cruising subject would find himself in a forlorn, and pre-emptive, paralysis.[13]

We could link the threat of the face, along with its accompanying body in motion, to the unsettling potential of what psychoanalyst Christopher Bollas calls "the sexual logic of intercourse." Intercourse appears as a key figure of disruption in the three-year-old child's sexual epiphany that, "apart from Jesus (or 'the Holy Family'), the child did not enter existence through maternal immaculate conception."[14] Instead of being the centre of the universe, the child

---

Judith Butler, *Bodies That Matter: On the Discursive Limits of "Sex"* (London and New York: Routledge, 1993).

13  "The pervert walking in the real is always on the prowl . . ." He produces "an illusion of omniscience, as the world seems to constantly serve up exact objects of desire." Christopher Bollas, *Hysteria* (London and New York: Routledge, 2000), 170.

14  Notice how the three-year-old's sexual epiphany comes just after the child has her body cut up by language and meaning into organs and limbs, ridding her further of oneness with the (m)other.

may actually just be "an after-effect of parental sexual passion sought after for its own sake." The crux of such a narcissistic crisis represented by the notion of the "intercourse"—as opposed to some kind of divine alignment of the stars to produce His Majesty, the Baby—is the idea that the self may be rendered as mere fallout from an act that wasn't meant to be productive, but merely conducive. The disruption is one that takes the child away from a desired outcome, or *raison d'être*, to assuming the existential position of a barebacking accident. A movement from cooked-up fantasy to accidental rawness: barebacking makes babies, barebacking is heterosexual, heterosexuality is barebacking.[15]

The difficulty in distinguishing movement from stillness has been the most basic precondition for the genesis of cinema. We can see a mirroring version of such confusion, and its exploitation, in what Tim Dean calls aimless cruising, when the Subject moves around in a physical space—without the aid of new media gadgets—seeking an effigy of (hetero)masculinity that could only last convincingly as such in darkness and in stillness. When such cruising happens through the digital, the Subject's movement becomes even more calculated and exclusionary, Dean argues, but less literalized, as the body is lost to its avatar, a much more hermetic effigy.[16]

The digital condition involves a repetitive and traumatic loss of the body, or of *a* body, and with cruising, the infinite postponement of its resurrection. Digital cruising (re)dramatizes the experiences of alienation that, according to Lacan, the child experiences even before she is born, as language describes the infant's place in the world prior to birth, "thus imposing a primordial split between culture and nature in the causality of being."[17] After that, at age two, the child will suffer a second alienating experience, which

---

15   All quotes in this paragraph are from Bollas, *Hysteria*, 169.
16   Dean uses the term "aimless cruising" to describe the democratic way of seeking the object that doesn't foreclose chance ("contact" is possible here), which "digital cruising" and its relationship to the privatization of desire (only "networking" is possible here) seems to foreclose. Tim Dean, *Unlimited Intimacy: Reflections on the Subculture of Barebacking* (Chicago: University of Chicago Press, 2009).
17   Ellie Ragland, *Essays on the Pleasures of Death: From Freud to Lacan* (New York and London and New York: Routledge, 1994), 118.

Lacan refers to as a form of castration, as language crops the body into parts and organs through meaning, all potentially laden with symbolic investments inherited from the parents ("you have Uncle Joseph's nose," "Grandpa's legs," or "Auntie Joan's hot blood," et cetera).[18] Digital cruising lends itself to the inscription "on various parts of the body, naming or designating (i.e., cutting up) the body," remaking an(other) Subject for an(other) Other.[19]

Digital technology isn't the first to fashion the fleshy body assigned male at birth into some kind of phallic effigy. In the early history of men's suits, a certain fantasy of manhood was also fabricated, as tailors built the illusion of a homogeneously masculine body through the ingenious utilization of cloth, an astute sense of design, and by harkening back to muscular sculptures of Greek antiquity as blueprints for a universal set of male body proportions.[20] But in digital cruising, it is the Subject himself that assembles the *trompe l'oeil*, to the beat of his own symptom. His reconstruction is meant to mobilize this alienating function, the carving of the body through meaning, for his own libidinal profit, based on the assumption of what the Other would like to see represented (phallic masculinity, whiteness, hairlessness, able-bodiedness), and what he would like to be kept off frame. Even if claims of masculinity and other kinds of re*naming* (through the development of hair/lessness and muscle) may be at odds with what these bodies actually want done to them. Whether on Grindr or in Craigslist's Casual Encounters section (where posts were short-lived and with significantly more room for descriptive writing and explication), limbs are cropped out of context and thereby gain a certain generality. As Subjects resort to canned notions of masculinity (decidedly masculine signs), a blankness is staged (when the face is finally put forth, it is often a

18    We can presume a tendency toward failure and alienation in such identificatory attempts when addressed to queer subjects who would likely be linked to relatives and attributes not coinciding with their queerness, or with what is queer about their authenticity. This isn't to say that the identificatory attempts to link children to relatives when it comes to supposedly normative subjects are any less violent.

19    Ragland, *Essays on the Pleasures of Death*, 118.

20    Anne Hollander, *Sex and Suits: The Evolution of Modern Dress* (New York: Knopf, 1994).

disaffected poker face): torsos, buttocks, and penises aim to seduce by being read as masculine/white/hairless/able-bodied enough. This allows the whoever-Other to project the whatever-fantasy that will make rejection less likely.[21] A rejection is, in this context, a deadlier interruption than a deadly virus itself. It derails the clockwork circularity of the symptom that covers us with the illusion of a stable identity—a name—in the first place. After all, by the time the Subject is caught up in the regular circularity of digital cruising, an unconscious decision has already been made, and remade at every cruising iteration, about the deadliness of the virus that haunts and shapes psychic and digital economies alike. Its deadliness has been neutered, or at least harnessed, phantasmatically, through the dynamics of cruising itself: the repetition and the numbing *frisson* that it begets, provided the narrative isn't severed.

The fact that Lacan describes objects, or things in the world, as inscribed within a place of lack (a hole) serves as the symbolic backbone for the digital cruising subject's repetitive experience of finding nothing behind the image. Or, rather, finding something that always turns out to be lacking (masculinity), which helps explain the impression that digital cruising has become increasingly a solitary masturbatory end, not a means for sexual intercourse, as gay men seem more interested in demanding (more images, more masculinity) than risking a physical encounter, or even just movement: the demands remain rooted in still images in all of the phallic confluence that only a static effigy, or the phantasmatic acting out of such an effigy in barebacking, could successfully re-present continuously. While the figure of the pervert in psychoanalysis produces a carefully coded closed field to put his fantasy at play, one that involves a ready-made love without gambles or surprises, the hysteric gives his self as a malleable perfect gift to the Other, the master who can sculpt him as though he were clay. Psychoanalyst Néstor Braunstein calls it a "sacrificial offer," which the hysteric follows with acts of scolding, accusation, self-pity, and violent complaints that will only

---

21    "The net of determinants was spread out far enough to catch the prey in any case." Sigmund Freud, *Totem and Taboo*, trans. Abraham A. Brill (London: Empire Books, 2012), 89.

prove that the Other is deceitful, that the deceit is in the Other. Then the hysteric will move on to another Other, who may seem worthy of his sacrifice, and may finally bring him plenitude.[22]

It's easy to read the hysteric's strategy of the sacrificial offer in the dynamic of gay men's obsessive search for the perfectly masculine Other in cruising. This may in fact put gay men in a relationship of kinship with heterosexual men, who themselves—and just as desperately—look for legitimization of (their) masculinity in the masculine Other, albeit through less sexual—although certainly not less erotic—means. But for gay men in the digital cruising economy, the chorus is omnipresent in its drive to build a master out of the Other only to unveil his inability to *masterfully* occupy such a position. "No femmes," "masculine only," "masc 4 masc," and their various versions can be said to form the very crux of this digital cruiser's demand and complaint—a demand whose purpose is perhaps rooted in the certainty of the complaint that follows it.[23] An expression of an ideal immune to the femininity that taints, exposes, and mirrors lack, simultaneously stated with a horrific (paranoid?) dread of a femininity that lurks and risks surprising the self, and exposing the chasm between his diligently composed fantasy object and the objects that actually turn up. The demand for an airtight masculinity borrowed from the ready-made ideal of hetero-masculinity is interpellated as hysterically as the fear, or certitude, that such a figure is there to simply (cock)block the view of literalized lack: there where there is nothing.

If the lack (of spotless masculinity) is pre-emptively produced/projected in the Other in digital cruising, in a way that echoes the sleight of hand that very same subject performs vis-à-vis viral deathliness, this may displace the self's own (history of) inadequate masculinity. The fantasy of sameness, or equality, masculine for masculine, which is so prevalent in the demands of online personal

---

22   Néstor Braunstein, *La Jouissance, un concept Lacanien* (Paris: Erès, 2005), 208. My translation.

23   Darian Leader reminds us that the neurotic is interested in collecting injustices, generating situations in which he is refused the breast. See Leader, "Is Jouissance Really Such a Great Concept?," (presentation, Centre for Freudian Analysis and Research public seminar, London, UK, November 3, 2018).

ads, makes the fantasy of an ideal masculinity of the self (which it presumes to be what the Other desires, in hysteric fashion) contingent on the ideal masculinity of the Other. In a contract of fiction—*I believe you are It, if you believe I am It too*—it is as though the repetitiveness of such a game, and the expendability of the Other, the entertaining of the idea of an encounter or intercourse, provoked more pleasure because it doesn't need to ever stop. The self's strategy is to bank on the masculinity of the Other being a ruse before that ruse reveals itself as such, catching the Subject by surprise. The Subject would rather catch the Other red-handed than be caught off guard himself.[24]

Following this logic, the alleged/presumed courting of death through barebacking risks the bearing of death as a pregnancy that will never deliver, thanks to pharmacological technology (the period of incubation perennially extended), in order to disarm death as a necessarily premature surprise. Once death isn't disavowed or kept at arm's length, but contained in the virus that is such an intimate variable in the Subject's everyday equation of desire—courted, swallowed, incorporated, and expelled a million times—death *qua* death is disdained as pre-emptively belated.

**ALL KNOTTED UP: ON PHANTASM AND PHARMACOLOGY**

While the technologies of cruising have evolved to enable a com-pression of the chasm between *fort* and *da* to potential immediacy, it is rather significant that the Subject works to produce an infinite interval between the pushing and the pulling, and makes of this deferral the space and time of pleasure.[25] It is also worth noting that

---

24 It must be noted that this strategy mirrors that of heterosexual masculinity itself, which is perhaps more successful in its presumed confluence but just as in need of keeping it up—through sports, laughter, language, clothes, tattooing, and rape culture writ large.

25 Sigmund Freud famously described a game played by his grandson involving a cotton reel, which the little boy would repeatedly throw out of his crib, saying "Gone!" and "There!" depending on whether the makeshift toy was next to his body or far from it. Freud, "*Beyond the Pleasure Principle,*" in *The Standard Edition of the Complete Psychological Works of Sigmund Freud*, vol. 18, trans. James Strachey (London: Hogarth Press, 1955) 14–17. Ragland highlights the vacillation between

the extension of this spatio-temporal chasm (between encountering the image of the Other and witnessing its fleshy version), which seeks to maintain cruising as a voyage without a destination, has been accompanied by health technologies' own extension between the contracting and the experiencing of HIV. This pharmacologically produced delay also becomes the time and space, and somatic condition, of pleasure as even the worst-case scenario for a not-yet-positive barebacking Subject wouldn't phantasmatically mean death, but its pharmacologically managed gestation. "In sexual intercourse the hysteric's sex object is internal only, and the sexual Other is engaged as a masturbation partner who shall screen carnal contents, which verge on guided imaginings," says Bollas.[26]

For those who are already HIV-positive, or PrEP users, the chronic or ultimate and sacrificial *swallowing* of power only allows for cruising to happen even more smoothly, without the interruptions that anxiety begets, or the practical putting on of the condom itself. The phantasmatic termination of death *qua* death reaches its zenith. For some, having swallowed the virus may function as a nano-technological connection to, if not the Father, then quite literally the state. In New York City, for instance, having full-blown AIDS can mean getting a roof over one's head, basic services, "and all this other stuff," perhaps in a way similar to some destitute men for whom prison at least guarantees a roof over one's head, food, sobriety, and masculine kinship.[27]

The naturalized body of the normative subject is, of course, a fantasy body that, in its translation from idealized image to a body in practice, also becomes queer—not just because queerness is precisely the condition of desire (in all of its oceanic excess and instability), but because bodies move and "make holes." And as they do, both normative and queer bodies (in this logic of non-coincidence, they

a sense of "being 'there' (*Da-Sein*)" and being " 'gone' (*Fort-Sein*)," which is at the root of all human experience (or the experience of all humans), in her remarks on Lacan's concept of *jouissance*. Ragland, *Essays on the Pleasures of Death*, 98.

26   Bollas, *Hysteria*, 166.

27   Maral Noshad Sharifi, "The Men Who Want AIDS—and How It Improved Their Lives," *Out*, August 8, 2013, http://www.out.com/news-opinion/2013/08/02/men-who-want-aids-bronx-new-york?page=0%2Co.

are one and the same) expose the body *tout court* as mere image animated by whatever tools the Subject can (re)signify it with. The digital cruising Subject, however, appropriates and reverses this botched translation, or trajectory, from idealized imagistic body to failed queer body-in-the-world vis-à-vis an inevitably heterosexual Symbolic logic. The dynamic now goes from an initially failed queer body, alienated from a symbolic system it desires but has no access to, unable to accede a normative mimicry (or confluence), repairing itself through the idealized imagistic body that the digital enables, or demands, and back to the body-fallen-short in the flesh (in the case that a fleshly body is produced at all). Since the digital cruiser seems to know, or dread, that the boy on the screen may be the product of a similar trajectory—a botched passing—enjoyment becomes more likely if the body of the Other remains a theoretical body ad infinitum. The best moment of love is thus no longer "when the boy leaves in the taxi," as Foucault once had it, but when the boy remains there and never arrives.[28] That way a confrontation with lack (there where there is nothing) is avoided. Enjoyment is produced through its very deflection.[29]

If the Other is so easily spoiled, such that it does not coincide with the phallic promises of its still and faceless image—its effigy—barebacking has emerged as a shortcut for fantasies of hermetic hetero-masculinity. There is, after all, something phallic about the Other who can, if not perfectly perform masculinity, at least annihilate it by the proxy of a virus. Barebacking may thus be not so much about the Subject's own body, but rather the body of a phallic Other who dares to bareback and must therefore be impenetrable to the virus or, at the very least, rendered impossibly destructive through its harbouring. But even that phantasmatic solution can be disarmed by its own practice. The casting of actual straight men into the fantasy of the self would, then, seem to guarantee a more

---

28   Michel Foucault, *Politics, Philosophy, Culture: Interviews and Other Writings, 1977–1984* (London and New York: Routledge, 1990), 297.

29   The pervert knows something about "that where there is nothing," he knows something of the female body's enigmas. We may liken these enigmas to the vagina, but also the anus, as well as the symbolic "nothing." Lucien Israël, *La Jouissance de L'hystérique* (Paris: Éditions Arcanes, 1996), 98. My translation.

sustainable solution, which can be achieved by the cross-dressing of *gay man*'s body for sexual purposes. I here make the confluence between the cross-dressing *gay man* and trans not as a flippant provocation, but as the theoretical culmination of the argument I have thus developed—that is, the idea of *gay man*'s desire for *gay man* being an existential misnomer that could be solved through his/her renaming. Which, I argue, is precisely what *gay man* might do when s/he barebacks.

## CROSS-DRESSING VIOLENCE:
## BAREBACKING AS SYMBOLIC DRAG

As described elsewhere,[30] I recently caught myself posting online ads in which I impersonate a husband looking for a "bull" to come over and play with my wife (performed by myself) while "I," the husband, am gone. Not only that. The bull is to borrow my wife in front of a webcam so that "I" can watch the act of cuckoldry remotely and record it. Since the wife will probably ask for the bull to wear a condom, the fantasy goes, I ask the bull to discreetly pull the condom off during sex, without her noticing it. It is true, a bull originally responds to an ad that says nothing about the cross-dressing condition of the wife, but also doesn't seem to mind when such details are revealed, in the third or fourth email exchanged between us. Such a bull must be hailed away from his original, and originally normative, trajectory, it seems, so he can still be contaminated by his original normative intentions when he comes over.

When the bull arrives, I am lying in bed as if trapped in this lacuna between a man I know, and who only exists in my remote impersonation of him (the husband), and a man I don't (the bull). I lie there, like a little lamb, letting the men carry out their plans. I feign oblivion and obedience. I, the figurative woman, desire nothing. I lend my body to the desire of the men, which they negotiated among themselves, in my apparent/assumed absence and the insignificance of what I want.

---

30   Semerene, "Playing Dead," 235–53.

The bull's ignorance of the fact that, in reality, the one being tricked is himself seems to hollow him out, enhancing his size, his weight, his force. By contrast, I become increasingly helpless and smaller. I need to give him an opportunity to seal the deal and take the condom off without my knowing it. For the condom to count as being off, its usage needs to be derailed mid-act. Except that the bull is the one who doesn't know. Or does he . . . but still? At the moment he begins pulling off the condom and sticking his penis back inside me, I turn around and ask where the condom is. I catch him red-handed. This is where my fantasy—co-scripted by the fact that at the time I am HIV-negative and not on PrEP—ends: with the disappearance of the condom, for which no one is willing to take responsibility.

Famously, in Lacan's playing with the Name-of-the-Father (*nom du père*) sound,[31] which fixes the Father's prohibitive function, he establishes that *les non-dupes errent* or "those who do not let themselves be caught in the symbolic deception/fiction and continue to believe their eyes are the ones who err most." *Les non-dupes errent* sounds, phonetically, like *le nom du père*, and it is most often translated along the lines of "the non-duped err." It can also be translated as "the non-duped wander (in circles)," or quite simply, "the non-duped cruise."[32]

Maud-Yeuse Thomas notes that for a regime that exerts control through the regulation of opposites (heterosexuality-homosexuality, *gay man–straight man*), the figure of the cross-dresser or the transvestite occupies the domain of the lie and of dupery: "The transvestite is the ultimate pariah, especially when he [*sic*] becomes undetectable." Thomas also associates the transvestite with the figure of the *flâneur*—the wandering around (in circles) of the non-duped, which Dean links to the analog gay cruising subject, and the "sexclub patron" in particular, "who readily loses himself in a stream of bodies and whose individuality thus consists in the disappearance

---

31    The Name-of-the-Father has to do with the restraints and laws that control desire with the help of the Symbolic.

32    Slavoj Žižek, "With or Without Passion? What's Wrong with Fundamentalism—Part I," http://www.lacan.com/zizpassion.htm.

of individuality."[33] Dean speaks here of a general "cruising ethos" that "conduces to this impersonalizing effect."[34]

The jump from gayness to T-girlhood (cross-dressing subjects assigned male at birth are largely referred to and refer to themselves as "T-girls" online) makes visible, even audible ("Hi hunny," "How are you babe?"), the strategy of sweetness and chivalry *straight man* uses to dress the hole-making violence (can we speak of a transmaterial barebacking that requires no flesh?) of the heterosexual sex act in some kind of love scene.[35] While the gay sex scene is often one of constraint and absence of chivalry in order to avoid any of the subjects being tainted as the more feminine object out of the two, the heterosexual sex scene forged here involves a kind of swindling, a drag of interests of another kind. As a T-girl, these men, unlike gay men, are quick to offer me things—a drink, a ride, cash, the best moment of my life, sperm, and even face pictures.

Their attempts at conveying sweetness and selflessness aim to reduce the feminine object lying before them to as weakened a state as possible in order to potentialize whatever it is that they do as sufficiently phallus-like. They err on the side of a hollow politeness that reiterates my role as literalized object and theirs as active agents, a position they hide behind a chivalry that, in the end, is its opposite. My consent will always be partial when compared to the pleasure they are sure to derive from it. And it is always a "they," which makes themselves present in the figure of my cuckold husband or in the slew of verifications that certain hook-up sites, such as Fabswingers in the United Kingdom or Wyylde in France, allow for: heterosexually identified men singing the praises of a T-girl's ass or blowjob skills, essentially pitching her to fellow comrades. Their strategy seems to reiterate the masculinist fantasy that the feminine position is one that is ultimately not that pleasurable (the woman is expected to resign her self to man's pleasure if he is sneaky

---

33    Cited in Maud-Yeuse Thomas, "Éthnologie du travesti(ssement)," *Miroir/Miroirs* 2, no. 1 (2014): 55. My translation.
34    Dean, *Unlimited Intimacy*, 36.
35    Thierry Schaffauser, "Drag Queen Feminism," *Miroir/Miroirs* 2, no. 1 (2014): 91. My translation.

enough to apparently fool her), and it is particularly evident when discussing if a condom will be used or not.

The majority of heterosexually identified men I meet online delegate that decision to the T-girl, as if only my body were vulnerable to disease. They tend to either claim it makes no difference for them or avow preferring one way or another (usually without it) but that they would be happy to do whatever as long as I (partially) consent to the sex act: "I don't care if I use one"; "I'll leave it up to you how rough you want it"; "I'm into rough sex, follow her rules of course"; "It is always up to the woman if she wants it bare or condoms"; "No rules here I follow yours!!"; "I'll satisfy your needs and desires"; "Condom or bare up to you but I do want to creampie that pussy all nite then cuddle up." Freud describes tenderness as a way of managing hostility, and he relates such a strategy to the relationship between mother and child, and married couples. In both cases, dressing violence with sweetness reveals the veneration of the person in the position of power, "their very deification" to be "opposed in the unconscious by an intense hostile tendency, so that, as we had expected, the situation of an ambivalent feeling is here realized."[36]

The adherence to violence is sometimes done through overt speech or through association to certain subcultures whose sartorial signs and other associations (S&M, leather, uniforms, gangbangs, slings) articulate the desire for violence so that the subject doesn't have to. In fact, the admission may even be welcome in that it mimics a supposedly masculine interest in aggression. Violence, that which touches the unprotected, is exposed as the guarantor that heterosexuality has taken place. The men replying to my online ads seeking to cast a bull to have sex with a wife, who turns out to be a T-girl, often utilize violent language as a way to convince the supposed husband that they should be chosen for the job: "would def take [her] Down"; "have a black belt in eating pussy"; "beat that pussy up in every way possible"; "experienced Dom here to ruin her"; "I will damage that white pussy"; "I'll put [her] in [her] place because

---

36    Freud, *Totem and Taboo*, 46.

I make the rules since I've got the Dick"; and "You could not handle what I have."[37]

Barebacking in a *gay man–gay man* arrangement appears, then, as the guarantor of heterosexual violence (violence as heterosexual) for those who cannot enjoy the violence of heterosexuality proper.[38] A virus could indeed ravage the body despite the quality of the phallic performance by the top, or "active" sexual partner. A lethal virus is naturally priapic. If the phallus fails, as it is wont to do once it's forced to perform, the failure of an undetectable virus to damage the body in the feminine position will never be found out, for even its alleged/apparent successful wrecking won't show its signs but in the future, if at all.

This fantasy of violence pays respect to a fantasy that nature will take its course; the achievement of the Other's performance (of masculinity) isn't even needed when in the end biology will take care of it. If there is a desire for shattering in bareback-aimed cruising, it is primarily a desire for the fantasized invincibility of the phallus to be made evident by not being attestable. By the time the subject knows if transmission has taken place, she will never be able to match the virus to the culprit. She alone will bear the effects of the anonymous act. Like a mother; the virus and the phallus, like gender: copies for which there are no originals.

AEbttmBoi from Barebackrt.com, for instance, writes on his profile that "BB [barebacking] is natural and i always BB now, Cock belongs in ass bare!" He then expresses his desire to "exploit" his "hole & throat by having it stretched, fucked, RAPED, & seeded (preferably by a group of UNCUT guys!)." His ultimate fantasy is a recurrent one in many barebacking accounts: "to be gangraped & breeded [sic] by enough guys to have my boicunt & mouth leaking

---

37  In Take1WildRide's profile on TSdating.com, he describes himself as a sucker for "passable young gorgeous girls" and feels compelled to explain the driving force behind his search in this way: "It's not so much your parts of body type as much your face [sic] I need a chick to release all this pent up aggression & rage." See http://www.tsdating.com/members/Take1WildRide/.

38  In my T-girl fantasy of cuckoldry I double down on guaranteeing heterosexual violence by managing to hail *straight man* into the scene and scripting it so that he threatens barebacking violence, so that barebacking is enacted—even if promptly aborted—as a threat.

nut. Use & verbally degrade this worthless CumSlut // Latinos a plus /." We can see signs of aggression the user associates with an impotence to guarantee the violence that the fantasy demands. A rape is desired not only by one, but by a group of men, potentialized by fantasies of virility attached to their race, the verbal reassurance that one is being degraded, and the visual confirmation of wreckage, as sperm flows out of his orifices like an ejaculating hemorrhage ("my boicunt & mouth leaking nut").[39] Ironically, the excreting of the sperm, often associated with breeding fantasies, functions as liquid evidence of the absence of breeding. The sperm has leaked out, not gone inside some kind of phantasmic womb. In this context, the excreted sperm gains what Arnaud Alessandrin describes as "the double movement" of vomiting in its queer "incapacity to swallow and incapacity to digest."[40]

Monique Schneider speaks of the belittlement of the desired object as a condition for one to approach it. We can see this belittlement in classic heterosexist masculinity, in which the reducing of the feminine object is a *sine qua non* (played up in porn, but stirring the sexual practice of everyday life): "A disdainful attitude constitutes a necessary subterfuge for the temptation to love, whether it is addressed to art or women, making oneself protected against the risk of losing."[41]

This belittlement apparatus creates a psychosomatic relationship between the symbolic violence of heterosexuality itself and the literal violence of a viral annihilation of the body. Barebacking can work as an underwriter for exacting difference through the latent/phantasmatic/imagistic violence of infection. This is true for subjects under the threat of sameness (the ruse of *gay man–gay man* equality in the equation of desire), in which a difference must be

---

39   See https://www.barebackrt.com/members/view.php?id=273460.

40   Arnaud Alessandrin, "Les Fluides comme médiateurs du dégoût: L'Exemple des corps trans," in *Miroir/Miroirs* 7, no. 2 (2016): 23. My translation.

41   Monique Schneider, "Freud et Le Combat Avec L'Artiste," in *L'Artiste et Le Psychanalyste*, ed. Joyce McDougall (Paris: Presses universitaires de France, 2008), 52, 53; my translation. Sylvia Payne sees the need to be pregnant in terms of the need to "have control over a feared object." Burton Lerner, Raymond Raskin, and Elizabeth Davis, "On the Need to Be Pregnant," *International Journal of Psychoanalysis* 48 (1967): 288–97.

found beyond ready-made genital difference, as in gay subjectivity more evidently, but not exclusively. Barebacking is fantasy material for heterosexuality as well. Even genitally locatable difference is always already under threat, as it is contingent on the fragility of repetition (of gender difference) and centred on the ever elusive phallus (the original *there where there is nothing*).

If the penis fails to mimic the invincibility of the phallus as if both were one, and we can bet that it will, we can at least count on the potential transferring of the virus as the "trick" that the active partner (man) harbours under his sleeve. Curiously, man's promise of the great phallus and delivering the mere penis mirrors the T-girl's own game of presenting seeming feminine lack and its accoutrements while hiding the penis, except that man knows the penis is there, and it is hers, which makes its revelation foreseeable and yearned. Horror, as such, is pre-emptively averted.

**REFERENCES**

Alessandrin, Arnaud. "Les Fluides Comme Médiateurs Du Dégoût: L'Exemple des Corps Trans." *Miroir/Miroirs* 7, no. 2 (2016): 15–31.

Bollas, Christopher. *Hysteria*. London and New York: Routledge, 2000.

Braunstein, Néstor. *La Jouissance, un concept Lacanien*. Paris: Erès, 2005.

Butler, Judith. *Bodies that Matter: On the Discursive Limits of "Sex."* London and New York: Routledge, 1993.

Dean, Tim. *Unlimited Intimacy: Reflections on the Subculture of Barebacking*. Chicago: University of Chicago Press, 2009.

Flugel, J.C. *The Psychology of Clothes*. London: Hogarth Press, 1930.

Foucault, Michel. *Politics, Philosophy, Culture: Interviews and Other Writings, 1977–1984*. London and New York: Routledge, 1990.

Freud, Sigmund. "Beyond the Pleasure Principle." In *The Standard Edition of the Complete Psychological Works of Sigmund Freud*, vol. 18, translated by J. Strachey. London: Hogarth Press, 1955.

———. *Totem and Taboo*. Translated by Abraham A. Brill. London: Empire Books, 2012.

Hollander, Anne. *Sex and Suits: The Evolution of Modern Dress*. New York: Knopf, 1994.

Israël, Lucien. *La Jouissance de l'hystérique*. Paris: Éditions Arcanes, 1996.

Leader, Darian. "Is Jouissance Really Such a Great Concept?" Paper presented at the public seminar of the Centre for Freudian Analysis and Research, London, UK, November 3, 2018.

Lerner, Burton, Raymond Raskin, and Elizabeth Davis. "On the Need to Be Pregnant." *International Journal of Psycho-Analysis* 48 (1967): 288–97.

Penny, James. *The World of Perversion: Psychoanalysis and the Impossible Absolute of Desire.* Albany: SUNY Press, 2006.

Preciado, Beatriz. *Testo Junkie: Sexe, drogue et biopolitique.* Paris: Grasset and Fasquelle, 2008.

Ragland, Ellie. *Essays on the Pleasures of Death: From Freud to Lacan.* London and New York: Routledge, 1994.

Richter, Gerhard. "Benjamin's Face: Defacing Fascism." In *Walter Benjamin and the Corpus of Autobiography.* Detroit: Wayne State University Press, 2002.

Schaffauser, Thierry. "Drag Queen Feminism." *Miroir/Miroirs* 2, no. 1 (2014): 91–93.

Schneider, Monique. "Freud et le combat avec l'artiste." In *L'Artiste et le psychanalyste*, edited by Joyce McDougall. Paris: Presses Universitaires de France, 2008.

Semerene, Diego. "Playing Dead: On Part-time Transvestism, Digital Semblance, and Drag Feminism." *Revista Periódicus* 5, no. 1 (2016): 235–53.

Sharifi, Maral Noshad. "The Men Who Want AIDS—and How It Improved Their Lives." *Out*, August 8, 2013. http://www.out.com/news-opinion/2013/08/02/men-who-want-aids-bronx-new-york?page=0%2Co.

Stockton, Kathryn Bond. *The Queer Child, or Growing Sideways in the Twentieth Century.* Durham, NC: Duke University Press, 2009.

Thomas, Maud-Yeuse. "Éthnologie du travesti(ssement)." *Miroir/Miroirs* 2, no. 1 (2014): 53–66.

CHAPTER 10

# RAW EDUCATION: PrEP AND THE ETHICS OF UPDATING SEXUAL EDUCATION

## Adam J. Greteman

*Queer culture already offers us some alternatives we need. We just have to learn how to recognize, how to value, and how to champion the queer cultural traditions that have come down to us.*[1]

Gayle Rubin concluded her landmark essay "Thinking Sex" by arguing, "those who consider themselves progressive need to examine their preconceptions, update their sexual educations, and acquaint themselves with the existence and operation of sexual hierarchy."[2] Decades later, such work continues to be necessary for progressives. Rubin, writing in the early 1980s, at the onset of what would become the AIDS crisis, recognized that

fear of AIDS has already affected sexual ideology. Just when homosexuals have had some success in throwing off the taint

---

1   David Halperin, *What Do Gay Men Want? An Essay on Sex, Risk, and Subjectivity* (Ann Arbor: University of Michigan Press, 2007), 10.

2   Gayle Rubin, "Thinking Sex: Notes for a Radical Theory of the Politics of Sexuality," in *Deviations: A Gayle Rubin Reader* (Durham, NC: Duke University Press, 2009), 181.

of mental disease, gay people find themselves metaphorically welded to an image of lethal physical deterioration. The syndrome, its peculiar qualities, and its transmissibility are being used to reinforce old fears that sexual activity, homosexuality, and promiscuity lead to disease and death.[3]

In what follows, I attempt to update thinking about our sexual education(s) by grappling with emerging understandings of and discourses on barebacking. HIV/AIDS, at the time of Rubin's writing, tragically illustrated a certain type of power over life, a power that disallowed queer life through forms of governmental and medical inaction along with homophobic disdain. Decades later, the powers impacting queer life have altered, due, in part, to technological and pharmacological advancements along with shifts in the political landscape, allowing some a place at the table.[4] There has been a certain reorientation in terms of how sexual minorities are viewed, for better and for worse. And there remains a need to explore the orienting devices of education—broadly understood—as they come to impact the possibilities of becoming queer. Barebacking may very well appear too perverse for education given the unease that still persists around discussions about homosexuality in the curriculum. However, as a queer subculture, barebacking provides educators with alternatives to envisioning education, sex, and more through its eroticizing of a virus and its replication of queerness. Pedagogically speaking, barebacking provides lessons at the limits of knowledge while pushing the limits of becoming a subject in the twenty-first century.[5]

As a philosopher of education, I enter this fray curious both about the ways emerging discourses around barebacking educate—what we learn from such scholarship—and about what barebacking can do to update our sexual education(s) in the twenty-first century—what we learn about medicine, technology, and health

---

3    Ibid., 170.

4    See Bruce Bawer, *A Place at the Table: The Gay Individual in American Society* (New York: Simon & Schuster, 1994).

5    See Adam J. Greteman, "Fashioning a Bareback Pedagogy: Towards a Theory of Risky (Sex) Education," *Sex Education* 13, suppl. 1 (2013): S20–S31.

education. However, this curiosity does not stop with learning, but extends to the ontological issues that arise as bodies come to matter through queer practices. Queers may have historically been denied or refused reproduction, but in a queer twist of fate they have embraced the replicative possibilities of a virus to create kinship and the perpetuation of queer practices. In an age of pre-exposure prophylaxis (PrEP) and the continued struggles people living with HIV/AIDS face globally, how does education grapple and move forward with shifting understandings of sexual practices and sexual subjects? As conditions have changed around HIV/AIDS, sex educations, and the inclusion of (some) understandings of marginal sexual identities in the curriculum, I ask: Does the figure of the barebacker provide ways to promote queerness that rubs raw the normative veneer of education through its promotion of raw sex? Queer emotions, of course, were rubbed raw during the AIDS crisis, orienting a generation of scholars and activists to ragefully articulate demands that shifted discourse and material realities of and for queer persons. Decades later, the re-emergence of raw sex rubs raw the emotions of respectability politics and the expert establishments that sought a certain control over the politics of queer life and sex. Those previous lessons were reproduced across educational venues, refusing to engage the resistant and fantastical practices of queers. Barebacking, then, disorients established sex education(s) centred on safety and the mitigation of risk. The education of barebacking, I argue, grapples with and unsettles political, medical, scientific, and educational advances by invoking the raw and provoking homonormative politics to grapple with queer sex that replicates itself through viral transmission.

Central to this work is the act of attending to the ways by which our sex education(s) have been oriented toward some forms of being and becoming human and away from others. Orientation matters, and, as Sara Ahmed has argued, "the concept of 'orientations' allows us to expose how life gets directed in some ways rather than others."[6] There is little question that (sex) education directs bodies,

---

6    Sara Ahmed, *Queer Phenomenology: Orientations, Objects, Others* (Durham, NC: Duke University Press, 2005), 21.

as teachers give directions implicitly and explicitly to students about a whole range of things. Debates within sex education grapple with what types of directions to give to students, and those debates illustrate how particular ways of living are or are not thinkable. Decades into a world that lives with the reality of HIV/AIDS, attending to the ways education—in and out of schools—has oriented our thinking toward particular types of being and becoming and away from others matters, and it matters greatly for addressing relationships between humans and the things humans encounter together. "Being oriented in different ways," Ahmed continues, "matters precisely insofar as such orientations shape what bodies do: it is not that the 'object' causes desire, but that in desiring certain objects *other things follow*."[7] Each of the forms of sex education(s) that pervade our world desires some object, be it abstinence from sex or comprehensive knowledge about sex, directing us to follow some paths and not others. They are lessons that implicate the work of reproduction and maintaining a particular type of "healthy" body. Barebacking, when brought into such conversations, challenges particular directions and opens up queer orientations toward sex educations that shift from reproduction toward replication. Barebacking may very well mimic reproductive sexuality through talk of "breeding," but inevitably its politics and ethics embrace replication—replication not of a living thing, but of a virus. There is no birth in such queer breeding, merely the transmission and replication of a virus.

My work here is not straightforward, and will probably fail to align itself with "mainstream" lines of thought on sex education(s). However, "queer orientations might be those that don't line up," as Ahmed argued, "which by seeing the world 'slantwise' allow other objects to come into view. A queer orientation might be one that does not overcome what is 'off line,' and hence *acts out of line with others*."[8] To take a queer orientation in education toward raw sex is less about approving or disapproving of particular sexual practices. Rather, it is to open up lines of thought and being that expose and

---

7    Ibid., 100 (emphasis in original).
8    Ibid., 107 (emphasis in original).

invent ways of encountering things in our world—both the human and the non-human—differently.

## PrEPARING EDUCATION AND IMMUNITY

Barebacking, in the first decade of the new millennium, was limited to, and pushed the limits of, queer sex. Eschewing identity politics in favour of eroticizing a virus, barebacking as a sexual practice refused the approved sex and health educations. Barebacking was seemingly a practice of resistance and a *cause célèbre* for queer intellectuals and activists, myself included. However, with the advent of Truvada, and its approval by the US Federal Drug Administration (FDA) in 2012 for use by adult HIV-negative individuals as a pre-exposure prophylaxis, barebacking became a less pathological, albeit still questioned, sexual practice.[9] It may be that such a move brought us into the "PrEP Moment" in the history of HIV/AIDS. In this transition from a transgressive sexual practice to a sexual practice made "safe(r)" via pharmaceuticals, queer sexual practices continue to illustrate the ongoing struggle for pleasure and becoming amidst the rise of pharmaco-power. As Tim Dean has noted, "via the expert technologies of PrEP, the long history of medicalizing homosexuality has embarked on a significant new phase."[10] Queer men, along with women, continue to face the bio-political demands for life, and these demands have become internalized. The advent of PrEP and its bio-political implications assist in further seeing the intimacy between the human and the non-human as the virus becomes eroticized, fetishized, and made to matter anew in the bodies of queer subjects. Once feared, the virus has become a gift, a form of kinship founded in and with a virus that once decimated (and continues to decimate) populations. The virus has similarly become a gift to Gilead Sciences, the bio-pharmaceutical company that manufactures Truvada, in that

---

9   In May 2018, as I was finalizing this chapter, the FDA approved the use of Truvada for at-risk adolescents. While I could not adequately address this new development in this chapter, future scholarship will hopefully address the implications of this on understanding adolescent sexual health and related issues.

10   Tim Dean, "Mediated Intimacies: Raw Sex, Truvada, and the Biopolitics of Chemoprophylaxis," *Sexualities* 18, no. 1–2 (2015): 228.

Truvada was one of the company's most profitable lines of business in 2015.[11] A queer task for education becomes engaging these changing realities, requiring that we reorient our connection to viruses for better and for worse. As Cris Mayo has asserted,

> Queering education and doing the kind of philosophy of education that is cheerfully queer may entail turning to tentative judgments and sideways forms of thinking and speaking, trying to use puzzles of invitation and challenge to get at difficulties of understanding among people, thinking through the problems associated with teaching and learning, and thinking more about the institutional structures that are turning energetic education into routines of testing and measurement.[12]

Queer men's health has, over the last four decades or so, become routine in some regards and complicated in others. While there are now recognized routines associated with the previously "universal" category of gay men, those routines are complicated by various forms of privilege rooted in one's race, class, gender expression, or geographic location, and which impact access to health care and information. Additionally, evolving forms of identification established within communities or created within public health, such as men who have sex with men (MSM), complicate who is addressed and recognized within public health and education campaigns. Within such complexities, queer men's health is defined, by and large, through testing, measurement, and prevention campaigns with different categories being addressed in different spaces and times. Queer men are taught—from quite a young age—about the importance of regular HIV testing by health campaigns, gay media, and sometimes mainstream media, along with other, often non-school-based curricula. Yet such campaigns are challenged by the

11    Jea Yu, "Gilead's 3 Most Profitable Lines of Business," *Investopedia*, March 6, 2016, http://www.investopedia.com/articles/active-trading/030616/gileads-3-most-profitable-lines-business-gild.asp.

12    Cris Mayo, "Philosophy of Education is Bent," *Studies in Philosophy and Education* 30, no. 5 (September 2011): 474.

diverse variety of queers, and by developing campaigns that specify and attend to this diversity. After all, if one cannot see oneself addressed by such lessons, one may very likely refuse or ignore them.

Amidst this complicated realm of queer men's health, it is necessary to develop broader understandings of queer male sexuality, as Eric Rofes has articulated quite persuasively. Rofes has argued that "the health of gay men ought to be conceptualized in an affirmative, holistic, politically imaginative fashion."[13] This conceptualization becomes ever more important as the languages around and of queerness change. It furthermore challenges writing about sexuality as its terms and identities shift in ways beyond the time of publication. While HIV/AIDS traumatized a particular generation, the continued use of crisis language may be holding back the reorientation of queer male subjectivity in ways that are not merely pathological or medicalized. After all, as David Halperin has noted,

> It is gay men themselves who have continued to define, and to redefine, the limits of safety through an ongoing history of sexual experimentation and mutual consultation, and who have thereby produced, over time, workable compromises and pragmatic solutions that balance safety and risk in proportions that have turned out to be both acceptable to a majority of gay men and successful in limiting the transmission of HIV.[14]

The medical and scientific communities have never fully embraced queer sexual practices, leaving it up to members of diverse perverse communities, in their ever-evolving milieus, to do this work on the ground. While education often prefers to draw upon expert discourses of accountability, it may be the case that we need to return to the ground where individuals in their cultural ethos are the experts of their becoming.[15]

---

13   Eric Rofes, *Reviving the Tribe: Regenerating Gay Men's Sexuality and Culture in the Ongoing Epidemic* (Binghamton, NY: Haworth Press, 1996), 227.

14   Halperin, *What Do Gay Men Want?*, 19.

15   Peter M. Taubman, *Teaching by Numbers: Deconstructing the Discourse of Standards and Accountability in Education* (London and New York: Routledge, 2009).

Within education, as Deborah Britzman has articulated, HIV exposed the uncertainties of knowledge and presented a variety of psychic consequences.[16] Education, writ large, along with sex education specifically, was challenged to grapple with such an epidemic and the subjects, particularly queer male subjects who were implicated as "at risk." HIV/AIDS made death visible along with, in the early period of the crisis, the disposability of queer populations. Schools freaked out in a variety of ways, seen most tragically in the treatment of Ryan White.[17] However, much has changed since the 1980s, such that, according to Rofes, by the mid-1990s there was a sense that a "Post-AIDS Moment" had been entered.[18] The post-AIDS moment, Rofes argued, occurred "when mainstream gay communities backed away from an energetic and narrow focus on HIV and began to integrate AIDS as an ongoing and unremarkable feature of community life."[19] This moment also illustrated that, while mainstream gay communities gained access to medications and other treatments to make living with HIV "manageable," communities with limited access continued to experience devastation. Living with HIV became manageable and chronic so that individuals with privilege and access could live "normal" lives and, arguably, take up the cause of gay marriage. It remains the case that HIV is manageable for those with access to medications, and it is a reality that barebacking may turn out to be a sexual practice connected to particular types of access. As Tim Dean has argued, questions about access and cost are important—pragmatic really—yet it remains the case that "broader ethical questions about expanding medicalization of sexuality—and about what it means to have our erotic lives mediated by pharmacology—remain under-examined."[20] We need

16  Deborah Britzman, "On Some Psychical Consequences of AIDS Education" in *Queer Theory in Education*, ed. William Pinar (Mahwah, NJ: Lawrence Erlbaum, 1998), 321–35.

17  See Catherine Lugg, *US Public Schools and the Politics of Queer Erasure* (New York: Palgrave Macmillan, 2015), 38–40.

18  Eric Rofes, *Thriving: Gay Men's Health in the 21st Century* (Self-published, CiteSeerX, 2007) http://citeseerx.ist.psu.edu/viewdoc/download?doi=10.1.1.694.2275&rep=r ep1&type=pdf.

19  Ibid., 33.

20  Dean, "Mediated Intimacies," 232.

a pluralistic way of addressing and examining the challenges and possibilities that HIV/AIDS raises for queer populations historically and contemporaneously.

HIV/AIDS defined the last decades of the twentieth century as it ravaged the ability of the body to defend itself against any number of infections and illnesses. In historicizing the immune system, Donna Haraway argued this system itself was "pre-eminently a twentieth century object . . . a map drawn to guide recognition and misrecognition of self and other in the dialectics of Western biopolitics."[21] Or "that the immune system is a plan for meaningful action to construct and maintain the boundaries for what may count as self and other in the crucial realms of the normal and the pathological."[22] HIV/AIDS, as it came to dominate the political, medical, scientific, moral, and educational discourses, created boundaries less at the level of "identity"—although identity played a role—than at the level of the immune system. Those with suppressed or weakened immune systems became society's pariahs. Individuals within "at risk" communities came to be defined by their immune systems as new language around "T-cell counts" and "viral load" became part of an emerging HIV/AIDS lexicon, and the immune system was made visible, particularly during the years in which Kaposi sarcoma ravaged bodies. Such visibility morphed with the advent of various pharmaceutical interventions that caused other physiological changes, from facial wasting to lipodystrophy. These visual cues may have changed somewhat as pharmaceuticals evolved, but they persist nonetheless, illustrating the centrality of the immune system in conceptualizing HIV/AIDS.

The immune system, in Donna Haraway's estimation, "is an elaborate icon for principal systems of symbolic and material 'difference' in late capitalism."[23] Early AIDS activists recognized this as they pushed against the FDA, the National Institutes of Health, and pharmaceutical companies, both for failing to address the urgent

---

21  Donna Haraway, "The Biopolitics of Postmodern Bodies: Constitutions of Self in Immune System Discourse," in *Biopolitics: A Reader*, eds. Timothy Campbell and Adam Sitze (Durham, NC: Duke University Press, 2013), 275.
22  Ibid.
23  Ibid., 276.

need for HIV/AIDS treatments and for profiting off those very needs. These needs have broadened. Pharmaceuticals have become a new market and a new way to discipline bodies. The barebacker's eroticization of a virus that impacted the immune system in early accounts was viewed as something pathological, and queer scholars have worked to depathologize barebacking. However, the practice of barebacking looks slightly different with the emergence of both post-exposure prophylaxis (PEP) and PrEP. The discourse has shifted, as has the nomenclature surrounding barebacking, such that "what used to be called *bareback*—and before that *unsafe sex*—is now described simply as *raw*."[24] However, as Tim Dean has argued,

> The idea of sex as raw, unmediated contact with another body or being is nothing more than a fantasy—albeit a powerful one—that responds to the intensively mediated conditions of modern existence. If our erotic lives were not so filtered through technology, pornography, pharmacology, and other forms of expertise, then perhaps the yearning for unmediated intimacy would not be so strong.[25]

Although raw sex might ascribe to such intimacies a certain "naturalness," this is questionable given the ways in which our bodies are in contact with all sorts of chemicals, technologies, and more in everyday life. "We live in a punk hyper-modernity," Paul Preciado[26] has argued, and "it is no longer about discovering the hidden truth in nature; it is about the necessity of specifying the cultural, political, and technological processes through which the body as artifact acquires a natural status."[27] Raw sex and its predecessor, barebacking, highlight the evolving forms of power on and over

---

24  Dean, "Mediated Intimacies," 225 (emphasis in original).

25  Ibid., 224.

26  Since the 2013 publication of the chapter cited here, Preciado has transitioned and changed their name to Paul.

27  Beatriz Preciado, "The Pharmaco-Pornographic Regime: Sex, Gender, and Subjectivity in the Age of Punk Capitalism," in *The Transgender Studies Reader*, 2nd ed., eds. Susan Stryker and Aren Aizura (London and New York: Routledge, 2013), 269.

life. Yet, in their perceived perversity, they illustrate that no sex can be natural in the pharmaco-pornographic era.

## BAREBACKING'S EDUCATION

Barebackers, as a subculture, have been positioned as expressing a desire for the transmission of HIV. The object of their attention is the virus—real or fantasized—as individuals seek to be "giftgivers" or "bugchasers."[28] Yet, following Ahmed's queer line of thought, we might instead recognize that barebackers, in desiring a virus and its related intimacies, open up other lines of thinking about and through sex, education, and living in the twenty-first century. These things are not easy—for some they may be provocative, for others perverse, and for still others perhaps passé—but they illustrate the changing terrain of sex, sexuality, pleasure, and the bio-political demands for life. Sex education(s) have a history of defining what is and is not considered healthy, and in doing so create particular hierarchies that discipline bodies and the things bodies encounter.

The phenomenon of barebacking illustrates shifting relations between living and dying in what Eric Rofes called a post-AIDS moment.[29] Post-AIDS not in the sense that we have gotten "past" AIDS, but that we are still "after" or "in search of" the virus's implications for living and dying in our increasingly networked worlds. Barebackers quite literally are "after" the virus, both born "after" the epidemic years in some cases and in search of transmission. Yet their perverse practices are not merely suicidal, since the advent of various medical treatments has made HIV/AIDS a manageable, albeit chronic, illness.[30] Rather, barebackers open up new lines of thought regarding living a queer life in the midst of changing conditions. And

---

28  The concept of bugchaser and giftgiver were brought to popular attention, in part, through an article by Gregory Freeman. See Freeman, "In Search of Death," *Rolling Stone*, February 6, 2003, https://web.archive.org/web/20080304003441/http://www.rollingstone.com/news/story/5939950/bug_chasers.

29  Rofes, *Thriving*, 33.

30  I use "perverse" here not in the pathological sense, but as a term that addresses sexualities that are not reproductive, which is not meant to imply they are immediately subversive.

such lines of thought matter in creating possibilities for maintaining queer projects amidst the ongoing normalization of LGBTQI+ identities. The scope of barebacking is unknown. The subculture is contested insofar as it is not a subculture that seeks political recognition and rights, nor are the lines around who is and is not within the subculture neatly drawn. Barebacking as a sexual practice and subculture has, as such, become a subject of significance within medical, psychological, political, and queer discourses. While seen as objectionable by some, as queerness has historically been seen in education, following queer sexual practices may well provide us with queer orientations to the body, pleasures, and forms and scenes of becoming. They may update our sex education(s) by treating the pleasures of replication and our relation to the viral as another line of thought wherein subjects come to be. Identity matters less than the presence of the virus, exposing sex education(s) to alternative ontological questions.

HIV/AIDS still suffers from what Paula Treichler, in the first decades of the crisis, called an epidemic of signification.[31] The discursive, material, and psychic challenges that HIV/AIDS raises persist in spite of, or perhaps due to, the evolving understandings of its implications for the health and well-being of individuals and communities. It continues to be significant in the world, but its significance is contested in various ways due to geography, access, and various moralistic discourses. It has become manageable for some populations who have access to health care and social services, while for others it remains unmanageable. By way of various political, scientific, and medical advancements, we have gotten "past" the genocidal implications of the 1980s and early 1990s. However, HIV/AIDS still greatly impacts global and marginalized populations that lack access to these new and emerging pharmacological and biotechnological materials. What HIV/AIDS signifies is varied and contested; while this poses significant challenges, it is nonetheless central to navigating a sexual subculture that is often viewed as "out of line" with contemporary educational lessons on "safer sex"

---

31    Paula Treichler, "AIDS, Homophobia, and Biomedical Discourse: An Epidemic of Signification," *Cultural Studies* 1, no. 3 (1987): 263–305.

and healthy living. We cannot think of barebacking without HIV/ AIDS, even in the age of such medical advancements as PEP and PrEP, and forms of sexual education(s) cannot ignore its changing faces, realities, and associated practices.

Given that HIV/AIDS and barebacking are orientated toward each other, they make some things possible and others impossible. The subject of barebacking within educational discourses is limited, but it is emerging in the ongoing work of updating our sexual educations. Eric Rofes presciently addressed barebacking in the early 2000s through engaging the work of sexual-health campaigns, arguing, "not only did safe-sex campaigns function to create a hegemonic view of 'acceptable' gay male sexual activity, but these health promotion campaigns may have also included elements that functioned as triggers for resistance."[32] Such resistance—in the form of sex without condoms—raised serious questions about the hetero- and homonormative politics that drove educational ideas and campaigns about safety and safe(r) sexual practices. "Does an appeal to safety and social responsibility as central to these campaigns," Rofes asked, "actually spark a counter response from many gay men, especially those gay men who overtly adopt renegade identities and subcultural norms?"[33] Since such renegade realities have been established, there remains a need within education to question its own logics about safety, health, and sexual subjectivity. In orienting education toward safety and health discourses focused on rational messages, a queer sexual subculture emerged that now exposes the orienting device that education was and still is. Within sex education(s), we can now question how the move from external prophylaxis (condoms) to internalized prophylaxis (PrEP) challenges education's understandings of safe or safer sex and reinserts penetrative sex as an "approved" practice—if, of course, accompanied with a daily dose of Truvada. However, the thing itself—be it a condom or a pill—is not the focus. Both require a certain level of rational action, capacity for choice, and the ability to access either or both. Rather,

---

32  Eric Rofes, *A Radical Rethinking of Sexuality and Schooling: Status Quo or Status Queer?* (Lanham, MD: Rowman & Littlefield, 2005), 128.

33  Ibid.

what they point toward or open up is of significant importance. The "pill" reorients us to contemplate the internalization of "protection" and further complicates barebacking—a subculture that emerged, as Rofes noted, in response to a particular time: a time before PrEP.

Queer scholars, notably Tim Dean, Leo Bersani, and David Halperin, have taken up Rofes's questions in various ways.[34] Each of them, grounded in different strands of queer theory—Bersani utilizing psychoanalysis, Halperin invoking Foucault, Dean engaging anthropology and psychoanalysis—investigated gay male subjectivity and barebackers' perverse (in the best sense of the word) responses to contemporary sexual politics, ethics, and education(s). The education(s) of barebackers were ones that had come to operate, quite literally, at the limits, since they refuted "best practices" of safe(r) sex to establish alternative models—of kinship, resistant politics, and temporality. They challenged mainstream gay and straight cultures while mimicking the language of reproduction. These challenges sought to expose changing norms and open up alternative modes of becoming queer in the world. The human may very well seek protection, produced through discourses of risk management, but the queer practice eroticizing a virus opens up—through rather perverse actions—new ways of becoming.[35] As I have argued in an earlier essay, barebackers were implicated in creating ways to fashion the self, albeit a very queer self with unknown ontological consequences for queer culture.[36] "Queer culture," as Halperin reminds us in the epigraph to this chapter, "already offers us some alternatives we need. We just have to learn how to recognize, how to value, and how to champion the queer cultural traditions that have come down to us."[37] The challenge here is that we live in the midst of the histories of sexuality and are seeing advancements—most notably in the form of PrEP—in

---

34  Tim Dean, *Unlimited Intimacy: Reflections on the Subculture of Barebacking* (Chicago: University of Chicago Press, 2009); Leo Bersani and Adam Phillips, *Intimacies* (Chicago: University of Chicago Press, 2008); Halperin, *What Do Gay Men Want?*

35  See Mel Chen and Dana Luciano, eds.,"Queer Inhumanisms," *GLQ: A Journal of Lesbian and Gay Studies* 21, nos. 2–3 (2015).

36  Greteman, "Fashioning a Bareback Pedagogy."

37  Halperin, *What Do Gay Men Want?*, 10.

how sexual practices operate, are disciplined, and are understood. If barebacking is now simultaneously both a historical and a still present part of queer culture, we have to come to recognize and encounter the pedagogical possibilities such a culture provides and opens up. In the ever-changing landscape of sex and sexual cultures, it is vital that education continue to update its work in cultivating the politics of and for queer life—a project at which it has woefully failed, favouring instead a politics that engages the mere protection of queers. Can we reorient sex education so that it helps queers thrive despite the continued homophobic violence? Can the replicative politics of bareback sex intervene in the work of normalization to promote queer forms of enjoyment?

## EDUCATION AT THE LIMITS

Queer work in education cannot simply rely on the work of identity, despite the political salience and necessity of identity politics at times. Identity matters, of course, but so do the ways in which such identities come into presence through various orienting devices. The shift to normativity over the last several decades, Halperin has argued, aimed "to distract straight people from everything about gay culture that might make them feel uncomfortable with it, suspicious of it, or excluded from it, and to get them to sympathize instead with our political (and therefore less viscerally upsetting) demands for equal treatment, social recognition, and procedural justice."[38] While LGBTQI+ identities have gained certain levels of acceptance and recognition, serious challenges remain when it comes to such a liberal project and its successes, particularly as it relates to sex, which numerous scholars have noted has become strangely absent from queer theoretical scholarship, including educational scholarship. "Sex remains a sticking point—including," Dean suggested, "for the academic discipline of queer theory, which often seems more comfortable discussing multicultural identities and their overlapping vectors of oppression than it is in confronting the libidinal investments of those constituencies the discipline osten-

---

38    Ibid., 5.

sibly represents."[39] To update our sexual educations, which Rubin has argued is necessary, requires attending to the role of sex—in other words, that we think sex, even at its limits, even in education.

Jen Gilbert has argued that "sexuality will push education to its limit, and education, despite this debt, will try to limit sexuality."[40] Education, as a broadly conservative enterprise, seeks to orient students toward particular ways of being and acting. Education as an orienting device limits what counts as sex education proper—those curricular possibilities within its institutional purview. Discourses around barebacking, by and large, seek to limit its practice, most often by attending to rational and heavily cognitive understandings of sex that fail to account for the non-rational, even at times irrational, unreasonable demands of sexuality. Barebacking, brought into existence as a distinct practice and subculture in the late 1990s, pushes us to see how our own limits are being exposed and redirected elsewhere.[41] Barebacking disorients us, and that is not a bad thing as it exposes the ways in which we have been oriented. After all, as Gilbert argued, the fates of sexuality and education are intertwined, and as such emerging sexual practices and subcultures invariably come to matter in exposing the work of education and its limits. The history of sex education is fraught, tied to eugenics and other hygienic movements.[42] Yet there remains a need to push for broader and more expansive understandings of sexuality and education's role in widening those possibilities.

Jonathan Silin thought as much, arguing, "the curriculum has too often become an injunction to desist rather than an invitation

---

39   Dean, "Mediated Intimacies," 226.

40   Jen Gilbert, *Sexuality in School: The Limits of Education* (Minneapolis: University of Minnesota Press, 2014), x.

41   The educations of barebacking are primarily seen and explored through pornography. Pornography, as a medium, has been important to various engagements with barebacking. See Dean, *Unlimited Intimacy*, particularly chapter 2: "Representing Raw Sex"; Stuart Scott, "The Condomlessness of Bareback Sex: Responses to the Unrepresentability of HIV in Treasure Island Media's Plantin' Seed and Slammed," Sexualities 18, nos. 1–2 (2015): 210–23.

42   Jonathan Zimmerman, *Too Hot to Handle: A Global History of Sex Education* (Princeton, NJ: Princeton University Press, 2015).

to explore life worlds."[43] There has arguably been a net gain for LG-BTQI+ persons' civil and social rights over the past few decades in the Global North/West.[44] We are seeing, as well, a backlash against such gains. LGBTQI+ persons may have achieved access to the civil order, but there persists resistance to such civility and the rights attributed to civil populations. This resistance illustrates the continued interest in and demand for pushing against the ongoing processes of normalization and the continued invention of ways of being in the space of ever-changing historical conditions. I think very broadly that queer theory—if it is to remain present in education—has an obligation to carefully attend to those perverse practices that emerge and the challenges of being considered a "perverse" subject that disrupts productive and reproductive understandings of becoming a subject.[45] Barebacking raises questions, quite literally, about coming into presence and the carrying on of queer subcultures. As a subculture, it operates at certain limits, but in doing so allows us to see alternative ways of being in the world. As a phenomenon and a practice, it operates in our current moment as a figure that raises ontological questions. Sex education(s) have historically taken up an epistemological project attending to the need to know about sex. However, if ontology on a very basic level asks questions about the nature of being, barebacking teaches us ways to be(come) queer in the twenty-first century that attend to our relationship to the viral in surprisingly (generative?) ways.

This is a shift toward articulating and thinking through ontological vulnerabilities in our sex education(s). This involves moving away from a sole focus on biological vulnerability to the processes and practices that impact how human life unfolds in all its complexities and paradoxes. As Eric Santer has argued,

---

43  Jonathan Silin, *Sex, Death, and the Education of Children: Our Passion for Ignorance in the Age of AIDS* (New York: Teachers College Press, 1995), 49.

44  For a nice overview of these changes and challenges in education, see Cris Mayo, *LGBTQ Youth and Education: Policies and Practices* (New York: Teachers College Press, 2013).

45  See Adam J. Greteman, "Queer Educations: Pondering Perverse Pedagogy," *Thresholds in Education* 39, no. 1 (2016): 44–56.

we could say that the precariousness, the fragility—the "nudity"—of biological life becomes potentiated, amplified by way of exposure to the radical contingency of the forms of life that constitute the space of meaning within which human life unfolds.[46]

Limits enter here again—both as that which we need to recognize as being imposed on us by any variety of institutions and discourses, and as an opportunity to experiment with ways of moving beyond them. Life unfolds against and because of the limits imposed on it. As conditions have changed around HIV/AIDS, sex education, and the inclusion of (some) queers in the curriculum, the figure of the barebacker provides ways to investigate queerness that rub raw the conception of human life imagined by educational discourses to engage the non-human, the viral, and its impact in how subjects come to be seen, recognized, and understood. We can live with the virus, eroticize it, fantasize about it, and resignify it to create and expose new ways of encountering and being in the world.

Education has been oriented by various political, economic, moral, and theological discourses, and it has disciplined subjects to do, think, and act in a variety of specific ways in relation to the state and civil society. Queer scholarship has illustrated and exposed the homophobic logics that had come to discipline queers in the hallways. This work necessarily pushed against such disciplinary logics. However, disciplinary mechanisms of control have shifted. "In disciplinary society, technologies of subjectivization controlled the body externally," argues Preciado.[47] Sex education born out of the HIV/AIDS epidemic disciplined sexualities through external prophylaxis (e.g., condoms) and demands for abstinence. Sex without risk may not exist, but donning a rubber, so the story went, was the safer route as queer male subjectivities were disciplined in a search for respectability. Yet, as Preciado points out, in "a pharmacopornographic society, the

---

46    Eric Santer, *The Royal Remains: The People's Two Bodies and the Endgames of Sovereignty* (Chicago: University of Chicago Press, 2011), 5–6.

47    Paul Preciado, *Testo Junkie: Sex, Drugs, and Biopolitics in the Pharmacopornographic Era* (New York: Feminist Press, 2013), 78.

technologies become part of the body: they dissolve into it."[48] Power, as such, operates less at the external level, and instead "acts through molecules that incorporate themselves into our immune system."[49] In our "PrEP Moment," we ingest Truvada, a combination of various chemical substances that, when taken daily, is internalized by our immune systems and becomes part of our very being. These conditions challenge education, which has yet to adequately grapple with the manner by which these molecules have come to impact students— often through other pharmaceutical products (such as Ritalin). In reorienting our sex education(s), the attention to putting (or not putting) drugs in bodies moves us toward the forms of being and becoming that are created with and by the pharmacological. This is for the better and for the worse, as Santer reminds us:

> Because for human beings the enjoyment of life and goods is always intertwined with processes and procedures of symbolic entitlement or investiture, the very value of human life—what makes life worth living, what causes it to matter—is subject to enormous fluctuation.[50]

To update our sex education(s) requires attention to, and the ability to take risks around, such fluctuations, as well as an attention to the possibilities of enjoyment that extend beyond the given norms to create new ways of mattering in and for the world.

## CONCLUSION

Education, given its history of disciplining subjects and impacting the politics of everyday life, plays a role in thinking about and through contemporary conditions and the changing ways life, sex, and pedagogies intersect. Updating our sex educations and engaging the ever-changing understandings, technologies, and politics around AIDS are no simple tasks. It is an ongoing project that at-

---

48    Ibid.
49    Ibid.
50    Santer, *The Royal Remains*, xx.

tends to the desire for justice and the possibilities of enjoyment for queer bodies. The emergence of a subculture that has disoriented particular understandings of safer sex and "health" challenges us not to simply repathologize queer sexuality, but to address the ways in which such desires open up new lines of thought regarding being. However, as Britzman argued almost two decades ago,

> even as we attempt to offer less damaging information and ready ourselves to rethink current representations of the virus, its global trajectory, medical interventions, at-risk bodily practices, and community campaigns, we also know those appeals to a rational, cohesive, and unitary subject in the name of toleration, role models, and the affirmation of and reliance on identity return the damage.[51]

While Britzman engaged the psychic consequences of AIDS—through the work of the ego—the advent of bareback sex and PrEP asks that we attend to our internalization of pharmaceuticals and the dissolution of substances to protect our immune systems. The psychic and the pharmaceutical come head to head in grappling with and reorienting our ways of living amidst and with AIDS. The continued appeals to rationality—including the rationalized ingestion of medication—and hysteria that emerge around queer sexual practices illustrate the continued need to update our sex education(s) and engage the ways we are oriented and continue to orient discussions.

HIV/AIDS may not be an object that sex education will ever direct students toward—after all, health prevention campaigns direct us away from transmission, and treatments seek to minimize viral replication to produce humans in particular ways. Yet the virus is an object that individuals are currently oriented toward in various ways. "Orientations toward sexual objects affect other things that we do, such that different orientations, different ways of directing one's desires, means inhabiting different worlds."[52] Over the last several decades, the different worlds of queerness have been

---

51    Britzman, "On Some Psychical Consequences of AIDS Education," 321–22.
52    Ahmed, *Queer Phenomenology*, 68.

minimized through various means. As Sarah Schulman illustrated, AIDS itself contributed to the gentrification of San Francisco and New York City. As gay men died lacking particular rights, their empty apartments opened up real estate developments in previously rent-controlled areas.[53] Similarly, Samuel Delany poignantly historicized the devastation of queer worlds brought about by the Times Square renovations of the 1990s, as spaces for interracial, inter-class, and intergenerational relations were cleaned up.[54] The external worlds that queers inhabited—particularly for sex—have tragically declined as such spaces become mediated by social technologies (dating apps for instance). Queer worlds have been internalized, privatized, and hidden from the respectable mainstream. Yet barebackers in their queer and complicated ways illustrate an orientation to the world, its pharmaceuticals and their consumption, that continue a rather queer and non-normative project and may update our sex education(s) to do different work that centres on becoming through replication's queer possibilities.

## REFERENCES

Ahmed, Sara. *Queer Phenomenology: Orientations, Objects, Others.* Durham, NC: Duke University Press, 2005.

Bawer, Bruce. *A Place at the Table: The Gay Individual in American Society.* New York: Simon & Schuster, 1994.

Bersani, Leo, and Adam Phillips. *Intimacies.* Chicago: University of Chicago Press, 2008.

Britzman, Deborah. "On Some Psychical Consequences of AIDS Education." In *Queer Theory in Education*, edited by William Pinar, 265–77. Mahwah, NJ: Lawrence Erlbaum, 1998.

Chen, Mel Y., and Dana Luciano. "Queer Inhumanisms." *GLQ: A Journal of Lesbian and Gay Studies* 21, nos. 2–3 (January 2019): 183–222.

Dean, Tim. "Mediated Intimacies: Raw Sex, Truvada, and the Biopolitics of Chemoprophylaxis." *Sexualities* 18, nos. 1–2 (April 2015): 224–46.

———. *Unlimited Intimacy: Reflections on the Subculture of Barebacking.* Chicago: University of Chicago Press, 2009.

---

53  Sarah Schulman, *The Gentrification of the Mind: Witness to a Lost Imagination* (Berkeley: University of California Press, 2012).

54  Samuel Delany, *Times Square Red, Times Square Blue* (New York: NYU Press, 1999).

Delany, Samuel. *Times Square Red, Times Square Blue*. New York: New York University Press, 1999.

Foucault, Michel. "What Is Enlightenment?" In *The Foucault Reader*, edited by Paul Rabinow, translated by Catherine Porter, 32–50. New York: Pantheon Books, 1984.

Freeman, Gregory. "Bug Chasers: The Men Who Long to Be HIV+." *Rolling Stone*, February 6, 2003. https://web.archive.org/web/20080304003441/http://www.rollingstone.com/news/story/5939950/bug_chasers.

Gilbert, Jen. *Sexuality in School: The Limits of Education*. Minneapolis: University of Minnesota Press, 2014.

Greteman, Adam J. "Fashioning a Bareback Pedagogy: Towards a Theory of Risky (Sex) Education." Supplement, *Sex Education* 13, no. 1 (February 2013): S20–S31.

——. "Queer Educations: Pondering Perverse Pedagogy." *Thresholds in Education* 39, no. 1 (2016): 44–56.

Halperin, David. *What Do Gay Men Want? An Essay on Sex, Risk, and Subjectivity*. Ann Arbor: University of Michigan Press, 2007.

Haraway, Donna. "The Biopolitics of Postmodern Bodies: Constitutions of Self in Immune System Discourse." In *Biopolitics: A Reader*, edited by Timothy Campbell and Adam Sitze, 274–309. Durham, NC: Duke University Press, 2013.

Lugg, Catherine. *US Public Schools and the Politics of Queer Erasure*. New York: Palgrave Macmillan, 2015.

Mayo, Cris. *LGBTQ Youth and Education: Policies and Practices*. New York: Teachers College Press, 2013.

——. "Philosophy of Education Is Bent." *Studies in Philosophy and Education* 30, no. 5 (September 2011): 471–76.

Preciado, Beatriz. "The Pharmaco-Pornographic Regime: Sex, Gender, and Subjectivity in the Age of Punk Capitalism." In *The Transgender Studies Reader* (2nd ed.), edited by Susan Stryker and Aren Aizura, 266–77. London and New York: Routledge, 2013.

Preciado, Paul. *Testo Junkie: Sex, Drugs, and Biopolitics in the Pharmapornographic Era*. New York: Feminist Press, 2013.

Rofes, Eric. *A Radical Rethinking of Sexuality and Schooling: Status Quo or Status Queer?* Lanham, MD: Rowman & Littlefield, 2005.

——. *Reviving the Tribe: Regenerating Gay Men's Sexuality and Culture in the Ongoing Epidemic*. Binghamton, NY: Haworth Press, 1996.

——. *Thriving: Gay Men's Health in the 21st Century*. Self-published, CiteSeerX, 2007. http://citeseerx.ist.psu.edu/viewdoc/download?doi=10.1.1.694.2275&rep=rep1&type=pdf.

Rubin, Gayle. "Thinking Sex: Notes for a Radical Theory of the Politics of Sexuality." In *Deviations: A Gayle Rubin Reader*, 137–81. Durham, NC: Duke University Press, 2009.

Santer, Eric. *The Royal Remains: The People's Two Bodies and the Endgames of Sovereignty*. Chicago: University of Chicago Press, 2011.

Schulman, Sarah. *The Gentrification of the Mind: Witness to a Lost Imagination*. Berkeley: University of California Press, 2012.

Scott, Stuart. "The Condomlessness of Bareback Sex: Responses to the Unrepresentability of HIV in Treasure Island Media's *Plantin' Seed* and *Slammed*." *Sexualities* 18, nos. 1–2 (April 2015): 210–23.

Silin, Jonathan G. *Sex, Death, and the Education of Children: Our Passion for Ignorance in the Age of AIDS*. New York: Teachers College Press, 1995.

Taubman, Peter. *Teach by Numbers: Deconstructing the Discourse of Standards and Accountability in Education*. London and New York: Routledge, 2009.

Treichler, Paula. "AIDS, Homophobia, and Biomedical Discourse: An Epidemic of Signification." *Cultural Studies* 1, no. 3 (October 1987): 263–305.

Yu, Jea. "Gilead's 3 Most Profitable Lines of Business." *Investopedia*, March 6, 2016. http://www.investopedia.com/articles/active-trading/030616/gileads-3-most-profitable-lines-business-gild.asp.

Zimmerman, Jonathan. *Too Hot to Handle: A Global History of Sex Education*. Princeton, NJ: Princeton University Press, 2015.

CHAPTER 11

# MERELY BAREBACKING

## Christien Garcia

I t's just sex.

That's not a phrase you hear tossed around a lot in cultural studies circles, even if some of its practitioners may have harboured the sentiment on occasion. Indeed, one of the overarching theses of sexuality and queer studies is that sex is never *just* sex, that sex is always cultural, social, economical. Or, as Judith Butler argues in "Merely Cultural," sexuality cannot be understood as merely an afterthought of the "real" business of politics.[1] In borrowing from Butler's title, this piece shares with her a preoccupation with affirming the validity of sexuality and sex as frameworks of analysis, but ultimately my use of the term "merely" is very different. Butler's ironic use of the adverb evokes the disparagement of what is "merely" cultural by certain (Marxist) segments of leftist political debate. Her piece seeks to undo this "mereness" insofar as she challenges the tendency to see culture as ancillary to politics. My objective, however, is to leave the mereness of sex in place. My argument is that by framing "merely" as a formal and textual means in and of itself—rather than as a deficit

---

1    Judith Butler, "Merely Cultural," *Social Text* 52–53 (Autumn–Winter 1997): 265–77.

that must be corrected—it becomes possible to think about sex outside a question of latent potentiality. Playing off of the expression "it's just sex," the aim of this piece is to consider seriously the impulse not to think about sex as more than itself. The intention is not to belittle sex's significance (social, subjective, political, or otherwise), but rather to consider the forms sex takes that cannot withstand the labour of more.

Since barebacking and bareback porn, in particular, have been the subject of much impassioned, contentious, and (according to some) overblown debate, it is perhaps the perfect context in which to read against the grain for the it's-just-sex-ness of sex. As my discussion of the pornographer Paul Morris shows, barebacking has sometimes been the context for reading sex as a basis of a subversive queer politics or in terms of "its promise of utopian potentiality," which is how Susanna Paasonen describes it in her interview with Morris published in GLQ.[2] The problem I see with the language of radical queer potentiality is that it implies that sex is somehow valuable for something "greater" than itself. Specifically, it reinforces the idea that sex must be justified in terms of value as defined by social discourse, and in terms of its ability to speak a truer version of ourselves than we can. A problem arises in the discussion of the queer potentiality of certain sex acts. How do we draw the line between utopian visioning and the construction of disciplinary or moral hierarchies between different sexual practices?

Discussing what she terms a "sex critical" framework, Lisa Downing has recently critiqued the tendency to evaluate sexual activity as either negative or positive from a social standpoint. Downing warns that the appraisal of specific sex acts for their liberatory potential risks buying too freely into the repressive hypothesis that Michel Foucault so devastatingly critiques.[3] The risk is that the emphasis on the way certain sex acts might represent the subversive or utopian aspirations of a particular subculture contributes to the "specification

2    Paul Morris and Susanna Paasonen, "Risk and Utopia: A Dialogue on Pornography," *GLQ: A Journal of Lesbian and Gay Studies* 20, no. 3 (2014): 237.

3    Lisa Downing, "Safewording! Kinkphobia and Gender Normativity in *Fifty Shades of Grey*," *Psychology & Sexuality* 4, no. 1 (2013): 92–102.

of individuals,"[4] whereby practice becomes the basis of identity, or as Downing puts it "*doing* becomes a matter of *being*."[5] The question becomes whether the positive (as well as negative) assessment of barebacking *in comparison with other sex practices* goes hand in hand with the classificatory apparatus of "sexuality," thus "contribut[ing] to constraints on social subjects to perform assigned identities, and to invest in the medical, psychological meaningfulness of those identities."[6] Indeed, my suggestion is just this: that the establishment of barebacking's significance as a queer foil to the restrictive confines of normative gay sex ultimately feeds the disciplinary production of sexual identity. For Morris, the potential of bareback porn lies in its ability to cut through the manipulative effects of the dominant, risk-averse sexual culture, to reveal something of the rawness of queer desire. But as others have argued, the queerness of sex is not a question of the authentic expression of queer subjects, but rather the cleavages it forms within the disciplinary regimes that produce the very idea of authentic selfhood. Reading sex as something that has the potential to repair social, subjective, and political inadequacies is also its potential erasure insofar as the meanings of sex are not translatable in the disciplinary terms of sex's cultural significance and subjective intelligibility. For this reason, my emphasis is on reading sex acts, not as expression, but as the forms desire takes that don't measure up under the discursive apparatus of sexual identity.

In resisting the labour of more, this chapter draws from a recent flourish of writing on the recessive and the minor. Anne-Lise Fran-çois, for example, proposes "a theory of recessive action,"[7] by which she reads literature in terms of that which "cannot withstand the work of articulation."[8] And in the arena of film studies, Eugenie Brinkema has recently advanced a "radical formalism" that reads

---

4    Michel Foucault quoted in Downing, "Safewording!," 97.
5    Ibid.
6    Lisa Downing, "What Is 'Sex Critical' and Why Should We Care about It?" *Sex Critical: Musings of a Curmudgeonly Sexuality Studies Scholar*, July 27, 2012, http://sexcritical.co.uk/2012/07/27/what-is-sex-critical-and-why-should-we-care-about-it/.
7    Anne-Lise François, *Open Secrets: The Literature of Uncounted Experience* (Stanford, CA: Stanford University Press, 2008), 1.
8    Ibid., 225.

cinematic form less as a code that must be analytically mined than as an "insistent exteriority" that refuses the interpretive imperative that we read in order to affirm something *in* or *for* the reader.[9] Although the present text relies on a psychoanalytic conception of desire, which in many respects differs from Brinkema's idea of "a subjectless affect,"[10] her work is nonetheless instructive in the way it conceptualizes the imbrication of formalism and textuality as a means of reading outside the expressivity hypothesis. For my own part, this link between form and text is centred on the adverbial nature of the terms "merely" and "just." In particular, it is the fecundity between slightness and absoluteness that is implicit in these terms that interests me. I argue that an analysis of sex can be thought of as an attempt to grapple with something that is, in both senses, *barely* there—fully exposed even in its insignificance. Through the concept of mereness, I read porn not as something waiting for its value to be made clear, but as already fully formed even in its inconsequence as a basis for social meaning.

I begin, in Part 1, with a discussion of why an ethnographic approach to reading pornography is an inadequate basis through which to form notions of authentic queerness. This is followed by a reflection on how the adverbial nature of terms like "just" and "mere" might help offer a reading of sex that is less influenced by expectation and becoming. Part 2, a close reading of Morris's commentary on the cinematic language of queer sex, attempts to put this adverbial reading into practice. Focusing on the rhythms, shapes, and durations of acts, I read his reading against the grain—not as a lexicon of queer identity or the promise of signification, but as the *mere* form desire takes.

## PART 1

Paul Morris has been one of the key figures in the critical analysis of bareback sex in gay pornography. The reclusive yet charismatic

---

9    Eugenie Brinkema, *The Forms of the Affects* (Durham, NC: Duke University Press, 2014), 37, 20.

10    Ibid., 45.

figure behind Treasure Island Media (TIM)—the studio commonly regarded as one of the first to explicitly and unapologetically reject the use of condoms in its films—has garnered significant attention from those interested in the pornography and subculture of gay male bareback sex.[11] Much of this writing focuses on the documentary and ethnographic nature of TIM porn. Morris himself has commented at length on the distinction between the ethnographic nature of his pornography and the sanitized "sexworlds"[12] of the pornographic mainstream.[13] "Danger, accident and specificity in porn insofar as they are honestly depicted (that is to say, documentary)," Morris writes, "enhance the possibility of a more complex, demanding and therefore productive relationship to power."[14] What Morris calls the "political basis of pornography"[15] rests in its ability to document queer sex lives as they really are, rather than reproducing culturally idealized and institutionally sanctioned ways of fucking.[16]

---

11    See Tim Dean, *Unlimited Intimacy: Reflections on the Subculture of Barebacking* (Chicago: University of Chicago Press, 2009). Dean discusses Morris's films and writing at length, especially in chapters 1 and 2. See also Lee Edelman, "Unbecoming," in *Post/Porn/Politics: Queer-feminist Perspective on the Politics of Porn Performance and Sex-work as Culture Production*, ed. Tim Stüttgen (Berlin: b_books, 2009); and João Florêncio, "Breeding Futures: Masculinity and the Ethics of CUMmunion in Treasure Island Media's *Viral Loads*," *Porn Studies* 5, no. 3 (2018): 271–85.

12    Paul Morris, "No Limits: Necessary Danger in Male Porn" (presentation, World Pornography Conference, Los Angeles, August 1998), http://www.treasureislandblog.com/community/pauls-corner/pauls-papers/.

13    It is worth noting that the distinction between mainstream and bareback porn is not as tenable as it was when TIM began releasing films in the late nineties, or even in 2009, when Dean published *Unlimited Intimacy*. Today, it is commonly noted that condomless sex in gay porn is fast becoming the norm—if it isn't already. By the same token, it would be difficult not to count TIM among the mainstream, given its public and commercial notoriety.

14    Morris, "No Limits."

15    Jerome Stuart Nichols, "Paul Morris, Treasure Island Media's *Maverick*, Sets the Record Straight about Porn, HIV, and 'the Complex Behavioral Language' of Gay Sex," *Let's Talk About Sex*, April 25, 2011, https://jerome-nichols.squarespace.com/home/2011/4/25/paul-morris-treasure-island-medias-maverick-talks-about-porn.html.

16    Can't the authenticity that Morris describes be found in the mainstream, too? For example, can't the detachment he associates with models who perform for "the wrong reasons"—for the cheque or in search of fame—represent a kind of cruel authenticity that speaks to the "truth" of sex? In a similar vein, I wonder about the ways in which using condoms (or other "inhibited" ways of fucking)

For Morris, the regime of safe sex is far more than the legal and cultural mandate to wear condoms; it is the commercializing and normativizing construction of sex as something we can put safely to one side, and occasionally dip in and out of without ever actually experiencing it and its inherent dangers. As Morris describes it, queer sex challenges the idea of sex as a social good, and his comments on this topic are as suggestive as they are insightful. There is, however, a problem that arises in the distinction Morris draws between authentic and idealized pornographic representation. The problem is that this distinction becomes a way of centring the subject in the false security of a one-for-one relationship between representation and desire. Under the assurance that queer desire can be represented in pornography, bareback identity emerges as the basis of a more desirable social order.

Morris repeatedly emphasizes that his pornography depicts regular guys rather than models seeking a paycheque, and that the scenes he films are not scripted or controlled by the director. In TIM films, the strict division between the men fucking and the men doing the filming often breaks down as they engage with each other verbally and, sometimes, physically. Furthermore, there is no effort to hide the video equipment in order to create the illusion of the scene existing in a closed-off reality. The production value is basic, and the settings are hotels or the performers' apartments, rather than the fancy rental suites used by other companies such as Sean Cody and Bel Ami. In this context, the absence of condoms is framed as just another testament to the ethnographic basis of bareback porn, and the idea that this is the way these men would be fucking even if the cameras weren't around.[17] What matters for Morris is not simply that the men are fucking bareback, but rather that they

has been—for certain people and at certain times—a way of taking, rather than avoiding, risk. That condoms might imply a continuation, rather than an interruption, of the "danger" that Morris sees as inherent to queer desire, complicates the dichotomies we might try to use to distinguish risky/safe, subversive/normative, or good/bad sex practices, which again harkens back to Lisa Downing's call to move away from the "either/or dichotomy of 'positive'/'negative' language" around sex. Downing, "Safewording!," 95.

17   As Dean points out, "it is considerably more than the absence of rubbers that distinguishes bareback from mainstream gay porn." *Unlimited Intimacy*, 106.

are fucking in a way that is honest. While we might think about porn as being about bringing fantasy to life, for Morris it is always a matter of accurately portraying something that is already there.

Of course, as students of postmodern criticism, we might be quick to point out that documentary realism is itself a carefully constructed genre. In pornography, as in all other forms of representation, there is no perfect boundary between actual reality and scripted fantasy. In my previous writing on barebacking, I was concerned precisely with this question.[18] I suggested that Morris's perspective on his pornography drew too simplistic a line between authentic and artificial (mainstream) representations of sex. While Morris's intention may be to simply and accurately portray what is already there, his porn is also the product of its own subjective determinants and representational regimes. Honesty, like falseness, is a contingent signifier within the fray of symbolic meaning. For this reason, although he positions himself as witness rather than author, Morris is necessarily an active participant in the production of what counts as empirical and what counts as *mere* fiction. And therefore the problem with Morris's account of queer honesty is that it perpetually veers toward implicating bareback porn in the very process he laments—the evaluation of sex according to a specific value, which can be reproduced and disseminated in the name of the social. In other words, bareback discourse—and Morris's in particular—risk disciplining queers in the act of authentic queerness, just as the regime of "safe sex" helps to regulate the idea of the "good gay."

However, this critique is perhaps flawed to the extent that it subjects all porn to a state of relativism, foreclosing any potential for thinking about the comparative effects of different examples of porn. Morris's search for authenticity may privilege certain representational signifiers—"danger, accident, and specificity," which are inherently amorphous terms capable of shifting in different contexts—but it is also about trying to capture, if paradoxically, the dimension of sex that does not answer to the call of representational

---

18    Christien Garcia, "Limited Intimacy: Barebacking and the Imaginary," *Textual Practice* 27, no. 6 (2013): 1031–51.

regimes. In his analysis of the 2006 TIM film *Breeding Season*, Lee Edelman makes just this point. He argues that Morris's work figures sex outside the stabilizing determinants of the Symbolic in favour of an encounter with the symbolic formlessness of the Real—or, in other words, that it "allegorizes the dissolution of form, including the form imposed upon the subject *as itself*."[19] *Breeding Season* features a dildo/popsicle made entirely of frozen cum. As a substance materialized by its own dissolving form, this "devil's dick" comes to represent, in Edelman's reading, the fundamental discontinuity between desire and representation. Given such an analysis, it is all the more intriguing how easily the discourse around bareback porn slips into the reproductive logic of identity.

In her interview with Morris, Paasonen writes of barebacking as a form of non-filial becoming:

> The issue here would be one of becoming gay, and queer, as a process where seropositive status links with resistance and viral contagion replaces hereditary production. In other words, forms of queer breeding do not reproduce the species but a sexual subculture based on alliance. The notion of queer kinship created through breeding and seeding involves a sexual and communal utopia that is detached from what Lee Edelman calls reproductive futurism.[20]

It is worth questioning how the vision of a communal utopia could ever be squared with Edelman's critique of futurity. Replacing one form of heredity with another only goes to show the veracity of the reproductive futurism that Edelman critiques. This is because it is not simply sexual procreation that he excoriates, but rather the mimetic process by which the logic of identity is constantly reborn through new patterns of particularity. In other words, it is precisely the ability of identity to feel new and full of potential, like the figure of the child, that ensures that the same old political logic remains firmly in place. Further to this point, Edelman argues

---

19   Edelman, "Unbecoming," 40.
20   Morris and Paasonen, "Risk and Utopia," 220.

that, "however radical the means by which specific constituencies attempt to produce a more desirable social order, [politics] remains, at its core, conservative insofar as it works to affirm a structure, to *authenticate* social order."[21] For Edelman, queerness is not something that links who we are on the inside to a corresponding social form—extant or utopian—but rather the force that garbles all correspondence between desire and its translation into the representational order of the social.

Vis-à-vis the promise of ethnographic truth, Morris sublimates the destabilizing effects of the queerness that Edelman describes into the coherence of alterity: "The sex of gay and queer men is without doubt a core behavior that in every sense delineates, defines and creates our identity. I've said it countless times: it is a language and because it tells us who we are it must be depicted with honesty."[22] Morris describes sex as a language. But if sexuality correlates with language, it is not because it tells us who we are, but rather because of the concomitant ambiguity both sexuality and language instill in the lives of speaking subjects. As Jacques Lacan describes it, "desire begins to take shape in the margin" between desire and what can be named of that desire in language.[23] In other words, desire exists precisely because the articulation of desire always comes up short. How, then, might we read this failure to reach the threshold of articulated meaning as itself the substance of sex? How can we think about the patterns and rhythms sex takes without demanding that they take on the shape of coherence?

One answer to these questions might be to shift our attention from the register of naming to the register of merely describing. In other words, rather than focusing on what certain sex acts say about certain people, we might shift our attention to the ways and means by which sex happens without necessarily speaking anything on the part of the subject engaged in that sex. A corollary to this distinction

21    Lee Edelman, *No Future: Queer Theory and the Death Drive* (Durham, NC: Duke University Press, 2004), 2–3.

22    Josh Robbins, "Gay Pornographer Paul Morris Is Taking on Weinstein," *I'm Still Josh*, October 10, 2016, http://www.imstilljosh.com/exclusive-paul-morris/3/.

23    Jacques Lacan, *Écrits: The First Complete Edition in English*, trans. Bruce Fink (New York: W.W. Norton & Company, 2007), 689.

lies in a consideration of the modifying function of adverbs as compared with other parts of speech. Whereas nouns, verbs, and adjectives name the things, actions, and qualities of the world, the role of adverbs is more ambiguous and incidental. That is to say, rather than naming the things that make up the world, adverbs describe the manner and degree of their being and doing. Take the *Oxford English Dictionary* example of "Gary, a silent boy, merely nodded."[24] Both nouns, "Gary" and "boy," identify the subject of the sentence. They name something that can be placed in the world. The boy's action in that world is to nod. And while the silence of the adjective "silent" is clearly a property of the boy doing the nodding, what about the mereness of the adverb "merely"? Is it a quality of the boy, the nod, the observer, the sentence itself? A distinctly eclectic category of word, adverbs condition without themselves being conditions or states. The nature of the suffix "-ly," which turns words into adverbs, is merely to inflect what is already there. In other words, it changes words that refer to things, qualities, and actions into words that refer to *the ways* in which those things, actions, and qualities are and act. Furthermore, adverbs are themselves marginal in that they are inessential to the construction of a coherent sentence. In these senses, all adverbs have a kind of mereness to them.

As a modifier, the specific adverb "just" denotes precision or specificity: "exactly, precisely; actually; very closely."[25] But in a different set of meanings, the term implies "limiting the extent or degree denoted by an expression; . . . barely; . . . by a slight margin."[26] Here, the exactitude of "do it *just* like that" opens onto the slightness of "only just," which is another way of saying "almost not at all." The etymology of merely reveals a similar ambiguity. In a set of obsolete or rare meanings, the term implies purity: "without admixture or qualification."[27] In this sense, it has the positive connotation of

---

24  *Oxford Dictionaries*, s.v. "merely," https://www.lexico.com/en/definition/merely.

25  *Oxford English Dictionary Online*, s.v. "just (*adv.*)," https://www.oed.com/view/En try/102192?rskey=jU5SwD&result=7&isAdvanced=false#eid.

26  Ibid.

27  *Oxford English Dictionary Online*, s.v. "merely (*adv. 2*)," http://www.oed.com/view/ Entry/116740?rskey=wpjw2G&result=2.

"absolutely, entirely; quite, altogether."[28] The root "mere" comes from the Latin *merus*, meaning undiluted, and in Middle English it meant pure, sheer, downright. But with time, merely takes on the negative connotations of being *only* this or that (lesser). Etymologically, then, merely can be thought of as a form of completion that draws attention to its own limits: "without any other quality, reason, purpose, view, etc.; only (what is referred to) and *nothing more.*"[29] Here the fullness of universality slides ambiguously into the limitedness of particularity.

Ultimately, what interests me about the prepositional function of terms like merely and just is that their seemingly contradictory meanings—undiluted and limited—are often far from discrete. Indeed, the ambiguity of this distinction is precisely what defines the mereness of such terms. The way just and merely modify their objects suggests that not all slightness exists for want of more. Observing this mutual determinacy between adequacy and limitedness can be useful in terms of how we think about sex and its interpretation. The *inadequacy* of that which distinguishes fulfillment and want, exactitude and insignificance, might itself be the substance of desire. Such an inadequacy is not the declaration of the potential for greater experience, but, rather, underscores the fact that we encounter fulfillment and need as overlapping. That inadequacy is familiar, for example, in the phrase "I'm just fine," where the more one emphasizes "just" as a sign of certitude, the more its sense of limitation seems to creep in: "*just* fine?" Is barebacking perhaps not itself a kind of preposition or modifier, like merely in the sense that it has, over the past several years, governed a discussion of sex in terms of both exactitude and deficiency—indeed, has made the two terms inseparable in thinking about the significance of specific sex acts and cultures?

Thinking retrospectively about barebacking, as both a practice and a topic of critical writing, reveals something of a contradiction. On the one hand, the idea of bareback sex has profoundly reshaped contemporary Anglo-American discourses of sexuality. But on the other hand, among those most invested in this discourse, there is

---

28 Ibid.
29 Ibid.

perhaps the lingering sense that barebacking is supposed to be more.[30] Barebacking seems now to be neither the liberatory nor the culturally destructive phenomenon it might have been when debates about it were at their peak. In a sense—at least for certain people in certain contexts—it has simply been folded into "just sex." No big deal. *Just* the way people are having sex. By this I do not mean simply that gay bareback sex has been normalized—although I think that, to various degrees within the North American context, it has. What I mean to invoke by the idea of "just sex" is that, as more people bareback, it becomes increasingly obvious that one can do so outside the cultural ethos of barebacking that Morris describes. Perhaps the waning of bareback's radicalness suggests the reluctance sex itself shows in delineating, defining, and creating identity.

What follows is a close reading of Morris's account of the "native language" of queerness,[31] which is itself a close reading of thirty seconds of bareback porn (quoted at length below).[32] I read Morris's description for the mereness of forms, silences, and indecipherability that unfolds alongside and against the satisfaction of thinking about sex as an experience of reciprocal meaning. By thinking about sex in terms of the formalism or styles of slightness and mereness, the goal is to decouple it from the labour of articulation, and the threshold by which it is sublimated into social value.

---

30   The academic focus on barebacking—perhaps especially in retrospect—would seem to be a kind of excessive expenditure, not unlike the seminal expenditure that so excites the barebacking imaginary. How much more ink will be spilt on this topic, which surely has by now run its course as a matter of urgent social relevance? Perhaps this is precisely what is interesting about barebacking now: the very fact that its critical output looks a lot like the pure expenditure of desire itself.

31   Nichols, "Paul Morris, Treasure Island Media's *Maverick*."

32   Close reading of a close reading amounts to a version of what Brian Glavey has called, and not unfavourably, a "too-close-for-comfort close reading" (4). In his own discussion of "the mereness of mere description" (13), which he explores in the context of literary modernism, Glavey suggests that there is always something potentially queer about a critic's proclivity for "caring too much" about a given piece of writing (2). Brian Glavey, *The Wallflower Avant-Garde: Modernism, Sexuality, and Queer Ekphrasis* (Oxford: Oxford University Press, 2016).

## PART 2

In a 2011 online interview, Paul Morris was asked if he might be reading too much into the simple sex acts that his films portray. His response was a characteristically erudite, thousand-word visual analysis of a thirty-second clip from a TIM gangbang scene. The analysis he provides is remarkable, in part, because its analytic tone and level of detail are so at odds with the superlative descriptions used in the marketing of porn. Through his analysis of rhythm, duration, repetition, shape, angle, and scale (zooming in and out), Morris stretches the temporality of porn, at once attenuating and thickening its unfolding actions. His close reading is itself worth a close reading, especially in terms of the way it draws out desire as, in Brinkema's words, "a problematic of form in a text"[33]:

A man has just shot a load up the ass of the blindfolded man. The bottom turns around to suck the semen off the cock. At 00.00.05, his left hand presses precisely between the abdominal fat and the pubic hair of the top. The connection functions as acknowledgment, control ("Stay still and let me suck your cock, even though it's very sensitive.") and a gauging of the body of the top (the bottom is, after all, blinded). . . .

At 00.00.07, the bottom's hand moves to the shaft of the top's cock. This removes the connection with the top as "person" and focuses on the top as "cock." The bottom is allowing himself to focus all of his attention on the phallus. At this point (00.00.09), the camera pulls back (you hear the bottom moan in appreciation for the cock and the taste of semen) and you can see that the top has had his hand on the side of the bottom's head, a gesture of connection, control, acceptance and gentle dominance. The sounds that the men are making are recognizably spontaneous and sincere. At 00.00.11, simultaneously, the bottom slaps the top's cock against his tongue and the top gently slaps the side of the bottom's head. Both gestures have complex meanings and

---

33  Brinkema, *The Forms of the Affects*, 40.

are meant to acknowledge the pleasure and satisfaction of the experience as well as the fact that it's ending (the top is leaving now that he's shot his load). At 00.00.12, there's a cut to a tripod camera that shows the larger group. In the background you can see a man stroking his cock. On the left (in the foreground), a man is standing with his hips forward and his hands almost behind his back. The top (in the light) pats the bottom's head strongly enough so that you can hear the slapping sound. Simultaneous to the end of the top's slapping, both other men—younger than the more dominant top who has just finished—reach out toward the bottom's head. The man on the left has acted first, so the man in the background quickly defers and pulls his hand back. At 00.00.16, we cut to the cameraman's held camera, seeing the action close again. . . .

Now the top's hand is resting on the wrist of the bottom. The other man's hand is now cupping the bottom's head. Following the action from here to around 00.00.19, you'll see that the older top's hand on the bottom's wrist signified to the bottom that he was leaving, that it was time to let go. At 00.00.19 you can see the bottom releasing the top's cock as the top takes his cock in both hands. Techniques of connection and disconnection in complex situations like this are extremely important. In the meantime, the younger top pats the bottom's head just as the older (and more dominant) top had, but he does so more tentatively, more gently. As his hand pulls back, you can see a tiny movement from the wrist that suggests equivocation and uncertainty.

At 00.00.23, as the older and more dominant top backs away, the younger top (his cock hanging flaccid) steps in, places his cock over the head of the bottom. They are very close together, but it's hard to tell if there's any actual contact between the cock and the bottom's face. The younger top doesn't place his cock in the mouth of the bottom, doesn't lift up the bottom's head. He seems to pat his cock on the face of the bottom and stroke himself. This leaves the bottom's mouth open. The bottom rubs his own tongue for a moment. The second young top, the one who had been in the background stroking his cock and had reached out (at around 00.00.12) but had deferred to the other young top, now reaches in (at 00.00.30) and places his hand between the other top's cock and the bottom's mouth.[34]

We can see in the opening lines of Morris's analysis a desire to read the scene in terms of communicative exchange between the bottom and top(s) in the scene. But in Morris's writing there is also careful attention paid to forms of waning and absence, which circumvent the framing of sex as a kind of reciprocal dialogue. As much as Morris focuses on "connection," "acknowledgement," and "control," there is also a distinct focus on the ongoing momentum of "deferral," "drawing back," "conceding." Indeed, the scene's "actions" seem always to be mediated by the barely active, barely articulated, and barely perceptible: a "moan," a "taste," a "gesture," all of which fall below the threshold of coherent speech. These minimal modes and utterances disentangle sex from the imperatives of communication, reciprocity, and disclosure. Meanings recede; they "back away," and it is precisely in this waning of signification that the inertia of desire takes form and is taken by form, like a syntax without semantics. All remains "tentative," "equivocatory," "uncertain." Yet at the same time, that mereness seems complete to the extent that there is "nothing more."[35]

It is intriguing that the clip Morris chooses to illustrate the "native language"[36] of queer sex is one that takes place just after the fact ("a man has just shot a load"), especially given, as Dean puts it, "the subculture's commitment to internal ejaculation."[37] But there is something about the scene being both over and ongoing—*complete* both in the sense of finished and full—that helps to underscore the

---

34 Nichols, "Paul Morris, Treasure Island Media's *Maverick*." The segment Morris describes appears at the end of the second scene of *What I Can't See 3*, directed by Paul Morris and Liam Cole (San Francisco: Treasure Island Media, 2011), DVD.

35 *Oxford English Dictionary Online*, s.v. "mereness (*adv.* 2)," http://www.oed.com/view/Entry/116740?rskey=wpjw2G&result=2.

36 Nichols, "Paul Morris, Treasure Island Media's *Maverick*."

37 Dean, *Unlimited Intimacy*, xii.

relationship between bareback porn and the notion of mereness. One of the important features of bareback porn and the discourse around it is that they can eschew the traditional arch of the pornographic event. Scenes like the one described above complicate the idea that sex is a discrete act with a clear start, climax, and finish. As in many TIM films, the scene that Morris describes depicts a "session" with multiple participants, sometimes centred on a particular bottom who serves as the anchor for a series of overlapping encounters, sometimes involving more than one location as in the 2012 TIM film *Slammed*. Participants often linger in the background of the scene, stroking themselves and others before and after breeding the bottom. The circulation of multiple participants as they enter and leave the physical space of the scene and the camera's field of vision establishes the rhythm of bareback porn as markedly different from conventional porn scenes. The perpetual comings and goings create a permeable periphery of movement around the central action of the scene. Rather than a singular narrative arch leading to and ending with ejaculation (foreplay, sex, cum shot), there are multiple coexisting and interwoven temporalities. The result is that there can be no one event, no consummate money shot to give a scene a definitive climax. Especially because so many tops cum, and because the bottom may or may not cum, it is difficult to pin resolution down as a reciprocal act between sets of bodies. In lieu of a grand release, there is merely the rhythm or "tiny movement" of the scene's motions and utterances, signalling the strange mutuality of deferred and continuous action.

The blending of withdrawal and ongoingness is also evident in the blurring of the line between the acts of holding and release in the scene. Morris writes, "you'll see that the older top's hand on the bottom's wrist signified to the bottom that he was leaving, that it was time to let go." How does an act of holding become a signal for leaving? Such "techniques of connection and disconnection" mean that there is overlap between a body's being *there* and the conciliatory *there, there* of its departure. He's come, so he's leaving, so he's staying for a while ("stay still and let me suck your cock"). The men in the scene linger and leave in ways that are literally intertwined: fingers over a wrist, a cock in a mouth, figures inside forms. These jointed forms are paired with hollow ones: a cupped hand, and an empty mouth made even emptier when the man to whom it belongs rubs his own tongue, a gesture that seems to be about satiation and hunger all at once. Not dissimilarly, the "satisfaction" of the scene seems to be a function of the "fact that it's ending," the fact that all that cum has come to just this.

In the context of the Freudian view of sexuality as a kind of tension that is resolved by the end-pleasure of the orgasm, John Paul Ricco has written about the perceived danger or taboo of forsaking the orgasm altogether, of lingering over the preparatory sexual acts, and deriving more pleasure from the "fore" of sex than the sex itself. "A certain satisfying pleasure," Ricco writes, "can be derived from its *incompletion* rather than its end."[38] That same logic can be applied to the "post-." What about when completion rather than incompletion is the context for lingering, as in the scene Morris describes? The lingering is not simply a question of there being "unfinished" business. Rather, it shows that completion can itself be the form desire takes. Or in other words, it shows that satisfaction can be a description of longing, rather than simply resolution. In this light, desire exists not when something is plainly, identifiably *missing*, but precisely when there is *nothing more besides*—when sex is *just* sex.

Another evocation of the mereness of sex comes with Morris's description of the moment when "person" becomes "cock." As the bottom shifts his focus and hand from the top's abdomen to his penis, what takes place is both a kind of underscoring and a divestiture. The top is somehow made both more and less, his body somehow more precise in this depleted state of *just* cock. Or to put this differently, the cock isn't *just* cock, the cock is also just-like in the way it denotes the amplitude of that which is reduced to a metonymic state. As a device of both negated and heightened senses, the blindfold also feeds into this mereness. It functions as a sign of the bottom's receptive or submissive state, but also his haptic activity. Like the adverb "just" itself, the blindfold draws emphasis to a particular thing ("allowing himself to focus all of his attention on

---

38    John Paul Ricco, *The Decision Between Us: Art and Ethics in the Time of Scenes* (Chicago: University of Chicago Press, 2014), 119.

the phallus" . . . *just* the phallus), but it also moderates the breadth of that thing through the subtraction of vision. Cock represents a kind of making do, or to borrow from François's vocabulary, a kind of "enoughness."[39] But this is not to say that this mereness is a kind of chaste, self-satisfied withdrawal from desire. Rather, it suggests a recalibration of how we understand its intensities.

When Lacan speaks of "desire's incompatibility with speech,"[40] frequently that incompatibility is envisioned as something powerful lurking in the Real, which threatens to dissolve the fabric of the Symbolic. But there is also a way of thinking about that remainder as a kind of inconsequence or insignificance, less a rival to the symbolic order of language than a diffuse pattern of barely register-ing instances woven throughout it. Here the remainder of desire's translation in language would be not only formed "in the margin," to recall Lacan, but also marginal to its core. One such instance is Morris's description of the way in which the top "pats" the bottom's head "strongly enough so that you can hear the slapping sound." Is a pat that makes a slapping sound not a slap? This is at once a serious and a somewhat facetious question. My concern is not a question of proper labelling—is it a slap or a pat? If, once again, we switch our focus from naming to merely describing, we see that there can of course be a "slappish" kind of pat. And it seems to me that there is something about the particular space this "ish" opens up, separate from the logic of naming, that speaks to the ways and means of sex in the shared arena of language and the body. It speaks, in Wil-liam Haver's words, to "the infinitesimal, empirical poiesis of what bodies can do."[41] Somehow the feeling of *both* a pat and a slap in the context of the TIM scene seems all the more precise given their potential interchangeability. In Morris's interpretation, the differ-ence between "a pat" and "a slap," coming and going, closeness and distance, is too slight to be resolved, and thus all the more vivid. In the same way, desire might be less about the satisfaction of a need,

---

39  François, *Open Secrets*, xx.
40  Lacan, *Écrits*, 535.
41  William Haver, "Queer Research: Or, How to Practise Invention to the Brink of Intelligibility," in *The Eight Technologies of Otherness*, ed. Sue Golding (London and New York: Routledge, 1997), 283.

or its fundamental insatiability, than about the attenuation of such a distinction, and the intensity that arises as a result.

Later in the same interview, Morris contextualizes his visual analysis by describing gay sex as "a process of education, experiment and learning." "All of it is driven," he says, "by both sexual and social desire and the promise of variants of fulfilment and satisfaction and self-definition."[42] For Morris, queer sex can be read as a pedagogical exchange between older and younger, top and bottom, but also between pornographer and viewer, the sex act and the social more broadly. In his writing on the topic of queer pedagogy, Haver offers a very different understanding of the possibility, and even desirability, of such a queer pedagogy. He argues that queer pedagogy fails when it looks to particular objects of study in search of a recognizable "us," no matter how appropriately queer that object might be.[43] For Haver, such identification is necessarily the evacuation of the erotic, because the erotic is necessarily an encounter with the undoing of the self. Haver goes so far as to describe pedagogy as "an instrumental technique or strategy for the occlusion of the erotic."[44] In the place of queer pedagogy, Haver calls for research as "an unworking without destination, thinking as departure . . . a hiatus in the very possibility for cultural (re)production."[45] In Haver's text, this "unworking" is a kind of radical interruption, a revolution, a grand *what if.* But it is also possible to think about this unworking as forms of letting go and making do. Indeed, the "erotic pragmatics"[46] that Haver calls for resonate with the mereness of desire I have been describing here. For all its investment in identifying authentic queerness, Morris's description also works in lesser, more adverbial ways. By focusing on this adverbial mereness, what Morris's reading of bareback sex ultimately reveals is a kind of pragmatics (from the Greek *pragma*: deed, act, affair, matter) of mutually generating withdrawal and continuity. More so than knowledge exchange, there are the forms

---

42    Nichols, "Paul Morris, Treasure Island Media's *Maverick.*"
43    Haver, "Queer Research," 287–8.
44    Ibid., 289.
45    Ibid., 284.
46    Ibid., 290.

and means of uncertainty and proximity. After all, "it's hard to tell if there's any actual contact" between the men, as Morris notes.[47]

Morris's idea of a "native language" of queer sex evokes the bind whereby the seemingly radical potential of subversive cultural practices gets woven into the disciplinary process of linking those practices to certain ways of being, reproducing the logic of identity that "queer" purportedly challenges. Following Edelman's insistence that "queer" refers to the fundamental disconnect between desire and its translation as representation, my consideration of mereness provides an alternative to reading sex for its social and subjective expressivity. More specifically, it frames bareback sex in terms of that which is *insignificant* in the light of social achievement, including the achievement of alternative kinship structures based on breeding and seeding. However, thinking about the capacity of "queer" to hold mere form suggests both a departure from and an elaboration of the recent emphasis on negativity that has guided much of the criticism of identitarian manifestations of queerness. It refashions queer negativity less as an "anti" in opposition to the social than as a slightness that doesn't add up to the symbolic order that the social demands. In other words, this mere theory, as it were, frames queer as a kind of minorness rather than a subversiveness. And it allows for the failure of queer expressivity within the social realm without envisioning a counter-realm where the value of queerness is "made right." Mereness is therefore a part of a tradition of queer critical- ity that questions the desire to frame sex as a basis self-knowledge. "Queer sex" in this sense might not so much denote a "type" of sex, as it does the very impossibility of framing sex as the basis of who "we" are or what "we" might become.

---

47  Nichols, "Paul Morris, Treasure Island Media's *Maverick*." This image of not quite knowing one way or another if there is any actual contact implies the impossibil- ity of absolute knowledge, but it also mirrors the ways in which desire, like the adverbial generally, modifies experience without being direct properties of (or being in actual contact with) the things and actions of the world. This diffuse relationship between the ways and means of desire and the specific details of, say, bareback porn, explains the difficulty of ascribing *certain* kinds of sex with pedagogical value for *certain* kinds of people.

## REFERENCES

Brinkema, Eugenie. *The Forms of the Affects*. Durham, NC: Duke University Press, 2014.

Butler, Judith. "Merely Cultural." *Social Text* 52–53 (Autumn–Winter 1997): 265–77.

Dean, Tim. *Unlimited Intimacy: Reflections on the Subculture of Barebacking*. Chicago, University of Chicago Press, 2009.

Downing, Lisa. "Safewording! Kinkphobia and Gender Normativity in *Fifty Shades of Grey*." *Psychology and Sexuality* 4, no. 1 (December 2012): 92–102.

———. "What Is 'Sex Critical' and Why Should We Care about It?" Sex Critical: Musings of a Curmudgeonly Sexuality Studies Scholar. July 27, 2012. http://sexcritical.co.uk/2012/07/27/what-is-sex-critical-and-why-should-we-care-about-it/.

Edelman, Lee. *No Future: Queer Theory and the Death Drive*. Durham, NC: Duke University Press, 2004.

———. "Unbecoming." In *Post, Porn, Politics: Queer-Feminist Perspective on the Politics of Porn Performance and Sex-Work as Culture Production*, edited by Tim Stüttgen, 28–45. Berlin: B_Books, 2009.

Florêncio, João. "Breeding Futures: Masculinity and the Ethics of CUMmunion in Treasure Island Media's *Viral Loads*." *Porn Studies* 5, no. 3 (May 2018): 271–85.

François, Anne-Lise. *Open Secrets: The Literature of Uncounted Experience*. Stanford, CA: Stanford University Press, 2008.

Garcia, Christien. "Limited Intimacy: Barebacking and the Imaginary." *Textual Practice* 27, no. 6 (October 2013): 1031–51.

Glavey, Brian. *The Wallflower Avant-Garde: Modernism, Sexuality, and Queer Ekphrasis*. Oxford: Oxford University Press, 2016.

Haver, William. "Queer Research: Or, How to Practise Invention to the Brink of Intelligibility." In *The Eight Technologies of Otherness*, edited by Sue Golding, 277–92. London and New York: Routledge, 1997.

Lacan, Jacques. *Écrits: The First Complete Edition in English*. Translated by Bruce Fink. New York: W.W. Norton, 2007.

Morris, Paul. "No Limits: Necessary Danger in Male Porn." Paper presented at the World Pornography Conference, Los Angeles. August 1998. http://www.treasureislandblog.com/community/pauls-corner/pauls-papers/.

Morris, Paul, and Susanna Paasonen. "Risk and Utopia: A Dialogue on Pornography." *GLQ: A Journal of Lesbian and Gay Studies* 20, no. 3 (June 2014): 215–39.

Nichols, Jerome Stuart. "Paul Morris, Treasure Island Media's *Maverick*, Sets the Record Straight about Porn, HIV, and 'the Complex Behavioral Language' of Gay Sex." *Let's Talk about Sex*. April 25, 2011. https://jerome-nichols.

squarespace.com/home/2011/4/25/paul-morris-treasure-island-medias-maverick-talks-about-porn.html.

Ricco, John Paul. *The Decision Between Us: Art and Ethics in the Time of Scenes.* Chicago: University of Chicago Press, 2014.

Robbins, Josh. "Gay Pornographer Paul Morris Is Taking on Weinstein." *I'm Still Josh.* October 10, 2016. http://www.imstilljosh.com/exclusive-paul-morris/3/.

# THE RAW AND THE FUCKED

## Tim Dean

**A**re we still barebacking?
Considered collectively, the chapters in *Raw* make clear that bareback does not exist as a stable category or practice. Its definition remains subject to disagreement and debate, even as its frequency as a practice seems to have exploded in recent years. Paradoxically, as more men fuck without condoms, we become less certain about what that means. The epidemiological consequences of pre-exposure prophylaxis (PrEP) for the uninfected are not yet definitively known. Rapid alterations in conditions for men who have sex with men, stimulated by not only PrEP but also new digital technologies, remain incompletely understood, their social and political implications ambiguous. When men relinquish condoms in favour of pharmaceutical prophylaxis, does their sex still qualify as unprotected? The sexual terrain has changed so much during the past few years that this volume's stock-taking is welcome and timely.

If the term "bareback" carries varying significance for men having sex, it also connotes a range of meanings for the contributors here. My aim is less to adjudicate among these disparate meanings—a fool's errand to try pinning down a single meaning as the correct one—than to assess how they are evolving and functioning. The terminology for sex without condoms, as well as its import, continues to morph. What used to be called, in the early years of the AIDS epidemic, "unsafe sex" has been variously renamed as "unprotected," "risky," "bareback," "raw," "real," "natural," or "skin." Far from neutral, this shifting nomenclature inscribes competing values that suggest a lack of consensus regarding the phenomenon under consideration. What you call sexual practices affects what they are and how they are experienced; the terminology matters. For the contributors to *Raw*, bareback signifies variously risk, freedom, community, filiation, masculinity, queerness, vulnerability, irresponsibility, closeness to others, and disregard for others. The signifier "barebacking" is highly overdetermined, now more so than ever.

What becomes evident from these chapters is that "barebacking" calls forth not just different meanings but diametrically opposed ones. Should we consider barebacking as transgressive or conformist? Filthy or sanitized? Healthy or pathological? A practice of the margins or of the mainstream? Is it an expression of radical individualism or, conversely, a mark of filiation and kinship? A sign of violence or of love? Has barebacking become normalized, or does it still count as queer? It is also worth asking: What has changed such that the practice appears to occupy both poles of these dichotomies simultaneously, as transgressive *and* conformist, marginal *and* mainstream, et cetera? How has one particular erotic practice (or set of practices) come to carry such a burden of meaning? Why does barebacking serve so readily as a metaphor for competing values and ostensibly incompatible ideas?

The category of bareback is being asked to perform huge symbolic and ideological labours in queer discourse. Some contributors, such as Christien Garcia, suggest that barebacking sometimes fails to meet our elevated expectations. It does not always deliver, whether pornographically, rhetorically, or ideologically. As with our expectations of love, so too with barebacking: we might be asking too much of it. Reading these essays, I'm struck by bareback's oscillation between various dichotomies. Some of this is attributable to our present historical moment—the "invisible condom" of PrEP (which can make it seem like you're barebacking when you're not), the mainstreaming of condom-free gay porn, and the mass migration of practices and styles from a subculture to gay culture more generally.[1]

However, some of bareback's oscillation between opposing poles has to do with the way in which conceptual categories shape social reality via binary oppositions. Here I'm referring to a structuralist anthropological account of how any culture makes sense to and for itself—specifically, Claude Lévi-Strauss's thesis in *The Raw and the Cooked*.[2] Drawing on Saussurean linguistics, Lévi-Strauss shows how empirical categories such as rawness may be used as conceptual tools for the cultural work of sense-making, thanks to their functioning in binary pairs. Culture/nature is one of the most elementary of such binary pairs, and never more so than when it comes to conceptualizing sex and sexuality. I've titled this afterword "The Raw and the Fucked" partly in homage to Lévi-Strauss, but mainly to suggest how raw sex has come to occupy both sides of a basic conceptual opposition. The fact that barebacking now can be viewed as *both* raw *and* cooked (that is, as sanitized, normative, inside culture rather than an outlaw to it) is "fucked up" in a way that's highly instructive. It tells us something fundamental about contemporary sexual culture.

On one hand, fucking without condoms could not be more natural. Bareback was how people had sex before rubber was invented. The activity seems pre-cultural, primitive, primal—and sexually arousing for just that reason. On the other hand, however, bareback today is the outcome of highly specific cultural processes of eroticization that involve the following: institutions of medicine, immunology, and virology; evolving semiotic codes of pornography and digital technology; plus an entire history of gay sexuality, including successive attempts to form community outside familial schemas. Nothing could be more culturally mediated than barebacking. The

---

1   For a discussion of the idea of "invisible condoms," see Tim Dean, "Mediated Intimacies: Raw Sex, Truvada, and the Biopolitics of Chemoprophylaxis," *Sexualities* 18, nos. 1–2 (2015): 239–41.

2   Claude Lévi-Strauss, *The Raw and the Cooked: Introduction to a Science of Mythology*, vol. 1, trans. John Weightman and Doreen Weightman (New York: Harper and Row, 1969).

notion of "raw" at stake here is, in fact, as "cooked" as anything can be. The tension between opposing conceptions of bareback sex animates every chapter in this volume.

The tension gets played out mainly in terms of the equivocal status of barebacking as queer. Because research in queer studies offered ways of understanding the phenomenon apart from its pathologization by public health experts, there has been a tendency to judge barebacking as a definitively queer practice, and therefore as politically salutary.[3] Our appropriation and "resignification" of the term "queer"—the way it has been converted from a pejorative to an honorific—has misled us into crediting anything that counters norms as automatically progressive or good. Since this mode of thinking sows confusion, I want to be clear. We are right to resist the pathologization and social marginalization of people and practices traditionally labelled as queer: the gender non-conformists, the sexually peculiar, people with disabilities, racialized minorities. In that respect, the de-stigmatization of queer has been an unalloyed good.

But queer is not, in and of itself, an unalloyed good. Queer theory and politics have generated their own kinds of conformism and, indeed, practices of social exclusion. The problem with treating queer as a cardinal virtue is that it leads to purity testing and, indeed, ideological cleansing, whereby certain people, practices, or ideas are denigrated as *not queer enough*. Sometimes this produces a kind of queer essentialism, in which one's status and bona fides require authentication by the self-appointed guardians of political credentialing. The hierarchy of value that queer was supposed to displace gets reinstated, with those crowned queerest at the top, while the less queer—the ideologically impure—are relegated to the lower rungs, if not dismissed altogether. Often, "queerest" is understood to mean "most oppressed," so an inverted racial hierarchy gets reinstated too. Within the fields of queer studies and queer politics, these hierarchies are no less pernicious than they are pervasive.[4]

---

3    See Oliver Davis, "A Special Issue of *Sexualities*: Bareback Sex and Queer Theory across Three National Contexts (France, UK, USA)," *Sexualities* 18, nos. 1–2 (2015): 120–26.

4    The problem is compounded by the way in which, over time, queer has congealed into an identity category. Once it becomes identitarian, queer needs

When framed in such terms, the question motivating many of these essays—*how queer is bareback now?*—appears misplaced. That was a question I tried to avoid in *Unlimited Intimacy* by approaching barebacking with judgment suspended.[5] It seemed to me then, and still does now, that deciding whether bareback sex is progressive or conservative, radical or compromised, queer or otherwise makes it too easy to elide the complexity of the phenomenon. The common human impulse to mark potentially disturbing behaviour as good or bad—to simplify it by either identifying with or violently disidentifying from it—shuts down thought. Specifying bareback as radical or conservative can discourage thinking about it seriously. Any proclamation that barebacking is indisputably queer is a sure sign it's being held at bay via superficial and stereotypical handling. Embracing barebacking wholesale may be, in the end, as dismissive as rejecting it out of hand.

Another way of getting at this problem entails acknowledging how queer theory and politics came into focus, toward the end of the AIDS epidemic's first decade, by opposing less heterosexuality than heteronormativity. Queer concerns not sexual identity but resistance to what Michael Warner called "regimes of the normal."[6] Following critical histories of medicine by Georges Canguilhem and Michel Foucault, *queer* challenges the division between normal and pathological by opening a viable alternative to the stifling binary options of healthy or sick.[7] Queer gave us a rationale for explaining

---

defending—and its boundaries need policing—like any other identity category. Minoritized identity categories manifest the pathologies of identitarianism—defensiveness, exclusionary tactics, paranoid border patrols—just as much as majority or unmarked identities. The pathology flows not from the category but from its reduction to identity.

5   See Dean, *Unlimited Intimacy: Reflections on the Subculture of Barebacking* (Chicago: University of Chicago Press, 2009).

6   Michael Warner, "Introduction," in *Fear of a Queer Planet: Queer Politics and Social Theory*, ed. Michael Warner (Minneapolis: University of Minnesota Press, 1994), xxvi.

7   See Georges Canguilhem, *The Normal and the Pathological*, trans. Carolyn R. Fawcett (New York: Zone Books, 1991); Michel Foucault, *History of Madness*, ed. Jean Khalfa, trans. Jonathan Murphy and Jean Khalfa (London and New York: Routledge, 2006); Michel Foucault, *The Birth of the Clinic: An Archaeology of Medical Perception*, trans. A.M. Sheridan Smith (New York: Random House, 1973); and

how, even if HIV-positive, we were not thereby pathological. Neither pathological nor normal, we were—and are—queer. Such ways of thinking have been lifesaving. But they also have produced, as a troubling side effect, the misconception of queer theory and politics as being opposed to *all* norms. This misconception, in turn, spawns a belief that anything quantifiable as non-normative must therefore be queer. The field of queer studies is still trying to dig itself out of this mess.[8]

What counts as normal or normative depends heavily on context. For example, during the early years of the epidemic, North American gay men established a socio-sexual norm that involved scrupulous condom usage for anal sex. That was a norm in the sense that it became widely understood as the thing to do—even if statistics about HIV transmission revealed that this norm of scrupulous condom usage was not adopted universally. It remains normative in an evaluative sense, even as the declining frequency of condom usage among gay men makes it less of a norm in the mathematical sense. In this context, anal sex with a condom is still normative—we know that it's how we're supposed to fuck—although increasingly it is not the norm for how men are actually having sex. Here is where the question of bareback-as-queer becomes especially tricky. Does barebacking qualify as non-normative if that is statistically how the majority of men fuck these days? Naming the practice as bareback might be a way of holding on to a frisson that has become obsolete. I'm wondering whether the term "bareback" already feels nostalgic—bareback as a look back to the moment before pharmaceuticals, when dispensing with condoms really meant something.

In spite of these shifts, bareback subculture is far from dead. *Unlimited Intimacy* approached unprotected sex in subcultural terms because I saw value in describing a set of erotic practices less as individual choices than as socially organized behaviour, with a meaningfulness that exceeds any particular participant. Diego

Michel Foucault, *The History of Sexuality, Volume 1: An Introduction*, trans. Robert Hurley (New York: Random House, 1978).

8    See, for example, Robyn Wiegman and Elizabeth A. Wilson, "Queer Theory without Antinormativity," *Differences: A Journal of Feminist Cultural Studies* 26, no.1 (2015).

Semerene begins his contribution to *Raw* by claiming that "the majority of early barebacking scholarship has assumed it to be a subcultural practice." But, in fact, I wrote *Unlimited Intimacy* because *none* of the existing scholarship assumed barebacking was a subcultural practice. The choice not to use a condom has tended to be understood in individualized terms—usually as an individual's failure—and I wanted to question that. Reframing it as subcultural enabled me to describe the distinctive styles and codes that make a practice intensely meaningful to those who undertake it. Since subcultural meanings are often invisible to outsiders, I tried to translate between the subculture and mainstream culture, including the mainstream gay culture that seemed so appalled at the prospect of organized barebacking.

Thinking about erotic practice in terms of a subculture allows one to see how the purpose of subcultures is to challenge the values of dominant culture. Subcultures are, in this sense, always counter-normative. Yet, in order to function, subcultures must develop their own distinctive values, and barebacking is no exception. The subculture has its own normativity—a set of values and conventions that defines it—central to which is the principle that condoms will not be used, at least not for protection. Bareback subculture's sexual permissiveness thus is based on a strict prohibition: no condoms! But barebacking differs from other subcultures in that it is uniquely permeable. Sex without condoms remains the default option for most men. Today, anyone with Internet access can locate bareback pornography and be stimulated by the fantasies it depicts. Bareback fantasies, practices, and iconography have become so widespread in recent years that, rather than counter-normative, they may appear as the new normal. The division between mainstream culture and subculture, while it has not disappeared, has become increasingly attenuated. We encounter a situation now in which gay sexual culture paradoxically adheres to competing norms—and this is what, in the end, thwarts every attempt to adjudicate the queerness of gay erotic practice.

*Raw* enters this confused and contested terrain with a range of valuable interventions. Jonathan Allan addresses HIV-prevention from the oblique angle of the foreskin, asking what queer theory can teach us about this anatomical morsel. The belief that male circumcision helps to prevent HIV transmission—a belief routinely mistaken as an established scientific fact—is treated as a discourse subject to analysis and critique. Allan reads circumcision discourses rhetorically, arguing that they serve to defend national security and, indeed, national heterosexuality. He wonders why queer studies has had so little to say about the prepuce or its significance for images and fantasies of the body. From my perspective, the answer to Allan's question is evident in his chapter's almost total neglect of the issue of pleasure. In its haste for social justice and its convenient forgetting of the complex materiality of sex, North American queer studies has abandoned erotic pleasure as politically insignificant.[9]

Pleasure resists ideological instrumentalization or use. That turns out to be one reason for neglecting it. Further, if we subscribe to the hygienicist assumption that erotic delight should be subordinated to normative conceptions of health, then loss of foreskin pleasure thanks to circumcision appears unimportant too. The question of whether circumcision makes a difference to viral transmission should be debated, without its being allowed to erase either the question of pleasure or the substantial history of pathologizing the foreskin.[10] An adult male foreskin has approximately fifty square centimetres of highly innervated tissue, so removing this erotogenic genital structure, especially without informed consent, is hugely consequential. Routine infant circumcision has become controversial from a global perspective because, outside the United States, it is seen as medically unwarranted genital mutilation. In the United States, however, infant male circumcision remains statistically normal, culturally normative, and less controversial than it should be. The US dominance of queer studies thus may help to account for the neglect of these issues among queer scholars.[11]

9   This claim is developed in Tim Dean, "No Sex Please, We're American," *American Literary History* 27, no. 3 (2015): 614–24, and Dean, "The Biopolitics of Pleasure," *South Atlantic Quarterly* 111, no. 3 (2012): 477–96.

10   See Robert Darby, *A Surgical Temptation: The Demonization of the Foreskin and the Rise of Circumcision in Britain* (Chicago: University of Chicago Press, 2005).

11   The best queer theoretical consideration of foreskin pleasure comes from a Finnish scholar. See Harri Kalha, "Fantasy Uncut: Foreskin Fetishism and the

It needs to be said that the pleasures associated with the foreskin are not strictly heterosexual, even for straight men; rather, they are autoerotic and homoerotic. The practice of cock-docking, which Allan refers to only in passing, offers a vital example of one foreskin-specific erotic pleasure that circumcision annihilates. Insofar as docking creates a sensual sheath out of a foreskin for the head of another man's penis, one might say that it enables one cock to fuck another. By way of a foreskin, docking makes the penis a site of receptivity rather than simply of penetration. It subtly shifts conventional imaginaries of the male body, and could be considered as queer—even as potentially feminist—for that reason. But I insist that docking is worthy of consideration as an erotic practice and, indeed, is valuable in its own right, *not* because it might have feminist or queer implications. The practice—and the anatomical structure on which it depends—are fully defensible in terms of erotic pleasure.

In the US medical community, foreskins are regarded as dispensable because they are viewed as useless, devoid of function. Erotic pleasure is likewise deemed irrelevant because it is not susceptible to the calculus of use. This way of thinking affects knowledge production beyond the field of medicine, such that our objects of study in the humanities and social sciences tend to be measured by their utility. In queer studies, where the governing metric is political utility, erotic practices have to demonstrate their ideological usefulness before they can qualify as worthy of attention. Pleasure is never enough. We want our sex to be revolutionary in order to talk about it.

In his chapter on PrEP, Octavio González claims we're in the midst of a gay sexual revolution. He is right that the new pharmaceuticals are significantly changing the sexual landscape for those who have access and choose to take them. He is also right that PrEP has not been unequivocally embraced in the gay community. Much of the controversy surrounding PrEP has played out on social media, where positions quickly become polarized, and the medium

Morphology of Desire," in *Porn Archives*, eds. Tim Dean, Steven Ruszczycky, and David Squires (Durham, NC: Duke University Press, 2014), 375–98.

itself discourages nuance or any acknowledgement of ambivalence. In the face of what González calls "a cultural backlash," it can feel imperative to defend PrEP as a silver bullet and to cast its advent as "revolutionary" for queers. But that oversimplifies the issue's complexity in the service of political expediency.

Many of the cultural anxieties surrounding PrEP are condensed in the figure of the "Truvada whore," a pejorative term meant to designate the gay man who, having discovered chemoprophylaxis, fucks without condoms indiscriminately. González situates this figure in a genealogy of AIDS panic icons whose primary function has been to terrorize people into not having sex. The Truvada whore is the twenty-first century's version of Patient Zero. He also updates the late-nineties figure of the barebacker. And, as the "whore" label indicates, this figure draws on broader cultural anxieties about sexuality as uncontrollable. The Truvada whore, implicitly a bottom taking raw loads with impunity, is, as González suggests, anticipated by Leo Bersani's critique thirty years ago in "Is the Rectum a Grave?"[12] But Bersani's position, in what is now an ur-text for queer theory, was not that we should demystify such stigmatizing figures. Rather, he discerned in these icons of *jouissance* a remarkable insight about the ontology of the sexual: "The value of sexuality itself is to demean the seriousness of efforts to redeem it."[13] The image of the Truvada whore captures something that, far from incidental or false about gay sexuality, should be celebrated, not demystified.

Here I am taking González's valuable account of the current sexual landscape in a slightly different direction. He claims that the PrEP revolution may precipitate a "demise of the culture of stigma and fear that arose as a way to combat the epidemic." While he's right to want an end to fear and erotophobia, I'm less sure that gay sexual culture wants to dispense altogether with stigma. The figure of the Truvada whore is a phobic construction, but also an erotically exciting one: it signals sexual disinhibition. The Truvada whore is

---

12    Leo Bersani, "Is the Rectum a Grave?," in *AIDS: Cultural Analysis/Cultural Activism*, ed. Douglas Crimp (Cambridge, MA: MIT Press, 1988), 197–222.
13    Ibid., 222.

akin to the mythical father of the primal horde, in *Totem and Taboo*, with apparently unlimited sexual access.[14] We need that figure to exist, at least mythically, in order to have any erotic pleasure at all. Demystification is rather beside the point.[15]

There are additional motives for gay men to be wary about distancing ourselves from whores. To suggest that one is *not* a Truvada whore sounds a little too much like a gambit of respectability politics. (One does not need to be actually taking Truvada to embrace the whores.) It may be worth recalling that, before men who enjoy sex with other men adopted "gay" as their preferred designation, the word was used as a slang term for female prostitutes.[16] Gays were originally whores. Lexicographer Alan Richter notes that "*gay man* is a 19th-century British term for whoremonger, a man who seeks prostitutes."[17] North American homosexuals becoming politicized in the 1960s borrowed a term associated with commercial sex, as if embracing the stigma shared by erotic deviants. At that historical moment, people labelled "whores" and "fags" were deemed social outcasts by virtue less of who they were than what they did. Socially unsanctioned sex inadvertently gave common cause to those who, by the 1970s, became known as gay men and sex workers. However, by the end of the twentieth century, many gay men in the United States were campaigning to expunge their stigma by distancing homosexuality from—of all things—sex. Full social acceptance seemed to entail emphasizing what gays have in common with

---

14  See Sigmund Freud, *Totem and Taboo* (1913), in *The Standard Edition of the Complete Psychological Works of Sigmund Freud*, ed. and trans. James Strachey, vol.13 (London: Hogarth, 1955), 1–161.

15  The question of eradicating stigma is too complex to do justice to here. Many gay men are stigmaphiles, that is, they love tattoos and other bodily markings. Since stigma remains an important basis for arousal, bonding, and kinship in sexual cultures, I'm doubtful it could or should be eradicated completely. The classic text on this issue is Erving Goffman, *Stigma: Notes on the Management of Spoiled Identity* (New York: Simon and Schuster, 1963).

16  Alan Richter, *Sexual Slang: A Compendium of Offbeat Words and Colorful Phrases from Shakespeare to Today* (New York: HarperCollins, 1995), 92. Richter classifies "female prostitute" as the primary meaning of "gay," since this usage dates back to the fourteenth century and was superseded by the secondary (to us, more familiar) meaning only in the twentieth century.

17  Ibid.

straights rather than with sex workers. As a result, the specificities of erotic practice were relegated to footnotes, when not elided
altogether. Embracing the whores—including the Truvada whores,
the cum sluts, and the least sexually respectable among us—may
help to counter that deleterious trend.

Sexual penetrability is heavily gendered. Put simply, women are
supposed to be penetrable, whereas men are not: for this reason,
masculine penetrability provokes cultural anxiety. Conversely,
however, men who enjoy being penetrated may find less stigma in
the "whore" label than women are wont to do. It is easier to be a
male slut than a female one, thanks to gendered cultural expectations about multiple partners. These gendered expectations affect
the issue of barebacking in heterosexual contexts, as Frank Karioris explains in his discussion of narratives of virility and virality.
Having focused on barebacking in a predominantly gay context, I
learned much from Karioris's analysis of the case of straight porn
icon James Deen.

Karioris plays on the homonym Deen/Dean to compare my
account of all-male bareback sex with what goes on in the world
of contemporary heterosexual hardcore, which takes unprotected
rough sex as a norm. James Deen is a salient example because,
having amassed a substantial following among female viewers, he
subsequently was accused of rape and sexual assault by multiple
women. Karioris takes this situation to exemplify how masculine virility is enhanced, in a heterosexual context, by the risk of
"virality" that displaces physical vulnerability onto women. If, in
the gay context, men fucking bareback assume a certain risk, in
the straight context that risk is borne disproportionately by the
women involved. The distinction between gay and straight bareback
scenarios is neatly encapsulated when Karioris writes, "James Deen
is thus the Jesse James to Tim Dean's Robin Hood. Whereas Robin
Hood stole from the rich and was part of the community, James
took only for himself."

Frank Karioris could hardly be expected to know that my father
was named James Dean or that, possibly for this reason, I too have
followed the career of James Deen with considerable interest. But
his account, making more of my patronym than I ever could, helps

to clarify a distinction I was trying to draw in *Unlimited Intimacy*. The case of James Deen makes clear that heterosexual barebacking concerns not only masculine self-aggrandizement or selfish pleasure, in contrast to the intimate kinship that gay barebacking aspires to create. Rather, both involve male bonding, but in the gay context, masculine intimacy is not at the expense of women. Indeed, part of what intrigued me about the viral kinship described in *Unlimited Intimacy* was that it appeared to be a practice of creating social cohesion that did not depend on processes of exclusion or othering. Bareback communities are far from utopias, but the practice of bonding without excluding is notable. Here one cannot avoid recalling Freud's claim that "it is always possible to bind together a considerable number of people in love, so long as there are other people left over to receive the manifestations of their aggressiveness."[18] We might say that committed barebackers bond over fucking with a virus so that they don't need to bond by fucking over women.

If, in place of the heteronormative traffic in women we discern a queer traffic in viruses, it may be worth noting that the virus (or "bug") is neither human nor gendered.[19] Rinaldo Walcott's contribution to this volume asks whether the virus is racist—or what it might mean to understand HIV in terms of the history of racism, and the disproportionate impact of HIV on communities of colour.[20] Is the non-humanity of the virus connected to the positioning of Black people outside the community of the fully human? How might what Karioris designates as virality be cognate with historical associations between Blackness and death—specifically, the idea of "Black

---

18  Sigmund Freud, *Civilization and Its Discontents*, in *The Standard Edition of the Complete Psychological Works of Sigmund Freud*, vol. 21, ed. and trans. James Strachey (London: Hogarth Press, 1955), 114.

19  On the sexual exchange of women between men as a mechanism of alliance, see Gayle S. Rubin, "The Traffic in Women: Notes on the 'Political Economy' of Sex," in *Deviations: A Gayle Rubin Reader* (Durham, NC: Duke University Press, 2011), 33–65. This classic article builds on, even as it offers a feminist critique of, Lévi-Strauss's structural anthropology.

20  I first tried to address the intersection between HIV and histories of racism in Dean, "The Germs of Empires: *Heart of Darkness*, Colonial Trauma, and the Historiography of AIDS," in *The Psychoanalysis of Race*, ed. Christopher Lane (New York: Columbia University Press, 1998), 305–29; and subsequently in chapter 3 of *Unlimited Intimacy*.

sex" as a harbinger of death? Bearing down on erotic pleasure more concertedly than many of the other contributors, Walcott examines pleasure via the figure of the "Black cumjoy," a not-so-distant relative of the Truvada whore.

The Black cumjoy emerges as a dialectical figure, with a doubled relation to mortality: both giver and receiver. He's the Black man who has raw sex with other men, whether gay or straight, Black or otherwise, and whose semen stereotypically threatens contagion. At the same time, he's the Black man we see as always already dead. He's an embodiment of a whole constellation of racial stereotypes— Black hyper-sexuality, BBD ("big black dick"), man on the down low, Black rapist, lynched body, half-dead slave, Black man with AIDS. In evoking these contradictions of the Black cumjoy, Walcott raises the possibility of Black men taking erotic pleasure in the stereotypes. This strikes me as a vital point, insofar as it refuses to cede libidinal satisfaction to political propriety.

Walcott wants Black cum because, though it threatens fatality, it is also potent with joy. Referring to joy more than pleasure—and intensifying it through his incantatory repetition of the phrase "Black cumjoy"—Walcott conjures up the psychoanalytic concept of *jouissance*, which lies beyond the pleasure principle. If *jouissance* contaminates eros with death, then Blackness overdetermines the mixture by marking sex with an excess that renders it almost intolerably exciting. This may be put more straightforwardly by asserting that "sexuality is always already racialized and race is always already sexualized."[21] What remains to be said here is that *jouissance* typically operates as a mechanism of social exclusion, whether of racism or homophobia or some combination thereof. The Black cumjoy, like the Truvada whore, is a figure for someone enjoying too much, and thereby soliciting punishment. Most folks cannot remain unmoved at the prospect of someone wallowing in cum.

The rawness of cum is reconfigured in the next chapter through blood, as Elliot Evans brilliantly supplements bareback breeding fantasies with lesbian bleeding fantasies. Including lesbians and trans

---

21    Shannon Winnubst, *Way Too Cool: Selling Out Race and Ethics* (New York: Columbia University Press, 2015), 140.

men in the conversation about barebacking is significant for various reasons, not least the revelation that fantasies of corporeal union through erotic practice are far from exclusive to a cadre of gay men.[22] Evans's focus on Monique Wittig restores to our understanding of this crucial figure a much stronger appreciation of the role of sex and eros in her work. The version of Wittig we inherit from Judith Butler's appropriation of her is a sanitized, rather bloodless figure, but Evans foregrounds the messy—even violent—erotics in *The Lesbian Body* by redescribing the book's fragmented sections as BDSM scenes. "*I* catch your sickness, you know it *I* am so sick from you that *I* am extremely happy," declares one speaker in Wittig's book, sounding for all the world like a contemporary bugchaser. Here lesbians and gay men are bonded less by shared oppression than by extreme erotic desire.

Some lesbians who share the intense, perverse lust more usually associated with gay barebackers have chosen to become trans men. In this case, Evans focuses on Patrick Califia and, to a lesser extent, Paul Preciado, both of whose writing about public sex has significantly influenced my own thinking about gay sexuality.[23] Gay men can learn from trans folk not just about the plurality of gender and sexual identities but also, more viscerally, about the intensity of erotic practice. For example, Califia's eroticization of blood exchange, even at the height of AIDS panic, indicates just how far some were prepared to go for the pleasures and intimacies that matter to them. In this respect, they are kinsmen of the committed barebackers described in *Unlimited Intimacy*. Eroticized blood exchange converts the entire corporeal integument into an erotogenic zone, even as it reduces the boundaries between bodies.

---

22  For more on lesbians and barebacking, see Kathryn Bond Stockton, "Reading as Kissing, Sex with Ideas: 'Lesbian' Barebacking?" *Los Angeles Review of Books*, March 8, 2015, https://lareviewofbooks.org/article/reading-kissing-sex-ideas-lesbian-barebacking/.

23  Elsewhere, Evans has discussed very insightfully Preciado's relationship with the notorious Parisian barebacker Guillaume Dustan; see Elliot Evans, "Your HIV-Positive Sperm, My Trans-Dyke Uterus: Anti/Futurity and the Politics of Bareback Sex between Guillaume Dustan and Beatriz Preciado," *Sexualities* 18, nos. 1–2 (2015): 127–40. See also Beatriz Preciado, *Testo Junkie: Sex, Drugs, and Biopolitics in the Pharmacopornographic Era*, trans. Bruce Benderson (New York: Feminist Press, 2013).

What Evans makes clear is the distinctive ethics involved in these erotic practices and commitments—an ethics that, though it revolves around fantasies of incorporation, may nonetheless honour the otherness of the other.

The scrupulous ethics that Evans delineates could not be more different from the moral bankruptcy of mainstream porn's commodification of barebacking as a marketing ploy. When bareback porn first emerged on the scene with films such as Dick Wadd's *NYPD* (1997) and Paul Morris's *Breed Me* (1999), the absence of condoms violated industry norms for gay porn at the time, without appearing as merely cynical commercialism. Most viewers understood that these films depicted men having sex with each other in the way they had it when the cameras were not rolling. That kind of faith in porn as documentary sounds naive to people outside the subculture, but it was articulated as a production principle very forthrightly by Morris, and it influenced how I discussed bareback porn in *Unlimited Intimacy*. Things have changed substantially since then. Increasingly, gay porn companies have dispensed with condoms, though their decisions have nothing to do with subcultural ethics. Often these decisions are purely commercial, and appear as exploitative. Under such conditions, viewers tend to remain unimpressed.

The desire for what is considered authentically raw in pornography helps to account for the popularity of "unfettered amateurism," as Evangelos Tziallas describes it in his discussion of Raging Stallion's film *Focus/Refocus*. This amateur aesthetic is an effect of technological developments that, with universally available camera phones capable of making Internet-ready video clips, render us all potential pornographers.[24] The fact that performers, camera techniques, and production values may be recognizably non-professional is a distinct source of pornographic excitement. Through the category of amateurism, rawness proliferates.

But it remains, nonetheless, conventionalized rawness, a mediated real. Gay porn today, whether amateur or professional, is mediated

---

24   I elaborate on these developments in "Introduction: Pornography, Technology, Archive," in *Porn Archives*, eds. Tim Dean, Steven Ruszczycky, and David Squires (Durham, NC: Duke University Press, 2014), 1–26.

by an industry that faces commercial pressure to show the real thing. Condoms are no longer understood to be part of real sex. The popularity of Treasure Island Media productions means that other porn studios are being pushed for commercial reasons to go bareback. Unprotected anal sex in gay porn is now less about documenting a subculture than about yielding to market demand. As a result, the ethics around bareback porn have mutated considerably over the past two decades—though Paul Morris appears disinclined to acknowledge the fact. His dialogue with Susanna Paasonen, while fascinating, reproduces a set of claims that read to me as rather outdated, and almost wilfully naive.

Morris is one of the most interesting pornographers working in the United States today; his published dialogues with Paasonen, a Finnish media scholar, offer insight into his personal philosophy at the same time as they reveal the limits of his individualist ethic.[25] Morris's oft-stated conviction that he's not really part of the porn industry—a conviction buttressed by his apparent disdain for other pornographers and porn companies—does not, in fact, exempt him or his work from industry conditions and constraints. Wishing doesn't make it so. This becomes evident in the discussion of how he uses money in porn, which focuses exclusively on his financial arrangements with individual performers without saying anything about the money his company makes. The business dimension of Treasure Island Media is repeatedly obscured in Morris's statements—an elision that is compounded by Paasonen's remarkable disavowal: "TIM is fundamentally embedded in late-capitalist commodity formation as a commercial production studio trading in pornography, but without being reducible to its operations." *I know very well* (that this is a commercial porn company), *but all the same* (it escapes the operations of capital). . . .[26] Treasure Island Media eludes the logic of late-capitalist commodity formation by a

---

25    See also Paul Morris and Susanna Paasonen, "Risk and Utopia: A Dialogue on Pornography," *GLQ: A Journal of Lesbian and Gay Studies* 20, no. 3 (2014): 215–39.

26    On the verbal structure of the psychic mechanism of disavowal, see Octave Mannoni, "Je sais bien, mais quand même," in Mannoni, *Cléfs pour l'Imaginaire, ou l'Autre Scène* (Paris: Seuil, 1969), 9–33; translated by G.M. Goshgarian as " 'I Know Well, but all the Same,' " in *Perversion and the Social Relation*, eds. Molly

miraculous assertion of will that a single moment's critical reflection reveals as pure illusion. The hyperbolic neo-Marxian rhetoric of revolution and utopia crumbles the minute one considers the company's capitalist business model.

We have to wonder about Paasonen's role in propping up Morris's illusions. The chapter contains two voices, though it's unclear whether we are witnessing an actual dialogue. The idea of a porn-maker collaborating with a cultural theorist is appealing, but here the collaboration reads as a process of bolstering ultimately untenable claims. For example, the claim that Morris's company focuses on "underrepresented practices within the gay male community" makes it sound like Treasure Island Media heroically gives voice to the marginalized and "underrepresented," when in fact bareback has become the gay porn norm. The claim sounds good, yet is misleading. My critique is not of bareback sex in pornography, but of the disingenuous terms in which it is being justified here.

It is striking to witness a feminist cultural theorist nodding along unquestioningly with the gender essentialism and unreconstructed identitarianism that Morris invokes.[27] Primal masculinity, male desire, queer nature—all are essentialized as culturally unmediated forces to which Morris bravely gives free rein. "Queer sex is the primal experience from which identities develop," he claims, ignoring the political motive of *queer* as counter-identitarian. The notion of "queer identity" he blithely invokes is a pure product of neoliberal consumer culture; doubtless it serves his commercial enterprise. I claim the opposite of Morris: sex dissolves the illusions of identity. But, if you're committed to essentialist views of sex, gender, and sexuality, then it makes perfect sense to advance claims on behalf of the innate superiority of queerness: "Our sex is the highest form of creation and communication," he says. That sounds like the kind of sentence one expects to hear from the Vatican.

---

Anne Rothenberg, Dennis A. Foster, and Slavoj Žižek (Durham, NC: Duke University Press, 2003), 68–92.

27    Elsewhere Paasonen's critical faculties appear intact: she takes counter-essentialist positions on gender in her book *Carnal Resonance: Affect and Online Pornography* (Cambridge, MA: MIT Press, 2011).

Paasonen never demurs. Instead, she swaddles Morris's opinions in references to concepts and theories that only occasionally fit. For example, she endeavours to couch his hardcore essentialism in terms of Foucauldian ethics. It would be hard to imagine a less Foucauldian thinker than Paul Morris. His view of power is Manichean; he's committed to sex as the foundation of identity, and he denies the cultural mediations of his own media in the name of an aggrandized outlaw agency. Most precious of all, Morris claims that he imbibed Foucault's ideas not by reading his work, but by fisting him: "Rather than studying with him, I absorbed Foucault through my left hand and arm."[28] Graduate students take note: fist-fucking is the new speed-reading.

In the midst of all of this, Morris offers a genuinely Foucauldian claim that undercuts almost everything else he's said: "We don't have a clue as to what queer agency is." What queerness is, or what it might be able to do, remains undetermined precisely because it is neither an essence nor an identity. Rather, it is a purely contingent relation to historically shifting socio-sexual norms. Since the situation of those norms vis-à-vis what Lacan designates as the symbolic order is a matter of some dispute (should the symbolic be understood as a sedimentation of norms or as a function of language that remains irreducible to them?), psychoanalytic critics tend to be divided on the subject of queerness.[29] Moreover, specifically Lacanian critics complicate the question of queerness vis-à-vis socio-sexual norms by focusing not only on agency, pleasure, and symbolic law but also on *jouissance*.

Akin to Walcott's notion of the Black cumjoy, *jouissance* offers a conceptual category that Gareth Longstaff employs to discuss bareback porn produced by UK director Liam Cole. A transatlantic associate of Morris's Treasure Island Media, Cole has become notorious for representing in his films the subcultural practice of combining hardcore drug use with unprotected sex—what is known

---

28    Morris and Paasonen, "Risk and Utopia," 220.
29    For an excellent sampling of the divergent views, see Noreen Giffney and Eve
       Watson, eds., *Clinical Encounters in Sexuality: Psychoanalytic Practice and Queer
       Theory* (New York: Punctum Books, 2017).

in the United Kingdom as "chemsex" and in the United States as "PnP" (party and play). Crystal methamphetamine, the principal illicit drug in these scenes, has fuelled bareback sex since the subculture emerged in the 1990s, thanks to its propensity for enhancing physical sensation, annihilating inhibition, intensifying sexual desire, and providing tremendous energy. If you wish to indulge the fantasy of getting fucked raw by multiple men in a single marathon session, then it is probably the ideal recreational drug—at the same time as it is highly addictive, corrosive to the human body, and widely regarded as destructive of community. Since *jouissance* takes eros beyond the pleasure principle into the realm of suffering and pain, it appears as a highly apposite concept with which to discuss chemsex and its pornographic representation. Indeed, Longstaff's contribution suggests a snug fit between hardcore slamming and fucking, on the one hand, and hardcore Lacanianism, on the other.

If today barebacking is enabled by the medically approved drugs of PrEP, then it also is facilitated by the illegal and widely disapproved drug cocktails of crystal methamphetamine, GHB, MDMA (ecstasy), and other stimulants. In other words, raw sex remains heavily mediated by pharmaceuticals: the ostensibly raw is always already supplemented, processed, and cooked. Yet the illegal drugs of PnP—by contrast with the prophylactic drugs of PrEP—are meant not simply to enhance pleasure but to push the desiring subject's body beyond the usual limits. Pharmaceuticals have their own erotic logic, and it may be the logic of *jouissance*. Longstaff is right that Liam Cole's pornography attempts to visualize and thereby authenticate *jouissance*; the question is whether Cole succeeds—or whether any visual text could ever fully capture the extremities of *jouissance*. How much excess can pornography contain on our behalf?

Barebacking has become a site where our strongest desires and wildest expectations intersect. For Diego Semerene, as for many of the other contributors, bareback sex is always so much more than it appears at face value. Forever in excess of itself, barebacking perpetually raises questions that demand interpretive solutions. In classic Lacanian mode, Semerene poses as a master demystifier. Since all is divided and doubled by virtue of the unconscious, everything dissimulates; hence, the Lacanian pose implies, nothing is beyond his hermeneutic grasp. Here we see exemplified the paranoid style of reading that, unleashing an interpretive frenzy, confirms the regrettable view of psychoanalysis as little more than a hermeneutics of suspicion.[30] But what distinguishes Semerene is that, by the end of his chapter, he turns this hermeneutics on himself. The dissimulations he laments in online images and cross-dressing are reproduced in his own weird attempt to trick his unsuspecting trick into surreptitiously going bareback. It's as if he had to act out his own duplicity, and then announce it in writing, to verify his assumption that others cannot be trusted.[31]

While other contributors doubt bareback's capacity to deliver on its exorbitant promises, Semerene claims conversely that barebacking can resolve lingering doubts about masculinity. For it is above all masculinity that he mistrusts. "Barebacking has emerged as a shortcut for fantasies of hermetic hetero-masculinity," he argues. "There is . . . something phallic about the Other who can, if not perfectly perform masculinity, at least annihilate it by the proxy of a virus." Later, he writes, "a lethal virus is naturally priapic." According to Semerene's logic, if masculinity appears as authentic (and hence most desirable) only when violent or lethal, then an untreated viral infection might be considered reliably phallic. Quite apart from his ignoring the expanded role of antiretroviral medications, this logic over-pathologizes the pathogen. It resembles Larry Kramer's reprehensible position twenty years ago, when he characterized barebacking as a form of homicide. How are HIV-positive men supposed to feel about this argument?

Certain prejudices apparently never die. That is why, as Adam Greteman insists, we stand in ever greater need of "updating sexual education." Particularly in the age of PrEP, as the calculus of erotic risk changes, our sexual education needs to adapt accordingly. It needs to

---

30　In queer studies, the *locus classicus* for the paranoid style is Eve Kosofsky Sedgwick's "Paranoid Reading and Reparative Reading; or, You're So Paranoid, You Probably Think This Introduction Is about You," in *Novel Gazing: Queer Readings in Fiction*, ed. Sedgwick (Durham, NC: Duke University Press, 1997), 1–37.

31　It is apparently necessary to repeat in print this tale of duplicity. See Diego Semerene, "Playing Dead: On Part-Time Transvestism, Digital Semblance, and Drag Feminism," *Revista Periódicus* 1, no. 5 (2016): 235–53.

adapt in a way that's mindful of the disproportionate burden borne by sexual and racial minorities in this epidemic. In order to be effective, sex education can never take a one-size-fits-all approach. The problem is especially acute in the United States, where federal and state governments have drastically defunded sex education in schools, except for "abstinence only" programs. This denial of young people's sexuality is all the more extraordinary in a social context where online pornography has never been so accessible. Without realistic sex education that's sensitive to diversity (as well as to questions of pleasure), young people—especially young men—learn about sex primarily from Internet porn. As several contributors observe, pornography has attained a disproportionate role in contemporary gay life. It is hard to grasp that porn is fantasy (rather than something to blindly imitate) when the reality with which it might be compared has not been supplied. Concerns about how bareback porn bamboozles its viewers are, in my view, misplaced: the concern should be directed instead at how US society has failed to provide remotely adequate sexual educations for any of its citizenry.

Greteman wants us to develop an ethical disposition in which we can learn from raw sex; "barebacking provides lessons at the limits of knowledge," he argues. Sympathetic to this view, I nonetheless question the impulse to make barebacking pedagogical. Why can't it suffice that sex be primarily about pleasure? When we take cognizance of the psychoanalytic claim that sexuality is overdetermined by the unconscious, then the question of education becomes infinitely more complex. Expertise, combined with sensitivity, is no longer enough. Greteman suggests something in the spirit of psychoanalysis when he recommends *listening* to the people who are having bareback sex: "While education often prefers to draw upon the expert discourses of accountability, it may be the case that we need to return to the ground where individuals in their cultural ethos are the experts of their becoming."[32] This represents a welcome shift in perspective,

---

32    Greteman's suggestion is also in the spirit of Rancière's philosophy of education, as expounded in Jacques Rancière, *The Ignorant Schoolmaster: Five Lessons in Intellectual Emancipation*, trans. Kristin Ross (Stanford, CA: Stanford University Press, 1991).

though it does not fully reckon with the extent to which, when it comes to *sex* education, the slippages of the unconscious irrevocably compromise expertise that comes from below as well as from above.

The role of the unconscious in sex, understood as a constitutive failure of erotic expressiveness, is addressed directly in the volume's final chapter. Slicing through ideological hyperbole, Christien Garcia wishes to cut barebacking down to size, and to view it with a refreshing dose of realism. The hyperbole "implies that sex is somehow valuable for something 'greater' than itself": we have needed bareback to be radically queer, revolutionary, counter-normative. Garcia is right that those expectations have accelerated the reversion to stultifying logics of identity, including in bareback porn. Nevertheless, he subtly elaborates a Paul Morris moment against itself, in order to reveal this pornography's "mereness," as well as its resistance to meaning. Garcia's subtle reading of this moment merits comparison to Paasonen and Morris's not-so-subtle aggrandizement of Treasure Island Media porn.

There is always a risk that resistance to meaning will congeal into its own meta-meaning, and that, by way of an almost irresistible logic of inversion, "mereness" or "minorness" will become the new queer major. Garcia's wish to think about sex "outside a question of latent potentiality" necessarily locates the unconscious on the side of failed or blocked meaning rather than the side of excess meaning. Despite itself, his brilliant chapter illustrates how difficult it is to keep sex in the minor position of *just sex* when one remains committed to thinking and talking about it. No matter our intentions, each time we treat barebacking allegorically, as a sign or symptom of something beyond itself, we stumble over the capacity of sex "to demean the seriousness of efforts to redeem it," in Bersani's words. The chapters in this volume deserve enormous credit for pushing barebacking to that limit—a limit that frustrates, even as it galvanizes, our capacities to think it.

**REFERENCES**

Bersani, Leo. "Is the Rectum a Grave?" In *AIDS: Cultural Analysis/Cultural Activism*, edited by Douglas Crimp, 197–222. Cambridge, MA: MIT Press, 1988.

Canguilhem, Georges. *On the Normal and the Pathological.* Translated by Carolyn R. Fawcett. New York: Zone Books, 1991.

Darby, Robert. *A Surgical Temptation: The Demonization of the Foreskin and the Rise of Circumcision in Britain.* Chicago: University of Chicago Press, 2005.

Davis, Oliver. "A Special Issue of *Sexualities*: Bareback Sex and Queer Theory across Three National Contexts (France, UK, USA)." *Sexualities* 18, nos. 1–2 (April 2015): 120–26.

Dean, Tim. "The Biopolitics of Pleasure." *South Atlantic Quarterly* 111, no. 3 (2012): 477–96.

———. "The Germs of Empires: *Heart of Darkness*, Colonial Trauma, and the Historiography of AIDS." In *The Psychoanalysis of Race*, edited by Christopher Lane, 305–29. New York: Columbia University Press, 1998.

———. "Introduction: Pornography, Technology, Archive." In *Porn Archives*, edited by Tim Dean, Steven Ruszczycky, and David Squires, 1–26. Durham, NC: Duke University Press, 2014.

———. "Mediated Intimacies: Raw Sex, Truvada, and the Biopolitics of Chemoprophylaxis." *Sexualities* 18, nos. 1–2 (April 2015): 224–46.

———. "No Sex Please, We're American." *American Literary History* 27, no. 3 (Fall 2015): 614–24.

———. *Unlimited Intimacy: Reflections on the Subculture of Barebacking.* Chicago: University of Chicago Press, 2009.

Evans, Elliot. "Your HIV-Positive Sperm, My Trans-Dyke Uterus: Anti/Futurity and the Politics of Bareback Sex between Guillaume Dustan and Beatriz Preciado." *Sexualities* 18, nos. 1–2 (April 2015): 127–40.

Foucault, Michel. *The Birth of the Clinic: An Archaeology of Medical Perception.* Translated by A.M. Sheridan Smith. New York: Random House, 1973.

———. *History of Madness.* Edited by Jean Khalfa. Translated by Jonathan Murphy and Jean Khalfa. London and New York: Routledge, 2006.

———. *The History of Sexuality, Volume 1: An Introduction.* Translated by Robert Hurley. New York: Random House, 1978.

Freud, Sigmund. *Civilization and Its Discontents.* In *The Standard Edition of the Complete Psychological Works of Sigmund Freud*, vol. 21, edited and translated by James Strachey, 57–145. London: Hogarth Press, 1955.

———. *Totem and Taboo.* In *The Standard Edition of the Complete Psychological Works of Sigmund Freud*, vol. 13, edited and translated by James Strachey, 1–161. London: Hogarth Press, 1955.

Giffney, Noreen, and Eve Watson, eds. *Clinical Encounters in Sexuality: Psychoanalytic Practice and Queer Theory.* New York: Punctum Books, 2017.

Goffman, Erving. *Stigma: Notes on the Management of Spoiled Identity.* New York: Simon and Schuster, 1963.

Kalha, Harri. "Fantasy Uncut: Foreskin Fetishism and the Morphology of Desire." In *Porn Archives*, edited by Tim Dean, Steven Ruszczycky, and David Squires, 375–98. Durham, NC: Duke University Press, 2014.

Lévi-Strauss, Claude. *The Raw and the Cooked: Introduction to a Science of Mythology*, vol. 1. Translated by John Weightman and Doreen Weightman. New York: Harper and Row, 1969.

Mannoni, Octave. "Je sais bien, mais quand même." Translated by Gary M. Goshgarian. In *Perversion and the Social Relation*, edited by Molly Anne Rothenberg, Dennis A. Foster, and Slavoj Žižek, 68–92. Durham, NC: Duke University Press, 2003.

Morris, Paul, and Susanna Paasonen. "Risk and Utopia: A Dialogue on Pornography." *GLQ: A Journal of Lesbian and Gay Studies* 20, no. 3 (June 2014): 215–39.

Paasonen, Susanna. *Carnal Resonance: Affect and Online Pornography*. Cambridge, MA: MIT Press, 2011.

Preciado, Beatriz. *Testo Junkie: Sex, Drugs, and Biopolitics in the Pharmacopornographic Era*. Translated by Bruce Benderson. New York: Feminist Press, 2013.

Rancière, Jacques. *The Ignorant Schoolmaster: Five Lessons in Intellectual Emancipation*. Translated by Kristin Ross. Stanford, CA: Stanford University Press, 1991.

Richter, Alan. *Sexual Slang: A Compendium of Offbeat Words and Colorful Phrases from Shakespeare to Today*. New York: HarperCollins, 1995.

Rubin, Gayle. "The Traffic in Women: Notes on the 'Political Economy' of Sex." In *Deviations: A Gayle Rubin Reader*, 33–65. Durham, NC: Duke University Press, 2011.

Sedgwick, Eve Kosofsky. "Paranoid Reading and Reparative Reading; Or, You're So Paranoid, You Probably Think This Introduction Is about You." In *Novel Gazing: Queer Readings in Fiction*, edited by Eve Kosofsky Sedgwick, 1–37. Durham, NC: Duke University Press, 1997.

Semerene, Diego. "Playing Dead: On Part-Time Transvestism, Digital Semblance, and Drag Feminism." *Revista Periódicus* 1, no. 5 (2016): 235–53.

Stockton, Kathryn Bond. "Reading as Kissing, Sex with Ideas: 'Lesbian' Barebacking?" *Los Angeles Review of Books*, March 8, 2015. https://lareviewofbooks.org/article/reading-kissing-sex-ideas-lesbian-barebacking/.

Warner, Michael. "Introduction." In *Fear of a Queer Planet: Queer Politics and Social Theory*, edited by Michael Warner, vii–xxxi. Minneapolis: University of Minnesota Press, 1994.

Wiegman, Robyn, and Elizabeth A. Wilson. "Queer Theory without Antinormativity." *Differences: A Journal of Feminist Cultural Studies* 26, no. 1 (2015).

Winnubst, Shannon. *Way Too Cool: Selling Out Race and Ethics*. New York: Columbia University Press, 2015.

## ABOUT THE CONTRIBUTORS

**JONATHAN A. ALLAN** is Canada Research Chair in Men and Masculinities and Professor of English and creative writing and gender and women's studies at Brandon University. He is the author of *Reading from Behind: A Cultural Analysis of the Anus*; *Men, Masculinities and Popular Romance*; and a co-editor of *Virgin Envy: The Cultural (In)Significance of the Hymen*. His forthcoming book is called *Uncut: A Cultural Analysis of the Foreskin*.

**TIM DEAN** is a student of human sexuality. He teaches in the Department of English at the University of Illinois, Urbana-Champaign, and lectures widely. His book *Unlimited Intimacy: Reflections on the Subculture of Barebacking* was named by Amazon.com as one of the Top Ten Books of 2009. He has published five additional books and more than one hundred and fifty journal articles, book chapters, and reviews. Currently he is completing three projects: *Sex, Literature, and Psychoanalysis* for Cambridge University Press; with Rancière scholar Oliver Davis a co-authored book, *Hatred of Sex*, for University of Nebraska Press; and *Untouchable*, a study of sexual harassment and stalking in the university.

**ELLIOT EVANS** is a lecturer in modern languages at the University of Birmingham, in the United Kingdom. They work on the intersections of feminist, queer, and transgender theories, with a particular interest in psychoanalytic theory, literature, and visual art. Publications include the articles " 'Wittig and Davis, Woolf and Solanas (. . .) Simmer within Me': Reading Feminist Archives in the Queer Writing of Paul B. Preciado" for *Paragraph* (2018); "Your HIV-Positive Sperm,

My Trans-Dyke Uterus: Anti/Futurity and the Politics of Bareback Sex between Guillaume Dustan and Paul B. Preciado" for *Sexualities* (2015); and the monograph *The Body in French Queer Thought from Wittig to Preciado: Queer Permeability* (Routledge, 2019). Elliot is co-organizer of the interdisciplinary seminar series Critical Sexology.

**CHRISTIEN GARCIA** is a scholar of literature, film, and visual cultures, focusing on British and North American queer aesthetics, politics, and theory. He is currently a Social Sciences and Humanities Research Council postdoctoral fellow and a visiting fellow at the Centre for Film and Screen at the University of Cambridge.

**OCTAVIO R. GONZÁLEZ** teaches transatlantic modernism and literary queer studies at Wellesley College. His monograph *Misfit Modernism: Queer Forms of Double Exile in the Early Twentieth-Century Novel* is under contract with Pennsylvania State University Press. González's scholarship appears or is forthcoming in *Ariel, Modern Fiction Studies, Cultural Critique,* and *ASAP/Journal,* as well as in various edited collections, including Cambridge University Press's *American Literature in Transition: 1960–1970* and *American Gay Autobiography.* In his spare time, besides watching reruns of *Buffy the Vampire Slayer,* González is at work on a second poetry manuscript, tentatively titled *The Wingless Hour.* His first, *The Book of Ours* (Momotombo Press, 2009; www.tianguis.biz/shop/the-book-of-ours/), was a selection of the Letras Latinas series at the University of Notre Dame/ the Institute of Hispanic Studies. A sonnet from the second collection was recently selected for *Lambda Literary's* "Poetry Spotlight."

**ADAM J. GRETEMAN** is an assistant professor of art education and director of the Master of Arts in Teaching program at the School of the Art Institute of Chicago. His teaching and research interests lie at the intersections of feminist, queer, and transgender theories, philosophy of education, aesthetics, and teacher education. He is the author of *Sexualities and Genders in Education: Toward Queer Thriving* (Palgrave-Macmillan, 2018) and the co-author (with Kevin Burke) of *The Pedagogies and Politics of Liking* (Routledge, 2017). His work has been published in various journals, including the *Journal of*

*Homosexuality, Educational Theory, Educational Philosophy and Theory, Discourse: Studies in the Cultural Politics of Education, Studies in Art Education,* and QED: *A Journal in* GLBTQ *Worldmaking.*

**FRANK G. KARIORIS** is visiting lecturer of gender, sexuality, and women's studies at the University of Pittsburgh, and director of the Center for Critical Gender Studies at the American University of Central Asia. They are the editor (with Andrea Cornwall and Nancy Lindisfarne) of the recent collection *Masculinities under Neoliberalism* (Zed Books, 2016) and have published on the topic of sexuality, masculinities, and education in various peer-reviewed journals, including the *Journal of Men's Studies,* the *Journal of Gender Studies,* and *Culture Unbound.* Their current work has explored issues related to men's friendships, education, and Foucault; Andy Warhol's masculinity; and the role of teaching in the neoliberal university. Their first monograph, *An Education in Sexuality & Sociality: Heteronormativity on Campus,* was published in 2019 by Lexington Books.

**GARETH LONGSTAFF** is a lecturer in media and cultural studies at Newcastle University in the United Kingdom. His teaching and research interests are primarily concerned with queer theory, gender and sexuality, celebrity, discourses of self-representation, pornography, and psychoanalysis. In his forthcoming monograph *Celebrity and Pornography: The Psychoanalysis of Self Representation* (I.B Tauris, 2020) he engages and applies queer theory to Freudian and Lacanian psychoanalysis, the celebrification of desire, and the mediated screening of subjectivity and *jouissance* in self-representational photography, pornography/sexual representation, and digital/networked media in celebrity culture. He is a queer activist and chairs the staff LGBTQ+ network at Newcastle. He also works at the intersections of queer history, culture, and heritage and is currently working toward an AHRC bid to create and sustain a Queer Creative Archive and Hub of the North of England.

**PAUL MORRIS** is an American pornographer, and the founder and owner of San Francisco–based gay pornography studio Treasure Island Media, which specializes in barebacking pornography.

**SUSANNA PAASONEN** is professor of media studies at the University of Turku, in Finland. With an interest in studies of popular culture, sexuality, affect, and media theory, she is most recently the author of *Carnal Resonance: Affect and Online Pornography* (MIT Press, 2011) and *Many Splendored Things: Thinking Sex and Play* (Goldsmiths Press, 2018); co-author, with Kylie Jarrett and Ben Light, of *NSFW: Sex, Humor, and Risk in Social Media* (MIT Press, 2019); and, with Ken Hillis and Michael Petit, co-editor of *Networked Affect* (MIT Press, 2015). She serves on the editorial boards of the journals *Sexualities, Porn Studies, New Media & Society, Social Media + Society*, and the *International Journal of Cultural Studies*, and is the PI of the Academy of Finland project "Sexuality and Play in Media Culture" (2017–21).

**DIEGO SEMERENE** is media scholar-practitioner working at the intersection of queer theory, fashion theory, and psychoanalysis. He is a senior lecturer in film and digital media at Oxford Brookes University, in the United Kingdom. He holds a PhD in media arts from the University of Southern California and an MA in cinema studies from New York University. Before joining Brookes, Semerene taught digital media, cinema, and fashion studies at Brown University and the American University of Paris. Diego's film work has been screened at film festivals around the world, the Anthology Film Archives, and the IFC Center in New York. He is a film critic for *Slant Magazine* and has published widely on new media technologies, gender, and sexual practices. His work has most recently appeared in *Discourse, Frames Cinema Journal*, and CM: *Communication and Media Journal*. Diego is working on a book on digital masculinities.

**EVANGELOS TZIALLAS** is a Toronto-based independent scholar whose research expertise includes pornography, queer film and culture, and surveillance.

**RICKY VARGHESE** received his PhD in the sociology of education from the Ontario Institute for Studies in Education of the University of Toronto. He serves as an associate editor for *Drain: A Journal of Contemporary Art and Culture* and has edited a special issue of the journal on the theme of the "Ruin," which came out in October 2014, and another on "AIDS and Memory," released in September 2016. He has been invited to edit a special issue of *Porn Studies* on the theme "Porn on the Couch: Sex, Psychoanalysis, and Screen Cultures/Memories," expected in 2019, and will also be co-editing (along with David K. Seitz and Fan Wu) an issue of the *Gay and Lesbian Quarterly* on "Queer Political Theologies," to be released in 2020. Alongside his scholarly work, he has also developed a rigorous art-writing practice, having written about the works of artists such as Gerhard Richter, Angela Grauerholz, Michèle Pearson Clarke, Erika DeFreitas, Francisco-Fernando Granados, and Vincent Chevalier. His writings on art have appeared in such publications as *Canadian Art, esse arts+opinions, C Magazine*, and *Modern Horizons*. Further to his academic training and art writing, he is also trained professionally as a social worker, having acquired both his BSW and MSW, and runs a private practice as a psychotherapist in downtown Toronto. As of September 2017, he has been a candidate in clinical training at the Toronto Institute of Psychoanalysis.

**RINALDO WALCOTT** is professor of Black diaspora cultural studies at the University of Toronto, where he is a member of the Department of Social Justice Education at OISE and the Women and Gender Studies Institute, as well as the Graduate Program in Cinema Studies. His teaching and research are in the area of Black diaspora cultural studies and postcolonial studies with an emphasis on questions of sexuality, gender, nation, citizenship, and multiculturalism. He is the author of *Black Like Who: Writing Black Canada* (Insomniac Press, 1997, with a second revised edition in 2003) and *Queer Returns: Essays on Multiculturalism, Diaspora and Black Studies* (Insomniac Press, 2016); he is also the editor of *Rude: Contemporary Black Canadian Cultural Criticism* (Insomniac, 2000). He is also the co-editor, with Roy Moodley, of *Counselling across and beyond Cultures: Exploring the Work of Clemment Vontress in Clinical Practice* (University of Toronto Press, 2010). He is the general editor of *Topia: The Journal of Canadian Cultural Studies*.

# INDEX